Contents

Information Systems
for you

FOURTH EDITION

Stephen Doyle

Nelson Thornes

First published in 1995 by:
Stanley Thornes (Publishers) Ltd
Revised edition 1996
Second edition 1999
Third edition 2001

Fourth edition published in 2011 by:
Nelson Thornes Ltd
Delta Place
27 Bath Road
CHELTENHAM
GL53 7TH
United Kingdom

11 12 13 14 15 / 10 9 8 7 6 5 4 3 2 1

A catalogue record for this book is available from the British Library

ISBN 978 1 4085 1519 8

Illustrations by David Lowe and Paul McCaffrey of Sylvie Poggio Artist Agency,
Mike Bastin and GreenGate Publishing Services
Page make-up by GreenGate Publishing Services

Printed and bound in China by 1010 Printing International Ltd

Introduction

The aim of this book

The aim of this book is to build up your knowledge of information communication technology and to develop your skills in this area. By the time you reach the end of the course you should know about ICT and be able to use the skills and knowledge you have acquired to solve your own problems. It is not necessary to study the chapters in the sequence they are presented in the book. However, if you study them in another order you may encounter unfamiliar terms that have been explained in previous chapters.

The starting point

Since many of the questions, tasks, projects, etc. presented in the book involve a knowledge of word processing, spreadsheets, graphics, desktop publishing, multimedia, control, measurement and database software, you should make sure that you know what these are and how to use such software at a basic level.

How to use this book

The book is divided into two sections, the first part dealing with the material for the theory examination and the second part covering skills assessment.

Chapters 1 to 27 cover the theoretical part of the specification, although they also include a variety of practical tasks. Chapters 28 to 35 are Skills chapters, the aim of which is to help you gain skills and knowledge about software.

All O Level, IGCSE and other course marking schemes show a certain percentage of the marks allocated to skills (either in an examination or by completing coursework) and this book gives you useful advice in this respect. At the end of most chapters there is a 'Test Yourself' section which tests on the material presented in the chapter. Boxes marked 'Things to do' are also included. These contain a variety of problems, including some examination-style questions. Some chapters contain projects, entitled 'Investigations', and these encourage you to do some research on a particular topic and use your skills to present your findings. Such projects will add to your overall knowledge of information technology.

Questions within the text

Questions have been included within the text to help you understand concepts as you come to them. In this way you do not have to wait until the end of a chapter before testing your understanding.

'Skills Building' exercises

These exercises are scattered throughout the book and provide opportunities to build your hardware and software skills in solving real problems.

Investigations

'Investigations' provide an opportunity to carry out a project on a particular topic (or topics). The aim of such investigations is to reinforce your knowledge of the subject as well as developing a variety of skills in finding the information and then presenting it.

Examination questions

At the back of the book there is a section of actual examination questions which you can use for practice.

Glossary

There is a glossary at the back of the book: it is a sort of dictionary of computer words, showing their meanings. If you come across a term that you do not understand, you can do one of two things to help you find out what it means. You can turn to the glossary, where you will find a brief explanation of what it means. However, if you want a fuller explanation, use the index to find the relevant pages.

Looking up words in the glossary will reinforce your knowledge of the subject. You will find that several of the smaller examination questions ask what is meant by certain computer terms. It is a good idea to try to learn some of the words in the glossary, along with their meanings. One approach to this is described next.

Learning the glossary

Find some paper or cardboard and cut it into rectangular pieces. Taking two cards at once, write a computer term on one card and its meaning on the other (see Figure 1). Shuffle all the cards and then try to match the terms with their meanings. Once you have done this, check your answers using the glossary.

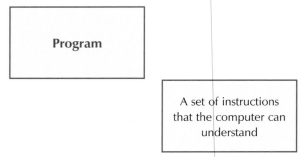

Figure 1 *Make up revision cards like these*

Acknowledgements

The authors and publishers wish to thank the following for permission to use copyright material:

Page 2, Figure 1.3: MurrayData Ltd; page 3, Figure 1.5: Capita SIMS; page 4, Figure 1.6: Capita SIMS; page 9, Figure 2.7: Fotolia; page 15, Figure 3.5: Fotolia; page 18, Figure 3.14: NASA; page 27, Figure 4.2: Fotolia; page 29, Figure 4.4, Figure 4.5: Fotolia; page 73, Figure 11.1: Corbis/Roger Ressmeyer; page 74, Figure 11.2: Fotolia; page 86, Figure 13.5: Fotolia; page 102, Figure 15.3: iStockphoto; page 134, Figure 18.4: iStockphoto; page 134, Figure 18.5, Figure, 18.6, Figure 18.7: Fotolia; page 149, Figure 20.10: iStockphoto; page 150, Figure 20.11: iStockphoto; page 167, Figure 23.1, Figure 23.2: iStockphoto; page 168, Figure 23.3: Getty Images/Greg Pease; page 168, Figure 23.4: iStockphoto; page 169, Figure 23.5: Alamy/Image Source; page 179, Figure 25.1: iStockphoto; page 180, Figure 25.3: iStockphoto; page 183, Figure 25.5: Fotolia; page 184, Figure 25.6: Fotolia; page 185, Figure 25.8, Figure 25.9: iStockphoto; page 186, Figure 25.10: iStockphoto; page 186, Figure 25.11: iStockphoto; page 191, Figure 25.14: Superstock; page 192, Figure 25.15: Gizmag.com; page 193, Figure 25.16, Figure 25.17: iStockphoto; page 194, Figure 25.18: Fotolia; page 195, Figure 26.1: Virgin Media; page 197, Figure 26.2: Virgin Media; page 200, Figure 26.3 Figure 26.4, Figure 26.5: Google Chrome; page 201, Figure 26.6: Fotolia; page 203, Figure 26.7: © 2011 Google – Imagery © 2011 TerraMetrics, Map date © 2011 LeadDog Consulting, Mapa GISrael, ORION-ME, Tracks4Africa; page 223, Figure 28.5: Grammarly.com; page 317, Figure 34.2: Fotolia; page 292, Figure 34.3: iStockphoto; page 292, Figure 34.4: Getty Images/Miguel Navarro

Microsoft Office screenshots reprinted with permission from Microsoft Corporation. Microsoft and its products are registered trademarks or trademarks of Microsoft Corporation in the United States and/or other countries.

Every effort has been made to contact the copyright holders and we apologise if any have been overlooked. Should copyright have been unwittingly infringed in this book, the owners should contact the publishers, who will make corrections at reprint.

The publishers are very grateful to Mr Noorami Naseeb for his assistance.

What Is an Information System?

Data

We call raw facts and figures **data**. Facts and figures often have little meaning until they are sorted or until we calculate something from them. This sorting or calculation is called **data processing**. When data is processed, it provides **information** (see Figure 1.1).

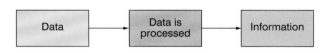

▲ **Figure 1.1** *Processing data produces information*

Information

Information is the meaning we attach to the data. For instance, a red traffic light is a form of data. The meaning we attach to this data (i.e. STOP) is the information. Sometimes data can give rise to ambiguous information. If you are driving a car and a car travelling in the opposite direction flashes its lights at you, what does it mean? It could just mean that a friend has spotted you and is saying hello; it could also mean that there is an accident further up the road. The information that may be obtained from data depends on the way that the data are interpreted and the context in which they are used.

Data are often meaningless. For instance, consider the number 250299. We could interpret this in any number of ways. For example, it might be:

- your video club membership number
- the date, for example, 25 February 1999
- the number of cars going down a certain road in a week.

The three stages of doing tasks

All tasks can be broken down into three stages: input, process and output. These are shown in Figure 1.2.

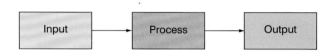

▲
Figure 1.2 *The three stages of doing tasks*

Manual information systems

We are all used to dealing with some sort of manual information system. A telephone directory is an example. There may be several hundred thousand entries, but if we know the surname and address of the person we are trying to contact, we can find the number, provided that it is in the directory.

Manual information systems have many disadvantages. Let's look at an example.

Suppose you have a friend whose phone number and surname you know but whose address you need to find. You do not know their parents' initials and their surname is, unfortunately, Jones. You could find the address by taking the following steps:

1 Look up the section for Jones.
2 Start from the beginning and work through the phone numbers, looking for the area code, for example, look for 928 and see if the rest of the number coincides.
3 Once the phone number has been found you can read off the address.

An even worse problem might be if you had a phone number of a person scribbled down on a piece of paper and you wanted to find out who you were ringing first. The telephone directory is ordered alphabetically according to surname and not in numerical order according to telephone number, so to find the number would prove an immense and time-consuming task.

Computerised information systems

Computerised information systems are much more flexible than manual ones and a lot faster. With a computerised system you could type in a phone number and, if the number was stored in the system, the name and address could be provided immediately.

Examples of computerised information systems

Vehicle databases

Governments often keep a huge collection of information concerning every driver and each vehicle in the country. Such a huge collection of data is called a database. Summarised details of this database are passed to the police to help them in their fight against crime.

Suppose there has been a hit-and-run accident and a witness is able to remember only part of the registration number, for example, _704 N___. Imagine trying to search through the thousands of car registrations having those letters or numbers in them. Even a computer can take some time doing these sorts of searches. Even worse, what would happen if we only knew that the car was a Ford Mondeo with partial registration L___ N___. This type of situation happens all the time when the police are trying to trace cars. Computerised information systems are one of the main weapons in the fight against crime.

A computerised school management system

Consider your school or college. In the secretaries' office there will be a computer containing information on all the students in the school. What are the requirements of a school information system?

Here are some of the tasks that the system would need to deal with.

1 The system must record the attendance details twice a day for all the pupils. It must be able to identify pupils who have poor attendance records so that they may be investigated.
2 It must list a pupil's personal details. This would include such things as name, address, date of birth, name of parent or guardian, daytime contact numbers and addresses, sex, religion, medical problems, form, form teacher's name, mode of travel to school, whether students stay for school dinners and so on.
3 It must be easy to produce the various lists, such as lists of pupils for registration groups, teaching groups, parents' evenings and school trips.
4 It must be possible to get information easily from the system so that letters may be generated and sent to certain pupils.
5 The system must be able to cope with the administration of examination entries.
6 It must cope with all the financial aspects of running a school.
7 The system should be able to help organise a timetable, making the best use of the teachers and the rooms.

As you can see from the above list, a lot of work goes on behind the scenes in a school.

▲
Figure 1.3 *Pupil profile forms are read automatically using an optical mark reader*

Advantages of a computerised information management system

1 You don't need lots of filing cabinets to hold all the pupils' files and other forms. A single computer can store all the information needed.
2 Terminals can be used, so that many people can access the information in different places at the same time. Whenever data are updated they are instantly available to all the people using the system.
3 There is no duplication of information. The pupils' details need only be entered once and then used for different tasks. It is possible to produce year lists, class lists, option lists, etc. using the data from the pupil file.
4 The system can be used in conjunction with a word processor to produce mail shots to pupils' homes.
5 Some information can be transferred to the system without using the keyboard. For instance, Figure 1.3 shows marks on a document being read by an optical mark reader.

Disadvantages of a computerised information management system

1 Everything depends on the computer system. If there is a power failure or if the system breaks down, an alternative system will need to be used.
2 To use the system, the staff will need to be trained. When staff leave, their expertise will be lost and new staff will need to be trained.
3 Security will need to be provided to protect personal pupil and staff information from prying eyes.

▲
Figure 1.5 *A computer being used to view a pupil's personal details.*

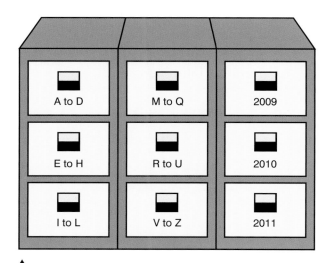

▲
Figure 1.4 *With manual systems, large numbers of filing cabinets are often needed to store records. With a computerised system, one computer could store all this information*

Pupils' personal details need only be recorded once on the system. Even a photograph can be put onto it. The system is easy for everyone to use and can use the **Windows** style of menus, as shown in Figure 1.6. All aspects of the school's administration can be dealt with by the system, from running the school library to recording pupils' option choices. The form shown in Figure 1.7 is used to record pupil option choices. Each option has a different barcode, which can be stuck to the form. The details can be read by using an optical character reader.

The school's information management system enables the headteacher of the school to run the school as efficiently as possible for the benefit of all the pupils. Tasks that would have taken a long time now can be done quickly.

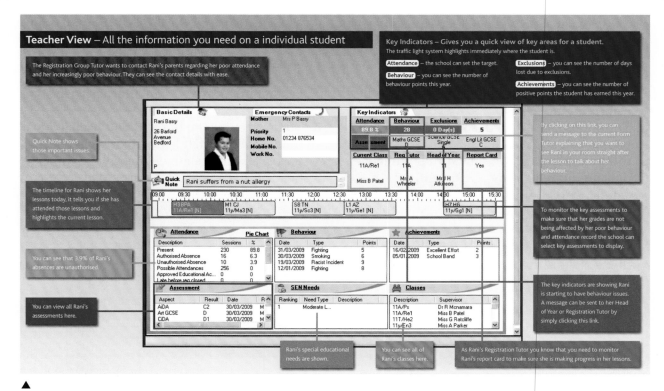

Figure 1.6 *A computer screen showing the school's information management system*

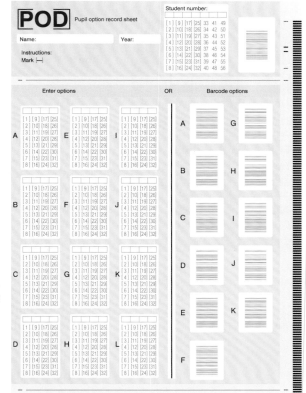

Figure 1.7 *This form is used to record pupil option details. Each option has a different barcode, which is stuck to the form. The details can be extracted using an optical mark reader or a barcode reader*

Things to do

1 Write a list of manual information systems that you use in your everyday life.
   Here are a few to start you off:
   ● Dictionary
   ● Library catalogue
   ● Mail order catalogue
   ● Guinness Book of Hit Singles
   ● Bus timetable
   See how many more you can think up.
   When you have finished, compare your list with your friends' lists.

2 You have been asked to produce a geography project on a particular country, such as Iceland.
   You intend to do this using traditional reference books. What manual information sources
   would you use? Write a list.

3 Find out about the information systems (manual or computerised) used in your school office.
   You need to investigate each of the following:
   (a) How do the data get into the system?
        If the school uses a manual system, explain how the system deals with the various tasks
        mentioned in the text. If a computerised system is used, how are the data entered into the
        system? Also, what information does the system provide?
   (b) Find out what sort of information needs to be held about each pupil, including you. Write
        a list of the information and explain for each one why it is held.

4 A school uses a database to store details about each pupil.
   (a) The details stored about each pupil include the following items:
        ● Pupil number
        ● Name
        ● Address
        ● Date of birth
        ● Class
        ● Sex
        (i)   Write down three more items of information the database would probably store about
              each pupil.
        (ii) Each pupil is given a unique pupil number when they join the school. What is the
              reason for this?
   (b) At the start of the year (or when a new pupil joins the school) pupils are asked to fill in
        a form which gives the school information to be put on the pupil database. Using an
        A4-sized piece of paper, design such a form.
   (c) Many pupil database systems, as well as displaying the personal details about each pupil,
        also display a recent photograph of the pupil. Why might this be useful to the school staff?

The Components of an Information System

Hardware and software

There are two parts to all computer systems: the hardware and the software. Hardware is the term used for the parts of the computer that you can touch and handle. Hardware is the collective name given to all the devices that make up a computer system. Some examples of computer hardware are shown in Figure 2.1. Basically these devices may be split into:

- **input devices**, which are used to get the data into the computer
- the **central processing unit**, which is the brain of the computer
- the **backing storage**, which consists of the disk drives used to store data when the power is switched off
- the **output devices**, which include such units as printers and VDUs, which are used to provide output in the form of printouts, screen displays, etc.

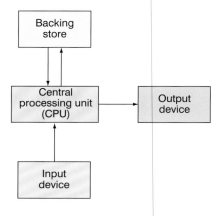

▲ **Figure 2.2** *A simple computer system*

The arrangement of these in a typical computer system is shown in Figure 2.2.

Software is the word used for the actual programs that allow the hardware to do a useful job. Without software, hardware is useless. Software is made up of a series of instructions that tell the computer what to do.

Why use computers?

Computers are extremely fast

A large computer used for producing weather forecasts is able to perform over one million calculations per second. This may appear to be excessive, but many millions of calculations are needed to produce a weather forecast, and forecasts need to be produced quickly.

Computer systems used by the gas and electricity companies have to produce bills to be sent out every three months. Without fast and powerful computers this would be impossible.

Computers are very accurate

We have to remember that when we see stories in newspapers about computers making huge mistakes it is the people who have programmed them or entered the data

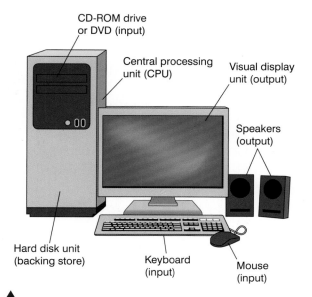

▲ **Figure 2.1** *The parts of a typical microcomputer*

that have made the mistakes. Computers only do what they are told to do. We often use the saying 'garbage in, garbage out' (GIGO for short): what it means is that if incorrect data are put into a computer, the computer won't realise that they are incorrect so it will produce a strange answer. If the computer is given the right information, then provided the hardware and software are working correctly, it will always produce the right output.

The clerical cost of filling a three-drawer filing cabinet is reckoned to be about $1,500. In addition, annual maintenance of the files would cost about $1,200

Some 70 per cent of paper filed is lost. However, the average document is copied seven times and this increases the chances of finding it again. What a waste!

▲
Figure 2.3 *Manual filing systems can take up a lot of space and are difficult to organise*

Computers can keep large amounts of information in a small space

Keeping all the information we need written on paper in files is an enormous task. Once you have gone through the tedious task of making up the files and cataloguing them, there is the problem of finding the file you want; sometimes you may have millions of them to hunt through! But if you use computerised storage you can keep millions of files in a very small space and get the information from them in seconds. You can also have a spare copy in case of accidents – imagine having duplicate written files (Figure 2.3).

Computers can work continuously for 24 hours a day

Computers don't become ill, they don't take lunch breaks or tea breaks and they don't go on strike (Figure 2.4). Computers can easily work 24 hours per day, 365 days per year. There are many things that are probably best left to humans though (Figure 2.5).

Computers can do some jobs that would be impossible without them

Airline booking, the use of credit and debit cards, weather forecasting and space exploration would all be much more difficult without computers.

▲
Figure 2.4 *Computers don't have tea breaks and they don't go on strike*

Figure 2.5 *Many things are best left to humans*

Are there any drawbacks in using computers?

Computers can replace people

There is no doubt that the use of computers has led to unemployment.

Computers hold personal information which may be misused

It is very easy to misuse the personal information held about individuals on computers. This will be looked at more closely in Chapter 18.

Problems arise when computers cannot be used

Sometimes a computer system breaks down, so things have to be done manually or postponed until it is fixed.

Staff need to be trained

Training can be expensive and if the staff leave, then new staff will need to be trained.

Processing data

Computers are used to process data. What we mean by 'processing' is doing something to the data.

Processing includes:

- **calculating** – for example, working out how much pay an employee gets
- **sorting** – your teacher may require a class list arranged in alphabetical order
- **searching** – your headteacher may want to produce a list of all pupils who stay for school dinners
- **storing** – information may be stored on the computer instead of using a paper-based system; old letters or memos may never be needed again, but it might still be worth keeping them for a few years
- **drawing** – you might use a paint package in your art lesson or a computer-aided design (CAD) package in your technology lesson to design a product.

The central processing unit

The central processing unit (often called the CPU or simply the processing unit) processes the raw data and turns these into information. We need not look too deeply into how it works because, as you can imagine, it is quite complicated. If you ever need to open up the case of a microcomputer you will see that there is a series of circuit boards containing the main processor, along with various memory chips.

You will also find a transformer and sometimes a fan, which is responsible for the hum that you get from a computer. Chips give out quite a bit of heat during operation, so a fan is used to cool them down.

There are three main elements of the central processing unit:

- the **control unit**, responsible for coordinating the input and output devices
- the **arithmetic and logic unit** in which all the calculations and logical decisions are made
- the **immediate access store**, which provides immediate memory for holding data and programs.

The immediate access store (IAS) is on a chip or a series of chips inside the computer. Data held here can be accessed immediately, unlike data held on disk, which can take some time to load.

Figure 2.6 shows how these three main parts of a computer are arranged. In this diagram the solid lines are the data signals passing between the various sections or units. The dotted lines show the signals that are used to control the peripheral devices.

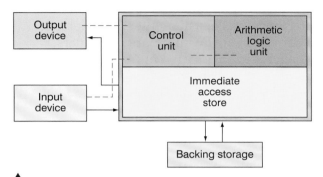

▲ **Figure 2.6** *Central processing unit with peripherals*

Processing units for large mainframe computers look like metal cabinets. Smaller microcomputers, as shown in Figure 2.7, come in a variety of types, such as desktop, notebook and palmtop computers.

Laptop computers

Many people use computers in situations where there is no mains power. They may want to complete work while they are on the move, such as when they are on planes or trains. Portable computing is very important and many people now use laptops that are smaller, have their own internal batteries and can often access the internet.

▲ **Figure 2.7** *Laptops are designed to be portable so that they can be used away from a desk*

Laptop computers do not have quite as high a specification as computers designed to be used on a desk (called desktop computers). This is because they need to be kept small and light. Compromises have to be made, so the processors are not usually as powerful because powerful chips use more power and have to be cooled. Both of these would drain the batteries more quickly.

Desirable properties for processors in laptops

Apart from the desirable properties for processors in any computer, such as high processing speed, there are a number of properties particularly desirable for laptops, such as:

- they should not generate lots of heat, as this can make it uncomfortable when using a laptop on your knees
- they should not need a fan or fans to cool the chip down, as these consume power – this will also extend battery life between charging
- the processor must be low-power consumption, so that more time can be spent away from a source of mains electricity.

Peripheral devices

Peripheral devices are devices outside the central processing unit but under its control. They may be input devices, such as keyboards, used to get the data into the computer, output devices, such as printers, or storage devices, such as disk drives.

Microprocessors

A microprocessor is a single chip that performs the functions of a central processing unit. A chip consists of millions of tiny electronic components etched on a piece of silicon. A microcomputer comprises a microprocessor, together with other chips such as memory chips.

Microprocessors are used to control devices such as washing machines, video recorders, burglar alarms and microwave ovens. In fact, it is hard to think of any electrical or electronic device that could not employ a microprocessor to help control it.

Microprocessors controlling microwave ovens

You can now buy intelligent microwave ovens that use barcodes to automatically set the power and time settings for cooking the food.

In the oven there is a microprocessor that contains information about powers and times. When the oven is used, the user scans the barcode on the packaging on the food and the information in the barcode is used to look up and input the values for the power and cooking times. The values for power and cooking times are set automatically.

There are several advantages of the system:

- The cooking conditions can be variable.
- You cannot make a mistake pressing the wrong buttons.

- It is faster because you do not need to input the settings manually.
- It is safer because the food will always be cooked thoroughly.

Embedded computers

Embedded computers serve as the 'brains' of a larger piece of equipment or machine. They are basically miniature computers. Their software is stored in the computer's own electronic circuits, not on disks. They work just like personal computers and have the same components, but have no monitor, keyboard or drives. Their purpose is to control the devices into which they are embedded.

Embedded computers (also called microprocessors) are found in devices from toasters and mobile phones to aircraft. Cars use them to control antilock braking systems and they are found in medical equipment such as heart–lung machines, dialysis machines, defibrillators and scanners.

Test Yourself

Using the words in the list below, copy out and complete sentences **A** to **H**, underlining the words you have inserted. The words may be used once, more than once or not at all.

programs   GIGO   hardware   information

software   searching   quick   peripheral

backing   microprocessor

A A computer system consists of two parts: _____ and _____.

B Software is the name given to the _____, which enable a computer to perform a useful task.

C A simple computer system consists of a CPU, input and output devices and some external storage called _____ storage.

D Gas and electricity boards use computers because they are very _____ at producing bills.

E A computer will give the wrong result if you feed it incorrect information to start with. This is often referred to as _____.

F Computers are often used because they are able to hold lots of _____ in a very small space. They are also quick at _____ for this information.

G A _____ device is the name given to a device that is outside the CPU but still under the control of it.

H A single chip which performs the functions of a CPU is called a _____.

Things to do

1   On a copy of the following list, tick one box for each of the items to show whether it is hardware or software. If you get stuck, use the index or the glossary at the back of the book to help.

	Hardware	Software
(a) Keyboard	☐	☐
(b) Magnetic hard disk	☐	☐
(c) Visual display unit	☐	☐
(d) Mouse	☐	☐
(e) Central processing unit	☐	☐
(f) Word processor	☐	☐
(g) Operating system	☐	☐
(h) Joystick	☐	☐
(i) Spreadsheet	☐	☐
(j) Database	☐	☐

2   (a) Give the name of the chip that carries out the functions of a central processing unit.
     (b) If you buy a CD-ROM with a computer game on it, have you bought hardware, software or both?
     (c) Give three reasons why a computer is more efficient than a human being.

3   (a) Name two jobs that it would be impossible to perform without computers.
     (b) For the two jobs you have named, give reasons why it would be impossible to perform them manually (by hand).

4   Not all aspects of using computers are good, but their good points far outweigh their bad points; otherwise we would not use them.

     Write a short paragraph on any disadvantages in using computers.

3 The 'Ins' and 'Outs' of Systems
Input and Output

Input devices

Input devices are used to get data into a system. The ideal input device would be able to get data into a system as accurately as possible, in the least amount of time and preferably without human intervention. The device would also be relatively cheap. Unfortunately, no perfect input device is available and the choice is always a compromise. The fastest input devices are suitable only for a narrow range of applications. Here are some of the main input devices in use today.

Keyboard

The keyboard is the oldest and most familiar of all input devices. Keyboards are intelligent devices and contain their own chips. Basically each key acts as a switch that closes when the key is pressed. The microprocessor scans the keyboard hundreds of times a second to see if a key has been pressed; if it has, a code that depends on which key has been pressed is sent to the processing unit. The CPU translates this code into an ASCII code (the code that computers use to represent characters on the computer keyboard), which is then used by the computer program. A standard keyboard is called a QWERTY keyboard because of the arrangement of the letters of the top row of the alphabet keys.

Concept keyboard

The arrangement of keys on a traditional computer keyboard is very similar to that on a typewriter keyboard. On a typewriter this arrangement was chosen for its slowness. New keyboards, called concept keyboards, have been developed which make use of the latest research into ergonomics. Concept keyboards are less tiring to use and higher

typing speeds can be achieved. They do mean that people have to get used to them and this has prevented their widescale acceptance.

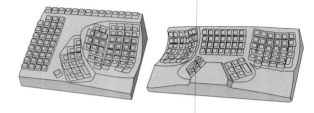

▲ **Figure 3.1** *These concept keyboards are very different from traditional keyboards*

Special keyboards for the disabled

Braille keyboards make it easy for blind users to input data into a computer.

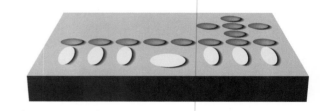

▲ **Figure 3.2** *A Braille keyboard*

For visually impaired users who have some vision, there are also keyboards with large coloured keys that are easier to see. Each key is about one inch square.

▲ **Figure 3.3** *A large-key colour-coded keyboard for the visually impaired*

Mouse

A mouse is an input device that translates its movements on the desktop into digital information – this is fed to the computer, which in turn causes the cursor to move on the screen. Many mice are now optical, which means they make use of an infrared beam to detect movement, and many are also wireless.

▲
Figure 3.5 *A laptop computer and track pad*

▲
Figure 3.4

Tracker ball

A tracker ball is like an upside-down mouse. The ball is rotated by the user, but in this case the 'mouse' stays still. The advantage of a tracker ball compared with a conventional mouse is that it takes up much less space, and this is why tracker balls are often seen on laptop computers.

Touch-sensitive pad

Touch-sensitive pads or track pads are commonly found on laptop, notebook and netbook computers. You move a stylus (or your finger) across a pad and this moves the cursor on the screen. Figure 3.5 shows a laptop featuring a track pad.

Joystick

A joystick is similar to a tracker ball. Whenever the stick is moved, the cursor moves in a similar direction on the screen. Joysticks are mainly used for games but you can also see them being used with scanners in hospitals, for example.

Light pen

A screen cursor can be moved by touching the screen with a light pen. Light pens are mainly used for design work and need special software to make them work.

▲
Figure 3.6

Touch screen

A touch screen is a special kind of screen which is sensitive to touch. A selection is made from a menu on the screen by touching part of it. These screens are ideal for use in banks and building societies, where customers who are not used to keyboards can obtain information about the services offered. You can also see touch screens in restaurants and bars.

Graphics tablets (digitisers)

Graphics tablets are rather like electronic tracing paper and, like paper, they come in all sizes, from a modest A4 size to a very large A0 size that will occupy the best part of a desk. A cursor or puck is used on a graphics tablet to trace over technical drawings put on the screen using a computer-aided design package such as AutoCAD.

Magnetic stripe reader

You can see magnetic stripe readers at the side of computerised tills (often called electronic point-of-sale (EPOS) terminals). Figure 3.7 shows one being used to read information contained in the magnetic stripe of a credit card.

Barcode readers

If you think that barcodes are used only in supermarkets, take another look. Barcodes are used in library systems, luggage handling systems at airports and for warehouse stock control. Barcode systems are now at an advanced stage and readers can record barcodes at distances of five metres or more. This has increased the number of applications.

In America, researchers have painstakingly glued barcodes to the backs of some bees. These barcodes are scanned every time a bee enters or leaves its hive, thus providing valuable information about pollination. Imagine the chaos this could cause if a swarm of bees entered a supermarket (see Figure 3.9)!

▲
Figure 3.8 *A bee with a barcode!*

▲
Figure 3.7 *A magnetic stripe reader*

▲
Figure 3.9 *Bees on the bill!*

Optical character readers and optical character recognition (OCR)

Optical character recognition is a method of inputting text using a scanner along with special software to turn the scanned image into standard ASCII code. In other words, the text is no longer treated as a picture, since each individual letter is recognised on its own and can therefore be edited using word-processing software.

Since OCR software must be able to distinguish between an S and a 5 or a B and an 8, the original text really needs to be typed. As well as recognising the different characters, optical character readers must be able to read different fonts (i.e. different patterns of letters), different type sizes and upper and lower case letters.

OCR software can also be used to scan financial documents such as company accounts directly into spreadsheets, as well as to scan text directly into word processors.

▲
Figure 3.10 *Recognising some characters is not easy*

Magnetic ink character reader and optical character recognition (MICR)

Magnetic ink characters are the rather strange-looking numbers that you see at the bottom of cheques, as shown in Figure 3.11.

The characters are printed using an ink which contains iron and may be magnetised. The magnetic pattern of the numbers is read by a special reader called a magnetic ink character reader.

When a cheque is printed, the account number, branch code and cheque number are all printed in magnetic ink. When someone writes a cheque, the receiver takes it to their bank and pays it into their account. The bank then has to type the amount onto the cheque using magnetic ink before the cheque is dealt with.

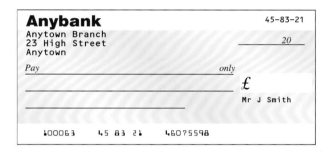

▲
Figure 3.11 *A cheque showing the magnetic ink characters*

Magnetic ink character recognition uses expensive equipment and is suitable only for very large-scale applications. The expense of the system is an advantage in banking since it is unlikely that people would be able to build the equipment and start to print their own cheques.

Optical mark readers and optical mark recognition (OMR)

Optical mark readers are able to sense marks made on a special form in certain places. Figure 3.12 shows a typical example of such a form used in a survey to collect details about customer opinions of service at a restaurant.

Uses for optical mark readers include multiple-choice answer sheet marking, capturing data from questionnaires and enrolment forms.

People who have never completed optical mark reading sheets can have problems filling them in. For instance, in a questionnaire to find out people's opinions of television programmes, the following 'variations' were obtained, despite the correct method of shading in the complete box being explained.

Just some of the variations were:

Did you enjoy the programme? YES NO

Did you enjoy the programme? YES NO

Did you enjoy the programme? YES NO

Did you enjoy the programme? YES NO

Advantages

1 The use of OMR means that details do not have to be typed in; typing could introduce errors and takes time.
2 OMR reduces the cost of inputting large volumes of data because people do not need to type the details.
3 The method is useful when results of tests are needed very quickly, for example, with an aptitude test for a job.

Disadvantages

1 If the forms are being filled in by the general public then very clear instructions are needed. A couple of examples should be chosen as an illustration. No matter how clear your instructions are you will find that a high proportion of forms are filled in incorrectly. The rejection rate is found to be around 30 per cent.
2 If the forms are creased or folded then they may be rejected or foul the machine. This will add to the time needed to read the forms. Badly damaged forms will need to be rewritten or keyed in manually.

Punched cards

Punched cards contain holes in different positions which mean something when they are read by a reader. Before screens and keyboards were widely used, punched cards were the main method of entering data into computers. They are seldom used now, but one use still remains, where a punched clock card is used to record the hours a person works so that their wages can be calculated.

▲ **Figure 3.12** *An OMR form used to collect customer opinions about service in a restaurant*

Voice recognition

With voice recognition you speak directly to the computer. It is particularly useful for people who have limited movement. It is now popular for inputting data into word-processing or database packages. A microphone is the input device for such systems.

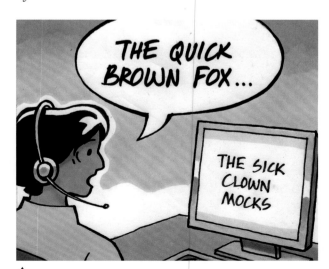

▲ **Figure 3.13** *Voice recognition*

Microphone

A microphone is used as the input device for a speech recognition system. The voice pattern of the user is then converted into instructions to the operating system or applications software, or into text on the screen.

A microphone may also be used as an input device to a voicemail system. Voicemail uses the internet to send, store and receive voice messages. The system works in a similar way to the email system, but instead of a text message being stored on disk, the user's voice is stored instead. The company providing the connection to the internet, called the internet service provider (ISP), stores the voice message on its server, and when the user logs on the system informs them that they have a voicemail message. The user can then play the message back using a loudspeaker as the output device.

Electronic point of sale (EPOS) terminal

EPOS terminals are the cash registers which also act as terminals to a main computer system. As well as providing customers with itemised bills, these systems also give useful management information.

Electronic fund transfer at point of sale (EFTPOS)

EFTPOS terminals are similar to EPOS terminals but with some additional features. For instance, they are able to transfer funds from your bank account directly to a store's account using a card called a debit card. If you have a debit card you can use it instead of a cheque and it is a faster method of payment. The advantage to a store is that the money is instantly transferred into its account, whereas with cheques and credit cards there is a delay before the money reaches the shop's account. You can also get 'cashback' using your debit card.

There are some disadvantages with such cards: they may be stolen or forged and they are said to encourage people to spend more money.

Scanner

Scanners are used to scan text or pictures into a computer's memory where they can then be manipulated in some way before being printed. They can be cheap hand-held ones, or flatbed A4 size or larger.

Optical character recognition (OCR) involves scanning in the image of a page of text with a scanner and then using special software to recognise each of the characters separately, so that they can be altered, if needed, using a word processor. Scanners often have OCR software included in the price.

Scanners are also used to scan in photographs and pictures for use in desktop publishing. One of the main problems you encounter when scanning images is the amount of space they take up on the disk. However, special file compression software can be used to reduce file sizes.

Digital cameras

Digital cameras are becoming very popular for a number of reasons:

- no film is needed
- there are no expensive developing costs
- you can put photographic images directly into a document without the need for a scanner
- the pictures, since they are in digital form, can be sent immediately over the internet
- you can size (enlarge and reduce) the image as well as crop it (cut out the part of the photograph you want) using software, without the need for professional darkroom work.

Digital cameras look just like traditional cameras except they have no film as such. Instead they have a memory which stores the image and many of them have special memory cards to give extra storage. The more memory they have, the greater the number of pictures which can be taken before downloading.

The amount of memory taken up by a picture depends on its resolution. The resolution is determined by the number of dots which make the picture; the greater the number of dots, the crisper the image. Higher resolution photographs take up more memory, so the camera will store fewer of them.

As well as the camera, you also need special software to edit, store and display your pictures on a computer. Using this software you can also remove things which you did not spot when taking the photograph. You could, for instance, remove a telegraph pole which looks as though it is sticking out of someone's head, correct red-eye and adjust the colour and contrast. It is even possible to take the outline of a person and put them into an entirely different picture or background.

Web cameras (webcams)

A web camera (webcam for short) is simply a digital camera that is used to capture still images and video images (i.e. moving images). These images can then be transmitted to a computer where they are stored in a suitable graphics format. If required, pictures can be used on a website.

Webcams are often included in complete computer systems, with the camera placed on top of the screen. Such a system allows videoconferencing.

Webcams are not, however, restricted to the tops of computers. There are webcams everywhere. Here are some of their uses.

Advertising

Cruise companies place them on ships so that potential customers can see what is going on inside a ship and where the ship is at a particular time.

Checking on children in nurseries

All parents worry about child abuse. When they put their children in nurseries they want to be sure that the children are looked after properly. Some nurseries have webcams so that parents can see their children on a computer while they are at work.

Checking on the weather in another part of the world

There are webcams just about everywhere. It is possible to see what the weather is like anywhere in the world if you have access to a webcam there.

Questions

1 Having your own web camera can be great fun, but like other features of the internet, it is not without its dangers.

What dangers might there be in using a web camera?

2 Here are some situations where you have to decide which would be the best input device to use. You should give reasons for your choice:

(a) Your teacher would like to keep a bank of past GCSE questions on a certain subject such as history. She does not want to have to type them all in, but she may want to alter them slightly using her word processor. What do you suggest?

(b) A firm runs an aptitude test with multiple-choice-style answers for all job applicants. The applicants first take the test and if they pass they are given an interview. The whole test (usually around 50 sheets) needs to be marked quickly and accurately whilst the applicants are having a coffee break. Which input device could be used?

(c) A library would like to have a new way of recording the membership number and video number when a video is rented. At present the six-digit number of the member and video are typed in and this causes a lot of errors. Which alternative method could they use?

(d) A building society is thinking of introducing a new cheque book account. Which input method would be best for the process of cheque clearing?

▲ **Figure 3.14**   *There are many webcams at the Kennedy Space Center. Log onto NASA to see what the latest space projects are*

Data from sensors

Sensors are used to obtain data automatically. For instance, traffic lights have a sensor which records the frequency of the traffic. A microprocessor can then alter the sequencing of the lights to improve the flow of the traffic. Burglar alarms and central heating thermostats both contain sensors. We will be looking at sensors in a later chapter.

Output devices

Output devices provide results in a suitable form after data processing. In many cases this will be in the form of a hard copy (printout) or on a screen. The widespread use of electronic mail means output is now often in the form of an electronic message to another computer.

Visual display units (VDUs) or monitors

VDUs or monitors are the fat screens you see being used with computers. They are used to display information on the screen and use a bulky cathode ray tube, which makes them large and heavy.

Liquid crystal display (LCD) screens

LCD screens are the more modern, thin screens you see being used with laptop and many desktop computers. Their main advantages over VDUs are that they do not occupy as much space on the desktop, in the case of desktop computers, and they are very light, which makes them portable in the case of laptop computers.

Laser printers

Laser printers offer both high speed and excellent print quality for text and graphics. Laser printers have toner cartridges that contain a fine powdered black plastic called toner.

Figure 3.15 shows a laser printer. As you can see it looks very much like a small photocopier.

▲
Figure 3.15 *A laser printer*

Inkjet printers

Inkjet printers are popular with home users because they are cheap to buy. However, they are expensive to run because of the high cost of the ink cartridges. They work by spraying ink onto the paper and can produce very high quality colour or black and white printouts. They are ideal printers for stand-alone computers, but are not good for networked computers as they are too slow.

The main advantages of inkjet printers are that they produce high quality print – ideal for printing photographs, brochures and illustrated text.

They are also very quiet when printing and this is important in an office, as telephone calls or conversations with colleagues can be conducted while the printer is printing. Another advantage is that they are cheap to buy.

▲
Figure 3.16 *An inkjet printer*

The main disadvantage of inkjet printers is the high cost of the ink cartridges. This is acceptable for low volume work, but for large volumes it is much cheaper to use a colour laser printer.

Other disadvantages are that the ink smudges and special, expensive, glossy paper is needed if you want to print out high quality photographs.

Dot-matrix printers

Dot-matrix printers are not as popular as other types of printers. There are some uses, however, for which dot-matrix printers are ideal.

Dot-matrix printers are impact printers, which can transfer print through layers of paper. This means that they are able to print multi-part stationery. So if you want to print a multi-part sheet where, for example, the white topsheet goes to the customer, the yellow goes to accounts, the blue to the stores, then you will need to use a dot-matrix printer.

▲
Figure 3.17 *A dot-matrix printer*

Colour printers

Colour printing is useful for improving the appearance of the output from a computer system. Imagine how much more interesting financial reports, posters, brochures, business letters and so on are when in colour.

Colour inkjet printers

These are the cheapest colour printers and are generally the ones chosen for home use, where they find a variety of uses such as printing birthday cards, invitations, menus and producing colour photographs from digital cameras. In order to produce high quality colour, inkjet printers need special glossy paper which is more expensive. When the image quality is not so crucial, ordinary paper can be used.

Although inkjets are cheap to buy, their running costs are quite high because the ink cartridges are expensive.

Colour laser printers

Colour laser printers do not produce as clear images as inkjet printers and are therefore not as suitable for the printing of photographs. They do cost more than inkjet printers to buy and their operating costs are high. They generally print at a higher speed than an inkjet printer.

Questions

Explain how a colour printer might be useful to:
(a) an estate agent
(b) a curtain design and fitting company
(c) a person who stores all their family photographs on their computer
(d) a pupil at school producing work for a project.

Advantages and disadvantages of laser printers

If you look at each type of printer you can see that the laser printer is probably the best overall printer, with the inkjet printer a close second. There are some advantages and disadvantages of laser printers, as we will see here.

Advantages of laser printers

1 Since they are page printers they are able to print a page at a time, which means they are very fast. The speed of a laser printer is typically about 10 ppm (pages per minute).
2 They produce high quality text and graphics. Typically laser printers print at 600 or 1200 dpi (dots per inch).

This improves the quality (called the resolution) of the image compared with other types of printer.

3 They are quiet in operation compared with dot-matrix printers, which are very noisy. The only sound laser printers make is the sound of the cooling fans and the paper moving.

4 Laser printers are equipped with paper trays for both the input and the output paper, which means that once the printer has been set up it does not need supervision.

Disadvantages of laser printers

1 Laser printers are more expensive than dot-matrix or inkjet printers.

2 They are quite large and can take up a lot of desk space.

3 They are quite complex, so the repair bills can be high.

4 Because they are non-impact printers, multi-part stationery cannot be used. With a dot-matrix printer, the impact can make marks on several sheets of paper at the same time. These thin sheets can then be sent to different departments within a company.

5 Laser printers are page printers, so they cannot be used with continuous stationery.

Graph plotters

Graph plotters enable accurate line diagrams to be produced on paper. They are ideal for plans, maps, line diagrams and three-dimensional drawings. Graph plotters use pens to produce images, and different pens may be used containing different coloured inks. There are two types of graph plotter. The drum plotter is shown in Figure 3.19 and the flatbed plotter in Figure 3.20. The drum plotter has the advantage that very large drawings can be produced.

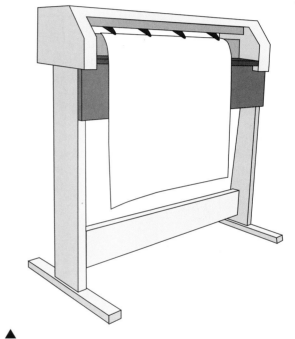

▲
Figure 3.19 *A drum plotter*

▲
Figure 3.18 *Toner cartridges are messy to change and can make you look as though you've been to a fingerprinting session at the local police station*

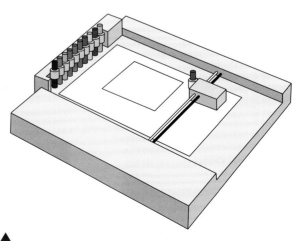

▲
Figure 3.20 *A flatbed plotter*

Voice output

Visually handicapped people find the spoken word from a computer invaluable. For instance, when special software is used with a word processor they can hear each letter on headphones as it is typed, and if they go to the start of a word then this is also indicated.

Electrical signals

Sometimes the output from one computer system can simply be a series of electrical signals. This is the case if one computer is being used as a terminal and the work that is done sent as electrical signals to a main computer, remote from the terminals.

Electrical signals can be output and used to control all kinds of devices, such as central heating systems or burglar alarms.

Robots

Electrical signals from a computer can be used to control a robot arm like the one shown in Figure 3.21. Robots are dealt with in Chapter 20.

Actuators

An actuator is a device that responds when signalled to do so by the computer. An example of an actuator is an electric motor.

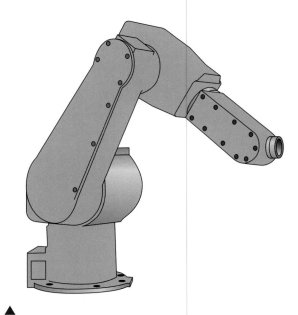

▲ **Figure 3.21** *Electrical signals can be used to control a robot arm*

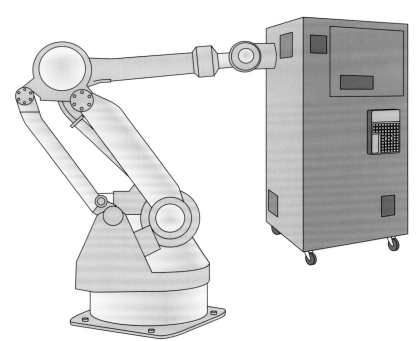

◄ **Figure 3.22** *Another robot arm (an output device) with a keypad, where the number code that controls it is typed in*

Test Yourself

Using the words in the list below, copy out and complete sentences **A** to **K**, underlining the words you have inserted. The words may be used once, more than once or not at all.

mouse   optical mark recognition   keyboard

laser   optical character reader

joysticks   light pens   barcode readers   inkjet

magnetic ink   character recognition   retail

A The most common input device, which comes with all computers, is the _____.

B A _____ is used to move the pointer around the screen and to make selections.

C _____ are used primarily with games.

D _____ _____ are used with computer-aided design packages to produce technical drawings on the screen.

E _____ _____ are used in supermarkets for recording the details of goods as they are passed over the laser scanner.

F Text may be read directly into a computer using a device called an _____ _____ _____.

G The method used by banks when inputting the details contained on cheques during the clearing process is called _____ _____ _____ _____.

H Optical mark readers are able to read the marks made on special forms. The process is called _____ _____ _____.

I EPOS and EFTPOS are systems that are used extensively in _____ outlets.

J The type of printer that produces the highest quality print and uses a toner cartridge is called a _____ printer.

K A cheaper printer, which squirts a jet of ink at the paper, is called an _____ printer.

IT Tasks

There are webcams everywhere. It is interesting and fun to look at some of them. Some sites allow you to control the camera by moving it and zooming in and out.

Use the internet to find sites that use a webcam. Write a list of the web addresses of the sites that you visited and write a short sentence to describe what you saw.

Things to do

1 A bathroom design company uses a computer to help plan new bathrooms. The company sends out a salesperson who measures up the bathroom and makes certain suggestions regarding the arrangement of the toilet, bath, basin, shower and so on. When the client is happy with the arrangement, the salesperson returns to the shop, where the bathroom design is transferred to the screen. The client is then sent a three-dimensional diagram of what their bathroom will look like.

(a) Name a device, other than a keyboard, that the designer could use as an input device and say why it is suitable.

(b) A very accurate and high quality printout is needed for the installers to work from. Name an output device that could produce a high quality plan.

(c) What other tasks could the computer perform other than those already mentioned?

2 The following diagrams show a variety of input or output devices.

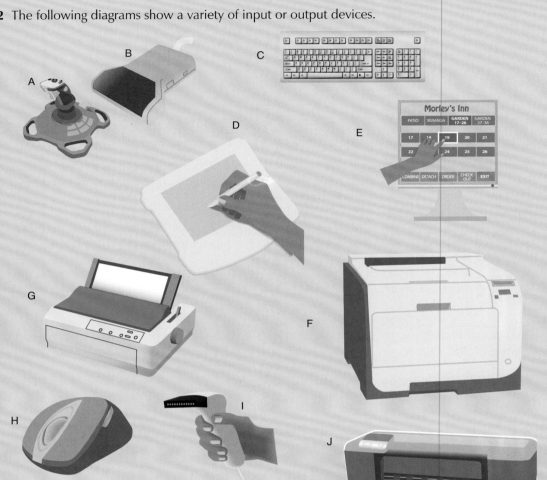

For each one:
(a) name it
(b) say how it is used
(c) give an application for it (e.g. you need to mention the type of job each is suited to).

3 A great many printers are now available, ranging from small, slow devices to versatile, fast printers. Describe various types of printer that are now in use, giving an indication of their comparative speeds and paying particular attention to:
(a) the different facilities that they provide
(b) typical applications for which they are appropriate.
(It is best to get your information for this question from recent copies of any computer magazine.)

4 A friend has asked you for your advice on buying a suitable printer. Write down a list of questions that you would need to ask them, before advising them.

Investigations

Betterbuys

Betterbuys is a small chain of food supermarkets. At present there are 10 shops scattered throughout a country.

The present manual system at the checkout is as follows:

1 The customer brings their basket or trolley to the checkout.

2 The price of each item is on a ticket that is stuck onto the goods when they are placed on the shelves. The till operator keys in the price of each item, presses a key to tell the till to display the total when ready and keys in the amount of money the customer has paid. The till automatically calculates how much change should be given.

3 The stock is checked each day by a person with a stock list going round the shelves and counting the stock of each item.

Some of the problems with the existing system are:

1 Sometimes goods are brought to the till with no label on them. Looking them up takes time and angers the shoppers in the queue behind.

2 All the main competitors are now using EPOS systems, where an itemised bill is produced, which gives all the names of the goods, along with their prices.

3 Changing prices for special offers is difficult, since it is necessary to stick new price stickers over the existing labels.

4 Customers are often complaining that the supermarkets frequently run out of certain items such as bread.

Task 1

Visit a large supermarket that uses EPOS terminals. Produce a word-processed report outlining the way in which EPOS terminals are used in the supermarket you have visited.

Task 2

Mr C. Masood, the recently appointed managing director of Betterbuys, wants to know what the main advantages are in using EPOS terminals compared with the existing manual system. In a word-processed document, explain what these advantages are. Are there any disadvantages to the supermarket or to the customers?

Task 3

It is eventually decided to go ahead with the EPOS system and you have been asked to produce a leaflet explaining how the system works and how it will be better for shoppers. This leaflet should be produced using word-processing or (better) desktop publishing software. This leaflet will be given to shoppers to help explain the new system.

4 Storing Data

Computers store data either in chips inside the main processor, in what is called memory (main store), or on other media such as a magnetic disk, in what is called backing store.

The storage of data

The number of instructions and amount of data a computer can store in its memory is measured in **bytes**. One byte contains 8 bits (short for binary digits, 0 and 1). Computers work by using pulses of voltage which represent either 0 or 1. A low-voltage pulse represents a 0 and a high-voltage pulse a 1. In most cases, 8 bits are needed to store one character. So a single character (letter, number or symbol on the keyboard) can be stored in one byte. We normally refer to storage capacities in terms of kilobytes (KB) or megabytes (MB).

1 KB = 1 kilobyte = 1,024 bytes
1 MB = 1,048,576 bytes
1 GB = 1 gigabyte = 1,000 MB
1 ITB = 1 terrabyte = 1,000 GB

From this you can see that for each megabyte we could store 1,048,576 characters.

Memory (main store)

There are two types of memory or main store:
- read-only memory (ROM)
- random-access memory (RAM).

Memory (or main store) is the name given to the group of chips inside the processing unit where data are held temporarily whilst processing takes place. The data held in the memory are instantly available to the computer, unlike backing storage which has to be accessed on disk or tape. The memory needed to run programs has increased enormously over the last few years as

they have employed more icons and other graphics. Even laser printers now have more memory than computers did only a few years ago (Figure 4.1).

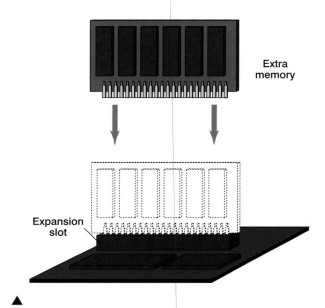

▲ **Figure 4.1** *Most computers have expansion slots for extra memory chips*

Memory is used to hold the following:

1. programs – these may be the operating system (programs which control the hardware) or applications programs (programs to do a particular task, such as word processing)
2. input data – these are put into the memory before processing
3. working area – this is used to store the data that are currently being processed
4. output data – these are put into the part of the store ready to be output to the printer.

Read-only memory (ROM)

ROM is held on a chip inside the processor and is used to hold data which cannot be changed by the user. Programs are stored on ROM chips when a computer is manufactured. Usually, the data held on ROM will be the software that tells the computer how to load the operating system (called the boot program). Since data are permanently stored on ROM they will stay stored even if the power is switched off. ROM is often referred to as non-volatile memory.

Random-access memory (RAM)

RAM is again held on a chip, but data in RAM are held only temporarily, which means that the data disappear when the power is switched off. For this reason, RAM is often called volatile memory. RAM is used to hold both data and programs during processing.

Both RAM and ROM are often referred to as immediate access store (IAS).

Magnetic media

Magnetic media are used to store data in the form of a magnetic pattern on a hard disk or series of disks.

Hard drives

Fixed hard disks consist of a series of disks coated with a magnetic material and a series of read/write heads which record data onto the surface or record it off the surface. Fixed hard disks are used to store operating systems, applications software (i.e. the software you use to complete tasks such as word processing) and any working data. All of these require that the data can be accessed quickly and stored onto the media quickly.

It is possible to buy additional hard disks for backup purposes. These hard drives are called portable hard drives and may be removed each night and stored safely.

Portable hard disks are also used to store very large files which need to be transported from one computer to another. Like fixed hard drives they can transfer data to and from the hard drive at very high speed, which is much faster than that for optical drives such as DVD.

Magnetic tape

Magnetic tape stores data on a plastic, magnetic-coated tape. Magnetic tape has a huge storage capacity and is used to back up the data stored on hard disks. Because it takes time to move the tape to the position where the data are stored, tape storage is much less common than disk storage.

Magnetic tape provides serial access. What this means is that it is necessary to access each record in turn on the tape until the correct file is found. This takes a long time and is the reason why magnetic tape is being taken over by fixed hard disk. Magnetic tape is useful for when every record on the tape needs to be accessed or stored in turn on the tape. This is the reason why magnetic tape can be used for backups of file servers for computer networks. These servers can have huge storage capacities and can be backed up on a single tape rather than a series of hard disks.

Optical disks

Optical disks are flat circular disks on which data are stored as a series of bumps. The way the bumps reflect laser beam light is used to read the data off the disk.

CDs are used to hold large files (more than 1 gigabyte) and are ideal for holding music and animation files. DVDs have a much larger capacity (4.7–8.5 gigabytes) and are used mainly for storing films and videos. Both CD and DVD can be used to store computer data and can be used for backup purposes.

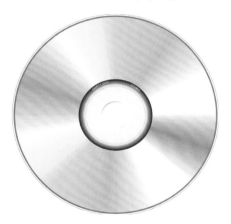

▲
Figure 4.2

CD-ROM (compact disc read-only memory)

CD-ROMs are used mainly for the distribution of software and the distribution of music. Although most home computers are equipped with DVD drives, a lot more computers, especially those used in businesses, still only have CD drives. You can read a CD using a DVD drive, but you cannot read a DVD with a CD drive. This is why software is still being sold on CD rather than DVD.

With CD-ROM:

- data are read only
- data are stored as an optical pattern
- there are a large storage capacity (600 MB)
- they can be used for the distribution of software.

DVD-ROM (digital versatile disc read-only memory)

DVD-ROM is used for the distribution of movies where you can only read the data off the disk. A DVD-ROM drive can also be used for reading data off a CD.

DVD is mainly used for the distribution of films.

CD-R (CD-recordable)/DVD-R

CD-R allows data to be stored on a CD, but only once. DVD-R allows data to be stored on a DVD once. Both these disks are ideal where there is a single 'burning' of data onto the disk. For example, music downloaded off the internet could be recorded onto a CD in case the original files were damaged or lost.

They are also used for archive versions of data. Archive versions are where old data are stored for reference purposes in case they are needed in the future. Storing archive data on the fixed hard disk would clutter up the disk, so it is better to store it on removable media and store it in a safe place. DVD-R is ideal for storing TV programmes when you do not want to record over them.

CD-RW (CD-rewritable)

A CD-RW disk allows data to be stored on the disk over and over again – just like a hard disk.

This is needed if the data stored on the disk need to be updated. You can treat a CD-RW like a hard drive, but the transfer rate is less and the time taken to locate a file is greater. The medium is not as robust as a hard drive.

DVD-RW (DVD-read/write)

A DVD-RW drive can be used to write to as well as read data from a DVD.

DVD-RWs are sometimes called DVD burners because they are able to be written to and not just read from. Like CD-RWs, they are ideal for storing data that need updating regularly.

Typical storage capacities are:

- 4.7 GB for the older DVD drives
- 8.5 GB for the latest DVD drives.

DVD-RAM (DVD-random-access memory)

DVD-RAM has the same properties as DVD-RW in that you can record data onto it many times, but it is faster and easier to overwrite the data. The repeated storage and erasure of data acts in a similar way to RAM, hence the name.

Blu-ray

The Blu-ray disk is a new optical disk that has a much higher storage capacity than a DVD. Blu-ray disks have capacities of 25 GB, 50 GB and 100 GB. These high-capacity Blu-ray disks are used to store high-definition video. They are used for storing films/movies, with a 25 GB Blu-ray disk being able to store two hours of high-definition (HD) TV or 13 hours of standard-definition TV. It is possible to play back video on a Blu-ray disk whilst simultaneously recording HD video. Some newer computers now come with Blu-ray drives.

Other memory devices

There are a number of memory devices which are used for backup storage and for the movement of data from one portable device to another:

- USB flash memory
- HD cards.

USB flash memory

USB flash memory is memory that is plugged into the computer via the computer's USB socket.

USB flash memory has several names, such as pen drive or memory stick, and they are very popular storage media which offer cheap and large storage capacities, and are an ideal medium for photographs, music and other data files. They consist of printed circuit boards enclosed in a plastic case.

The main advantages are:

- small and lightweight – easy to put on your keyring or in your pocket and can be used with any computer
- large storage capacity (up to 256 GB)
- no moving parts so they are very reliable
- not subject to scratches like optical media.

The main disadvantages are:

- their small size means they can easily be stolen
- they are often left in the computer by mistake and lost
- they do not have as high an access speed as magnetic hard disks.

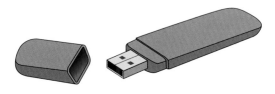

▲
Figure 4.3 *Memory sticks/pen drives are ideal for the transfer of relatively small amounts of data between computers*

HD cards

HD cards, often referred to as flash memory cards, are the small, thin, rectangular or square removable cards that are used for storage of digital images by digital cameras. They can also be used in any situation where data need to be stored, and so are used with desktop computers, laptops, palmtops, mobile phones and MP3/MP4 players. You can see the card readers in supermarkets and other stores where you can take your card containing photographs and get them printed out.

▲
Figure 4.4 *This flash memory card is being used with a mobile phone*

Memory systems used in MP3/MP4 players

MP3 players are used to store and play back music. MP4 players are used to store and play back both video and music.

Memory size is important for both MP3 and MP4 players as it determines how much media can be held by the device.

Because MP4 players are used to store video, and video files are much larger, they usually have a small magnetic hard drive for storage. MP3 players usually use memory on a chip similar to that used with USB flash memory.

▲
Figure 4.5 *An MP3/MP4 player*

Modern devices for the storage of music and films

People are more demanding in the way they want to watch films or listen to music. For example, they may want to download films and music and listen to/watch them on their large TV. There are storage devices that make use of magnetic hard drives that can be attached to TVs and computers and can be used as a store for all the media you need.

These devices, called HD media drives, have huge storage capacities (typically 1 TB – 1 TB = 1,000 GB).

HD recorders are also used to record TV programmes and many of these allow you to:

- watch one programme whilst recording a different programme
- record two different programmes that are broadcast at the same time on different channels – this requires more than one read/write head
- watch one recording whilst recording another programme.

▲ **Figure 4.6** *This HD media drive allows you to store and play music and videos, and to look at photographs from the internet*

Test Yourself

Using the words in the list below, copy out and complete sentences **A** to **H**, underlining the words you have inserted. The words may be used more than once.

character   one   byte   kilobytes   memory

megabytes   optical   CD-ROMs   magnetic tape

RAM   ROM   hard

A A bit is the smallest unit of storage and may be nought or _____.

B A group of 8 bits is called a _____.

C One byte is used to store one _____.

D Storage is usually measured in _____ or the larger unit _____.

E Data and program instructions currently being dealt with are held in _____.

F There are two types of storage: one retains data when the power is removed and is called _____; the other loses data when the power is turned off and is called _____.

G The most common backing storage media are _____ disks and hard disks.

H Optical disks, called _____, are used in multimedia systems.

Things to do

1 The words RAM and ROM are often used when computer memory is discussed.
 (a) What do the following abbreviations stand for?
   (i) RAM
   (ii) ROM
 (b) What are the main differences between RAM and ROM?
 (c) Backing storage is storage outside the central processing unit. Why is backing storage needed?

2 A general practitioner's surgery contains a personal computer on which all the patients' records are stored. What type of backing storage would it be most likely to have?

5 Software

What is software?

Software is the general name given to all the programs that can be run on computer hardware. There are two main categories of software: operating systems (systems software) and applications software.

Operating systems (systems software)

An operating system is a program that controls the hardware directly. Operating systems perform the following tasks:

- They provide a way for applications software to communicate with the hardware. For example, in your word-processing package (an application), if you click on the printer icon, the operating system gives an instruction to the printer to start printing.
- They manage the system resources such as memory and also allocate CPU time to the task being run.
- They manage the transfer of data to and from the various peripherals (keyboards, mice, scanners, printers, etc.).
- They manage system security. Many operating systems allocate certain rights to users. A user can only do certain things on entering a password.

The operating system provides an interface between the user and the computer hardware. Figure 5.1 helps to explain this. Without an operating system, a computer would be useless, so the first thing a computer looks for when it is switched on is the operating system. Once the operating system has been found, the computer loads it from disk.

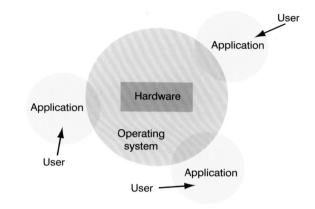

▲ **Figure 5.1** *The operating system acts as a 'shell' around the hardware. For programs to work, they need an operating system. For users to get useful work out of the computer they have to use applications programs and the operating system to communicate with the hardware*

Multitasking

Multitasking means the ability of a computer to run two or more programs at the same time. As a user it may be hard to see how you can do two things at once. One way would be to print out a large document (say 20 pages) whilst continuing to use the word processor to type in a new letter. The operating system takes care of the printing and the word processing at the same time.

Other examples could include sending a fax or transferring a large file over the internet whilst working on another task.

Multi-access

A multi-access system is a system that allows several users to make apparently simultaneous use of the computer. Network systems are multi-access systems and it appears to each user that they are the only user of the computer, when in fact the computers' processing time is being shared between other users.

User interfaces

The user interface is what you see when you turn on the computer; it consists of the cursors, prompts, icons, menus and so on, which allow you to get something done using your computer. Ideally the user interface should be as easy to use as possible, so it is obvious to someone who has never used the software before what they have to do.

User interfaces may be:

1 command-driven
2 menu-driven
3 graphical (referred to as a graphical user interface or GUI).

Command-driven interface

With a command-driven interface, you type in an instruction, which is usually abbreviated, in order to get something done. Command-driven user interfaces are not easy to use. If you are new to the software you have to remember many commands in order to be able to use the software quickly. Commands for different software packages are rarely the same, so people often get the commands mixed up. Some people, mainly those who are used to using them, prefer command-driven menus because they can be faster to use once you have learnt all the commands.

Menu-driven interface

This type of user interface produces a list of commands or options available within a program and the user can make a selection by using either a mouse or a keyboard. Both Microsoft® Windows® and Apple® Macintosh® programs are menu-driven.

Graphical user interface

A graphical user interface (GUI) provides a way for the user to communicate with the computer through pictures (icons) and pull-down menus. Windows®, is an example of a GUI. Windows® provides a common way of using programs, which makes them easier to learn. It also takes care of some common chores, such as working with the printer and the disk drive.

WIMP

WIMP stands for windows, icons, menus and pointing devices. The term describes the features of a graphical user interface (GUI) which make it easier for the user to get things done.

▲
Figure 5.2

Designing a user interface

To make an interface as user-friendly as possible it is necessary to take care when designing it and take into account the following.

- **Consistency** – each part of the software should behave in the same way as another, making the program easier to learn and use.
- **Positioning of items on the screen** – icons, menus and so on should be consistent, again making software easier to learn and use.
- **Use of colour** – some colours are easier for the eye, while others make things harder to see; colours should be chosen carefully.
- **Use of sound** – sound can be annoying to some people, so it is best to make sound an option that a user can turn off if desired.
- **Availability of help** – most software has online help, which means that it is often not necessary to refer to a manual; the user simply accesses the help screen for a particular function or topic.

Programming languages

A program is a set of instructions that the computer can understand. Since the computer can understand only binary code (a series of 1s and 0s), all computer languages must be reduced eventually to binary code, and the way this is done depends on the type of language used. Humans can use different languages to communicate and computers are no different. There are a variety of computer languages and the one that is chosen for a particular job depends on the job that is being done.

Low-level languages

Low-level languages are languages that are easy for the computer to understand, but more difficult for the programmer to understand. Assembly language and machine code are collectively called low-level languages.

Machine language (or machine code)

Machine language is the language directly understood by the machine. In other words, it consists of a series of 1s and 0s. All other languages must be translated into machine code before the instructions can be carried out, unless the program is already written in machine code. Machine code is often machine-specific, which means that one computer's machine code will not be understood by a different type of computer. A program written in machine code needs no translation and is therefore very fast. A lot of games or simulation programs are written in machine code for this reason.

Assembly language

An assembly language is a language that uses simple instructions, such as ADD, SUB and LDA, and is used in preference to machine code, since it is easier for the programmer to use and to debug (debugging means removing any mistakes from the program). Once a program has been written in assembly language it needs to be translated into machine code by software called an assembler before it can be understood by a computer.

▲
Figure 5.3

High-level language

A high-level language is developed with the programmer in mind rather than the computer. Such languages have the advantage that they are not as machine-dependent as machine codes or assembly language, so once a program has been written it can be used on different computers with very little alteration.

High-level language instructions are similar to English, which means that programming is made easier. Instructions in BASIC, a high-level language, include such commands as PRINT, GOTO and READ, which are easy for us to understand and remember.

Advantages of high-level languages

1 Simple instructions similar to English make high-level languages easy to understand.
2 It is easy to correct errors and test programs.
3 Programs written in high-level languages can be used on different makes of computer.

Some high-level languages have been developed with a particular problem in mind. Here are some, along with their main uses:

- **COBOL** is used mainly for business data processing because of its excellent file handling.
- **BASIC** is mainly used as a teaching language.
- **FORTRAN** is used mainly in scientific applications.
- **C++** is an increasingly popular language. It is very good for graphics and good for developing commercial software.
- **LOGO** is used primarily for teaching children about programming and using computers. Children are taught to write a series of instructions to control the movement of a 'turtle', which draws a line behind it on the screen.
- **JAVA** is a language especially suited for writing software used to search for things on the internet.
- **HTML** Hypertext Markup Language. A language used for the development of websites.

Translation programs

Translation programs are part of the systems software and are used to convert the program commands into machine code. There are three types of translation program: compilers, interpreters and assemblers.

Compilers and interpreters

Compilers and interpreters are both programs that change high-level language instructions into machine code, although the way they do this is different.

An **interpreter** takes each instruction in turn, converts it to machine code and then carries it out. It is rather like a person who cannot read French taking a word in a document, looking it up in a dictionary, translating it and then moving on to the next word. If the document needs to be read at a later date then the same process will need to be performed.

A **compiler** is software that converts the whole of a program written in a high-level language into machine code in one go. Provided that there are no mistakes in the program, the complete program is converted to machine code. Suppose an original disk contains a program written in a high-level language (called the source code), then after compilation another disk with the program written in machine code will be produced (called the object code). Whenever the program needs to be run, the disk with the program converted to machine code is used. This is like a person translating the whole

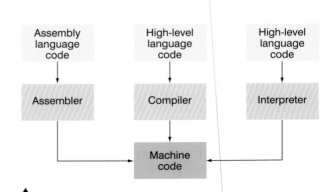

▲ **Figure 5.4** *The relationship between assemblers, compilers and interpreters*

of the document from French to English in one go and then using the English version if the document needs to be read again. If a program needs to be altered at a later date, the original source code is altered and the program recompiled.

Assemblers

Assemblers translate assembly language instructions into machine code. This translation is easy because one instruction in assembly language usually corresponds to one machine code instruction.

Test Yourself

Using the words in the list below, copy out and complete sentences **A** to **F**, underlining the words you have inserted. The words may be used more than once.

hardware   software   systems   operating

compilers   assembler

A Programs that may be run on a computer are called _____.

B Software may be classed into two groups: _____ software and applications software.

C Another name for the systems software is the _____ system.

D Without systems software the _____ would be useless.

E Translation programs which convert high-level language instructions into machine code are of two types: interpreters or _____.

F A translation program used to convert a low-level language instruction into machine code is called an _____.

Things to do

1 Systems software can be divided into three types: the operating system, utility programs and translation programs.
   (a) (i) Give the name of the system software that your computer uses.
       (ii) Give two jobs performed by the operating system.
   (b) Give two examples of a utility program and explain what each does.
   (c) Two types of translation program are used for translating high-level languages into machine code. Explain the differences in the way that compilers and interpreters translate instructions.
   (d) There is another type of program used to translate assembly language into machine code. Give the name of it.
   (e) There are many high-level languages to choose from. Name two of them and for each give the type of job for which they are particularly suited.

2 The following is a list of types of general-purpose package:

   word processing   spreadsheet
   database   graphics
   desktop publishing

Find out, using computer magazines to help you, which of the above categories each of the following packages falls into:

   Microsoft® Word   Microsoft® Access®
   Microsoft® Publisher   Adobe® Photoshop®
   Microsoft® PowerPoint®

3 LOGO is a computer program which may be used to control an arrow on the screen. When the arrow moves forward, it leaves a line on the screen. To control the movement of the arrow, commands are typed in. Some of the commands that may be used are as follows:

FORWARD distance   (in mm)
RIGHT angle   (in degrees)
LEFT angle   (in degrees)

For instance, the command FORWARD 20 would move the arrow forward 20 mm, and the command RIGHT 30 would turn the arrow through an angle of 30°, with the angle measured from the line drawn straight ahead from the arrow. Write down the instructions needed to draw the following shape.

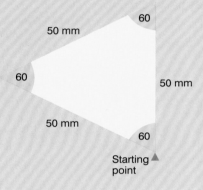

6 Collecting Your Data

The problems with college enrolments

Every year new students enrol on courses in colleges and each college needs to record the student details onto its computer system. Because the enrolments all happen at the same time, the main problem is with the time and the number of staff needed to enter the student details. Let's look at what details need to be recorded.

Questions

Write down a list of the details that a college would need to keep about each of its students. Show your list to a friend to see if you missed any items. It is a good idea to think about who is likely to use the details. Not everyone gets their fees paid for them. For example, some part-time students may have full-time jobs so they have to pay their own fees or their employers pay for them. So you need to distinguish between full- and part-time students.

Form design

In the student enrolment problem discussed above, students would have been asked to fill in a form. The students completed details that only they would know, such as name, date of birth, address, and the college added details such as course codes and fees. The design of forms is very important, as most of the information from forms will be placed on a computer system.

We all have to fill in forms sooner or later. Some forms, if they have been carefully thought out and designed, are very good, but others are appalling. Important information is left out while irrelevant information is included. Often, not enough space is left for the important information. How do we design a good form? To do this, we should bear in mind the following points.

Have people been consulted who will be using the form?

Some users of the form should be asked what the form should contain. Design of an important form is best not left to one person, who may forget to include something.

Headings

The title of the form should describe its use. Too much information on a form will clutter its appearance.

Instructions

Instructions should be in a prominent position and should be clear. If they are not clear, many forms will be returned with items missing or filled in incorrectly. For special types of form, such as those used by optical mark readers like that shown in Figure 6.1, you have to remember that people may not have seen such a form before. It is therefore a good idea to include an example of the way to fill in the form on the form itself.

Layout

The layout should be simple and follow a logical sequence. The items should be spaced out and the form made an appropriate size.

Sections

Many forms have a part which is filled in by the subject and another part which is filled in by the person who distributed the form. Sometimes the latter part says 'for official use only'. If you design such a form, make sure that you place all the parts to be filled in by the subject together and make sure that it is clear which parts have to be completed.

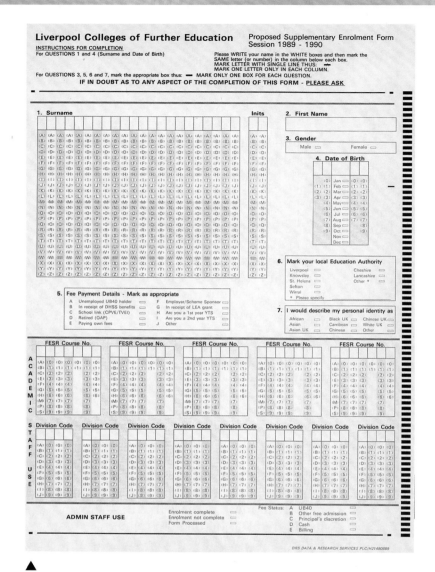

Figure 6.1 *Enrolment form to be filled in by a student writing and shading in boxes*

Testing

It is always a good idea after you have designed a form to ask people to fill it in and then to ask them whether they found it easy to understand. Doing this will also give you an idea about whether you have left enough space for users to write in.

Questions

At the time of enrolment students are required to fill in an application form. Some of the form will be pre-printed; part of it will be filled in by the student and another part will be filled in by the tutor when the correct courses have been decided on. Using your answer to the question earlier in this chapter, design a form that could be used to hold details about the student and the courses they are following.

Coding data

In many instances codes are used to represent information and these are useful provided we know how to interpret them. Why do we use codes? There are several reasons, including the following.

1 Codes are quicker to type in, both initially and for subsequent searches.
2 Using codes reduces the sizes of the files, which in turn increases the speed of searches and any processes performed on the data.
3 Codes are often unique. For instance, if we gave each student a unique code number we could use this to search for a student's details. Using a surname for a search might reveal several students with the same name.

Designing codes

There are certain points to remember when designing a coding system. These are:

1 Codes should always be the same length. This is a useful check (called a validation check). If the code is too long or too short, then we know a mistake has been made.
2 Codes must be easy to use. People will not use them if they are too cumbersome.
3 Codes must not be too short. Although they are easier to type in if they are short, there is the possibility of running out of codes.

Codes may be used in a student enrolment system for the course details. When the code is either typed in or scanned using a barcode

8510/93-4/T

INTRO TO WINDOWS(SUMMER)
HRS: 2   FEE: 45.00
Mode of Attendance 05

▲
Figure 6.2 *Self-adhesive label containing course information and code*

reader, the computer obtains the full details of the course, such as name of course, hours of attendance, fee payable, directly from the course file stored on disk by the computer.

Putting the details into the computer

Getting the information into a structure in which it can be processed by the computer is called **data capture**.

There are various methods that can be used and we will look at each one, with its advantages and disadvantages.

Questions

1 The self-adhesive label shown in Figure 6.2 contains a course code.
   (a) Why has a barcode been used?
   (b) If the information has been stored in a barcode, why is it then written underneath?
   (c) Someone has suggested that all the information contained on the student enrolment form could be put on a series of barcodes. What potential problems are there in doing this?

2 Your headteacher has asked you to come up with a coding system for options taken in year 8. You will need first to investigate the options. The headteacher would like some sort of coding system where the code refers to option, year and so on. Make sure that you fully explain how your coding system was developed. You should also mention any other systems that you developed along the way and the reasons for arriving at your final choice.

3 Design a form to be read by an optical mark reader that you could give to the members of your class to record their names, addresses and dates of birth.

Key to disk

The student enrolment form can be used as the source document and the details that it contains typed into the computer. The main problem with this is that it takes some time.

Typing can also introduce many errors. This method may be used if the number of students is small, but if a college has about, say, 8,000 students, then this could take too long.

Alternative methods of data capture

The use of keyboard entry has been dismissed because of the time it takes. If more staff were to be employed then they would not be fully occupied for the rest of the year, so this method has been discounted. It would be ideal to have some way of the computer automatically reading data from the forms. Several direct input methods can be considered and these are detailed below.

Questions

You have been appointed to be in charge of student enrolments in a college with 5,000 full-time and 6,000 part-time students (11,000 altogether). All the students need to be enrolled in the first two weeks of term so that the college receives funding and the tutors can be given class lists.

(a) Using the enrolment form you have already designed, work out how many characters (letters, numbers, punctuation marks and spaces) there would be in the details supplied by the student and the tutor for an average student. Remember that you do not need to include the information that is preprinted on the form.

(b) Using the total obtained from part (a) and the fact that a keyboard operator could input data at a rate of 50 characters per minute, find the total number of hours it would take for a single operator to key in all 11,000 student details using a keyboard.

(c) From your answer to part (b) report back to the college principal, outlining the problems of using keyboard input for this number of students.

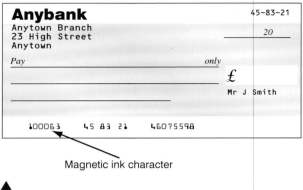

▲ **Figure 6.3** *A bank cheque*

Magnetic ink character recognition (MICR)

With MICR the reader detects characters written in magnetic ink. The problem here is that these characters are usually preprinted (as on a cheque) and only a small amount of data is typed onto the form before processing. Because of the volume of data that needs to be input, this method would be no quicker than typing the data normally. In addition, the equipment needed is very expensive so it is used only by banks for clearing cheques (Figure 6.3).

Optical mark reading (OMR)

With OMR the student would make marks on a form similar to that shown in Figure 6.1. A machine called an optical mark reader is then able to read the marks and convert them into characters in the student file. The instructions on such a form have to be made extremely clear, since many students will not have seen one before, although some may have come across this system with multiple-choice answer sheets. One of the main problems with optical mark forms is that they have a high rejection rate (see Chapter 3). Optical mark readers are not too expensive to buy and the reading speeds are quite high, although the forms are difficult to design. Nevertheless, the use of OMR is a distinct possibility for our enrolment system.

Barcode readers

Barcodes are really suitable only for preprinted information. You could not have a barcode for a student's details since you would not know these in advance. Although barcodes can be printed by laser or inkjet printers using special software (Figure 6.4), data would still have to be typed into a computer, so this would offer no advantage over keying to disk. However, barcode readers are cheap and accurate. We could use them to solve part of the problem. Each course could have its own barcode so that when a student enrols, barcodes for each of their courses are added to the form. With this method, student details, such as name, address and date of birth, would still have to be keyed in, but for a student doing, say, six IGCSEs, just six barcodes could be used instead of all the course information being typed in for each course.

First the bars must be related to the data that needs to be captured for each of the courses. Either an inkjet printer or a laser printer can then be used to print the barcodes. When the barcodes for each course are read with a scanner, time can be saved keying information.

Optical character recognition (OCR)

With OCR, the computer scans a page containing text, looks at each character in turn and compares it with characters it has previously stored. Although the reading speed is high, this method suffers from high rates of rejection and is really suitable only for reading material that has already been typed. For student enrolment the rejection rate would be high, so this method may be rejected.

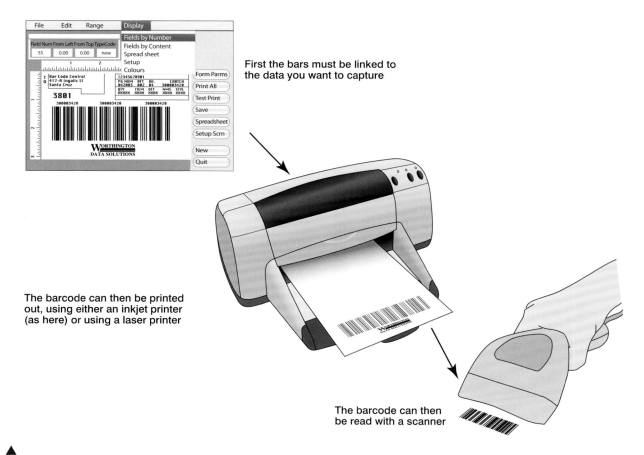

First the bars must be linked to the data you want to capture

The barcode can then be printed out, using either an inkjet printer (as here) or using a laser printer

The barcode can then be read with a scanner

▲

Figure 6.4 *Designing, printing and reading a barcode*

Taking orders quickly

In the UK, you can use a special package which, when you type a postcode and house number, provides all the address details automatically, together with the customer's full name. The system makes use of all 26 million Royal Mail postal addresses and the 44 million names on the Electoral Role (a file of everyone eligible to vote in local and general elections).

The system has advantages:

- It saves around 80 per cent of the keystrokes that would normally be needed.
- There are no problems with the operator having to understand a strange accent.
- It saves time with difficult spellings.
- Spellings are always accurate.

Talking to your computer – speech recognition

Many people are unable to type at high speed and this slows them down when entering data. Rather than type in data using the keyboard, we can now use speech recognition to dictate data into the computer.

▲
Figure 6.5

A speech recognition system usually consists of a multimedia computer with a microphone headset and special speech recognition software. When you talk into the microphone your words are turned into commands or text on the screen. Before the system can be used you have to allow the computer to get used to your voice. It may make mistakes at first, but like a child it will learn by its mistakes. Once you have told the computer about the mistakes it has made and corrected them, it makes fewer mistakes. The more you talk to your computer the better it gets at understanding you.

As well as dictating text into a word processor, you can issue commands using your voice. By saying 'dictate to Word' you could let the computer know that it needs to load the word-processing package Microsoft® Word.

Once you have dictated a document into the computer, you can get the system to speak it back to you via the loudspeakers.

Flood warning: an example of automatic data capture

Where there is low-lying land near to a large river there is always a danger that, after prolonged heavy rain, the river could burst its banks and cause extensive flooding. Flooding can cost insurance companies hundreds of thousands of pounds as householders put in claims for the damage caused by the water. If it is known that a river is likely to burst its banks, then remedial action may be taken to divert the water or use sand bags to build up the banks. The problem is that the river could burst its banks at any time of the day or night, not just during working hours! It is not feasible for a river's water level to be constantly monitored by human staff. Instead sensors are used to measure the water level. Radio links send the data from the sensors to the main computer, and if there is a danger of flooding the emergency services can be alerted and a flood warning issued.

Automatic data capture using signals

Not all data have to be entered using a keyboard or special forms. Some data can be entered directly into a computer in the form of electronic signals. These data usually come from sensors which produce a signal that depends on a physical property. For instance, components passing along a production line could break a beam of light as they pass. A sensor detects that the light is absent when each component passes and a signal is sent to a computer which enables the computer to count the components. Because a sensor receives data from the outside world it may be considered as an input device.

If local authorities wanted to know about the traffic flow along a certain road, they used to employ people (usually students) to stand at the side of the road monitoring and recording the traffic flow. With the flow of traffic we now have on many roads, this is not feasible. Instead pressure sensors are used which record a pulse every time a vehicle passes over them. You may have seen these; they look like thick black wires running across the road and there is sometimes a box at the side of the road to house the recording system. A diagram of this arrangement is shown in Figure 6.6.

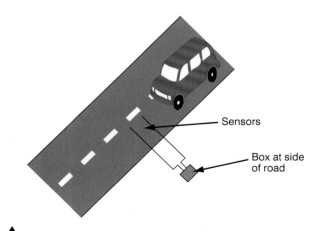

Sensors

Box at side of road

▲
Figure 6.6 *System for automatic monitoring of traffic flow along a road*

Remote sensing

Remote sensing means sensing at a distance. The electronic signals from remote sensors can be sent through telephone wires or via radio transmitters to a computer in another part of the country or even in another part of the world. Such a system is ideal for remote weather stations, where temperature, pressure and wind speed can be detected at thousands of remote weather stations which send the data to a central computer.

As well as using remote sensing to detect when a river is likely to burst its banks, river authorities also use sensors to monitor the water quality in our rivers and to give a pollution alert should the quality change.

Turnaround documents

Problem

A gas company sends out bills for payment. The customers can pay the bill in various ways: they can take the bill and payment to the local gas showroom and pay, or write a cheque and put it in the post. There are other ways to pay but we will concentrate on the postal method. When a payment is made, it has to be linked to the customer and this is done using the customer reference number. Given that the reference number is 15 digits long, a mistake could easily be typed, resulting in the wrong person being credited with the cheque.

Solution

Turnaround documents are used by most companies who receive payment by post. Credit card companies, water, electricity and gas companies all use these documents.

Turnaround documents are documents produced by a computer which are subsequently used as input documents by the computer. For instance, electricity or gas bills contain some preprinted information on them and the variable information (name, address, number of units used, etc.) is added by the computer. Figure 6.7 shows these processes.

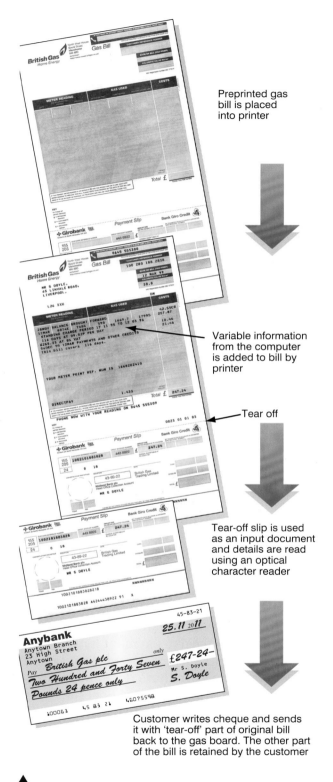

Preprinted gas bill is placed into printer

Variable information from the computer is added to bill by printer

Tear off

Tear-off slip is used as an input document and details are read using an optical character reader

Customer writes cheque and sends it with 'tear-off' part of original bill back to the gas board. The other part of the bill is retained by the customer

▲

Figure 6.7 *Using a turnaround document to record payment of a gas bill*

The bills are sent to customers for payment. If a customer writes a cheque to pay for electricity supply, this is sent back to the electricity board with part of the bill. The tear-off slip is used as an input document with an optical character reader. The computer then notes that the payment has been received and there has been no need to key in account or reference numbers.

Test Yourself

Using the words in the list below, copy out and complete sentences **A** to **G**, underlining the words you have inserted. The words may be used more than once.

MICR   key-to-disk   OMR   turnaround

sensors   data capture   laser   scanner

A Typing the details contained on a form into a computer using a keyboard and then storing the data on disk is called _____-_____-_____.

B _____ _____ is the name given to the process of getting the details into a form that can be processed by the computer.

C Banks use _____ for data capture because it is extremely quick and very difficult to forge.

D _____ involves using a form with boxes that are shaded in. Multiple-choice answer sheets are an example of the use of this method.

E Barcode reading involves using a _____ _____ to read a number or code contained in the barcode.

F Data may also be captured using electric signals from _____.

G Documents which are output by the computer and are subsequently used for input into the system are called _____ documents.

Things to do

1 A motoring organisation uses a computer to work out routes for its members when they go on a driving holiday.

The computer takes into account:

- date of travel
- type of route required (shortest, quickest, scenic, avoiding motorways)
- whether the car is towing a caravan
- the starting and finishing points
- the names of two places the route may go through.

Design a data capture form that could be sent to a member wanting to use this service.

2 The form in Figure 6.8 has been poorly designed. The person who designed the form has asked you for your opinion.

(a) The purpose of the form is to capture the information so that the form can be used as a source document for keying into the computer system. Explain what is meant by

   (i) data capture

   (ii) source document.

(b) Figure 6.9 on the next page shows the form after it has been handed to a parent for filling in. The blank parts of the form are then filled in by the headteacher. Examine the form carefully and say what is wrong with it.

(c) The headteacher has asked you to redesign the form. Redesign it, paying attention to making sure that it is arranged in a logical order, that the spaces left are long enough to accommodate the information, and that there is a clearly marked section to be filled in only by the headteacher.

```
Application form for entry into the 6th form

 DOB_____  Pupil number_____

 Name_____  Sex (M/F)_____

 Address_____
 _____

 Postcode_____
 GCSEs passed with grades
 (for 6th form applicants)_____
 _____

 Ethnicity_____  Religion_____

 Home language_____

 Mode of travel to school_____

 Parents and contacts_____
 _____
 _____

 Arrangements for lunch_____
 _____

 Form_____  Name of form teacher_____

 Name and address of previous school_____
 _____

 Admission date_____

 Hobbies_____
 _____

 Any special medical problems_____
 _____
 _____
```

Figure 6.8 *A blank application form*

Figure 6.9 *The application form after it has been completed by a parent but before the headteacher has added information*

Application form shown:

Application form for entry into the 6th form
DOB 26th March 95   Pupil number ?
Name Joanne Davis   Sex (M/F)
Address 5 Cartbridge Lane,
Crosby, Liverpool
Postcode L23 6TA
GCSEs passed with grades (for 6th form applicants) Mathematics (B) English Language (C), English Literature (B), History (C), Geography (C), Art (A), Biology (C), French (E)
Ethnicity British   Religion Christian
Home language English
Mode of travel to school School bus
Parents and contacts Mother: Jackie Davis 5 Cartbridge Lane, Crosby, Liverpool L23 6TA
Arrangements for lunch School Lunch
Form ?   Name of form teacher ?
Name and address of previous school Same school
Admission date ?
Hobbies Tennis, Swimming, Disco Dancing
Any special medical problems Has Asthma. Always needs to carry an inhaler. Has permission to miss school games if she feels unwell.

3 The driver number on a driving licence codes the date of birth and sex of the driver in the following way:
  digits 1 to 5 – first five letters of surname
  digits 6 and 11 – year of birth
  digits 7 and 8 – month of birth (if female 50 is added)
  digits 9 and 10 – day of month of birth
  digits 12 and 13 – initials of first names or 9 if none.
  (a) What information can you obtain from this coded driver number?
  KENNE409209SE9IB
  (b) By referring to the driver licence code above, briefly explain the difference between data and information.

4 You are a junior systems analyst and you are working on an order processing and sales invoicing system. You have been instructed by your boss to draft the invoice/advice note which will be printed out by the computer. On this advice note will be a variety of items, along with a space, called a data field, for the data to be inserted. You will need to decide how much space should be left for insertion of the data in each field. Your draft design should provide for the computer to print out the following data fields:
  (i) invoice address
  (ii) delivery address
  (iii) customer order number
  (iv) supplier order number
  (v) sales district code
  (vi) salesperson's code
  (vii) invoice date

(viii) product code
(ix)   product description
(x)   quantity
(xi)   unit price
(xii) total price for each product
(xiii) carriage and packing charge
(xiv) invoice total.

(a) Use a full A4 page to show the design of this document and state any assumptions that you have made. For the purpose of simplicity we will ignore the VAT calculations, which would normally be present on such a form.

(b) In order to prepare a usable document, you would need to obtain further information about the 14 data fields shown above. What further information would you need?

IT Tasks

The local newspaper has asked a record store to provide it with a list of the 10 top-selling CDs each week. The record store uses only an ordinary till, so there is no way of counting the sales other than manually. To make things easier for the shop assistants, the shop manager would like to design a form which could be filled in each time a CD is sold.

(a) The manager comes up with the form shown in Figure 6.10 and has asked you for your comments.

Bearing in mind that the shop sells around 800 CDs each week, explain why you think the form would be unsuitable.

There are other problems with the form. Imagine that you are trying to record the sale of CDs using this form: can you think of any additional problems you might have? Explain these.

(b) Design an alternative form and explain how it could be used to obtain the chart.

Name of CD	Artist/Artists	Number sold

▲

Figure 6.10 *Manager's suggested form for recording CD sales*

7 Checking Data

Reasons for errors

Computers can produce accurate results (e.g. payslips, bills, invoices only if the data put into them is accurate). In many systems an input document may be used and the data on this document keyed into the computer. In other systems, this document is input directly to the computer, thus avoiding the need for typing, which frequently introduces errors. Incorrect data can have consequences of varying degrees of seriousness.

Consequences of errors

1 Customers become angry if they are sent bills that are too large and companies lose money if bills are too small.
2 Wrong decisions are made by the managers because the decisions are based on incorrect information.
3 In the UK, a company could be prosecuted under the Data Protection Act 1998 if the incorrect information causes the person concerned some kind of loss. For instance, if someone lost a job because a computer contained wrong information about a criminal record, the unsuccessful applicant could claim compensation.

How are errors avoided?

Verification

Verification means checking that the data being entered into the ICT system perfectly match the source of the data. For example, if details from an order form were being typed in using a keyboard, then when the user has finished, the data on the form on the screen should be identical to that on the paper form (i.e. the data source). Also, if data were sent over a network, the data need to be checked when they arrive to make sure no errors have been introduced.

Here are some methods of verification:

- **Visual check / proofreading** – involves one user carefully reading what they have typed in and comparing it with what is on the data source (order forms, application forms, invoices, etc.) for any errors, which can then be corrected.
- **Double entry of data** – involves using the same data source to enter the details into the ICT system twice and only if the two sets of data are identical will they be accepted for processing. The disadvantage of this is that the cost of data entry is doubled. Double entry of data is often used when creating accounts over the internet. You may be asked to create a password and enter it twice. This ensures there are no mistakes that would prevent you from accessing the account.

Validation

Validation is the process of detecting any data that are inaccurate, incomplete or unreasonable. Validation is performed by a computer program. There are many ways that a computer can check to see whether the data are valid (i.e. allowable).

Validation programs will usually perform some or all of the following types of checks.

Character type checks

Character checks make sure that the right type of characters have been entered. Such checks detect numbers where characters should have been entered and vice versa (Figure 7.1).

Figure 7.1

Range checks

Range checks are performed on numbers to make sure that they lie within a specified range. If, for instance, a program deals with retirement pensions and all the recipients of the pensions have to be 60 or over, then if a typist enters 18 instead of 81, a range check would detect this. However, only absurd data may be detected, so if the typist enters 69 instead of 96, the range check would not detect this.

Presence checks

When entering data into a database the completion of some fields may be optional. For example, a field set up so that a telephone number can be entered in a personnel database may not always have data in it, as the person to which the field refers may not have a telephone.

There are certain fields which must contain data and the system will not allow them to remain blank. An example of this would be a National Insurance number in a payroll system.

Check digits

When any large number is input to a computer, either using a keyboard or using a direct input device such as a barcode reader, there is always a chance of error. These large numbers are important, since they could be product numbers in a supermarket, employee numbers for a payroll or account numbers in a bank; it is essential that they are input correctly. For this reason an additional number is usually included, placed at the end of the original number. This additional number is called a check digit and is calculated from the other numbers.

When an account number is input the computer cuts off the last digit, which is the check digit. It then uses the rest of the numbers to recalculate the check digit, which it then compares with the removed digit. If the numbers are the same then the account number has been input correctly.

Calculating a check digit

If you look at any book, including this one, you will see a number on the back and inside the book, called the International Standard Book Number (ISBN). This is a unique number and is used by bookshops and libraries to identify a particular book.

The computer calculates the check digit in the following way.

Suppose a book with the ISBN 0 09 172981 5 is input to a computer.

1 The computer removes the last number, which is the check digit, so that it is left with 0 09 172981

2 We now have nine numbers. Working from the left-hand side, the first number (i.e. 0) is multiplied by ten, the second number (also 0) is multiplied by nine, the third number (9) is multiplied by eight and so on. The total is then found:
$$0 \times 10 + 0 \times 9 + 9 \times 8 + 1 \times 7 + 7 \times 6 + 2 \times 5 + 9 \times 4 + 8 \times 3 + 1 \times 2 = 193$$

3 The total (193) is then divided by 11 (it is always divided by 11) and the remainder is noted: 11 divides into 193 17 times, with a remainder of 6.

4 The remainder is then subtracted from 11 to give the check digit:
$$11 - 6 = 5$$
so 5 is the check digit.

5 The check digit will sometimes be 10, in which case an X is used.

This may seem quite a complicated procedure to follow, but the method has to be able to detect where digits have been swapped around. Remember that a computer can perform millions of calculations each second, so a little calculation like this is very quick.

Spelling checkers

Spelling checkers are not just used in word-processing software. Any software where accurate text needs to be entered can have a spell-checker facility.

Custom dictionaries

Despite having a huge dictionary, most word processors still fail to recognise certain words. Generally these words are of two types:

- proper names – names of people or places, for example
- specialist words used in a narrow field – medical terms, legal terms, computer jargon, new slang words and so on.

It is possible to purchase supplementary dictionaries for foreign languages, medical terms and so on. Another alternative is to create your own customised dictionary with the terms correctly spelt. Once these words have been added to the dictionary, the spell checker will not question the words again unless they are misspelled.

Length checks

Sometimes a certain item of information is always of a certain length: it contains a set number of characters. A National Insurance number, such as YY232425A, always has nine characters. If a National Insurance number has more or fewer characters than this, then the length check will alert you to the fact that it has been entered incorrectly.

Lookup tables

Stock items are given a unique code to identify them. Whenever this code is used, it is checked against a table stored by the computer to make sure that it is a valid stock code. If the code is not in the table it is rejected, thus preventing any processing using incorrect codes.

Parity errors

When data are passed along a communication line it is important that the data are not corrupted in any way, and if they are, it is equally important that this is detected and the data re-transmitted.

The checking of data after they have passed along a communication line is performed by using a parity bit. Parity checking works in the following way. The computer adds up the number of bits in one byte, and if the parity is different to the parity setting the computer will report an error. It is possible to use either even or odd parity. Taking odd parity, for instance, suppose we are sending the letter C along a communication line. In ASCII code, the series of bits used to represent C is 1000011. Since there are three 1s in this code and odd parity is being used, a 0 is added to the left-hand side of the group of bits so that the total for the byte is odd. If even parity were being used, a 1 would need to be added so that total for the byte would then be an even number.

Modems have a chip inside them to deal with parity checks: the sending modem adds the parity bits and the receiving unit calculates what the parity bit should be. If an error has occurred, transmission parity will no longer be observed, and the corruption is detected. The problem with parity checks is that if more than one error occurs and the errors compensate for each other, parity can still appear to be correct.

Types of error

Transcription errors

Transcription errors occur due to misreading or mis-typing data. This may be caused by bad handwriting or confusing the number 5 with the letter S or zero with the letter O, for instance.

Transposition errors

Transposition errors occur when two digits or letters are swapped around. If you are typing in data at high speed you do not always look at the screen and it is very common to end up with say 'ot' instead of 'to' or '5124' instead of '5214'. It is estimated that about 70 per cent of all errors are transposition errors.

How to avoid errors

Despite all the checks that we can perform on the 'raw' data before it is accepted into a system some errors are bound to occur.

If data is entered into a system via a keyboard, the simplest way of reducing errors is for the person who is entering the data to proof read it carefully against the original document. This simple method reduces the chances of the keyboard operator introducing new errors.

Checking for errors in a wordprocessed document

There are two different situations to consider:

1 The first situation is where the typist has been given a copy of a document or where a document is on an audio tape. All the typist has to do is to key in the document.

In this situation the typist will be working at high speed (often in excess of 70 words per minute) and will be looking at the document or listening to the tape. They will not look at the keyboard and will only occasionally look at the screen.

At such high speed, mistakes are not noticed and any mistakes not corrected as the document is typed. Instead the typist can leave all the corrections until the document is typed. The spell-checking facility on the word processor can then be used. Secondly the typist will carefully proof read the document. Any mistakes spotted are corrected and a copy then printed out.

2 The second situation is where someone types their own document. This is generally a much slower process, since the person has to think about the meaning of what is being typed. Also, such a person is likely to type more slowly than a fully trained typist. A slow typist will probably correct any typing mistakes as the text is typed. The document will still need spell checking and proofreading at the end. In some cases, an important document goes through a series of drafts. Each draft is printed out, corrected and the corrections keyed in until a final copy is obtained.

Automatic spell checking as you type

Most software allows the user to input text and therefore has a spell-checking facility. Some software will check the words as you type them and will highlight any words that are not in the spell checker so that you can check them and correct if necessary.

Using direct input methods

To completely avoid keying in errors, alternative methods of inputting the data are needed, other than a keyboard. Such methods include OCR (optical character recognition), OMR (optical mark recognition), MICR (magnetic ink character recognition) and barcode recognition. The input documents for these methods are shown in Figure 7.2. Although all of these methods can introduce errors, they are so fast they leave plenty of time for the errors to be corrected.

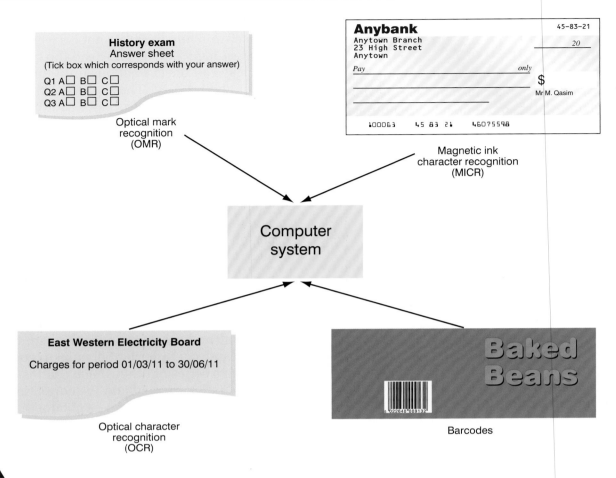

▲
Figure 7.2 *Direct methods of data input reduce errors and are much quicker*

Test Yourself

Read the chapter carefully. The following sentences are incomplete. Copy out and complete the sentences using the words in the list below.

transposition   range   verification   check digit

proofreading   character type   validation

processing

A One method of _____ is to let two people type in the same data. Only if they make identical keystrokes will the data be accepted for _____.

B Another, more feasible method involves getting someone to check carefully what has been typed in. This is called _____.

C _____ is performed by a computer program. Validation checks include the following: _____ _____. Checks to make sure the right type of character has been entered, _____ and checks to make sure that the data lie within a certain range.

D When a large number is entered, mistakes often occur, so an extra number is added at the end which is calculated from the other numbers. This extra number is called a _____ _____.

E The commonest type of error is the _____ error which is caused by letters or numbers being typed in the wrong order.

Things to do

1 One type of error that could be made when data are typed into a computer system is a transcription error.
   (a) A transcription error can be detected by a verification check. Explain how this check is carried out.
   (b) A date can be validated as well as verified. A date is to be input in the form 25 APR 2010 (a two-digit day, followed by a three-letter month, followed by a four-digit year). Describe the validation checks that could be carried out on dates in this form.

2 The following is a list of International Standard Book Numbers. Some of these numbers are correct and some are incorrect. Using the method shown in this chapter, check each of the ISBNs and, showing your working out, say whether each is correct or not.
   (a) 0 582 05179 6
   (b) 0 582 05165 7
   (c) 0 09 182438 9

3 Each of the items of data in the table below has been incorrectly typed. The following checks may be used on data:
   • range check   • character type check   • check digit.

   Copy and complete the table, placing a tick if the error can be detected using the above checks and also stating which validation check is the most appropriate for the data.

Type of data	Item	Tick if error would be detected	Validation check
(a) Name	John Brwn		
(b) Sex (M or F)	N		
(c) Date of birth (day/month/year)	310994		
(d) Examination subjects	English Physics		
(e) Exam fee paid	$2,350		

Investigations

You work part-time in a DVD rental shop that is part of a large chain of 100 shops scattered throughout the country. Each member is given a six-figure membership number when they first join. The number needs to be this large because it is possible for a member to hire DVDs from any of the branches. The shops are having problems with members of staff keying in wrong membership numbers when hiring out DVDs. This has several consequences. When a membership number has been incorrectly keyed:

1 the shops have an incorrect record of who has hired the DVD
2 if that DVD is returned late, letters are sent to the wrong member
3 if the DVD is not returned at all, the wrong member is invoiced for it.

All of this wastes time and loses customers.

The staff are not all to blame because some customers forget their membership card when renting, but just quote their membership number instead. Occasionally they may accidentally (or deliberately) quote the wrong number.

1 Figure 7.3 shows what the DVD membership card looks like. Would changing the design of the card help? If so, design a card using appropriate software and say why your design is better.

2 What procedures could be adopted by staff when DVDs are being hired out to reduce the problems mentioned above? You need to consider both verification and validation. It is best to consider various options to start with and then to choose a combination of the best ones.

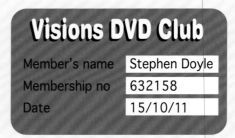

▲ **Figure 7.3** *Visions DVD membership card*

8 How Data Are Stored
Databases

A database is an organised collection of information or data. Putting information into a computer database gives you far more flexibility in organising, displaying and printing that information.

The parts of a database

Files

Think of a box of filing cards like those sometimes used in libraries. A computer's equivalent of the complete box is a file. The computer's file is usually stored on a disk, which may be optical or magnetic.

Records

Within the library card box are the individual cards, each of which contains information about one book. In a computer database, the cards are known as records and most databases will display one record on the screen at a time, just as if you were browsing through the cards in a card box.

Fields

On each card will be a number of different items of information: a library card might list the title, author, publisher and ISBN (a unique number for a particular book).

Each item of information on the computer record is known as a field, and it consists of two parts: the field name and the field data. The field names are the words 'Title', 'Author' or 'Publisher'. They are the same on each record and indicate what the field data represent. Figure 8.1 shows the relationship between fields, records and files.

A card box filing system

On a card in a card box you can squeeze extra information in by writing smaller, or by writing on the back of the card. This is not possible with the computer equivalent. With a database, one of the first things you have to do is to specify the size and design of the record screen. You need to consider how you want the information to be arranged on the record and how long the data for each field will be. It is no good specifying an author field to allow up to 10 characters when you have several books by an author with a surname such as Forbes-Hamilton in the library.

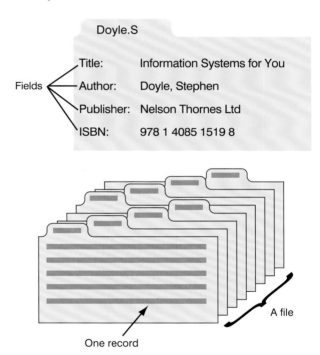

▲ **Figure 8.1** *The relationship between fields, records and files*

You could of course go to the other extreme and specify a field length of 30 characters for names of authors. The problem here is that larger fields will take up more space on your floppy or hard disk. Another problem is that longer files take longer to process. If you have 2,000 members or customers in your database, with a maximum surname length of 16 characters, then the surnames alone will take up 32,000 bytes on your disk. If you have allowed 30 characters for each surname, though, you have probably reserved 60,000 bytes, wasting 28,000 bytes in blank space!

As with most things, the best answer is a compromise. You should try to design your fields to cope with the largest entry you can imagine making, without reserving unnecessary disk space by over-specifying. You may find it worthwhile abbreviating the longest entries, if the overwhelming majority are shorter.

Record design

Modern databases give you freedom to design your own records. They give you an empty screen on which you can add the field names, fields and other background text, such as the title. On some databases you can put boxes around headings and even change the colour of the text.

Num	Field name	Field type	Width	Dec	Index
1	ADD-PROP	Character	50		N
2	AREA				
3	TOWN				
4	POSTCODE				
5	TYPE				
6	NO-BEDS				
7	RECEIPT				
8	GARDEN				
9	GARAGE				
10	FREEHOLD				
11	PRICE				
12	DOM				
13	PROP-AGE				
14	OWNER				
15	TELEPHONE				

▲
Figure 8.2 *Template for the design of the structure. Only the first line has been filled in*

Some databases require you to create a different type of field for different information. You usually have to specify the type of data to go into the field.

This can be:

1 numeric, which means it contains only numbers – make sure that a number does not have any starting zeros or dashes (e.g. a telephone number 0181-888-3456)
2 character text, which means that numbers, letters and other symbols can be entered
3 date, which means that the date is entered like this: 09/10/11
4 logical, which allows Y/N (for yes/no) or T/F (for true/false).

As well as selecting the field names and the type of data to be entered, some of the more sophisticated databases allow you to specify some validation checks to the field.

Figure 8.2 shows the template for the design of the database structure. The information for the first field has been filled in.

Questions

Figure 8.2 shows a database structure for a database to be used by an estate agency. A database package is to be used to store the details of all the properties that the agency has on offer. Copy out the table and fill it in with appropriate field types and widths. The column headed 'Dec' is used to specify how many decimal places there are in the numeric field, so you need to fill this in only if the field type is numeric. In the Index column you can just put N for no for all the fields.

Key fields

A key field is a field that may be used to search a file. It is always useful to have one field which is unique to a particular record. For example, each pupil starting at a school will be given an admission number. This is a number that no one else will have, so it is unique to a particular pupil.

With the library system, the key field would be a number given to the book when it is bought by the library. The International Standard Book Number (ISBN) would distinguish between different books, but it could not be used to distinguish between copies of the same book and therefore would not be unique.

Questions

Databases can use any field in order to perform a search.

(a) Why should we not use the pupil's surname as the key field?

(b) The school secretary says that there are only 1,000 pupils in the school, so we do not need an admission number of more than four characters. Do you agree? Explain your answer.

(c) A letter needs to be sent to a pupil who has an unreported absence from school of over a week. The teacher knows the name of the pupil but not the admission number. What other fields could be used to perform this search?

Personnel file

Employee Number: 1473

Surname: Mansoor

Forename: Ayesha

Date of birth: 15/01/74

Job title: Systems Analyst

Payroll file

Employee Number: 1473

Surname: Mansoor

Forename: Ayesha

Date of birth: 15/01/74

Salary: $22,000

Department file

Employee Number: 1473

Surname: Mansoor

Forename: Ayesha

Experience: 15 years

▲
Figure 8.3 *Data duplication with manual systems*

Manual filing systems

Figure 8.3 shows three records from three different files kept by departments in a company. As you can see, some of the data are the same on each file. This is called data duplication and is one of the main problems with manual filing systems. Data duplication means that more space is taken up by the files and more work is needed to retrieve the information.

The main problems arise in the following situations:

1 We may need to obtain information that is held on several files. Suppose we wanted to find out the names of systems analysts, with fewer than 16 years' experience and who earn over $22,000 per year. We would need to use all three files, which are held by three different departments.

2 Also, because the data are not shared, a change in information, such as a change in surname because Jane got married, would cause three files to need updating.

3 If two people need to look at information on the same file at the same time, it is necessary to photocopy the information, which is time-consuming and wasteful.

4 If a file is put back in the wrong place, finding it again can prove an awesome task (Figure 8.4).

▲
Figure 8.4 *The file for Qasim was in the Ms*

Computerised databases

Advantages

The main advantages of a computerised database are as follows:

1   It is usually necessary to store the information only once, since most database software allows you to access information from several files.
2   Files can be linked together, which means that if you update one of the files, all the other files that depend on the same information will automatically be updated. Not all databases are able to do this, but those that can are called relational databases.
3   If you find that the record structure needs changing after you have put a great deal of data into a database, this is easily done. To do this manually would be impossible.
4   Access to the information is rapid and there is less likelihood of the data becoming lost.
5   Validation checks may be made on the data as they are being entered into the database, which means that there will be fewer errors in the data.

Disadvantages

The main disadvantages of a computerised database are as follows:

1   If the computer breaks down, you are not able to access the details.
2   It is easy to copy computer files, so sensitive data should be protected by passwords.
3   Training is needed to use the system and this takes time and costs money.

Database management system (DBMS)

A database management system (DBMS) is a set of programs that allows the creation of datafiles, the alteration of the data in these files and the extraction of data from the files. The idea with a DBMS is that all the data are kept centrally and only authorised users can access data via the DBMS.

All database management systems allow the following:

1   the data files to be set up by creating tables (or datafiles) which may be linked together
2   the users to ask questions (known as queries) of the data (i.e. they allow the user to search for data meeting certain criteria)
3   the addition of more data (appending), the deletion and editing of existing data
4   alteration to the structure of the datafiles or tables
5   some security, by allowing only certain people access to each of the datafiles or tables
6   the user to import data into the database from other packages and data to be transferred to another package (exporting).

File organisation

There are several methods you can use to organise files.

Serial files

With a serial file, the records do not follow each other in any particular order, so if another record needs to be added it can just be added to the end of the file.

Sequential files

Sequential files are like serial files, except that the records are held in a certain sequence. For instance, you might decide to order the pupil file in admission number sequence.

Random files

Random files have to be stored on disk and, as the name suggests, they are not stored in any order on the disk surface. The disk operating system (the programs that control the storage on the disk) keeps a map of the disk surface, and using this map the read/write heads can go straight to the data. In this way the data are found without the whole disk having to be read. Random access allows data stored on disk to be found extremely quickly.

Methods of accessing files

Serial access

To read a serial file, a computer has to read each record until it reaches the one required.

Sequential access

With sequential access the records are in order, so if just one record is required then the method is slow, but if all the records are required then it is very fast.

Direct access (random access)

With direct access files it is possible to go directly to a record without having to look at any other records first. You can access both sequential and random access files directly.

Types of files

There are various types of files.

Master files

A master file is the most important file since it is the most complete and up-to-date version of a file. If a master file is lost or damaged and it is the only copy, the whole system will break down.

Transaction files

Transaction files are used to hold temporary data which are used to update the master file. A transaction is a piece of business, hence the name transaction file. Transactions can occur in any order, so it is necessary to sort a transaction file into the same order as the master file before it is used to update the master file.

Backup or security files

Backup copies of files are kept in case the original is damaged or lost and cannot be used. Because of the importance of the master file, backup copies of it should be taken at regular intervals in case it is stolen, lost, damaged or corrupted. Looking after your disks is not enough; you should always keep backup copies of all your important data, especially project work such as IT tasks and system tasks.

Transaction log files

Transactions are bits of business such as placing an order, updating the stock or making a payment. If these transactions are performed in real time, the data input will overwrite the previous data. This makes it impossible to check past transactions, so would make it easy for people to commit fraud.

A record of the transactions is kept (the transaction log file) which shows all the transactions made over a certain period. Using the log you can see what the data were before changes were made, and also what the changes were and who made them. Transaction log files therefore maintain security and can also be used to recover transactions lost due to hardware failure.

The grandfather–father–son principle

There is always a slight chance that the data contained on a master file may be destroyed. Data could be destroyed by an inexperienced user, a power failure, fire or even theft. For a large company, the loss of vital data could prove disastrous. But using the grandfather–father–son principle it is possible to recreate the master file if it is lost.

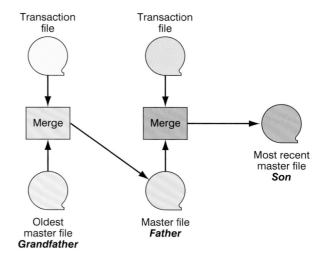

All these files are kept so that if one or more of the files is lost it can be recreated

▲ **Figure 8.5** *The grandfather–father–son principle, often used for file security*

The principle works like this. Basically, three generations of files are kept. The oldest master file is called the **grandfather** file and it is kept with its transaction file. These two files are used to produce a new master file called the **father** file which, with its transaction file, is used to create the most up-to-date file, called the **son** file. The process is repeated and the son becomes the father and the father becomes the grandfather and so on. Only three generations are needed and the other files may be reused. This system (sometimes called the ancestral file system) is usually used for tapes, although it could also be used for disks. Figure 8.5 summarises the principle.

Questions

1 Backup copies should always be taken at regular intervals.

(a) What is meant by a backup copy?
(b) Some programs such as databases and word processors automatically take backup copies. Your friend says, 'My word processor takes backup copies so I don't need to worry'. Explain what is wrong with her argument.
(c) John has a disk box in which he keeps all his disks. The box is labelled with his name, form, address and phone number. He realises that data can be lost, so in his disk box he also keeps his backup copies. Is he doing all he can to keep his data safe? Explain.

Common file processes

The beauty of any computerised filing system is the ease with which sorts, searches, merges and updates may be performed. With manual filing systems these tasks are performed only with great difficulty.

File updating

File updating involves bringing a file up to date with any changes that have occurred since it was last updated. There are various processes that can take place during updating.

Insertions

Suppose we had a file containing the details of pupils in a school. A new pupil may have joined the school, so that pupil's details will need to be added to the file.

Deletions

A pupil could have moved to a new school, so that pupil's details will need to be removed (deleted) from the file.

Amendments

A pupil has moved house, so the address field needs changing. This is called amending the details.

File manipulation

The common file manipulations are sorting and merging.

Sorting

Often a field needs to be sorted into a particular order. For instance, we may need a list of all the pupils in the school arranged in alphabetical order. It is also possible to sort according to several fields, so we could produce a list of all the pupils arranged in year order, with the list for each year arranged in alphabetical order.

Merging

Sometimes we want to combine the contents of two files to form a single file. The process of combining the files is called merging. If the two files to be merged are on magnetic tape, we must sort the tapes into order before merging them. The new tape file produced will also be in order.

Merging is very useful if we want to divide the work. For instance, if a school wanted to convert its manual files for 1,500 pupils, then to do this quickly, it may decide to split the work of inputting the details into the database. In effect, two separate databases would be created with the same structure. These could then be merged to produce the complete database. In this way, one person might type half the data and someone else could type the other half.

File interrogation

Interrogation involves getting information from a file. Fields are selected and the computer then searches through the records, finding all the records which match the field or fields being used for the search. A report (printout) is then produced which has either all the records found or only certain fields of those records.

Data analysis

Some databases allow the data to be analysed in some way once they have been entered. For instance, you can produce bar charts, pie charts and line graphs, using selected fields from the database. Tables can also be produced using fields from several different files.

Test Yourself

Using the words in the list below, copy out and complete sentences **A** to **J**, underlining the words you have inserted. The words may be used more than once.

master   records   database   duplication

security   grandfather   files   fields   structure

transaction   son

A An organised collection of data is called a
_____ .

B A database usually consists of many _____ which may be linked together.

C Files consist of a series of _____, each one about a certain company, person or item.

D Within each record we have _____ such as name, address, date of birth.

E When designing a database on a computer you have to specify the _____ of a record by telling the program what fields are needed, the type of each field and the length of each field.

F There are many problems with manual filing systems. Data _____ means that the same data are stored several times on different files.

G A _____ file is the complete, up-to-date version of a file on a certain subject.

H Master files are kept up to date with changes using a _____ file.

I Backup files are always kept for _____ reasons.

J So that a master file can be recreated if it is destroyed, the _____–father–_____ principle is used.

Things to do

1 You are responsible for updating a file which contains details of all the members of a sports club. Copy out and label the following changes to be made at the end of one month as I, D or A, according to whether they are insertions, deletions or amendments.

Change	Type of update
(a) Change of address	
(b) Resigned from the club	
(c) New member	
(d) Member changed her name through marriage	
(e) Changed from annual member to life member	
(f) Member died suddenly	
(g) Previous member has rejoined	
(h) Member resigned through ill health	
(i) Member's telephone number has changed	
(j) Member has emigrated to Australia	

2 A school keeps information on each of its pupils and part of the information contained on the computer file is shown below.

Admission number	Surname	Forename	Date of birth	Tutor initials
2312	Doyle	Stephen	19/12/94	KF
2344	Kendrick	Graham	23/06/95	PK
2367	Smith	Julie	12/09/97	HT
2380	Jones	Susan	09/01/96	BG
2381	Jackson	Joan	01/01/96	JS

(a) How many records are shown?
(b) How many fields does each record have?
(c) In all computer database systems there is a unique field.
   (i) Which is the unique field in this section of the file?
   (ii) Why is it important to have a unique field?
(d) Only part of the complete file is shown. Name two other fields that could be added to this file and give reasons for their inclusion.

IT Tasks

Task 1

Ahmed's Motors is a used car dealer which keeps a stock of around 300 used cars. Ibrahim, the garage's proprietor, has decided to computerise the records held about each car.

1 Look at the adverts in your local papers or a specialist publication for adverts for used cars. These adverts will give you ideas about what people look for when they are buying a used car. Here are a few to start you off.

Make: Mercedes
Model: CLK Convertible
Engine size: 1.8 litres
Mileage: 18,000

Write a list of the details you need to record for each car. Put them into a suitable order, with what you consider are the most important features of the car at the top of the list.

2 Now design a form which can be filled in each time a car is added to the stock. Compare it with a friend's form to see if you have missed anything important. It is important to make sure that enough space is left for the details to be inserted.

3 Ibrahim is pleased with your effort and has asked you if the details on the form could be put into a database.
(a) What advantages does a database have over the cards arranged in a filing cabinet?
(b) Ibrahim often receives telephone calls asking whether he has a particular make of car. How could the database be used to help him?

Task 2

Develop a suite of letters and standard paragraphs that your form teacher could use to send to parents, to inform them, for example, about school trips, parents' evenings and sports events. Ask your form teacher what kind of details should be included. Your form teacher is fairly new to computers, so will need some documentation as to how to use the system you have developed.

You frequently need to merge (i.e. combine) the contents of two files. Type in the following letter and then save it using the name SMO1.

Grange Hill Comprehensive School
Shawfield Road
Grange Hill
London
NW10 4AA

Telephone: 020-8220-2300

Today's date

Dear Parent,

I regret to inform you that your daughter has been found smoking in school and I am concerned that you should know. Apart from the bad example that this is giving to the other children, she is unwise to risk attachment to a habit which is widely regarded as both antisocial and damaging to health.

Yours sincerely

A Johnston

Mrs A. Johnston (Headteacher)

The following paragraph is often incorporated into other letters when pupils have been found swearing, smoking, fighting and so on. This paragraph is referred to as DET1. Type this paragraph into your word processor and save it with the filename DET1.

I should be grateful for your support in discouraging such behaviour by reinforcing the school's punishment of a school detention on Wednesday until 5 p.m.

Julie Hill has been found smoking, so the standard smoking letter is to be sent to her mother Mrs A. Hill. Load in the letter SMO1 and insert the variable details, such as her mother's name and Julie's, as well as today's date. The headteacher decides to place Julie on school detention, so she has asked you to incorporate (i.e. merge) the detention paragraph DET1 into SMO1. You should perform this task whilst in the SMO1 letter by inserting a file and not by retyping.

9 Types of Computer Operation

Real-time processing

With real-time processing, the system is automatically updated when a change is made due to a transaction occurring. So if I booked the only available seat on a plane from Manchester to Frankfurt at a travel agent's office, and then you went to another travel agent and tried to book the same seat, the computer would tell you that the plane is full. In the fast world we now live in, it is important that data are kept up to date, so real-time systems have to be used.

Since in a real-time system the terminals must be connected to the computer, you can see that a real-time system must also be an online system.

The advantage with real-time systems is that the current situation is always being shown. At a travel agency we can find out which flights or holidays are actually available. Many shop systems use real-time processing: as soon as an item is sold the system automatically deducts that item from stock, so the stock file always shows the true stock position.

Real-time processing is essential for computer control. Examples of computer control include traffic lights, robots, process control (e.g. steel works and chemical processes) and flight simulators.

Doing all the processing in one go: batch processing

Problem

An electricity board wants to send out over three million electricity bills, all within a few days of each other.

Looking at the system in its simplest form gives the following outline:

1 When a person moves to a new house they have to go to the electricity company's office to fill in a form for the supply of electricity.
2 The details contained on the form are input via a terminal to the main computer. These details are recorded on a main file called the customer master file.
3 Every three months the computer produces a list of customers, arranged in order of houses in a certain street for the meter reader to visit. The meter reader is given a sheet like the one shown in Figure 9.1, which is used to record the meter readings.

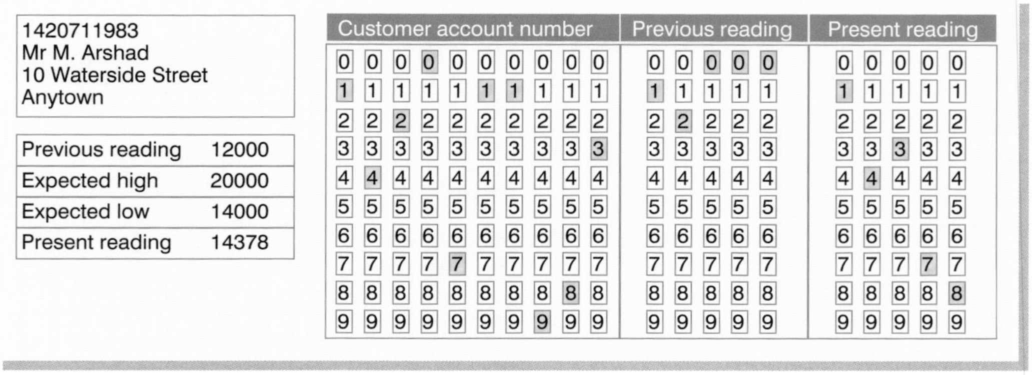

Figure 9.1 *A meter-reading sheet with mark sense boxes. Information is coded by shading in the boxes*

4 After they have been recorded, the meter readings are then sent to the computer centre for processing.

5 First of all, the meter reading sheets are read by an optical mark reader and the details placed on magnetic tape in what is called a transaction file.

6 This magnetic tape is then sorted into the same order as the master file to produce a new tape called the sorted transaction file. You cannot sort a tape and put it back on the same tape again, although you could do this if a disk system were used.

7 This transaction file is then processed with the master file, which is also held on tape. A new updated master file is produced along with the electricity bills to be sent out to the customers.

The production of electricity bills in this way is an example of batch processing. This is a system of collecting all the inputs together and putting them into the computer in one go or 'batch'.

Batch processing is used when a particular job needs to be done in one go rather than in a number of parts. All the relevant data are collected and processed together. The main advantage with batch processing is that the computer operator can load the data in only one operation, no matter how many meter-reading sheets there are in a batch. The programs in the computer go through the various processes and the final result is a pile of bills to be sent out to customers and an updated master file with the latest information added.

Batch processing has other uses. Preparing a company's payroll is a suitable application. Here, all the relevant information, such as hours worked, pay per hour, tax and National Insurance contributions, is collected for each employee and put into the computer. Batch processing is suitable because payroll processing is usually carried out once a week or once a month.

Multitasking and multiprogramming

Any processing unit works relatively quickly, so if it is working on just one task then most of its time is spent waiting for the slow peripheral devices to catch up.

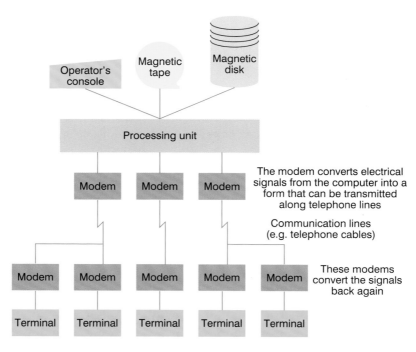

▲ **Figure 9.2** *How a multi-access system can be used by many people at different locations*

Rather than waste this valuable processing time, the processing unit can be made to process the data from several programs at once. The speed of the computer makes it appear as though it is doing two jobs at the same time, although what is happening is that the computer works on one task for a short period and then on the next. Such a system is called a multiprogramming or multitasking system.

Using Microsoft® Windows® software you can print out a job at the same time as working on a different task using other software.

Transaction processing

Transaction processing takes place when needed, rather than at set intervals like batch processing. Rather than wait for the data to accumulate, demand processing is usually performed on individual items of data. Suppose a monthly-paid employee leaves halfway through the month. Instead of waiting for the payroll to be done at the end of the month as a batch process, the data could be input to a disk-based system and the pay worked out for the one employee.

Multi-access and timesharing

With timesharing many users can have access to the same data apparently at the same time. For instance, in the airline booking example, other travel agents could be using the same airline database at the same time. Multi-access systems give the user the impression that he or she is the only one using the computer. In fact the computer serves other people during the time it takes one user to press the keys (see Figures 9.2 and 9.3).

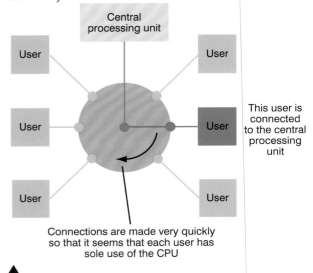

▲ **Figure 9.3** *A multi-access system with users at a single location*

Test Yourself

Using the words in the list below, copy out and complete sentences **A** to **H**, underlining the words you have inserted. The words may be used more than once.

timesharing   multi-access   on   interactive

control   real-time   batch   multiprogramming

A If a device is _____ line it means that it is under the control of the central processing unit.

B The type of system where the computer conducts a 'conversation' with the user is called an _____ system.

C _____ systems must always be real-time systems.

D The type of processing where changes are immediately acted upon and any files are immediately updated is called a _____-_____ system.

E _____ processing is used where a job is all done at one time rather than in parts.

F _____ allows the computer to work on several programs apparently at the same time.

G A _____ system allows many terminals to access the CPU.

H Each terminal has a certain amount of time allocated to it. This is called _____.

Things to do

1 Real-time processing is being used increasingly because the information is always up to date. Batch processing still has advantages for doing certain types of jobs.
   (a) What types of jobs are these?
   (b) What advantages does batch processing have over real-time processing?
   (c) What is meant by the term 'up to date'?

2 You go to a travel agency to book a holiday in Spain, travelling by air. The travel agent makes an initial enquiry for you, using the interactive computerised enquiry system.
   (a) What input device would you expect to see on the agent's desk?
   (b) What is meant by the term 'interactive'?
   (c) Why is an interactive system necessary for enquiries?

   You decide to make the booking.

   (d) Give seven items of data that the airline booking clerk will need before a flight can be booked for you.
   (e) The clerk gives you a booking immediately. How can the clerk be certain that the seats will not be double-booked?

   The booking will be recorded on the airline's backing store.

   (f) What type of access is necessary for booking information?
   (g) What backing storage would be most appropriate?
   (h) Give three reasons why the computerised booking system is more efficient than the previous manual one.

3 For each of the applications given below, state whether the method of processing would be real-time or batch. In each case give one reason for your choice.
   (a) A bank cash dispenser which can also give a report of the current balance in a customer's account.
   (b) An examination board system for collecting marks from examiners using mark sense forms.
   (c) A flood warning system which uses sensors to continually monitor the water level in a river.
   (d) The production of bank statements to be sent out to bank customers at the end of the month.
   (e) A supermarket POS (point-of-sale) terminal where, when an item is sold, it is automatically deducted from stock.
   (f) A central heating control system where each room can be kept at a different constant temperature.
   (g) A fast-moving, arcade-type computer game.

10 Data Transfer

It is common in computing to have to transfer data between different software packages and even between different computers. Some years ago you would have had great difficulty doing this, but today it is not too much of a problem.

Transferring files between word processors

The most common type of file transfer is between different word processors. Even within large organisations people often use different word processors or different versions of the same word processor, so it is essential that they can read each other's files. You may want to send someone some notes through the post, for instance. If you send them a disk of word-processing files, you could save on postage costs and it will also allow the other person to edit the files. Most word processors, but not all, have a file transfer facility so that, for instance, a Microsoft® Word file could be read by a WordPerfect word processor. The only sure way to transfer text between different word processors is to store everything as ASCII files. When you transfer files of ASCII code, the formatting commands (margins, tabs, etc.) and features such as underlining, bold and different fonts are all lost, but the body of the text will still be there.

Comma-separated variables

One common file format is comma-separated variables, or CSV for short. The CSV file format is useful because of the ease with which it is possible to transfer files. Files in this format can be read by most spreadsheets and databases.

Digital and analogue computers

Data can either be analogue or digital. Digital quantities have values which jump from one to the next without any 'in between' value. An on/off switch on a radio is a device that could be thought of as digital because there is no state between 'on' and 'off'. Some quantities can vary over a whole range of values. Temperature is an example, since it can be 10, 10.1, 10.01, 10.001°C and so on. In fact, temperatures can be an infinite number of values. Quantities that have an infinite number of values are called analogue quantities. For analogue quantities to be processed by a digital computer they need first to be converted into digital quantities using an analogue to digital converter.

There are two types of computer: digital computers and analogue computers. Most people use digital computers; in fact, analogue computers are quite rare. Analogue computers are used mainly for the control of processes in factories and for some forms of modelling.

Digital computers like to be given their information in the form of numbers (i.e. in the form of binary digits). All information eventually has to be turned into groups of binary digits (0s and 1s).

Digital data	Analogue data
The number of cars in a car park	Temperature recorded using a mercury thermometer
Traffic light sequences	Position on a compass dial
Digital watch	Old-fashioned watch with hands
Barcode	Room light dimmer switch
Data stored on a magnetic disk	Time read from a sundial

Peripheral device control

As well as working on program instructions to process data, the processor has to deal with the input from peripheral devices such as keyboards, mice and sensors, and with the output to the screen, printer and so on.

An **interrupt** is a signal to the processor from the peripheral device indicating that an event has occurred that needs its attention. If the interrupt is important, the processor will stop carrying out the current sequence of instructions and start a different sequence of instructions to deal with the interrupt. Because interrupts can occur frequently, the processor determines which interrupts should be given priority over others. This means that they are not always dealt with by the processor in the order in which they occur.

Another type of system is used, called a **polling system**, where the processor asks the peripherals if they have anything to report. If they do have anything to report, the processor instructs them to send the data. Unlike with interrupts, the processor remains in command.

When the computer sends data to the printer in order to be printed out, the processor will need to make contact with the printer. If the printer is switched off, then an interrupt is sent back to the processor and this will cause the processor to display a message to alert the user.

The process of the first signals establishing that the printer is able to communicate successfully with the printer is called **handshaking**.

A **buffer** is a temporary storage space in memory used to store data whilst these are being moved from one place to another. For example, the processor could send data to a printer at very high speed. The problem is that the printer cannot print at the speed the data are sent, so there needs to be a place for the data to be stored temporarily until the printer is ready to deal with them.

Buffers are used between the processor and the input/output devices to cope with the difference in speeds between the speed that the processor receives or sends data from and to input and output devices.

When data are being transmitted from one place to another, for example from the computer to the printer, there is a danger that the series of 0s and 1s that make up the numbers and letters will become mixed up. There needs to be some way of detecting whether this has happened.

A group of a fixed number of bits is called a byte, and a number of bytes together is called a block. By adding together all the bits in a transmission unit of data, the system can check that the receiver receives the same number of bits as was sent. The count of the number of bits sent is called the **checksum**.

Questions

1 Say whether the following devices would be analogue or digital:
   (a) a mercury-in-glass thermometer
   (b) the floor indicator on a lift
   (c) a radio tuning dial
   (d) the display showing the track that is being played on your CD player
   (e) a speedometer on a car.

2 More and more devices which previously had analogue displays now have digital displays. Why do you think this is?

Sound sampling

Provided you have a microphone either inside or connected to your computer, you can play a recording or live sound into the sound card of your computer. The sound card listens to the sound and takes a measurement of the height of the signal many times a second. The measurement is called the sound sample.

Sound is an analogue waveform, and for a computer to be able to process, store and play it back, it has to be turned into a digital signal. Figure 10.1 shows the waveform of the analogue sound signal being sampled at times t_1, t_2, t_3 and so on. At time t_1 the signal lies between 3 and 4, although it is nearer to 4 so it is given the value 4. At time t_2 the signal's sampling level is 3.

The sampling rate is the number of times the sample is measured per second and it is measured in kilohertz (kHz). The higher the sampling rate, the better the sound reproduction. There are implications in having perfect sound: the higher the quality of the sound, the larger the file will be. For a three-minute high quality recording the file can be as large as 30 MB.

Analogue to digital conversion (ADC) and vice versa

In chemical factories, the processes used to make chemicals are usually controlled with the help of computers. Often a batch of chemicals must be kept at a precise temperature. The signal from a temperature sensor is usually a continually changing analogue signal and this must be converted into digital form before it can be processed by a computer. This conversion is done with an analogue–digital converter (ADC). The computer may then control the process by outputting a digital signal through a digital–analogue converter (DAC) to an electric motor which can open or close a valve.

Modems are used to enable data to be passed from one place to another using communication links (telephone wires, optical cables, radio links, etc.).

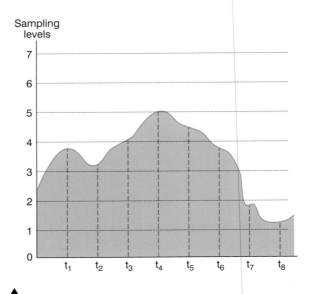

▲ **Figure 10.1** *Sampling a waveform*

A modem (modulator–demodulator) is used to convert the binary digits from a digital computer into an analogue signal that may be passed along ordinary telephone wires. The modem at the other end of the wire converts the analogue signal back into a digital one that the computer is able to understand.

IT Tasks

You are working with a friend on a joint project at school and have agreed to split the work between you. You will type half the work and your friend will type the other half. Since you are using the same word processor, joining the files will not be a problem. Find out and then write instructions so that a complete novice could join the two files together.

There are various ways that we can present computer output. We can present the data:

- as a screen display
- as hard copy, that is, as printouts on paper (text, pictures, graphs, charts)
- with multimedia presentations (sound, text, pictures, graphs and charts)
- using virtual reality
- using sound.

Hard copy

Printed information is still the main form of computer output. It is used because everybody is a 'subscriber' to the system. We all have letter boxes and know the various processes involved in sending mail. Paper's universal use and acceptability makes it a very difficult system to replace. Nevertheless, there are some disadvantages with paper. With electronic mail, messages can be created, sent and read completely on computers without ever being printed on paper. Many people think that the mail service will never be replaced, but others think that electronic mail will soon replace it. What do you think?

Hard copy (printouts on paper) may gradually be replaced and the reasons for this are:

1 paper is expensive to buy and to store
2 the use of paper encourages people to photocopy it so that they do not lose it
3 many bills, invoices and so on are preprinted and this is expensive
4 the use of paper is not environmentally friendly
5 moving paper around an organisation takes time.

There are, however, some advantages:

1 with legal documents, it is hard to prove that an electronic letter has been received and seen

2 everyone is able to use a paper-based system
3 paper is easier to read than a computer screen
4 it is easier to flick back and forth in a paper document
5 paper can be read on the move and in circumstances where a computer might not be available.

Questions

Produce a diagram, using a combination of graphics and text, which could be used to describe the steps involved in producing and then posting a letter. Assume that the letter has been created on a computer and printed out using a printer.

Presentation graphics

Graphics consist of a combination of diagrams, text and charts which are used to make a visual impact when people see them. Graphics may be presented as slides, transparencies to be used with overhead projectors, paper or even as computer displays. Salespersons frequently use screens to display their products or services to potential customers. Some of them now use multimedia.

Multimedia

Multimedia is the mixture of text and graphics with motion and sound, including video, audio, animation and photographs. Multimedia is interactive which means that the user can decide on different routes through the software. The images may be controlled using either a mouse or a keyboard. Multimedia is ideal for learning new things, because you can control the program to work as slowly or as quickly as you like and it will not tell you off if you get things wrong. In a way, multimedia software can be an ideal teacher. Learning boring topics can be made fun using multimedia. For instance, you can learn about decimal points via an adventure called 'Who stole the decimal point?'

Computer-aided learning (CAL)

Computers can interact with pupils to enhance the learning process. The development of multimedia has led to a huge growth in the use of computers as an educational tool in the classroom. Computer-aided learning can be used to instruct pupils and then test them on what they have learnt.

Producing multimedia software

You will have seen the wonderful displays, video clips and sounds provided by multimedia software, but how are these packages written? As you can imagine, a lot of equipment is needed to produce really good software. You can prepare your own multimedia software if you have a multimedia authoring package.

Sound

One feature of a multimedia system is the use of speakers. A special sound card contains chips and other circuitry that enable a computer to produce high quality sound. You can then feed the sound through speakers or headphones so that you can play games, look at and hear a variety of information on CD-ROM or just listen to your favourite music on an ordinary CD.

Virtual reality

You may have seen pictures of children wearing headsets and gloves wired up to a computer and wondered what they are. This is the world of virtual reality.

A lot of research in virtual reality is directed towards military uses. Virtual reality can be used to recreate a terrain where fighting is likely to take place. To a soldier wearing a headset and gloves, the battle situation can be as near to the real thing as possible.

Many other uses for virtual reality systems are being developed. One example is possible use for simulating traffic accidents for use in court. If a witness says that they saw an accident, the court can be shown exactly what the witness would have seen from a particular position on the road.

Figure 11.1 shows the headset and gloves in a virtual reality system.

▶ **Figure 11.1** *Part of a virtual reality system*

Using virtual reality for design

Architects and designers can use virtual reality to show clients and customers what their design of a building will look like from the inside or outside. The customer or client can virtually walk around the building on a screen and view the inside from any direction.

Many real estate agents use virtual reality to show prospective buyers a view inside a home without actually having to be there.

Virtual reality is popular with kitchen and bedroom design companies to show what a new kitchen would look like in the room it is being designed for.

▲ **Figure 11.2** *A newly designed kitchen as seen in virtual reality*

Test Yourself

Using the words in the list below, copy out and complete sentences **A** to **E**, underlining the words you have inserted. The words may be used more than once.

hard copy   electronic mail   multimedia

sound card   posted

A Output from a computer on paper is often referred to as _____ _____.

B Printouts have the advantage that they can be _____.

C The service that involves passing electronic messages from one computer to another is called _____ _____.

D A mixture of text and graphics with motion and sound is an example of _____.

E All computers contain a _____ in order to be able to output sound through speakers or earphones.

Things to do

Output from computers can be presented in many different ways.
(a) Software to log data in a science laboratory can present data on a screen or as hard copy. State one advantage and one disadvantage of these two methods.
(b) In publishing systems, it is necessary to combine text and various forms of graphics.
(i)   Why is it often necessary to import graphics files into a DTP package?
(ii) Why is it becoming increasingly easy to do this?

12 How to Describe an Information System

Describing systems

A system is a group of connected operations or things. We can describe systems in various ways. Often we can describe them in terms of inputs, processes and outputs (see Chapter 1). Figure 12.1 shows the simplest system.

▲
Figure 12.1 *The three steps involved in the processing of data*

A diagram like this doesn't really tell us too much, so we could draw a diagram like that in Figure 12.2, which tells us a little more. Don't be afraid of drawing your own diagrams like this to describe your systems. These diagrams do their job well because everyone understands them and they help you to think about the problem as you are drawing the diagram. Don't try drawing a diagram in one go; instead, try to concentrate on one aspect or part of the system. You can always draw several diagrams and then join them together to obtain an overall picture.

Structure diagrams

Structure diagrams can be used to describe information systems. An overall task is broken down into smaller, more manageable tasks. These may then be broken down further into smaller tasks. This way of describing tasks is described as the top-down approach.

The top-down approach

Let's take a look at drawing a structure diagram for a task we are probably all familiar with: doing the weekly shopping.

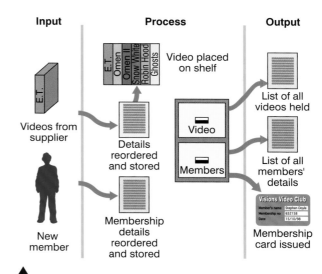

▲
Figure 12.2 *A video library system*

First we place the overall task at the top and we write a brief description of the overall task in the box (i.e. doing the weekly shopping) (Figure 12.3).

▲
Figure 12.3

This task is then divided up into a series of tasks required to do the main task. For instance to do the shopping we may have to:

- prepare a shopping list
- do the shopping
- put the shopping away.

So we now have the structure shown in Figure 12.4.

▲
Figure 12.4

| Check cupboards | Look in fridge | Write down items needed | Drive to shops | Select items | Pay for items | Unpack shopping | Put some food in fridge | Put some food in cupboard |

We write these in the order in which they are performed ⟶

▲
Figure 12.5

Again, this second set of tasks may be split up, as shown in Figure 12.5.

We can now put all the stages together to produce the final structure chart, as shown in Figure 12.6. When drawing structure diagrams, do not worry that yours might look different from other people's. They are rarely the same.

As you can see, the purpose of a structure diagram is to show the tasks in more detail as you move down. The top box is the overall view (doing the weekly shopping), hence the term top-down approach. You could carry on breaking each task down, but there comes a point where you have broken the tasks down into enough detail.

▲
Figure 12.6 *A structure diagram for doing the weekly shopping.*

Questions

1. Pick one of the following tasks (preferably the one you are most familiar with) and draw a structure diagram for it:
   (a) renting a DVD from a DVD shop
   (b) borrowing a book from your local library
   (c) programming your DVD recorder to record a programme
   (d) getting ready to go for a night out
   (e) washing the dishes.

2. Draw a structure diagram for making an evening meal with meat, rice, vegetables and coconut sauce. Figure 12.7 shows the top part of the diagram to start you off.

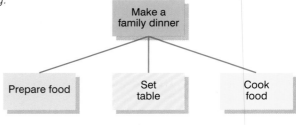

▲
Figure 12.7 *The start of a structure diagram to make a family dinner*

Data flow diagrams

Data flow diagrams are used to consider the data without bothering about the equipment used to store the data, and are used as a first step in describing a system. Four symbols are used in these diagrams and these are described on the next page.

The box

The box is either a source of data, such as an order form from a customer, or a part of the system which uses or consumes the data, called a sink. We are not concerned with what happens to data before they reach the box if they are a source, or what happens to data after they go past a sink.

The sausage

The sausage shape is sometimes replaced by a circle on some data flow diagrams and is used to denote a process performed on the data. A process is something which is done to the data, like a calculation. The process might be sorting the data or combining them with some other data. A brief description of the process should be placed inside the box.

The open rectangle

The open rectangle represents a data store. This is where the data are held. It could represent the data being held manually or on a computer. Basically, a data store is a logical collection of data. A description of the store can be placed inside the box.

The arrows

The arrows are used to show how the other symbols are connected.

Let us now draw a series of data flow diagrams for a system for a DVD library. The first diagram follows the data flow that takes place when a new member joins the library. To join the library it is necessary to fill in an application form and to show certain documents to provide proof of identity. If the potential member does not have this documentation, then the library manager will refuse membership. After the membership details have been checked (or validated) a membership card is produced and given to the new member and the member's details are recorded. If the member borrows a DVD or if the manager wants to know whether a particular person is a member, then the details can be found. Figure 12.8 shows the data flow diagram for this part of the system.

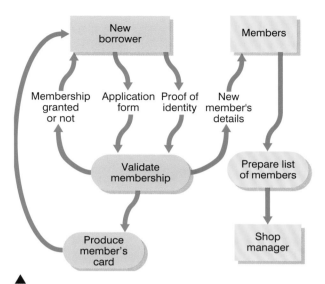

▲ **Figure 12.8** *A data flow diagram for a DVD library*

Now we can look at the data flow diagram for a DVD being added to the library. This is a simple system, with the details of the DVD, such as name and price being recorded and then stored. Figure 12.9 shows this part of the system.

Figure 12.10 shows the data flow diagram for the process of borrowing a DVD. Notice that the member data and DVD data are needed because the loans store of data will only contain the DVD number and the membership number. This is done to save space. By storing the DVD and member numbers together, it is possible to find out a member's details and the DVD details if they are needed.

We could, if we wanted to get an overall view of the system, join these diagrams together, but it is much easier to draw them for each part of the system and then to draw a diagram with them all joined.

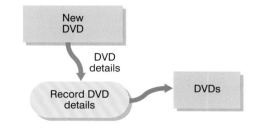

▲ **Figure 12.9** *The data flow diagram for adding a new DVD to the library*

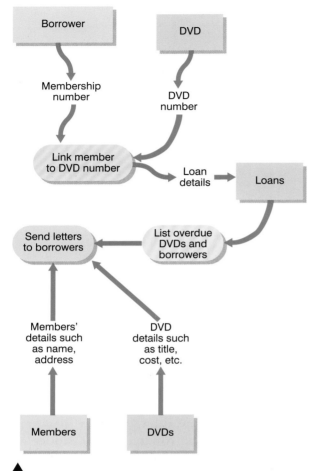

▲
Figure 12.10 *The data flow diagram for borrowing a DVD*

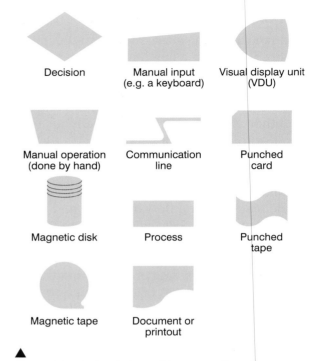

▲
Figure 12.11 *Symbols used in systems flowcharts*

Questions

Your form teacher marks the register twice a day. Find out what happens to these attendance marks and draw a data flow diagram for the system.

Systems flowcharts

A systems flowchart is a diagram which gives an overall view of a system. It shows the tasks that are performed on the data, such as sorting or updating, and also shows the type of media (magnetic disk, tape, etc.) used to hold the data. Figure 12.11 shows some of the usual symbols. The flow is always indicated by arrows. A tape will always have an arrow going into it or coming out of it, but a disk may have one in either direction or both.

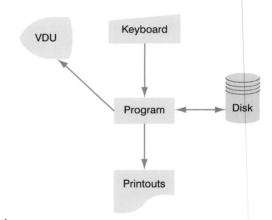

▲
Figure 12.12 *Systems flowchart for a simple database system*

For a small database system using a single computer, the systems flowchart shown in Figure 12.12 is very simple.

Notice the following:

- There is a double arrow going between the disk drive and program. This shows that data can be read into the computer and written to the disk drive.
- There are two ways of outputting the information, either on a VDU or as a printout (often called hard copy).

Systems flowchart for producing gas/electricity bills

The production of gas/electricity bills is an example of batch processing. Look back at Chapter 9 to see the steps involved in producing an electricity bill. Electricity companies each have millions of customers, so they use large mainframe computers. These usually consist of a separate processor or processors, backing storage devices such as tape or disk drives, and terminals.

Figure 12.13 shows the stages involved in producing the bills. The diagram itself is fairly easy to understand. Because every customer gets a bill and there are so many customers, batch processing is used, with magnetic tape as the storage medium. The transaction file containing all the meter readings has to be

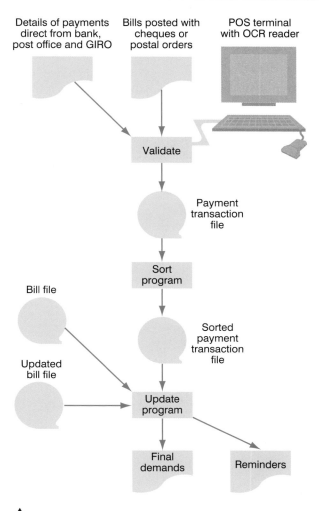

▲ **Figure 12.14** *Systems flowchart for processing the bills file*

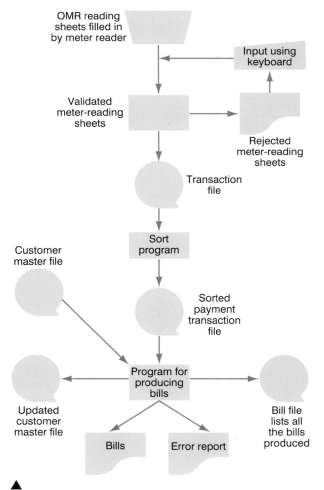

▲ **Figure 12.13** *Systems flowchart for producing gas/electricity bills*

sorted into the same order as the customer master file, otherwise the processing would be very slow, because tapes would need to be wound backwards and forwards until the records matched. The bills file, also on magnetic tape, contains details of the amounts owed by the customers and this will need updating as the customers pay their bills. Figure 12.14 shows the systems flowchart for processing the bills file. Notice that there are several ways of making the payments and the payments must be validated before being recorded on the transaction file. The update program is used to produce reminders and final demands to the people who have not yet paid their bills.

Systems flowchart for a payroll system which uses batch processing

The following system is used to produce the weekly wages for a large number of staff who work in a factory.

Each employee is given a clock card at the start of each week which contains the employee's name and works number. This card is placed into a special clock which records their arrival and departure time, and the date. For a complete five-day week, there will be 20 times recorded onto the card. The process of recording the times is called clocking in and clocking out.

The machine punches holes into the card to record each time and these cards can be placed directly into a machine which is able to read these coded data. The data are transferred directly to a transaction file, which may be on either magnetic tape or disk. The transaction file is validated and then sorted into employee works number order. Details of incomplete clock cards (e.g. from someone who has forgotten to clock out) will be output as a list called an error report. These clock cards will need to be dealt with by a separate system. A disk file is used to hold details regarding an employee's hourly rate, tax code, taxable pay to date and so on.

The systems flowchart used to represent the above system is shown in Figure 12.15.

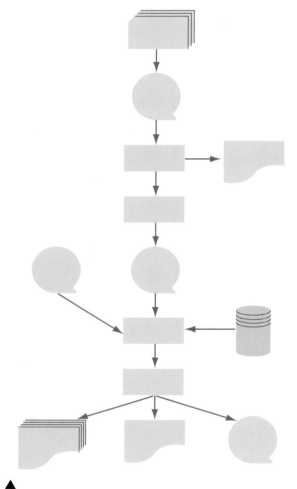

Figure 12.15 *A systems flowchart for a payroll system that uses batch processing*

Questions

Copy the systems flowchart in Figure 12.15 (now you can get to use your flowchart stencil!). Put each of the descriptions shown in the list below into the correct boxes in the flowchart you have drawn.

- transaction file
- wage slips
- tax tables on disk
- calculate wages
- sort program
- update master file
- updated master file
- sorted transaction file
- error report
- clock cards
- validation program
- employee master file
- error report

1 The following system is used to update the files for payments received from customers by a small firm. Customers send their payments to the firm's offices, where the details are entered into the computer using key-to-disk. These entries form the payments transaction file. After validation, the records are output to a second disk file. Any errors are corrected and re-input. The valid fields are then sorted and used with the customer master file to produce an updated file and a list of people who still owe money.

(a) On a copy of Figure 12.16, insert the letter for the correct expression into each space in the systems flowchart.

   A   sort payments records into customer account number order
   B   old customer file
   C   updated customer file
   D   error report
   E   error report
   F   validated payments transaction file
   G   payments transaction file
   H   payment records
   I   corrected payments records
   J   correct errors
   K   update
   L   sorted valid payments transaction file
   M   list of people who owe money
   N   validation

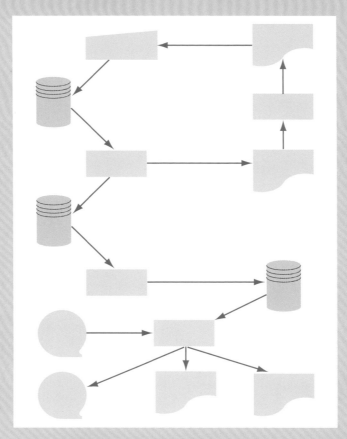

▶ **Figure 12.16**
Systems flowchart for payments update

(b) Why is the payment transaction file sorted to customer account number order?
(c) If the customers do not send part of the bill back when they are paying, which one piece of information is needed before the payment may be processed?
(d) What name is given to the field that contains that piece of information?
(e) Three days after paying her bill, a customer received a request for payment. Why has this happened?
(f) The flowchart shows three disk files and two magnetic tape files in use. Which file will become the new son file?
(g) Which file will be the new father file?
(h) After which two stages are errors found?
(i) Name the three files which must be kept for security reasons.

2 The systems flowchart in Figure 12.17 shows the process of updating the master file at the regional tax office using a transaction file.
(a) Explain why it is necessary to sort the transaction file.
(b) There are three different types of processes that are undertaken during an update. Name these three processes.
(c) Give two examples of errors that could occur during updating and which might be included in the error report.

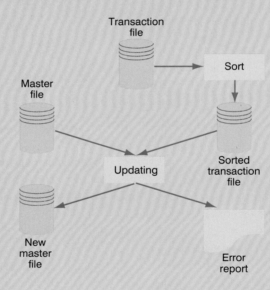

▲ **Figure 12.17** *Updating a master file at the regional tax office*

13 Systems Analysis

Sounds Hard. What Is It?

In this chapter we are going to find out what systems analysis is by looking at how we would perform one for a company called Harlequin Aquatics. The initial background to the company is given below.

Harlequin Aquatics

Harlequin Aquatics is a company involved in the selling of fish-keeping equipment to the public. Most of the company's business comes from a catalogue that is distributed with the monthly fish-keeping magazines. The customers select the items from the catalogue and either fill in the order form at the back of the catalogue (Figure 13.1) or, if they need the equipment very quickly (which is often the case), ring up, quoting their credit card number and the goods they require. The goods can be selected from the warehouse and dispatched to the customer. As well as the mail order business situated at the head office in Liverpool, UK, there are five smaller shops, situated in Chester, Manchester, York, Leeds and Birmingham. These shops do not get involved in the mail order side of the business, except when they have goods that are out of stock in the main warehouse.

USE THIS FORM TO ORDER DIRECT FROM US:-

Harlequin Aquatics

96 Hull Lane, Bootle, Liverpool L21 6OA

If you pay by CHEQUE please write your Bank Card number below (if available)
If you pay by CREDIT CARD please write your Credit Card number below.

Bank Card or Credit Card No.

Credit Card Expiry Date

Cheque/P.O.s payable to 'Harlequin Aquatics'

YOU CAN ALSO PHONE CREDIT CARD ORDERS

Give Access or Visa No and Expiry Date

0800 555555

USE OUR ANSWER PHONE SERVICE OUTSIDE NORMAL WORKING HOURS

Tick method of payment
Cash ☐ P.O. ☐ Cheque ☐ Card ☐

Name (BLOCK CAPITALS) ____

Telephone ____ Fax ____

Address ____

____ Post Code ____

Item Code	Quantity	Size	Price
			£
			£
			£
			£
			£
			£
			£
			£
			£
			£
			£
			£
		TOTAL PRICE	

If you have an account state the number below

ORDERS CAN ALSO BE PLACED BY FAX ON 0800-555666

CUSTOMERS WHO NEED A SPEEDIER DELIVERY PLEASE RING FOR SPECIAL SERVICES   PRICES CORRECT AT TIME OF GOING TO PRESS

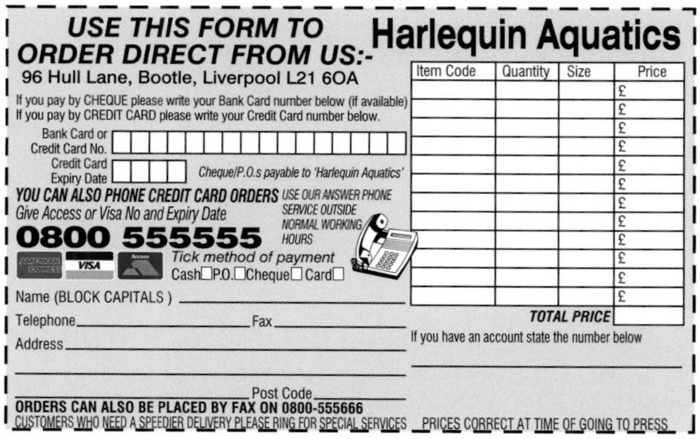

Figure 13.1 *An order form for Harlequin Aquatics*

At present all the tasks in the company are being performed manually and, although the company is very profitable, the directors realise that it has become very inefficient.

As a first step the directors wish to streamline the most profitable part of the company situated at the head office and main distribution centre in Liverpool. At the moment there are five telesales staff who take the orders over the phone and deal with occasional fax orders. There are also three other staff who deal with the orders through the post.

As soon as an order is received it is typed on a form which contains an order number. This form is in three parts: one to be sent to the warehouse, one to the accounts office and one to be sent to the customer with the goods.

The company bases its success on the fact that orders can be dealt with promptly (within 24 hours if the customer is prepared to pay for express delivery), but lately, with the volume of orders, this has become increasingly difficult to achieve. Increased competition has meant that a price war has started, with each company promising to beat each other's prices. This has meant that Harlequin Aquatics needs to be more efficient. The increase in orders has prompted the directors to look at the possibility of employing more staff, but they have now decided that they will try to deal with the greater volume of orders with the same number of staff as before. They are now looking to computerise the business and have recruited you as an outside consultant to investigate the possibilities for their business.

At present the head office of the company is located in an old converted church (used as the shop and the warehouse for the distribution of the mail order goods), with a small new office block of three storeys at the back.

In this chapter we will look at the steps involved in systems analysis. Harlequin Aquatics has not used a computer system before, so the company can start a new system from scratch. The steps involved in systems analysis are:

- fact finding
- a feasibility study
- an analysis phase
- system design
- implementation
- testing
- documentation
- evaluation.

We will look at what each of the above entails.

Fact finding

Fact finding is concerned with finding out about the existing system. It may be that computers are already used, but not to their full extent, or it may be that a manual system exists which needs computerising. In either case, we need to find out how things are done at the moment, before we can suggest any improvements.

There are four main ways of finding out about existing systems:

1 asking questions (interviewing people)
2 getting people to fill in carefully designed questionnaires
3 sitting with various people to observe how the job is done at the moment
4 inspecting any bits of paper, screen displays and files which are used in the present system.

The final step in fact finding is to produce a report that describes the existing system and its shortcomings, together with some description of the output needed from the new system.

Feasibility study

The feasibility study looks at the chances of being able to solve a particular problem at a reasonable cost. The feasibility report is the

Questions

1 Have another read of the scenario on Harlequin Aquatics. You are going to carry out a systems analysis on this company.

Imagine you have just received instructions to go and investigate their present system. You have no other background information apart from the scenario.
(a) Prepare a questionnaire which you could get the company to fill in before you arrange an interview. Your questionnaire should be general to start with, but then go on to ask more details later. Prepare this using suitable software.
(b) After receiving the completed questionnaire you decide to arrange a visit. Write a list of questions you would ask in the light of the results of your questionnaire. Try not to ask too many questions that are simply answered yes or no, but ask open-ended questions, such as 'Can you tell me what problems you have had with the existing system?'

2 One part of the fact-finding process is to collect the various pieces of paper used in the business and then examine them. Read the scenario again and decide which pieces of paper you would like to examine.

document produced at the end of the study and will give an idea of the time the project is likely to take, along with some estimate of cost. The aim of the feasibility study is to see whether it is possible to devise a system that can be implemented and will work at reasonable cost.

The feasibility study ends when a decision has been reached whether or not to proceed with the project.

The following are usually included in a feasibility study:

1 a description of what the system is required to do (called the objectives of the system); Figure 13.2 shows some of the objectives for the Harlequin Aquatics's system
2 some preliminary design so that the costs may be estimated

3 some alternative designs so that the most suitable one can be chosen

4 a cost/benefit analysis; this looks at the benefits and makes sure that they outweigh the costs. The costs of a system are not just the costs of the hardware and the software needed. Figure 13.3 shows some of the costs you might not have thought of

5 the conclusion, which states whether it is worth going ahead with the project and which design has been chosen.

5 the human, technical and economic factors:
- do the staff have the expertise to cope with the new system?
- is the technology available, that is, can it be done?
- is there enough money to go ahead?

6 a plan for the implementation

7 a proposed course of action (i.e. what the consultant/systems analyst suggests the company should do next).

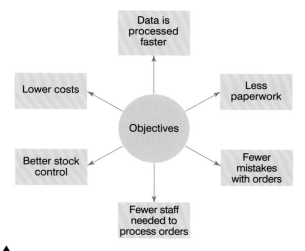

▲ **Figure 13.2** *Some of the objectives of a system for Harlequin Aquatics*

The feasibility report

The feasibility report is a written report given to the directors of Harlequin Aquatics and is really a summary of the results of the feasibility study. Usually the report is written, but it can also be given in the form of a spoken presentation.

The feasibility report should include the following:

1 a brief description of the business and any problems with the existing system

2 details of what part of the business is being looked at – for instance, with Harlequin we are looking at the processing of orders

3 the objectives of the proposed system

4 a list of some of the alternative solutions considered and why these alternatives were rejected

Questions

Figure 13.3 shows the headings for some of the costs which Harlequin Aquatics might have to pay during the development and eventual use of the system. Write a more detailed list under the headings in Figure 13.3.

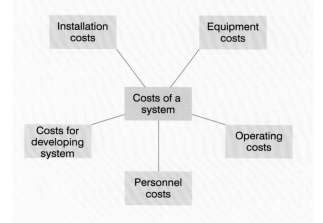

▲ **Figure 13.3** *The costs associated with an information system*

Action plan

Most ICT projects are too large for a single person to work on them. Instead project teams are put together containing people with different skills. For example, some of the project team may have expertise in systems analysis, while others have expertise in programming.

Once it has been decided to go ahead with a project, it is essential that the project team makes sure that the new computer-based system is implemented to an agreed timescale and to budget.

Without careful planning many projects can lose large amounts of money. This means that some projects have to be abandoned without anything being achieved.

A plan needs to be drawn up showing what activities need to take place and when, and various deadlines should be established where a review of the tasks completed to date can be compared against the plan. Any slippage in the timing of the project can be identified and steps can be taken (taking on extra staff, working overtime, etc.) to try to bring the project back on schedule again.

There are a variety of techniques and tools which may be used to help manage ICT projects and these are outlined here.

Critical paths

Determining the critical path involves the analysis of a large project to identify those tasks that can be undertaken in parallel, and which of these parallel tasks are critical to the project timescale. Once you know which tasks are critical to the project being completed on time you can concentrate more resources onto these tasks.

Project management software includes critical path software and this software can be used to see how a slight delay in one or more small tasks will affect the completion of the whole project.

Using spreadsheets for cost control

Cost control is an important part of any project, and since most companies include every cost (staff wages, rental of accommodation, use of consumables, even down to the bills), it is important to keep a careful check on the project costs and monitor them throughout the duration of the project.

The project manager needs to keep accurate records of the costs as they mount up, and this is usually done using a special software package or sometimes using an ordinary spreadsheet.

Gantt charts

Gantt charts are a type of horizontal bar chart used to schedule jobs. These diagrams show when the tasks that make up the whole job start and finish. They have a timescale going across the page and a list of the activities to be done going vertically down the page. The blocks that show the duration of the activities are shaded to show the time taken on each task. They are used as a planning tool since it is possible, by using a ruler placed alongside the chart, to determine which jobs are late and which jobs are running ahead of schedule.

It is usual to construct Gantt charts on squared paper so that times may be accurately read off. A transparent ruler placed at the present time aids reading off those activities that are behind schedule. Most project management software makes use of Gantt charts in some way.

	Tasks	1	2	3	4	5	6	7	8	9	10	11	12	13
1	Investigate existing system													
2	Feasibility study													
3	Fact finding													
4	Analysis													
5	Output design													
6	Input design													
7	File design													
8	System design													
9	System testing													

▲ **Figure 13.4** *A simple table of tasks*

▲ **Figure 13.5** *Project management software can produce Gantt charts*

PERT (Program Evaluation and Review Technique)

PERT is a project management technique which involves charting out the time and the other resources needed to complete a project. Although you can perform PERT just using a pen and paper, there are now many software packages for project management which contain PERT features.

Analysis phase

The feasibility study outlines what is required from the system, and in the analysis phase this study is used to design the new system. To perform the analysis, the systems analyst will need to look at the system in greater detail than for the feasibility study. When the present system is investigated, the systems analyst will find more weaknesses in it.

In the analysis phase, the charts (systems flowcharts and data flow diagrams) should be drawn as an aid to understanding the present system.

Included in the analysis phase are:

1 detailed objectives of the proposed system
2 facts about the parts of the old system being replaced by the new system
3 any constraints on the system: these are limitations on the solution to the problem. Many problems can be solved if the money, technical expertise and time are available. If any of these cannot be found, they are constraints on the system
4 an update of the cost/benefit analysis based on the new information
5 an update of the plan for further development of the system. This would include such things as the responsibilities of the members of the team involved with the project and deadlines by which the stages must be completed.

System design

If the directors of the company are convinced that a new system will be worth having, work can be started designing the new system.

Further investigation should be undertaken to consider what inputs, processes and outputs will be needed. Let's now consider each one in turn.

Outputs

Since the outputs from the system determine how the rest of the system operates, these are looked at first.

We need to look at each of the following areas.

1 What output is needed? For instance, we may decide that for our system we need the following:
   - an invoice (bill) which is sent out to each customer
   - a copy of the invoice to be sent to the accounts office
   - a dispatch note to be sent with the goods
   - a picking list for the storekeeper
   - a screen display so that we can find out if a particular item is in stock.
2 We must then look at what needs to be included on these documents and screens. We may be able to use the same document for different processes. In this way we could make several copies of the invoice using multi-part stationery and give one each to the customer, warehouse and accounts office.
3 How frequently do these documents need producing? For instance, we may need a list of all the stock at the end of each day or a list of all the past customers annually, when there is a sale on.
4 What is the volume of output? How many orders are dealt with each day? How many items are on each order? All of these determine the type of system we need to use and the input method chosen. If lots of orders are dealt with, methods other than keying need to be looked at.

Inputs

Questions the systems analyst will need to answer are as follows:

1 Where do the data come from? In our company the orders come in a variety of

ways. They are placed on an order form and posted, or they may be telephoned or faxed.

2 What data need to be input into the system? This would include catalogue numbers, descriptions, prices, quantities and so on.

3 How much data needs to be entered and how often does data need entering? For our company, it would be useful to determine how many orders were received in a day, what was the number of items on each order and so on. To determine the sizes of files we need to find out how many customers the company has and how many items there are in the catalogue.

4 Which input device should be chosen? This really depends on the volume of data and whether any of the data can be captured using OMR, OCR, barcoding and so on.

The systems analyst will also need to look at the design of the input screen, which should preferably match the design of the order forms.

Data preparation

Data preparation involves getting the raw data into a form that can be processed by the computer. Verification and validation are included in data preparation. Verification makes sure that, if a keyboard is being used, no typing mistakes have been made. Various validation methods can be used to trap some of the errors. Remember that validation is performed by a computer program.

Code design

We can use codes to save time typing and also save storage space. Codes need to be carefully designed if they are to be useful.

File design

We need to decide how many files are needed and then to design the structure of each of the files. To understand how this is done, look at Chapter 8 on databases. When designing files we should make sure that we do not duplicate any of the information.

Hardware configuration

If more than one computer is used, it makes sense to network them. Harlequin Aquatics needs a network, since paper would then not need to be transferred between the sales office and the other areas, such as accounts and the warehouse. Hardware configuration also includes deciding on the type of computer, and on peripheral devices such as disk drives and printers.

Software used

We first need to decide what software to use. We could hire someone to write it specially, which is very expensive. Alternatively, we could use a software package. For Harlequin we would use a database package. There are many database packages available and each would need to be evaluated. Once the application package has been chosen, we then need to look at the operating system it requires.

Testing the system

Before it is introduced the new system must be thoroughly tested. The testing of a system may be broken down into five stages.

1 The system is tested with data that contain no errors to see if it produces the correct results.

2 Known errors are now introduced into the data to see how the computer will process these. Ideally all the errors will be picked up by any validation procedures, but we must remember that it is impossible for the computer to detect all types of error.

3 We now start trying to process very large amounts of data to see how the system copes with this. This is really to see how the system copes with extra work that might be necessary in the future.

4 Some processing is only done now and again. For instance, we might need a stock report at the end of a month, so this will need to be fully tested.

5 Extreme data should be entered to make sure that the range checks included in the validation program will work.

If all goes well, we move on to the next stage which is the implementation of the system.

Implementing (or introducing) the new system

How you implement a new system really depends on its size. Solutions range from a microcomputer or two, to a system that uses a number of networked PCs or even a system based on larger computers.

Systems may be introduced into an organisation in three ways and we will look at each of these in turn.

Direct implementation

With direct implementation the users decide to start using the system on a given date. In practice, this method is only used for small computer systems, since in larger ones problems reveal themselves during the first month and the result can be havoc. Usually the number of computing staff is quite small compared with the administrative staff, so if too many problems occur they will be unable to cope.

Phased implementation

With phased implementation, each job is introduced separately rather than all jobs being introduced in one go, as with the previous method. For instance, we may decide to look at the order processing first and get this running before we deal with other areas of the business. One snag with this method is that it takes much longer and the benefits of the new system are delayed.

Parallel running

With parallel running, the new system is run alongside the existing system. If the new system fails, then because we still have the old system, we can use that until the problems are sorted out. Parallel running provides an ideal opportunity to compare the results from the new system with those of the old system, since both systems will be in operation at the same time. However, it does have the serious disadvantage that since each job is done twice, there is much more work for users while the two systems are running in parallel (Figure 13.6).

Documentation

Documentation is of two types: user and technical.

User documentation (or user guide)

A user guide or manual is documentation that the user can turn to for learning a new procedure or for dealing with a problem

▲
Figure 13.6 *Parallel running*

that has arisen. The guide should cover such things as how to load the software, how to perform certain functions, how to save and how to print. It is a good idea to include examples and exercises to help the user understand the system. Since users are usually non-technical, any specialist, technical language should be avoided.

The guide should detail what to do in exceptional circumstances. For instance, if the system fails to read a disk or data are sent to the printer without it being switched on and the machine is locked, a user will need to know what they have to do.

As always, users have the best view of a system and so should be asked to evaluate any proposed user guide. Their comments should be incorporated into the guide. You have probably tried to find things in manuals, so you will realise just how important they are.

Technical documentation

Technical documentation is used to explain a system to a specialist, either a programmer or a systems analyst. Since these people understand computer jargon, this guide does not need to be as simple as the user guide. This documentation is extremely important, since it might be used by someone new to the project and there may be no one around who was involved with the original project.

Changes always need to be made to a system at a later date, so this documentation will be needed when the system is improved or upgraded.

System evaluation

After a project has been implemented it should be reviewed periodically to make sure that it is still meeting its objectives.

A good way of evaluating a solution is to ask the users of the system. They will be able to tell you if a system does what they originally wanted or if there are any improvements needed.

There are always constraints placed on the system and these might include time, money and the lack of qualified staff involved in the project. Hence the solution has some limitations placed on it. Perhaps with Harlequin Aquatics a wide area network could be used to link all the shops to the head office, but the cost or lack of technically qualified people to look after it would prevent its use. Such a system could be considered in the future if Harlequin Aquatics has more money and when the staff are more familiar with computers.

System maintenance

Once systems have been developed, they need to be maintained to ensure they are able to cope with the needs of the business. Changes in the way the business or organisation operates will need alterations in the system. Programs may need to be written or altered. For example the percentage of sales tax could change, or fluctuations in income tax could trigger the need for changes. Businesses sometimes change direction or get involved in new ventures.

System maintenance can involve:

- setting up help-desk facilities to help users who experience problems with the new system
- extra functions being added to the existing system
- maintenance teams altering existing programs or creating additional ones
- operational issues such as poor performance, or software bugs identified by users that need to be corrected by appropriate staff
- system crashes being investigated to find out the reasons for their occurrence.

Test Yourself

Using the words in the list below, copy out and complete sentences **A** to **K**, underlining the words you have inserted. The words may be used more than once.

output   fact find   systems analyst   parallel

documentation   analysis   feasibility study

trained   evaluated   design   feasibility report

A A _____ _____ is the person who looks at the manual system to see which parts to computerise.

B She looks at the manual system in terms of three stages: input, process and _____.

C To begin with, she will perform a _____ _____ in order to find out a variety of facts about the business.

D Going on from this, she will then perform a _____ _____ which will look at whether an alternative system would be feasible.

E When she has completed this, she will submit a _____ _____ to the directors of the company.

F If the directors are happy with the report, they will give the go-ahead for the system and the analyst can start to _____ the system.

G Detailed systems _____ then follows, where outputs, inputs, files, software and so on are all decided.

H The personnel involved with the new system will need to be _____.

I Also, _____ will need to be written.

J There are three ways that a system can be implemented: _____ running, phased implementation and direct implementation.

K After a system has been in use for some time, it needs to be _____ to make sure that the objectives of the system are still being satisfied.

Things to do

1 John, the head of mathematics at a large comprehensive school, decided to take early retirement and start up a tutorial agency matching tutors to students. He advertises nationally for both tutors and students. He does the marketing and advertising, while his wife deals with all the paperwork. The business has been a huge success, but the amount of paperwork now generated is getting them both down. They are using a manual system at present, but would like a new computerised system.
  (a) The head of information technology at his old school suggests that they need to perform a feasibility study which will cover hardware, software, staffing and operating costs. Explain why such a study will help John and his wife select the best system.
  (b) Explain the steps involved in a feasibility study.
  (c) Once they have decided on a system, how should they go about getting their new system up and running?

2 A rail company uses an online system for reserving train seats. Documentation has been written for various users of the system. For each of the users below, explain what should be in the documentation.
  (a) A reservations clerk.
  (b) A senior supervisor.
  (c) A systems analyst, who has to maintain the system.

3 One stage in systems analysis is called fact finding, where the person performing the task, usually a systems analyst, will need to determine answers to a wide range of questions.

You have been asked to find out about an estate agent's system. The estate agent operates 20 agencies in a particular city and its surrounding suburbs. One of the larger shops acts as the head office.
(a) Write down at least 30 facts that you would need to find out about the estate agent's business in order to be able to advise the company on a suitable system.
(b) You are worried that you might encounter some opposition to the introduction of a new system. What can be done to ensure full cooperation from all staff?

IT Tasks

Task 1

You have been asked to build an information system for your school library from scratch. This is a substantial task and to perform it you will need to go through the various steps involved in systems analysis.

Some of the tasks you will need to perform include the following:
(a) You need to carry out a fact find of the manual system, which should include use of questionnaires and involve an interview with the library staff. Any forms, file cards and other documentation should be included in your initial report on the existing system.
You need to get an overall view of the existing library system in terms of the number of books, the number of borrowers, the number of loans per day/week, the average number of books per borrower and so on. You will need to find out how books are catalogued according to subject or author, and how the reminder system for overdue books works. At the end of this analysis you should be able to identify the strengths and weaknesses of the existing system.
(b) You will need to design a system. To do this you will need to look at the objectives of the system. You will then need to look at which software, hardware and peripherals should be used. In addition you will need to design input and output screens, database structures and any printouts needed.
(c) A pilot implementation should be done to check whether the system is likely to work. Any likely training implications should be identified, and finally an evaluation of the pilot should be undertaken.
(d) Some idea of the cost of the full implementation and the timescale should be given.
(e) A full-scale library system should be investigated, like the one used by your local library, and it should be compared and contrasted with the suggested system for your school library.

IT Tasks

Task 2

You have been asked by the owner of a DVD library to investigate its present manual system because they are thinking of computerising it. The DVD library has only one shop, about 1,800 customers and 2,000 DVDs. Prepare a list of questions in order to perform an initial fact find before a feasibility study.

Task 3

Harlequin Aquatics has decided to place stock details on the company computer. A section of the catalogue is shown below.

(a) Look at the section of the catalogue, which is only approximately one-hundredth of the whole catalogue. Think carefully about the uses to which the stock file will be put and decide what fields are needed. You will also need to decide on the type of field (numeric, character, date, logical, etc.). Now design the database structure for creating a stock file.

(b) A customer rings up and says, 'Can you let me know what internal filters you have in stock and what prices they are?' Could you answer this, bearing in mind that internal filters are just a small section in the total stock? If you can not, you will need to make some alterations in your stock file design. You could use a coding system to distinguish between the different sections.

(c) When you are happy with your structure, you can start putting the data into your database using the data in the list below and some data which you will need to supply yourself.

(d) Search for a website of a fish-keeping business and have a look at some of their prices. Using the information from the website, fill in your stock file until it contains 30 records.

(e) Give examples of reports (lists and results of searches and sorts) that you can get from your stock file.

(f) Finally, evaluate your system. Does it do what you intended and what shortcomings does it have?

Internal Filters

Catalogue number	Description of item	Price
52773	Rena Filty Internal Filter	$23.00
52774	Rena 225 Internal Filter	$30.50
52775	Rena 245 Internal Filter	$45.50
52776	Rena 245S Internal Filter	$45.50
52777	Rena 325 Internal Filter	$51.90
52778	Eheim 2252-200 L.P.H.	$129.9
52779	Eheim 2248-600 L.P.H.	$91.95
52780	Eheim 2209-80 L.P.H. inc. media	$53.90
52781	Eheim 2207-180 L.P.H.	$32.50
52782	Fluval 1 180 L.P.H.	$18.00
52783	Fluval 2 360 L.P.H.	$21.95
52784	Fluval 3 540 L.P.H.	$30.00
52785	Fluval 4 900 L.P.H.	$40.50
52786	Visijet IF 100-400 L.P.H.	$46.00
52787	Visijet IF 200-600 L.P.H.	$55.95

▲ **Figure 13.7** *Part of the Harlequin Aquatics stock list*

Weather Forecasting
An Application of Data Logging

Weather reporting: the old way

Figure 14.1 shows a typical school weather station. It consists of a slatted box, called a Stevenson's screen, in which are held certain instruments such as thermometer, maximum and minimum thermometer, and wet and dry bulb thermometer (used to measure the amount of humidity). Outside the box are a rain gauge, used to measure in millimetres the amount of rainfall, and an anemometer, which is used to measure the wind speed. A sunshine recorder reports on the number of hours of sunshine in the day.

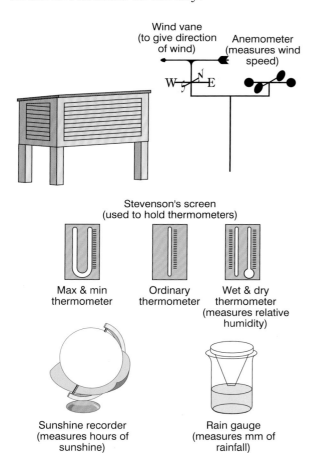

Figure 14.1 *Collecting weather data the old way: the instruments involved*

Collecting the data

The readings are taken by the pupils in the morning immediately before school starts. Two pupils take the readings and they fill in a form with the relevant data.

Questions

Design a form that could be used to obtain the weather data over a week. This form will eventually be used by pupils in maths and geography lessons.

Before you design the form think about what the requirements of the form should be. It would be better if all the data for one month could be placed on a single piece of A4 paper. Are there any other requirements?

The geography teacher decides that she would like more frequent readings made. Julie and John, who have to take the readings, are not very keen on this idea. Although they find collecting the data interesting, they do not find it that interesting!

Another problem is that readings are unavailable over the weekend, and if both pupils are away from school on the same day, no readings are taken for that day. Also, the equipment is not read over the summer holidays. Overall, the weather data collected are incomplete.

The problem

Ideally, the geography teacher would like the following:

1 complete records of weather data over 365 days of the year
2 more frequent measurements (say four times a day)

3 greater accuracy of readings (sometimes the instruments are read incorrectly).

The maths teacher, who has been illustrating the use of statistics with the data, would like:

1 computer printouts of weather patterns over various periods of time
2 to be able to use a computer package to draw the various graphs.

The solution

Some way is needed of recording the data at set intervals, automatically. This will solve the problems outlined above. If the equipment could transfer the data directly to a computer, without necessarily being connected to the computer all of the time, this would be another advantage. A data-logging system would be an ideal choice for this system.

Data logging

A data-logging system automatically collects data over a certain period of time. As well as being able to alter this time, you can alter the frequency with which the measurements are made. Since there is no human error, the measurements will be more accurate than before.

Weather reporting

Weather reporting is an application of data logging. Data logging involves recording quantities automatically over a set period of time. For weather reporting, these quantities are illustrated in Figure 14.2.

Most data loggers do not need to be connected to a computer all the time. Instead, they store the data in the logger for a period (50 hours for one particular package). It is also possible to display the data continuously, but this ties up a computer and prevents it being used for other things. Figure 14.3 shows an automatic data-logging weather station, with its various sensors.

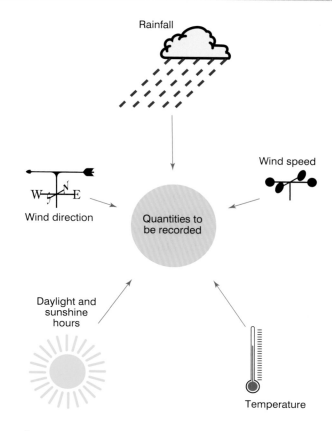

▲ **Figure 14.2** *For weather reporting, information about all of these needs to be recorded*

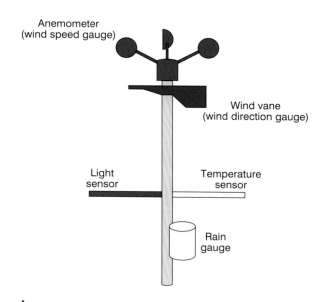

▲ **Figure 14.3** *An automatic data-logging weather station*

The sensors

Sensors act as the input devices into the computer. Figure 14.4 shows the detailed arrangement of the components of the Weather Reporter, a fully automatic data-logging weather station. The sensors measure the following elements.

Temperature

The temperature sensor gives an analogue temperature signal which is converted via an analogue-to-digital converter to a digital signal, which is then stored by the microprocessor.

Wind speed

An anemometer measures wind speed by using an optical sensor to generate a binary signal each time it rotates. The wind speed is recorded in kilometres per hour.

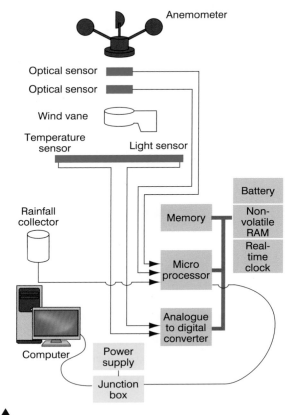

▲ **Figure 14.4** *Arrangement of the components in the Weather Reporter*

Wind direction

The wind direction is detected on a grey code disk. As the wind vane rotates, three optical sensors read the disk and generate a three-bit binary pattern. Each pattern represents one of the eight wind directions. For instance, the pattern 010 might represent north-west.

Rainfall

Rainfall is measured using a tilting bucket. As the bucket fills with water, it starts to tilt. When it is full the bucket tips the water out and brings another bucket into position, ready to collect more water. An optical sensor detects the number of tips and this digital signal is passed to the microprocessor.

Daylight and sunshine hours

Sunshine is detected by a special diode. The signal from this is then passed to the microprocessor, after it is converted from an analogue signal to a digital one. The digital signal is then used by the microprocessor to determine sunrise and sunset time, and also to measure sunshine hours.

Additional sensors

Additional sensors that measure atmospheric pressure and relative humidity (a measure of the amount of moisture in the air) may also be connected to the system.

Analogue-to-digital conversion

All the quantities measured by the Weather Reporter are analogue quantities, because they are continuously variable and do not jump in steps from value to value. For instance, temperatures do not jump from one degree straight to the next; there are many values in between. Quantities which have continuous values are called analogue quantities, and those that jump from one value to the next are called digital quantities.

A rain gauge measures rainfall, which in this system is an analogue quantity, but the sensor itself counts the number of buckets that are filled. This is only ever 1, 2, 3 and so on, so it is a digital value. Digital values can be fed directly into the microprocessor or computer but analogue values need to be converted to digital values using an analogue-to-digital converter, since most (but not all) computers process only digital values.

Questions

Fill in the table shown below, saying whether each physical quantity is either analogue or digital.

Physical quantity	Digital or analogue
Wind speed	
Wind direction	
Temperature	
Rainfall	

Now look at the section on the sensors used to detect these quantities and fill in the following table.

Sensor	Digital or analogue
Wind speed (optical sensor)	
Wind direction (optical sensor)	
Temperature (integrated circuit sensor)	
Rainfall (optical sensor)	

Advantages of data logging

Data logging is performed automatically, without the need for a human to make the measurement. Also, because of this, the data can be collected more frequently than would be possible doing it manually. The frequency with which the data are logged may also be varied. The electronic signals from the sensors can be relayed through communication lines (by radio or through phone wires), so the sensors can be situated anywhere in the world. Figure 14.4 shows a remote weather station as used by the Meteorological Office. Figure 14.5 shows how the weather data are presented on the screen, using equipment and software such as the Weather Reporter.

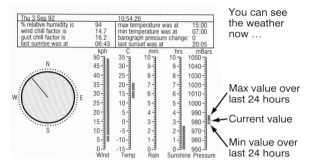

You can see the weather now …

Max value over last 24 hours

Current value

Min value over last 24 hours

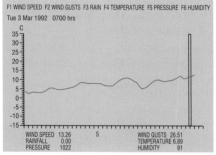

… or look at the changes in weather over the last 60 hours …

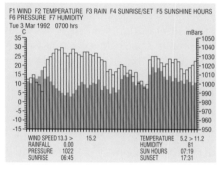

… or look at the variations of two quantities over the last 58 days (This one shows how the temperature and pressure changed each day).

▲

Figure 14.5 *Information that can be shown on the computer screen of a fully automatic data-logging weather station*

Transferring weather data to another package

It is possible to transfer weather data obtained from the Weather Reporter to another package. To do this, the weather data are converted to a special format which can be loaded into a spreadsheet package such as Microsoft® Excel® or a database package. Transferring data out of one package is called exporting. Transferring the data into another package is called importing.

Things to do

1 When the weather station is used on its own (i.e. not connected to the computer), the data from the sensors are stored in non-volatile RAM.
  (a) What does the abbreviation RAM stand for?
  (b) Why is it important that the RAM is non-volatile?

2 When the data are sent from the sensors to the microprocessor, the time must be sent as well. Why is this?

3 The program that controls the microprocessor is stored in ROM.
  (a) What does the abbreviation ROM stand for?
  (b) Why is it necessary to store the program in ROM rather than in RAM?

4 Compare and contrast the collection of weather data manually using a Stevenson's screen and so on, and by using an automatic data-logging system such as the Weather Reporter.

5 Manor Top is a secondary school that teaches a full range of subjects. Wherever possible, the teachers at Manor Top encourage the pupils to use computers as part of their studies. Manor Top has 20 computers that the pupils can use, but there are over 600 pupils. Mrs Logit, the teacher responsible for information technology, is anxious that the pupils should experience computers being used for data logging and control.

A group of senior pupils and Mrs Logit design and construct an automatic weather station. The weather station consists of such devices as a rain gauge, a sunshine recorder and an anemometer. Each device has to be connected directly to one of the school's computers. As it is important that the weather data are collected on a regular basis, Mrs Logit and her pupils have to write some computer programs that will run all the time.

Pupils and teachers who are involved in science, geography, the environment and statistics soon become very interested in the data that the weather station is collecting. Mrs Logit is therefore finding that she is under pressure to provide more and varied data.

The computer connected to the weather station stores, in a computer file, the amount of sunshine detected each day.
  (a) Name the software package that could be used to store the sunshine data.
  (b) A software package is used to produce the output shown in Figure 14.6.
    (i) Name the software package.
    (ii) The chart shows two things that cannot be true. State what they are.
    (iii) Explain why, in this case, the result of the average sunshine per day must be wrong.
  (c) Each day, the computer connected to the weather station stores the date and the rainfall in centimetres for that date. A database package is used to analyse the file of rainfall data. Describe what information would be given by the following database instruction:

IF RAIN IS MORE THAN 5 THEN OUTPUT DATE

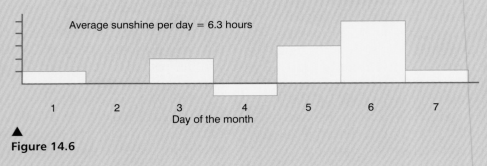

▲ **Figure 14.6**

(d) Tilda Shower is a geography teacher.
Tilda wants the rainfall data to be recorded every day for a whole year. She wants the results to be printed out in booklet form.
  (i) Describe how this amount of data could have been collected without the aid of a computer.
  (ii) Explain why, in a school, it would not have been practical to collect this amount of data without a computer.
  (iii) State one advantage to Tilda's pupils of having this amount of data.

(e) The instructions below are part of a computer program which, every 30 minutes, stores the temperature that the weather station detects.

```
WAIT 30
DETECT TEMP
STORE TEMP
```

Tilda now wants the temperature to be stored every 15 minutes.

(f) Show how one of the instructions will have to be changed.

(g) (i) Explain why these three instructions by themselves would not keep on storing the temperature.
  (ii) Show the extra instructions that would be needed so that the computer will store the temperature 'forever'. (You may invent your own instructions.)

(h) 50 °C is very very hot; −50 °C is very, very cold. Sometimes the weather station does not work properly, so silly temperature values are stored. Explain how the program could be improved to prevent the computer storing silly values for temperature.

IT Tasks

Task 1

1 Use electronic mail to transfer your data along the telephone lines to other schools and colleges. Use appropriate software to see the way the weather changes from one part of the country to another.

2 Use a weather recording system to obtain regular readings of wind speed, temperature, hours of daylight, pressure, wind direction, hours of sunshine, rainfall and humidity. Collect the data either manually or by using data-logging equipment, and transfer it to a computer for processing. Display the readings in a suitable way on the computer. Can you predict the weather tomorrow from your data? Produce a 'school weather forecast' and print it out. How accurate were you?

Task 2

Design a complete weather forecasting system over a period of several weeks or months. Collect your readings either manually or by using a data-logging system, and transfer these to the computer for processing. Processing could include producing graphs.

Transferring Data Around
A Company with a Communication Problem

Binscope is a retail organisation that is in business to sell high quality optical equipment: terrestrial telescopes, astronomical telescopes, binoculars and microscopes. In addition to the above, the company also sells books on astronomy, birdwatching and so on, as well as many accessories, such as eyepieces, camera attachments, tripods and cases. It also has a small workshop where optical equipment is repaired.

At present Binscope has seven shops: in Liverpool, Birmingham, London, Manchester, Leeds, Glasgow and Chester. The whole Binscope operation is controlled from the head office and warehouse next to the Liverpool shop. Figure 15.1 shows the Binscope 'empire'.

▲ **Figure 15.1** *The Binscope empire*

Much of the equipment comes from abroad and it all arrives at the Liverpool warehouse, where it is checked before being dispatched via carrier to the various shops.

John Bird and his wife Anne opened their first shop in Liverpool in 1989. Both of them had been teachers. The rapid expansion of the business to seven sites, along with the employment of a large number of staff, has caused many problems.

Many of the problems stem from the fact that the shops are scattered throughout Britain. Transfer of information between the shops and the head office causes problems and some of these are outlined here.

Problems with the existing system

1 Lists of stock are prepared by head office and sent to each branch by fax before the shops open in the morning. The shops have to send the head office a list of what they have in stock just before they close in the evening. Since stock is continually changing throughout the day, no one really knows what the actual stock situation is.

2 To compensate for point **1**, staff have to ring around the other branches to find an item that a customer wants, if it is out of stock in their own branch. This takes time and ties up sales staff. Customers frequently get annoyed waiting while this is done and inevitably sales are lost. In addition the phone bills have been excessively large.

3 New price lists, product literature and maintenance schedules are sent by post and this takes too long.

4 Sales figures have to be telephoned to the head office at the end of each day. This is tedious, since all the shops tend to try to phone at the same time and it can take a long time to get through.

5 Orders from the manufacturers are dealt with by the head office and this makes it difficult to inform a customer in one of the branches when a particular product will be delivered without phoning the head office first.

6 The company likes to keep in touch with its customers, so it sends them a list of new products and special sales from time to time. Since each branch keeps its own database, one customer who had shopped

at three of the branches receives three copies of these lists.

7   Because of the problem with stock, there are frequent delays in ordering goods from suppliers. The company runs out of goods which are in high demand, and sales are lost because customers go elsewhere.

8   Fax is used to send orders to suppliers, but suppliers would like to receive payment electronically. Much of the optical equipment comes from Japan or Germany, two technically advanced countries. Companies in these countries have suggested that Binscope uses EDI, but the directors of Binscope do not even know what it is.

9   John and Anne Bird frequently need information from the shops in order to manage the business effectively. This information takes time to get and this is very frustrating for them.

Binscope realises there is a problem, so the directors hire a computer consultant for some advice. The consultant, who is a qualified systems analyst, will look at the present system in detail, and will identify their needs and come up with some solutions.

After looking at the business and having talks with the various staff, the consultant suggests that they need the following:

1   a stock file that is accessible to everyone
2   a faster way of sending mail and pictures (for advertising) between the head office and the shops
3   a faster ordering system between Binscope and its suppliers
4   a central file of customers that is accessible to everyone
5   a way of paying the suppliers directly, using some form of fund transfer from the bank
6   as each sale is made at the various shops, the details of the transaction (piece of business) need to be sent automatically to the head office, where the stock file and the customer file can be automatically updated. Since this happens in real time it means that the stock file is continually updated and reflects the true stock position of Binscope.

Questions

1   At the moment faxes are used to transfer some important information between sites. Explain what is meant by faxes and how they are used. Use the glossary at the back of the book to find what a fax is if you do not already know.

2   Put yourself in the position of one of Binscope's customers. Write a list of the problems and frustrations you might have in dealing with this company.

3   Put yourself in the position of a manufacturer of telescopes. What problems might you have in dealing with Binscope?

The solution to Binscope's problem

The consultant decides that the company needs a communications system. She suggests that all the computers should be networked so that data are easily transferred between the sites. She decides that a local area network (LAN) is used in the head office, with a wide area network (WAN) between the sites. Also, the company needs to consider the possibility of using electronic mail. This all sounds very complicated to Anne and John, so the consultant has made some notes to explain how the system works. Here they are.

Networks

A network is a series of computer systems that are linked together so that they are able to share computing power or storage facilities. The link may be between computers in the same building or between computers in different parts of the country or even in different parts of the world.

Binscope needs to make sure that when a network is chosen, room is left for future expansion. Who knows, in five years' time the number of shops may have doubled. For this reason the systems analyst has suggested that a dedicated file server is used. This is generally a much higher specification than the other computers, with a very large hard disk drive. All the common data, such as the stock file will be held on the file server's hard disk. A dedicated file server monitors and controls the network, and while it is performing this important task it is not available to be used as a normal workstation.

Local area networks

Local area networks (LANs) are confined to a small area. Usually this small area is within a single building, although it need not be confined to just a single office. Sometimes LANs spread through several buildings on the same site. Messages can be sent between the terminals and this is very useful for sending memos between offices. Figure 15.2 shows the local area network proposed for the Binscope office.

Wide area networks

Wide area networks (WANs) cover a wide geographical area. For instance, banks and building societies have their main computers situated in one place, with connections made by telephone wires to all the various branches. Using WANs, computers may be linked together in different countries using satellites, microwaves or telecommunication links.

In practice, LANs are often connected to WANs via a special gateway. Using a gateway any computer system can be accessed, provided that it is connected to one of the many communication systems in use.

Advantages and disadvantages of networking

Advantages

1 Expensive peripheral devices such as laser printers and scanners can be shared between users.
2 Messages can be sent between users on the same site with LANs, or anywhere in the world with WANs.
3 All users can access the same files, so this avoids having to duplicate information.
4 Network software can be purchased, which is often cheaper than buying an individual package for each machine.
5 It is possible to access data or programs from any terminal/workstation.
6 Data and software can be stored centrally, which makes them easier to maintain and back up.
7 Users can easily be prevented from accessing those files that are not needed for their job. This means that someone in the accounts department, for instance, would not be able to access the personnel files.

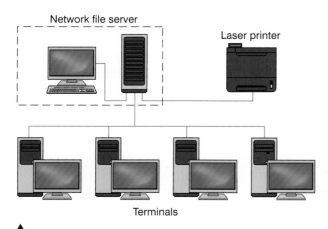

▲ **Figure 15.2** *The local area network in Binscope's head office*

▲ **Figure 15.3** *Sending messages across a local area network can be useful*

Disadvantages

1 If a WAN is used, sophisticated equipment is needed and the rental of telecommunication links makes it very expensive.
2 A loss in the ability to transmit data for even a short time can cause havoc, with tasks having to be performed manually.
3 File security is more important with networks, especially if they are connected to the public telephone system. For instance, if a virus were to get onto a network, it could affect all the networked terminals.
4 Wiring can be expensive, both to buy and to install. Wiring has to be sunk to avoid it trailing across a floor, where it would be dangerous.
5 In a type of network called a file-server network all the programs and data are stored on a main computer called a server. If this server breaks down, the whole network becomes unusable.
6 Networks are temperamental; they need an experienced person (a network manager) to keep them running successfully. Network managers are usually well paid and this adds to the cost of a network.

Network topologies

There are many different devices that may be connected to a network, such as CPUs, disk drives, printers and point-of-sale terminals. All of these need to be brought together in some way. Most often, cables will be used to connect the terminal and other equipment together, although radio communication links can be used.

When a diagram of a network is drawn, lines are used to show the communication links between devices. Devices in a network, called **nodes**, can be connected in a variety of different ways or **topologies**.

There are four common network topologies, called **ring**, **line (bus)**, **star** and **hierarchical**.

Ring topology

In the ring topology the terminals or other equipment are connected together in a circle (see Figure 15.4a). None of the computers in the network is any more important than any of the others. One of the main disadvantages of the ring topology is that if there is a break in any part of the communication line, all the devices on the network will be affected.

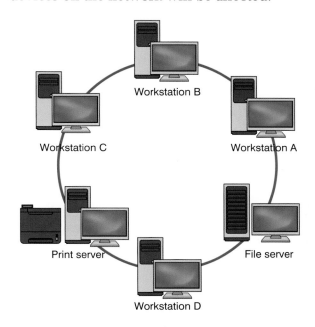

A schematic diagram of the ring network

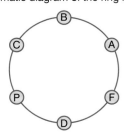

▲
Figure 15.4a *Ring topology*

Line or bus topology

In a line or bus network, the data are sent to all the devices on the network at the same time (see Figure 15.4b). This means that if a terminal is not working properly others are not affected. Like the ring topology, there is no central computer used to control the network, so each of the terminals has equal status. The main advantages of the line or bus network are that it is cheap and reliable.

Star topology

In the star topology, there is a computer at the centre that is used to control the whole of the network (see Figure 15.4c). If this machine breaks down, the whole network breaks down. Star topologies use more cabling and are therefore more expensive than other topologies. However, since there is a path from each terminal to the central computer, this type of topology is very fast.

Hierarchical networks

Hierarchical networks are those networks where one or more computers are more powerful than the rest. Hierarchical networks

are often called client–server networks, because a more powerful computer called the server is used to look after printing, file maintenance and other peripherals. Less powerful computers (sometimes without any processing power or disk drives of their own) called clients are connected to the network. These client computers are able to make use of the services provided by the server.

There are two types of server: the print server and the file server.

A file server is a computer used for managing the files on a network. Some file servers are dedicated file servers, which means that they spend all their time managing the network. These file servers are

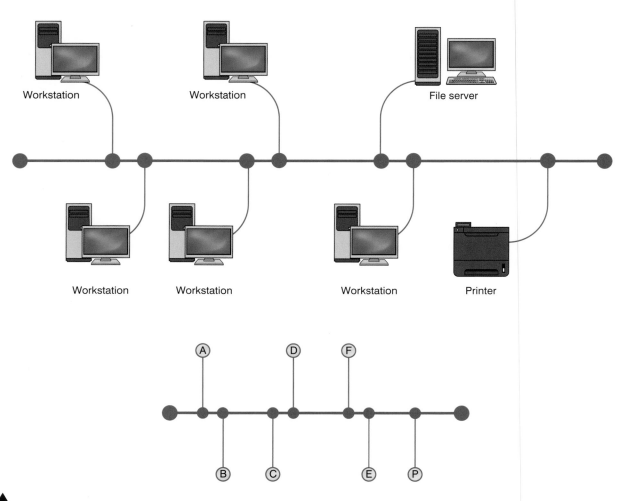

▲ **Figure 15.4b** *Line or bus topology*

not available for use as terminals. The file server is used to store both programs and data, and is generally a much more powerful computer than the others to which it is connected. In some ways a file server can be considered a giant hard drive to which all the other computers on the network have access.

A print server is the name given to a computer in a network that has a printer connected. This server manages all the print requests from users on the network. The advantage in using a print server is that the individual computers are no longer tied up managing their printers.

Modems

For Binscope's shop-based computers to communicate with the head office system, each computer in the shops will need to have a modem.

A modem (short for **mo**dulator–**dem**odulator) allows data to be passed along telephone lines from one computer to another. This device converts the digital signals produced by the computer into analogue signals. These analogue signals are sent along a telephone line to another modem, where they are converted back into digital signals for the receiving computer (Figure 15.5).

The speed at which data are transferred is measured in bits per second (bit/s for short). The faster the modem, the quicker the data can be transferred and it is possible to get up to speeds of around 56,500 bits per second. Speed is important in terms of the cost of transmission: the time spent connected to the phone line is directly related to the cost. If the time can be decreased, then the cost of transmission will be reduced. Some modems are able to compress data before sending them and this also reduces the transmission time and cost.

A schematic diagram of the above star network (notice the central controller node, S)

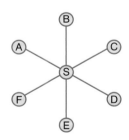

Figure 15.4c *Star topology*

Figure 15.5 *Using modems to transmit signals down telephone lines*

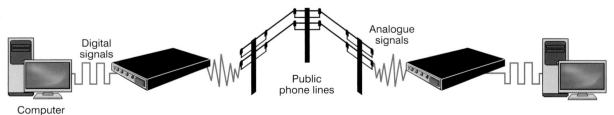

Dial-up service

This is a slower, more old-fashioned way of connecting to the internet. When you log on to the internet using a dial-up modem, it dials the number of your internet service provider (ISP). You are then asked for your user ID or screen name and a password. On providing this, you are connected to the internet. A dial-up service is slow because it takes time to connect to the internet, and once connected the speed at which data are sent and received is quite slow.

Broadband service

Broadband is an always-on service, so no time is wasted dialling and waiting for a connection to the internet. Broadband is much faster than dial-up and allows you to:

- use the telephone at the same time
- download and upload files at high speed
- watch online videos
- use web cameras
- listen to online radio
- watch TV programmes
- surf the internet very quickly.

The parts which make up a network

Networking is not simply connecting up a few computers with cables. Here are some parts that can be found in a typical network.

Software

Network software may be part of the operating system (such as Windows 7 or Windows XP) or it can be special software for managing a network.

Cables

Connecting cables are usually used to connect devices on a network, although some networks make use of radio or microwaves to provide the link. Cables vary in both performance and cost.

Connectors

Connectors are used to connect network cables to terminals or other devices.

Network cards

To use a personal computer as a terminal on a network, it is necessary to include a device called a network card inside the computer. The network card looks like a small circuit board and slots into one of the connectors on the main circuit board inside the computer (called the motherboard). Network cards have connectors on them for network cables.

Data transmission

Communication links

Terminals need to be able to 'talk' or communicate with each other. To do this there needs to be a communication link. These links are not necessarily cables, so you cannot always see or touch them. They can be radio or infrared signals, in which case the data are sent between the terminals as a series of pulses of infrared waves or radio waves.

Data are transmitted as signals (which can be electrical or light signals), with the signals carried on a wave. The material (or medium) that carries the signal passes on its journey from one computer to another, and this is called the transmission medium.

Data can be transmitted through metal cables (e.g. telephone wires or coaxial cables) or fibre optic cables made up of thin strands of glass. Where there is a great distance between the sending and receiving computers, it may not be possible to lay a cable or it might be too expensive. In this situation, a method is needed that does not make use of cables and so is called wireless media.

Cable media

Metal cable

Cable media consist of metal wires (usually copper) down which data are transmitted in the form of a varying current.

Fibre optic cable

Fibre optic cable works by transmitting data as a series of pulses of light along a thin glass fibre. One bundle of fibres is used to send messages and a second bundle carries messages in the opposite direction. They are very good for transferring data because they are fast and do not suffer from interference like metal cables.

Wireless media

With wireless media, electromagnetic waves provide the medium (a carrier signal) onto which the data are encoded as a superimposed signal.

There are several ways of transmitting the data, using different wavelength ranges:

Radio waves – here the data are transmitted as a series of radio waves.

Microwaves – the data are sent contained in microwaves. Mobile telephones use microwaves. They are ideal for linking computers in two separate buildings fairly near to each other. Satellite systems also make use of microwaves. Satellites are used when transmitting over large distances (e.g. from one continent to another). The data signal in the form of a microwave is beamed up to a satellite and the satellite then beams it back to another part of the world.

Infrared – this works a bit like your television remote control. Infrared signals can only travel a short distance and this limits their use. They are used to provide a link from a laptop to a printer or desktop computer, so that data can be sent between the two without the need for a cable. This is easier and saves time connecting and disconnecting mobile systems.

Advantages and disadvantages of wireless networks

Advantages

- There are no trailing wires, which can be a tripping hazard.
- They are cheaper, as there is no need to install wires in walls, floors and ceilings.
- Data transfer is faster as there are no wires to connect.

Disadvantages

- The level of security is reduced as it is possible for hackers to access a wireless network unless precautions are taken, such as use of firewalls or proper use of passwords.
- Some wireless networks have a limited range.
- You may be in a place where it is impossible to get a wireless signal to access a network.

Data transfer speeds and how they are apparent to the user

Data transfer speed (measured in Mbits/s) is the speed at which data are transferred between a server and a terminal. If the data transfer speed is low, the user will notice two things.

- The response is slow: it takes ages to get connected to a website.
- When you click on something you do not get a response right away.

Download time is the time taken to transfer a file from the server to the terminal.

Keeping unauthorised people out of networks

The difference between a password and a user ID

A user ID is a number or name that is unique to a person using the network. The person who looks after the network uses this to allocate file space for each user's work. It is also used to permit users to access certain files. A user ID tells the operating system that a certain person is using the terminal.

A password is a string of characters (letters and/or numbers) that the user (or the person who looks after the network) can select. It is used to authenticate the user to the system. Only if you type in the correct password will you be allowed access.

The user ID will normally be shown on the screen, but any password is hidden. As each character of the password is typed, an asterisk is shown on screen, to ensure that it cannot be read by anyone watching the screen as the log-on takes place.

Many networks only allow around three attempts at entering the correct password. Once this number of attempts has been exceeded you will be locked out of the system even if you then enter the correct password. The purpose of this is to stop hackers trying to guess at a password.

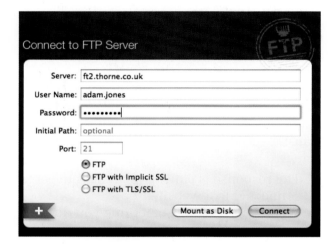

Access rights

Access rights are a facility offered by most organisations' network software. They enable certain rights to be allocated to files and users. For example, for a particular user some files can be viewed only and not altered, other files can be viewed and altered and some cannot be accessed at all.

This means that all the users of the network do not have complete access to every file or folder. If only the accounts staff are to be allowed to access the company's accounts, this can be done using the access rights as part of the network operating system.

◄

Figure 15.6 *The screen that you use to log onto the internet asks for a screen name (this is another name for a user ID) and a password. The screen name/user ID shows who is using the internet and the password makes sure that only the correct user is allowed access*

Figure 15.7 *A network opening screen which asks for a user ID and a password*

▼

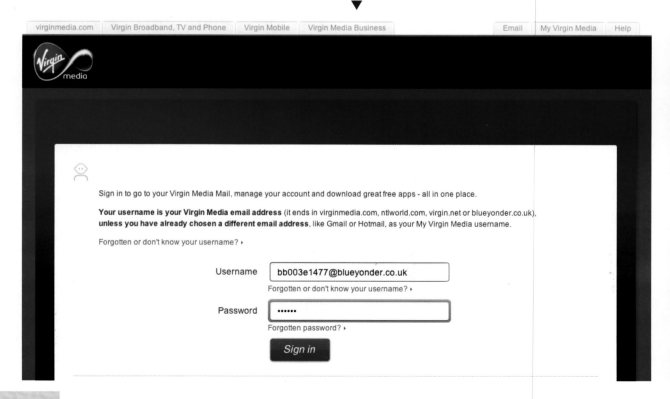

Monitoring all attempts to access the system

Networks normally monitor attempts to access the system. If a person enters the user name with the correct password, that person is then allowed access. The system will also monitor which files have been looked at. This is done to protect the privacy of files and also to discourage fraud, as it is possible to find out who altered a file.

Questions

The staff of an insurance company are mainly out and about talking to customers. They do have to come into the office at least one day each week to catch up with their administrative tasks. There are 200 insurance agents and it would be a waste of space and money if they were all to have their own desk and terminal. Instead there are 40 terminals that can be used by any of the insurance agents. Agents come in, find a vacant terminal and do their work.

1 Each insurance agent is given a user ID. Why is a user ID needed?
2 The network administrator suggests that each user's first name should be used as a user ID. Give one reason why this would not be a good idea.
3 Each insurance agent needs to think up a password. What is a password and why is it needed?
4 To log into the network both a user ID and a password need to be entered. Why are both needed?
5 Suggest two things these users should bear in mind when choosing a password.

Questions

Which three of the following developments have most enabled people to telework from their homes?
- the low cost of IT equipment
- fast train or tram links into town
- the internet
- the availability of chat rooms
- fast communication links to the organisation's data

Questions

Here is a list of advantages and disadvantages of networked ICT systems compared to stand-alone ICT systems.

The list is jumbled up and each item needs to be put under one or other heading. Copy and complete the table, putting each item under the appropriate heading.

- You can obtain access from any workstation.
- A network manager is needed.
- Cost of installation is high.
- Users' access rights can be controlled.
- There is usually complete reliance on the server.
- Expensive peripherals may be shared.
- There is a need for more security.
- Data and software can be stored centrally.

Advantages	Disadvantages

Intranets

An intranet is a private network that uses the same technology as that used by the internet for the sending of messages around the network. The main use of an intranet is to share organisational information and share resources. Usually only employees of that organisation are able to use it.

Note that an intranet need not be confined to a single site and it is still possible for people on an intranet to access the internet.

The differences between an intranet and the internet

- Internet stands for **inter**national **net**work.
- Intranet stands for **int**ernal **r**estricted **a**ccess **net**work.
- An intranet contains only information concerning a particular organisation.
- Intranets are usually only used by the employees of a particular organisation.
- Intranets are based on an internal local network.
- With an intranet, you can block sites that are outside the internal network.
- For the intranet to work, it is not necessary to use modems.
- The information is all stored on local servers.
- Intranets are usually behind a firewall, which prevents them from being accessed by hackers.
- The internet can be accessed from anywhere using a range of devices, such as computers, PDAs and phones.

The advantages in using an intranet

- Intranets are usually behind firewalls, which protect the information from being hacked into.
- Intranets are ideal in schools because they can be used to prevent students from accessing unwanted information.
- The internal email system is more secure than sending emails using the internet.
- Only information that is relevant to the organisation can be accessed and this saves employees accessing sites that are inappropriate or which will cause them to waste time.

Telecommunications

Telecommunications has been a big growth area over the last few years. More and more people are involved in working from home, using computers and telecommunications to transmit their work to an office or to other workers in the electronic chain.

Telecommunications can be used to link up to many online databases.

Message sending

Sending data down a communications line is not just a question of sending the streams of bits that represent each character. The problem is that each computer manufacturer has its own standards for encoding data. However, there is a standard for the connection of PCs which enables communication between all the components. This is called Open Systems Interconnection (OSI).

Protocols and handshakes

When human beings communicate with each other, we have a set of rules that we use. Although we do not think about them when we are holding a conversation, they still exist. For instance, we wait until the other person has finished talking before we say something, and usually acknowledge that we have understood what has been said by nodding occasionally. In other words there is a protocol between the individuals.

We also have protocols in telecommunications. Protocols ensure that each computer behaves predictably and provides information in an understandable way.

We have already come across a gateway. A gateway translates the protocols between computers so that different computers are able to communicate with each other.

Before sending data a computer performs what is called a handshake. The handshake is an exchange of signals which establishes the communication between the devices.

Data compression techniques

Data compression is a technique used to reduce the size of a file. By compressing a file you reduce the time taken to upload or download the file. This is particularly important when transferring multimedia files – for example, large video files.

Advantages of data compression:

- It is much faster to upload a file (e.g. transferring photograph files onto a photo-sharing site).

- It is much faster to download files such as software, films and music from the internet.
- It is faster to load a file when it is compressed.
- It is faster to transfer as an email attachment.

Disadvantages of data compression:

- Images are not as high quality as images without compression.
- The receiver of the compressed file may not have the software needed to decompress the file.
- Sound quality is not as high with compression such as that used with MP3 files, although not many people would notice the difference.
- Compression means it is much faster to transfer movie files, and this causes problems when people copy movies illegally.

Speed of access

The speed with which you can surf the web or view data over a wide area network depends on a couple of factors. The speed of your modem will determine how fast the pulses are sent, and the speed of the receiver's modem will determine the speed with which they can arrive. The speed of the slowest modem will determine the speed of the overall link.

Different types of cabling also influence the speed, with fibre optic cables being much faster than metal wire cables.

Together these factors determine the bandwidth that limits the quantity of data that can be passed along the link in a certain time period.

Bandwidth

When you are using the internet you may have wondered why on certain days it seems to take forever to load the website you require. The reason for this is to do with something called bandwidth. Bandwidth determines how fast the connection will be. A smaller bandwidth means data will

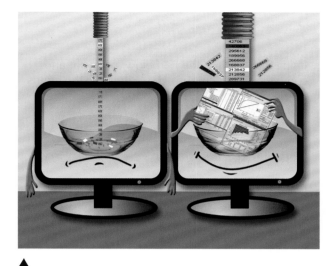

▲ **Figure 15.8** *The bigger the bandwidth, the greater the speed of flow of data*

arrive more slowly. Sending data along a communication line (like a telephone line) is like trying to get water through a pipe. The narrower the pipe, the slower the water comes out.

Bandwidth is determined by the medium through which the data are transmitted. Ordinary wire cable like that used with telephone lines has a lower bandwidth than fibre optic cable.

Cost of installation

The costs involved in the installation of a network are as follows:

- terminal costs
- server costs
- cabling costs (wire is the cheapest and fibre optic cable is the most expensive)
- network cards (each terminal usually has its own network card)
- software
- backup devices
- the cost of the modem or ISDN adapter if a LAN has to be connected to a WAN/internet
- internet service provider (ISP) costs, if access to the web is needed
- telephone or other communications charges
- connectors.

Test Yourself

Using the words in the list below, copy out and complete sentences **A** to **H**, underlining the words you have inserted. The words may be used more than once.

gateway protocol LANs WANs network

modems electronic analogue

A A group of computers linked together in order to share facilities is called a _____.

B Networks confined to a single site are called _____.

C Networks that use communication lines and are separated by a distance are called _____.

D Computers connected together using a communications line need two _____, one at each end of the line.

E Modems convert the digital signals from a computer into _____ signals which may be passed along the telephone line.

F _____ mail allows messages to be sent from one terminal to another, which may be in another part of the country or even the world.

G For computers to communicate with each other they must share the same _____.

H Different types of computers may communicate with each other provided that a _____ is used.

Things to do

Read the paragraph below and then answer the questions.

In a busy local office of a large motoring insurance company there are about 10 computerised workstations, linked to each other by an LAN. The system is controlled by a powerful file server with a 500 GB hard disk, which is accessible by all workstations. The file server also has a tape-streamer attached to it. Each workstation can access any one of the 20 black and white laser printers connected to the network. There are also two colour laser printers attached, which all workstations can access.

There is also a gateway that enables access to the internet.
(a) What does LAN stand for?
(b) Briefly explain what the purpose of a file server is.
(c) Why would it not be worth the company having a laser printer attached to each of the workstations?
(d) Give three advantages of using a local area network rather than individual, stand-alone computers.
(e) State three advantages to the company in being connected to the internet.
(f) Explain the purpose of a tapestreamer.

IT Tasks

Task 1

Use the internet or any other electronic mail system to contact pupils or students in a school in another country. If you have any penfriends you could try contacting them, or perhaps your town is twinned with another that you could contact.

Try to coordinate this task with your language or geography teacher. For instance, you could word-process a document to be sent to a French school and for them to reply to you in English.

Remember that this task needs to be looked at from an information technology point of view; when writing it up for your IT task you should consider the following:
- a description of what you are trying to achieve
- which software you used and why it was chosen against other types of software
- the hardware needed for the system and why it was needed
- what you actually did to perform the task and your reasons for doing it in this way
- the advantages of electronic mail over telephone, letters, fax and so on.
- evidence of the results you have obtained, such as printouts of the electronic mail messages (both those sent and those received).

Task 2

John and Anne Bird frequently like to attend sales exhibitions of optical equipment and any other opportunity for them to show their equipment. The problem is knowing where and when there are country fairs, shows and so on. What they need to know is which online communication systems are available and whether they would be of any use to them. You have been asked to investigate.

Task 3

John and Anne Bird frequently have to travel to various cities and towns by train. You are employed at Binscope and have been asked how to find out travel information from any railway databases available using the internet. In your documentation compare the way the computer system works with finding out the information using timetables and fare details available from the main stations.

Binscope would like you to design an advert for the company to be placed in a specialised magazine called *Bird Watching*. The advert is for the mail order part of the business, so only the head office's address, phone and fax number need be quoted. It is February, typically a quiet month for Binscope, so they have decided to stimulate sales by offering 10 per cent off all prices until the end of the month. The prices quoted in the advert will still be the original prices though.

Here are some of the things you will need to include in the advert. They are not in any particular order, so you will have to decide the order for yourself. You can also include your own information. Remember that the purpose of the advert is to sell Binscope's equipment.

- Binscope
  67 Crosby Road East
  Crosby
  Liverpool
  L23 6TY
- Phone: 0151-211-9000 Fax: 0151-234-8976
- February Special Offer: 10% Off Everything!
- You can use your ACCESS or VISA card to order by telephone.
- Goods dispatched promptly.
- Mail order: insurance, packing and postage are free.
- Mail order service available Monday to Saturday, 9 a.m. until 5 p.m.
- The friendly experts professionals recommend!

Include as many special effects, fonts and typefaces as your software allows.

Try to incorporate some diagrams or clip art into your advert. There are some diagrams on the next page that you may be able to scan in if you have access to a scanner. If not, have a look through any clip art with your graphics package and see if there are any suitable pictures. If not, do not worry. The magazine will probably charge more if there is artwork anyway. If you feel adventurous, you could try your hand at drawing some pictures yourself.

Produce a couple of drafts. Make sure that there are no spelling mistakes and show them to someone else, maybe your art teacher, for their comments.

Here are details of the equipment Binscope want to place in the advert.

Kowa telescopes

TSN 1	$699.00
TSN 2	$699.00
611	$632.00
612	$592.00
TSN 3	$1,298.00
TSN 4	$1,298.00

Kowa eyepieces

20 × Wide Angle	$148.00
25× /40 ×	$126.00
20–60 ZEP	$254.00
27 × Wide Angle	$218.00

Leica binoculars

8 × 32 BA	$1,298.00
7 × 42 BA	$1,396.00
8 × 42 BA	$1,436.00

Nikon binoculars

Compact 8 × 23	$198.00
Compact 9 × 25	$218.00
Sportstar 8 × 20	$238.00
Sportstar 8 × 30	$598.00

Skills Building

Nikon telescopes
Fieldscope 2 $758.00
Fieldscope245 $798.00

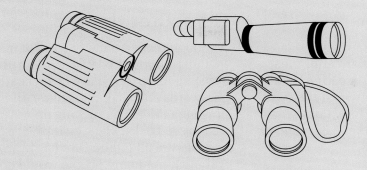

▲
Figure 15.9   *Some optical equipment which you could scan for your Binscope advertisement*

System Security

Computer security

Computer security is concerned with taking care of hardware, software and, most importantly, data. The cost of creating data again from scratch can far outweigh the cost of any hardware or programs lost. Loss of data can have various consequences, some of which are shown in Figure 16.1.

Bad business decisions

Loss of goodwill from customers

Cash flow problems (could lead to bankruptcy)

Loss of data

Adverse publicity from the press

Failure to receive payment

Late delivery of goods

▲ **Figure 16.1** *Some of the consequences of data loss*

Physical security

Computer equipment and its data need to be protected from physical harm. Hazards could include natural ones, such as fire, lightning, water damage and deliberate damage or theft.

Computer theft

Although there are many ways of making sure that unauthorised people are denied access to a system through the use of keyboard locks, passwords and so on, it is more difficult to prevent a thief from picking up a system and stealing it. Locks, bolts, clamps, alarmed circuits and tags are all methods of hardware protection. Although not many people would consider leaving a bicycle without a lock, people do often leave thousands of pounds worth of computer equipment unlocked and unattended.

Sometimes it is easier to improve the security around a computer system. Usually, if a building is secure, the computer system will be secure.

Having fewer entrances to buildings, using alarms on emergency exits, using security badges and having keypad locks on all rooms will all help.

Preventing computer theft

1 A note should be made of all the serial numbers of computers and peripherals, since this may be the only way that the police can identify stolen equipment.
2 It is possible with some computers to lock the case of the computer, which prevents the computer from being turned on. This should always be done when the computer is not in use, and the key should be safely stored in a secret place and not in the top drawer of the desk that the computer stands on.
3 Data should be backed up regularly and stored securely away from the computer. If the computer system is stolen then at least the data, which would be a lot more expensive to recreate, are safe.
4 All staff should be made aware of security and encouraged to question suspicious behaviour.

5 If an ID badge system is used (where staff and visitors have to wear a security badge that contains their photograph, name, etc.), then everyone from the chairman to the cleaners must wear them, since this indicates to outsiders that the firm is security conscious.

Protection from fires

Fires which start in computer rooms are rare. Usually they are the result of faulty wiring or overloaded sockets. It is more likely that a fire will start in adjacent offices or in storage areas. Fireproof doors help contain fires. Smoke detectors should be used to detect fires at an early stage. Gas flooding systems are used in large computer installations and are preferred to water ones because the damage done by water is often greater than that by the fire.

Protection from dust and extremes of temperature

Air conditioning is more important for larger mainframe systems, where the temperature and the humidity (amount of water in the air) must be controlled. The air must also be pure and is therefore filtered before it enters the room.

Software security

Viruses

Viruses are mischievous programs, the purpose of which is to disrupt the sensible use of computers. Many viruses do little more than display a message (usually insulting!) on the screen, but some are designed to act after a certain period of time and do such things as make the letters start to drop off the screen or even erase the entire contents of your hard disk. As their name suggests, viruses are able to spread by 'infecting' other disks; they do this by copying themselves onto other disks which are being used by the computer. Although there are many viruses (over 2,000 to date), the main problems are caused by a handful of very

familiar ones, with names such as: Cascade, Form, Jerusalem and Stoned. Since these viruses have been around for some time, they are well understood and easy to remove from computers by anti-virus software. Viruses are quite common, especially in situations where there is a large number of users, such as in a school or college.

I think my computer has a virus...

▲ **Figure 16.2**

Antivirus software

Antivirus software can be used to scan a computer's memory and disks to detect viruses. Any viruses detected are then removed using the software (disinfecting a disk, as it is often called). When choosing antivirus software, speed of checking is important.

Avoiding viruses

1 Don't buy secondhand software unless you can scan it first.
2 Check your computer for viruses if it has been recently repaired.
3 Do not download software from bulletin boards, since this is the easiest way for the people who produce viruses to distribute their handiwork.
4 Be suspicious of all software distributed freely, such as shareware and software which comes free with magazines, as these sometimes have viruses on them.
5 Try not to use too many different computers, since this will increase the risk of passing on a virus.

6 On your own machine, install antivirus software which checks for viruses on the hard disks every time the system is booted up and checks all disks before data are taken from them.

Backing up data

Backing up data means taking a copy of the data and keeping it away from the computer in a secure place. Obviously it is no good keeping a backup copy on the same disk.

The most common way to lose a file is through user error, where a person makes a mistake with one of the commands and deletes a file or a whole series of files which they did not intend to delete. Although there are software packages available to recover such data, these should not be relied on, and there is no substitute for having a backup copy of the data in a secure place.

Rules for backing up

1 Never keep backup disks near the computer. If the computer is stolen the thieves may take the disks as well. Never keep the disks in the drawer of a desk, since this is the first place thieves will look.
2 If you hold a lot of data which would be very expensive to recreate, you should invest in a fireproof safe to protect your backups against theft and fire.
3 Keep at least one set of backup disks in a different place (i.e. at a different site).

Archiving

Archiving means placing important computer files in a safe place so that they can be found easily if needed.

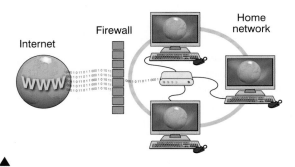

▲
Figure 16.3 *Firewalls only allow certain requests for access to the internal network*

Protecting your files

Software can be written which does not allow access to a computer unless a password is keyed in. The password, which is never shown on the screen, should be changed regularly and should never be written down. Obvious names, such as the surname of the person using the machine, should be avoided, along with other obvious passwords, such as 'access'.

Many large systems use software to limit each user's access to only those files that are needed for the performance of their particular job. For instance, an accounts clerk could have a password that allows access to files needed for checking invoices, whereas the accountant would have access to all the accounts files.

It is also important to try to restrict access to a computer's operating system, particularly for inexperienced users. A simple command at the operating system's prompt can erase an entire hard disk. Restricted access can also be used to prevent people from copying data from the hard disk.

Encryption

Sometimes files which contain sensitive data are encrypted (i.e. coded). If a tape or disk containing sensitive files is stolen it would then be impossible to read the data without the decoder.

Encryption is often used when important data are transmitted from one place to another. The data are coded before being sent and then decoded at the other end. Both processes are performed automatically by computers. Should the data be intercepted, they will be impossible to understand or alter. When people are making payments for goods bought over the internet using a credit or debit card, the details are always encrypted.

Firewalls

Firewalls are software, hardware or both, used to filter out unauthorised requests from outside users to gain access to a network. This keeps hackers out. Firewalls also filter data so that only allowable data are permitted into the system. This means that access to certain websites that contain undesirable material can be blocked. All networks that have access to the internet should have a firewall.

The difference between security and integrity

Data integrity

Data integrity is concerned with the 'correctness' of the data. Errors may be introduced into data in a variety of ways. They can be introduced when the person typing in the data misreads them off a source document or if a program or machine errors corrupt the data. Some types of corruption can be caused by simple typing errors. Validation and verification checks are performed on data to ensure their integrity, and further information about this can be found in Chapter 7.

Data security

Data security is concerned with keeping the data safe from the various hazards that could destroy them.

Transaction logs

When you make changes to the data in a file, you usually delete the old information and replace it with the new information. If you have a bank account, money added to your account (credits) or taken out (debits) needs to be recorded. Each bit of business is called a transaction. The account statement showing the amounts entering and leaving the account shows details of these transactions and is called a transaction log.

With databases, new details often overwrite the old information; once this has happened you cannot see the original details. To avoid this problem a transaction log is produced when files are changed. This records the changes that are made and also the date, time and person who made them, in the interests of security.

Test Yourself

Using the words in the list below, copy out and complete sentences **A** to **J**. Underline the words you have inserted. The words may be used once, more than once or not at all.

> water   data   physical   encrypted   backup
>
> gas   smoke   viruses   antivirus   tape
>
> keypads   passwords

A Computer security is concerned with protecting the hardware, software and _____.

B _____ security is used to protect against theft, fire and so on.

C As computers become smaller, they become more portable. To protect against theft, _____ may be used on doors to prevent unauthorised access.

D Copies of data or programs kept for security purposes are called _____ copies.

E _____ copies should always be kept away from the computer, since if the computer is stolen, the thieves will probably take the disks as well.

F To provide early warnings of a fire, _____ detectors are used and _____ flooding systems are used to extinguish the fire.

G Programs that are written to disrupt serious computer use mischievously are called _____.

H _____ software is used to detect viruses and to remove them.

I To copy the entire contents of a hard disk quickly a _____ streamer is used.

J Data is often _____ to prevent tampering before it is sent along communication lines.

1   It is Friday the 13th and yet another story is on the news about a computer virus which lies dormant until, on this date, it springs into life and destroys all the files.

(a) Your father does not understand what a virus is and how it is caught by a computer. Write a short paragraph to explain viruses.

(b) Your father uses a personal computer at work. After your comments in part (a) he starts to look worried.
 What can he do to:
 (i)   determine whether there are already viruses lurking on his computer?
 (ii) make sure that no viruses enter his system?

2   Michelle is an accounts executive for a large advertising agency. She uses a personal computer at work for storing the artwork for all the agency's major customers. No backup copies are kept, since to back up a 500 GB disk full of files takes a long time and 'in any case the computer has been very reliable so far'. Michelle often brings the machine home at weekends, partly to do some extra work, but mainly for the use of her son, who likes to play computer games. He has just received a copy of a disk from a friend of a friend and is looking forward to playing the game that is on it.

Michelle needs to be made more aware about security.

(a) Explain what a backup copy is and why it is made.
(b) Why should Michelle not depend on her machine's reliability?
(c) What security risks are introduced by bringing home the computer in her car and letting her son play games on it?
(d) Suggest a list of guidelines that Michelle should adopt regarding the security of her data.

3   Your teacher/lecturer is fed up with people not looking after their disks. Disks with no names on them are constantly being left in machines after the lessons. Some pupils are losing the data because disks have been mishandled. Pupils have not been taking backup copies on a regular basis. Your teacher has asked you to use a graphics package to design a poster that could be placed on the computer room wall. Using appropriate software, design and produce a suitable poster. (You may find it easier to work on paper to start with and then to do the final design using the computer.)

Look through some computer suppliers' catalogues at the security devices available for microcomputers. Write a brief report, using word-processing software, explaining how these gadgets work and how much they cost.

Investigations

In this project you will be given various situations which have actually arisen. You need to read about them carefully and then suggest improvements that would prevent each situation from occurring again.

1. Virus attack

A firm of typesetters used computers for desktop publishing. Their software package became infected with a virus called the 'Lazy Harry', which distorts the text on the screen and also causes the system to crash now and again. The company at first suspected that it was a hardware fault and its overall effect was to slow the company down and cause missed publication dates. This in turn caused financial problems. Eventually the firm discovered that the problem was a virus that had been brought into the company by the senior partner's son, who had been playing games on the office PC. The work dropped by 25 per cent and some customers were not sent invoices, which cost the company $40,000.

What strict guidelines would you lay down to make sure that this did not happen again?

2. Power failure

A minicomputer was installed in the offices of a food-processing plant high up in the mountains, in an area where lightning frequently occurred. As the lightning struck, the power supply would go off for one or two seconds, which was sufficient time for the computer system to fail. Backup copies had to be used to restore the data and sometimes this would need to be done four or five times a day.

What could be done to help this company?

3. Theft

A health authority had eight microcomputers in a busy department. The public had access to the department and the computers were visible from the street. One evening all the computers and associated equipment were stolen. The thieves gained access through the front door, which had only a single Chubb lock. The theft occurred at nine o'clock at night and was witnessed by several people who thought that the department was moving to another office.

What possible security measure could this authority have taken?

4. System failure

A young, inexperienced computer operator was working in a computer room with a minicomputer. He switched it on early in the morning and a grating sound was heard coming from the disk drive when he loaded the operating system. He took the disk out and placed the backup copy in the drive and tried to reload the operating system. He heard the same grating sound as before. He turned to the other drive and placed each disk in turn into it and again heard the grating sound. An engineer was called and he told the operator that both disks and drives were ruined. The problem appeared to be caused by dust on the disk.

What could the company do to prevent this happening again?

Investigations

You have been asked to review the security of your school's or college's computer operations. Write down a list of the questions you would ask the person in charge of the computers.

Here are a few questions to start you off.

1 How often are the passwords changed?

2 Does each person using the system have the same password or are the passwords used by a group of people?

3 Does a screen turn off if a user has not used a terminal for a while?

4 Can a user get into the operating system?

From the answers to your questions, write down, with reasons, whether you think the security could be improved. Then make suggestions of what could be done to improve security.

Data Protection Laws

Computers and privacy

The rapid explosion in the use of computers in the last 15 years has benefited us in many ways. Many things that we now take for granted, such as the use of credit cards and cash dispensers, would have been impossible without them. However, there are problems. As more computers are used, more and more information about each of us is stored on computers. By linking together the information gained from several computers, it is possible to build up a complete picture of a person's life. Figure 17.1 shows just some of the organisations that hold personal information about us.

Suppose that Misbah goes abroad for a fortnight. Let us see how much we could find out about what he did on the holiday if we had access to computers that stored information about him.

By linking in to travel companies' computers we could find out where he went on holiday, whether he went on his own, how long for and the dates. From the bank's computer we could find out how much money he took with him. We could find out from the travel insurance company's computer whether he had any existing illnesses before he went. If he paid by travellers' cheques or credit cards, we could find out what he bought while on holiday. If he was a member of a library we could even find out which books he took with him!

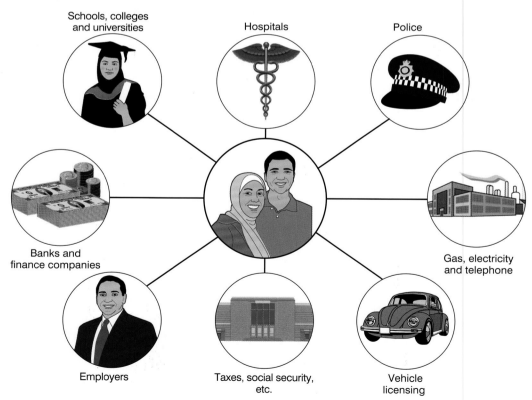

Figure 17.1 *Some of the organisations that hold personal information about us*

When mobile phones are switched on, their whereabouts can be located fairly accurately

Cameras at ports record the registration numbers of vehicles entering or leaving the country

Loyalty cards and credit cards link you to the purchases you make

ATMs (cash dispensers) record transaction details (date, time, location, amount withdrawn, etc.). Some will secretly take your photograph

Internet 'cookies', without you knowing, record details of the websites you have visited

▲ **Figure 17.2** *Your private life is becoming less and less private*

- When making their purchase either by cash, debit card or credit card, the loyalty card links the customers to their purchases.
- The card adds a certain number of points, based on their bill and the items bought, to the total.

As well as making the customer loyal to a particular store chain, the scheme can be used to provide useful marketing information about each customer and the items they have purchased. Before loyalty cards, if you paid cash, the store did not know who you were. They had no way of linking you to the purchases you had made. Now they can find lots of information about you and what you like to buy.

The customer fills in an application form

The card that the customer is given when the account is opened has a magnetic stripe, so that the account number can be read each time the customer buys goods

Loyalty cards

Most large store chains now have what is called a loyalty card scheme. Each time the customer uses the card, points are added. When the number of points earned reaches a certain value, customers are given vouchers that can be used in the store instead of cash. The scheme works like this (see Figure 17.3):

- The customer fills in an application form to join the scheme.
- The customer is given a reward/loyalty card that contains a magnetic stripe.
- Each time the customer goes to the shop they take the card with them.

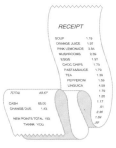

Based on the amount of money spent, points are added to the customer's account. Points can be exchanged for reward vouchers

▲ **Figure 17.3** *How loyalty cards work*

▲
Figure 17.4 *What the items in your shopping basket may reveal about you*

Here are some of the things store chains could find out about you:

- what newspapers, magazines and paperback books you read
- what drinks you like
- the method you use to pay for your purchases
- whether you have a petrol or diesel car
- if some or all of the members of the household are vegetarian
- what pets you have
- whether there are any young children in the family
- whether you or any member of the family is on a diet
- whether you or any member of your family smokes.

Questions

The above list shows just some of the many interesting facts about a person's lifestyle that can be found from the things they buy from a supermarket.
(a) List five additional things your shopping could reveal about you.
(b) Some people are concerned that the use of loyalty cards invades a person's privacy. Why might some of these concerns be well founded? Explain briefly.
(c) Loyalty card schemes can cost the stores a lot of money to set up. Give two reasons why it is important for the stores to know as much about their customers as possible.

Why electronically stored information is easier to misuse than information kept in conventional form

1 Cross referencing

It is easy using a computer to link the data from different systems.

2 Danger of hacking

If the system uses communication links then there is a risk of people gaining unauthorised access (called hacking), and looking at or changing confidential information.

3 Making alterations

If alterations have been made to data on paper then these can usually be seen. With a computer, there is no such evidence.

4 Faster access to data

It is much quicker to gain access to electronically held data and copy or print it out than it is to search through and photocopy manually held files.

Data protection laws

As more and more information came to be stored on computers, much of it personal data about individuals, there was clearly need for some sort of control over the way that it was collected and the way it could be used.

Any data protection laws have to deal with those things that cause loss of privacy, such as the monitoring of internet use, loyalty cards, CCTV cameras and the use of huge customer databases for marketing purposes.

Data protection laws vary from one country to another, but most place obligations on those people who record and process personal data, who are sometimes called data controllers. Data controllers must be open about their use of the data by telling the person who enforces the law that they are collecting personal data and how they intend to use these.

Data Protection Principles

Many countries have a series of Data Protection Principles which are listed as part of their data protection law. The list shown here applies to the UK, but other countries have similar ones.

Data protection principles

The principles state that:

1 The personal data shall be processed fairly and lawfully and, in particular, shall not be processed unless at least one of the following conditions is met:
   Processing conditions:
   - The data subject has given their permission for the processing.
   - The processing is necessary for the performance of a contract which involves the data subject.
   - The data controller has a legal obligation to process the data.
   - The processing is necessary to protect the vital interests of the data subject (e.g. the disclosure of a data subject's medical history to a casualty department after the data subject has had an accident).
   - The processing is necessary for the administration of justice or for a government department.
2 Personal data shall be obtained only for one or more specified and lawful purposes, and shall not be further processed in any manner incompatible with that purpose or those purposes.
3 Personal data shall be adequate, relevant and not excessive in relation to the purpose or purposes for which they are processed.
4 Personal data shall be adequate and, where necessary, kept up to date.
5 Personal data processed for any purpose or purposes shall not be kept for longer than is necessary for that purpose or those purposes.
6 Personal data shall be processed in accordance with the rights of data subjects under this law.
7 Appropriate technical and organisational measures shall be taken against unauthorised or unlawful processing of personal data and against accidental loss or destruction of, or damage to, personal data.
8 Personal data shall not be transferred to a country or territory outside the country or economic area, unless that country or territory ensures an adequate level of protection for the rights and freedoms of data subjects in relation to the processing of personal data.

Sensitive personal data

The law mentions data called sensitive personal data, which may not be disclosed, and this includes information about:
- the racial or ethnic origin of the data subject
- their political opinions
- their religious beliefs
- whether or not they are a member of a trade union
- their physical or mental health or condition
- the commission or alleged commission by them of any offence
- any proceedings for any offence committed or alleged to have been committed by them, and, if they are convicted, the sentence they were given.

Questions

1 The Data Protection Principles outlined above are very wordy and need to be translated into everyday language. Use a dictionary if you need to. Explain what the following words mean:

   lawfully   specified   purposes   disclosed
   incompatible   adequate   relevant   undue
   excessive   appropriate   unauthorised

2 Now write a set of summarised data protection principles, in your own words and without using any of the words in the list above.

A data controller is a person (by themselves or with other people) who determines the purpose for which, and the manner in which, any personal data are processed. The data controller is therefore the person who decides what to do with the data once they have been entered onto the system.

Notify the enforcer of data protection laws

The person who enforces the data protection laws must be notified by the data controller if they hold data not falling into one of the categories covered by the exemptions. The data controller must give certain particulars, including:

- their own name and address
- a description of the personal data which is being processed
- a description of the purpose for the processing of the data
- a description of the recipient to whom the data controller intends to disclose the data.

When the data controller notifies the enforcer, the data controller must say what security provisions there are to protect the personal data. There is a fee which needs to be paid with the notification.

What happens if an organisation does not register?

They will be taken to court and fined.

Is compensation payable?

If a person suffers damage or damage and distress because of things the data controller does which contravene the law, then they may be able to claim compensation.

Data subjects and data controllers

There are many examples where data collected for one purpose is used for another, and some of these are shown in Figure 17.5. For example, if you rent a television, then your details will be automatically passed to the TV licence centre. The organisation that records details of drivers and their vehicles is linked to the police computer. Banks automatically notify the tax office if a person receives over a certain amount of interest in a year.

The transfer of personal data between computers does have some advantages. For example, without the rapid transfer of records, the capture and conviction of criminals would be made more difficult.

However, there are dangers. Suppose your record gets mixed up with someone else's record, or incorrect data are entered into your record? This could have various results: you could be refused credit or benefits or even a job. In certain cases it could result in you being arrested. Figures 17.6 and 17.7 tell you more about who has computer records about you and the possible consequences of the information being incorrect.

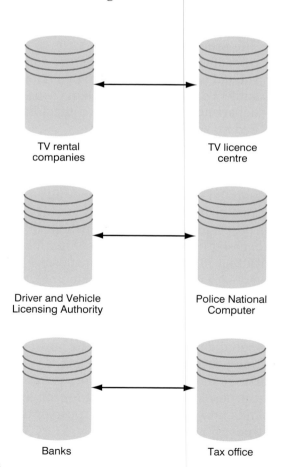

TV rental companies

TV licence centre

Driver and Vehicle Licensing Authority

Police National Computer

Banks

Tax office

▲ **Figure 17.5** *How data collected for one purpose can be used for another*

Data protection laws give us the right to see our personal data kept on computer and to get data corrected if they are wrong. They also give us the right to complain to the person in charge of the law if we do not like the way the data are collected or the way that they are used.

I was arrested driving my own car – the police reckoned it was stolen

According to my building society I died three years ago

I've been refused a loan. According to the computer I'm a bad credit risk

▲
Figure 17.6 *Serious problems can be caused when records become mixed up*

The tax office holds information about incomes on computer. If this is incorrect you could pay too much tax.

Mail order companies obtain names and addresses from many different sources. What do they know about you?

Employers can have a lot of information about you. Who else might they give this information to?

Banks not only know how much money you have in your account, they also know your income and where you spend your money. How might they use this information?

▲
Figure 17.7 *Who knows all about you?*

Do all the uses of personal data have to be notified?

Not everyone has to register their use of personal data, so, if you hold your address book or your birthday card list on your home computer, you can sleep at night.
The following use of personal data is exempt. In other words, you do not need to register your use of personal data if your use falls into any of the following categories:

1 when the data held are being used only in connection with personal, family or household affairs, or for recreational use
2 when the data are being used only for preparing the text of documents
3 when the data are being used only for the calculation of wages and pensions or for the production of accounts
4 when the data are used for the distribution of articles or information (e.g. unsolicited mail, that is mail that advertises goods or services that you have not asked for)
5 when the data are held by a sports club or a recreational club which is not a limited company.

Your rights as a data subject

You have the right to see any personal details about you held on computer or held manually. You also have the right to a description of the data being processed. This means if you do not understand what the data mean, you can have them explained. You are also entitled to know the logic behind any decisions made when the decision is made automatically. To see the details it is necessary to send a letter or email to the organisation concerned.

The organisation may ask for a small fee to cover the expense of providing the information. They have 40 days to respond to your request.

You do not, however, have the right to see all the information held about you. You may be denied the information if it is being used for any of the following purposes:

- the prevention or detection of crime
- catching or prosecuting offenders
- collecting taxes or duty
- medical or social workers' reports in some instances.

Personal data which consist of a confidential reference (for a course or for employment) is exempt from subject access. This means you cannot apply to see your personal reference.

Examination scripts and examination marks are also exempt from subject access. So you can not demand your exam scripts back or see your exam results before they are formally published.

> The Date
>
> Dear Madam,
>
> I wish to make an application under the Data Protection Law. Please supply me with any information which you hold about me to which I am entitled or confirm that none is held.
>
> If you require further information from me or a fee, please let me know as soon as possible.
>
> If you do not normally handle these requests for your organisation, please pass this letter to your Data Protection Officer or other appropriate official.
>
> Yours faithfully,
>
> *M Qasim*
>
> M. Qasim

▲ **Figure 17.8** *A formal letter asking about personal details held on computer*

Things to do

1 Banks use information technology to handle information about customers and their accounts.
   (a) List four items of information about customers and their accounts.
   It is possible for a bank to use this personal information for purposes of which the customer would not approve.
   (b) Describe such a potential use of the customer's personal data.
   (c) Explain why this is easier when the data are stored electronically than when they are just stored on paper.
   (d) Describe the possible effects of inaccuracies in the customer's data.

2 In the UK, when a baby is born, its record is immediately put on to the hospital's computer. After a week or so, the birth will be registered on the Register of Births, Marriages & Deaths. These data will then be passed to the Office For National Statistics (an extra person has been added to the population). The baby's details are also sent to the Department of Health. As the baby grows up, more and more organisations store information on computer about it.
   (a) Write down the names of four organisations which hold personal information about a 16-year-old.
   (b) Write down the names of five organisations which could hold information about you when you reach the age of 18 that they are unlikely to hold at 16.

3 Computerised information about individual people is held in separate databases by a wide range of organisations.
   (a) Name two organisations that might hold computer records about a teenager who has just applied for a job.
   (b) Many people are worried about the misuse of computer data. Outline four principles that you would lay down to reassure people that there would be no misuse of the information held about them.

4 (a) Mary has been feeling ill, so she goes along to her doctor who examines her and says there is nothing wrong with her. She thinks the doctor is hiding something so she asks to see her medical records held on computer. Is it likely that she will be allowed access?
   (b) John has committed a robbery. Later he is arrested by the police and released without charge. As time goes by he thinks he may have gotten away with it. He applies to see the records held about him on the Police National Computer. Will his request be granted?

5 A doctor is thinking of storing her patients' records on a computer system. She is very worried, however, about the confidentiality of the information and the problem of unauthorised access. Explain the various methods that could be used to ensure that the data remain confidential.

6 Part of the application form to be filled in by all potential XYZ Ltd employees is shown in Figure 17.9. If an applicant is successful then the information on the form is transferred to a database held on a personal computer in the personnel office.
   (a) Write down a list of any of the questions in the application form which you feel infringe on your privacy. Explain why you would not like the company to know these details.
   (b) Choose three of the more personal questions in the application form and for each one explain what use the answer would be to the company.

Application Form for XYZ Ltd

Name_____ Height _____ Weight _____

Address _____

_____

Tel No: _____

Date of birth _____

National Insurance Number

Married (Y/N) _____ If so, how long for?_____

Religion _____

No of children_____

If applicable, ages of children _____

Bank Account Number _____

Are you a union member?_____

If answer to above is Y, give name of union _____

Outstanding value of mortgage and other loans _____

Do you travel to work by public transport? _____

Have you visited your doctor in the last 12 months? _____

If so, what for? _____

Have you ever been refused credit? _____

▲
Figure 17.9 *Application form for XYZ Ltd*

7 The following situations concern the security of files held on computer. For each one of the following situations, write a short paragraph explaining what could have been done to prevent the breach of security.

You may need to look back at the previous chapter on security.

(a) Mrs Ali, a cleaner, is cleaning the personnel office and notices that her best friend's personnel record is displayed on a screen. There is no one around, so she presses the print screen button and obtains a printout which she then takes.

(b) Abel the sneak thief goes into his doctor's surgery to order a prescription. He notices a personal computer on the desk and since there is no-one around, he unplugs it, picks it up and carries it to his car.

(c) Latifa wishes to gain access to her manager's computer. She is leaving the company soon and since she is going to work for a competitor it would be useful to obtain a list of the names, addresses and value of the orders for all the customers. She switches on his computer and it springs into life. However, a message is displayed asking for a password to be entered. Not one to be put off, Dianne looks around and finds a piece of paper attached to the back of the monitor with a single word written on it. She tries it and it works. She now gains access.

(d) Pablo would like a reference for a job. Pablo applied for a job a couple of months ago which he did not get. He suspects he may have got a bad reference from his boss. He would like to see the reference, which he knows is on his manager's personal computer. Pablo goes into his manager's office and turns the power on and nothing happens. He notices that a key is needed. He tries the top drawer of the desk and finds the key. He starts up the computer and has a look at his reference.

Investigations

Read the following passage on the lifestyle database.

The lifestyle database

You have just been out to buy a copy of your favourite monthly magazine. When you get it home a small booklet drops out which promises a free entry to a prize draw for $5,000 if you take the time to fill in a questionnaire and send it off. There are questions such as how much you earn, how often you go on holiday, whether you donate to charity, how often you order goods through the post, down to which particular make of soap you use. There are six pages covering about 100 questions, which you start to fill in. In filling in the questionnaire, you are giving the company a complete profile of your lifestyle. So who wants to know this information? Well, almost any company involved in selling goods or services. For instance, suppose a particular charity is launching a postal appeal, it can send out letters to people who said in the survey that they donate

to charities and who hold a credit card. In doing this they are targeting a group of people who are more likely to respond. This is only one of the many ways that such a database could be used.

Task 1

You have decided to make your own 'lifestyle database'. Your first task is to make up a series of questions to find out when people are likely to buy goods or services. Design an attractive questionnaire using suitable software (you could use word processing, DTP, graphics or even spreadsheet software).

Task 2

Get all the members of your class to fill in your questionnaire. Look at the answers they have given to your questions and then decide how this information might be used to market goods and services. Write a short description on how the information could be used to market goods and services.

Investigations

Perfect Friend Searching Agency

You have just been appointed as the computer manager for the Perfect Friend Searching Agency which has been formed by the merger of three smaller agencies. You are in complete charge of the computer facilities and it will be up to you to run your department as you see fit.

Nearly all the clients (the people who are looking for friends) were enrolled with the smaller agencies before the merger. These clients had their details recorded on cards held in filing cabinets. At present there are approximately 6,000 clients on the books, but with a recently planned advertising campaign in most of the daily newspapers, the new agency hopes to double this number in about six months.

About 40 per cent of business comes from adverts in magazines, where people fill in and send to the agency forms with their names and addresses. As soon as the agency receives the forms it intends to key people's names and addresses into a database. This enables the agency to send letters using the mail merge facilities of a word processor. In doing this, the agency hopes to convert a greater number of enquiries into sales.

Each potential client is given a detailed application form which they are expected to fill in 'truthfully'. This form covers their own likes, dislikes and other attributes, along with the qualities they would like to see in their 'perfect friend'. When the forms are sent back, the details are then typed into a database. For each client, this database uses a program which searches for clients with as many of the desired qualities as possible who preferably live in the client's area.

As well as being used for the above task, the computer will also be used for working out the staff wages each month. At present there are 47 staff employed in the head office, but in addition, there are various agents who advertise in local papers, take the enquiries by telephone and then inform head office about potential new clients. These agents are paid by the number of enquiries they obtain, with a bonus for each person who signs up with the agency. There are 80 local agents and their pay is processed by the computer.

In addition, the company intends to keep records of the personnel files of all its staff on the computer.

Read over the scenario several times before looking at what you have to do. All your solutions to the following tasks need to apply to this scenario.

1 The directors of the company, who have had little exposure to computers apart from having to type a few private letters now and again on the word processor, have just heard about the data protection laws. They have asked you to produce a brief report outlining the main purposes of the laws, why they were introduced, and how they could apply to the type of business they are running.

2 The directors would now like to know if any of the following files stored on the computer would be exempt from the data protection laws:
   - the client database (it contains all the clients' information)
   - the name and address enquiry database (for sending mailshots)
   - the payroll file for staff and agents
   - the personnel file for staff and agents.

   Write a memo (a brief note) to your managing director explaining which of the above files are exempt and why they are exempt.

3 Realising that it is necessary for the company to register its various uses, the directors have decided that you, as the computer manager, should be responsible for this process. Explain what steps need to be taken in order to register.

4 One of the directors is very sceptical about all this. She feels that this is just another example of government interference in the running of businesses. She has asked you what you think. You are in favour of the law.

   Produce a brief written argument in favour of the law, giving examples of how the law can help ordinary individuals in their lives.

5 The same director is still sceptical and wants to know, 'What if we don't register?' Write down the various possibilities.

6 The seventh data protection principle states that 'personal data should be surrounded by proper security'. With reference to your company, outline the various security techniques that could be used to prevent data from falling into the wrong hands.

18 Computers and the Law

With the growth of computer systems there has been an increase in computer crime. There has been a move away from cash transactions – so much less cash is held by companies than it used to be. Many more employees are now paid by cheque or by direct payment into their bank accounts. The opportunity for the criminal to steal cash is limited. However, the ease with which transactions now take place has opened a whole new area of credit card fraud.

Credit card use

There are many types of card in use: credit, debit and cash cards. Debit cards are used as an alternative to cheques. When goods are bought using a debit card, the money is immediately transferred from the shopper's account to the store's account. Cash cards are used to obtain cash from a cash dispenser.

Credit cards, as the name suggests, enable people to obtain instant credit either against goods bought or for cash from a cash dispenser. Obtaining credit for goods involves the retailer filling in a docket either manually or by using the till and then asking the customer to sign the docket. If the card signature and the signature on the docket are the same then the customer is given the goods and the retailer sends the docket to the credit card company, where the transaction is recorded and the retailer paid. The cardholder receives a statement at the end of each month that outlines:

- the balance at the start of the month
- the interest payable on this outstanding balance
- the amounts and details of any transactions that have taken place during the month
- the balance owing at the end of the month.

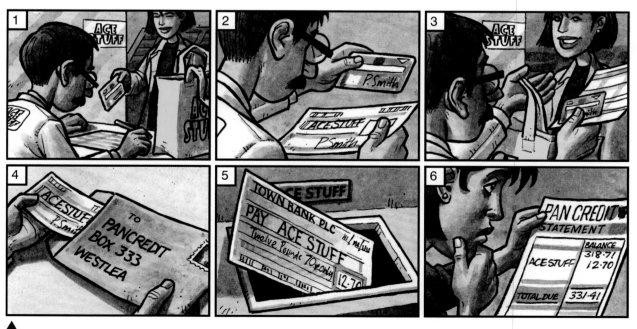

▲
Figure 18.1 *Using a credit card*

The cardholder is then able to make the decision on how much of the balance he wishes to pay off, provided that it is greater than the minimum payment specified by the credit card company. The whole of this process is summarised in Figure 18.1.

It is now very common for there to be no documentation at the time of purchase, since so many goods and services are bought by phone with credit cards or debit cards.

Automated teller machines (ATMs)

Cash machines are sometimes called automated teller machines (ATMs). The system for obtaining cash from a cash dispenser using a credit card is more secure, since a number called the PIN (personal identification number) has to be keyed before access to the machine is allowed. The PIN is known only to the cardholder, so the card on its own cannot be used to obtain cash from a dispenser. When the PIN is entered at the keypad, the dispenser compares the PIN entered with the number contained in the magnetic stripe on the back of the card. This method provides a higher level of security than when a credit card is used to buy goods, since signatures are so easily forged.

Figure 18.2 shows the reverse of a cash card and the magnetic stripe where the PIN is stored.

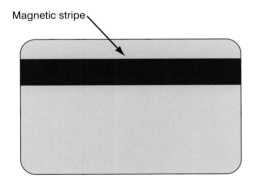

Magnetic stripe

▲ **Figure 18.2** *The PIN number is stored in the magnetic stripe*

More and more payments are being made with payment cards. They are rather like cheques in the sense that the money comes directly

from the holder's account, but payment cards have the advantage that they are quicker to use, since EFTPOS (electronic fund transfer at point of sale) terminals write out slips for users to sign. When a cardholder's signature is confirmed, the money for the goods is immediately transferred from the cardholder's bank account to the retailer's bank account. Again, because signature verification is used, the system is open to abuse if a card is stolen. Payment cards are also called debit cards.

Credit card fraud

Credit card fraud costs the credit card companies huge amounts of money each year. It is not surprising that ways of reducing this fraud have been looked into.

One way around the problem is to authorise each transaction as it occurs by checking via the phone or a special terminal whether the card has been stolen. Another way is to make people key in their PIN at the checkout when making purchases using credit or payment cards.

Biometric testing can also be performed, whereby the user places an index finger into a machine that compares the fingerprint with one previously recorded. Another method looks at the way a person writes a signature by concentrating on the timing, the rhythm and the invisible pen movements.

Figure 18.3 shows a fingerprint being checked. There are also systems that use the pattern on the retina of a person's eye.

▲ **Figure 18.3** *Biometric testing is an important weapon to protect against credit card fraud*

Chip and PIN

Most credit and debit cards are chip and PIN, which means there is a small chip on the card containing encrypted data that only the reader in the store can read. This means that when you enter your PIN, the store can be sure that you are the correct owner of the card.

Credit and debit cards can be used to make purchases either over the phone or using the internet. In both these cases the customer is not present when they pay for their goods. Instead they give certain details, such as name, address and their card details.

Chip and PIN has reduced card fraud when a card is being used in ordinary stores, but owing to the rise in transactions where the customer is not present (e.g. when buying goods or services over the internet), there has been an overall increase in credit and debit card fraud.

▲ **Figure 18.4** *The small chip on a credit/debit card*

▲ **Figure 18.5** *The reader being used to read the details in the chip on the credit card: the customer enters their PIN to verify they are the correct owner of the card*

Modern security systems

The use of smart cards

Smart cards are plastic cards that look similar to credit cards except they contain their own built-in microchip. They are used to gain access to computer rooms and computers, as well as to hold encrypted details that are compared with the PIN when credit or debit cards are used in chip and PIN machines in stores and restaurants.

Smart cards are also used in security passes to ensure that the holder is the true holder.

▲ **Figure 18.6** *This smart card is used to gain access to a secure computer room*

▲ **Figure 18.7** *This smart card is used to check the holder is the correct person allowed access to a VIP event*

Passports

Passports are very important documents as they allow their holder access to other countries. Passports are sometimes forged, so it is important for staff to check that the person using the passport is genuine.

The passports held by the residents of certain countries contain a chip and/or a loop circuit.

The reader is able to read the information in the loop or chip and this is used to check that the holder of the passport is the correct holder.

Software piracy

Software piracy involves the illegal copying of computer software. It is estimated to cost the software developers huge amounts of money each year.

If a company has developed its own software rather than used off-the-shelf software, it will have spent a lot of time and money on development. Large programs are usually written by a team, with each person writing a particular section or module. It can take a long time to write the programs. Suppose five programmers are working on a project and it takes each programmer 200 hours, then the total number of hours worked on the project is $5 \times 200 = 1,000$ hours.

Computer crime

There are many different ways computers or communication services such as the internet can be misused. Many of these instances of misuse are illegal, and if you are found out you can be prosecuted. Some examples include:

- deliberately planting viruses on computer systems
- copying computer programs illegally (i.e. software piracy)
- hacking into someone's system with a view to seeing the information or altering it
- using a computer to commit a fraud (i.e. to steal money using the computer).

Many computer crimes are committed by employees of the organisation who have access to the computer programs and data files. Other crimes are committed by outsiders who gain access to the organisation's computers using the internet. These people are hackers who crack inefficient security systems in order to gain access to the files they need in order to commit fraud.

Test Yourself

Using the words in the list below, copy out and complete sentences **A** to **F**, underlining the words you have inserted. The words may be used once, more than once or not at all.

credit card   hack   hacking   piracy
theft   PIN   phantom   smart

A The largest growth area of computer crime is that of _____ _____ fraud.

B Mysterious withdrawal of money from a person's account is often referred to as a _____ withdrawal.

C Cards which look a bit like a cash or credit card, but which contain a microchip, are called _____ cards.

D The number coded in the magnetic stripe on the back of a credit or cash card is called a _____.

E Illegal copying of software is called software _____.

F _____ means gaining access to private data using communication systems.

Things to do

1 You are in charge of a small computer network, with six terminals located in different offices, but in the same building. You have been worried about the threat from viruses and some of your staff have been putting their own programs onto the computers (particularly games that they play when you are out of the office!). You have decided to put up a notice that is to be placed near to each terminal listing a set of rules that must be obeyed when using the company computers.

Using suitable software of your choice (e.g. graphics, word processing, DTP), design a suitable, hard-hitting notice to discourage such practices.

2 It is often said that if software piracy could be eliminated, then so could most of the problems with viruses.

Using what you have learnt about software piracy and viruses, explain the above statement.

3 (a) Maria buys a copy of a popular word-processing package that she intends to use on her computer at work and on her home computer. She copies it onto each hard disk. Is she breaking the law?

(b) Umar buys a presentation package that he copies onto the hard disk of his computer. He puts away the program on the disks in a safe place. Is he breaking the law?

(c) Paolo has bought a new computer game that he shows to his friend. His friend asks him to make him a copy. Is he allowed by law to do this?

(d) Alma is approached by her boss who tells her that she will have to learn a new desktop publishing package in order to produce new company price lists. Her boss says that she needs to install the package on the computer and to photocopy the manual because her friend wants it back. Should Alma do this? Write a short but polite memo explaining to her boss why she will not do it.

Social and economic effects of IT

Before the industrial revolution nearly everyone worked in agriculture. Communication was by word of mouth or paper. When the industrial revolution came, life became more complicated. People started to work in factories and the factories needed offices to deal with administration. The amount of paperwork needed for trade started to increase. As time went on, technology was used to develop machines such as the typewriter, telephone and telex machines, and, eventually, the computer (Figure 19.1).

We are now in an 'information age' and our society is very dependent on information storage and communication. Many people are now using some form of information technology to help them.

▲
Figure 19.1

Is information technology a good thing?

Some arguments for and against IT are given below. You may agree or disagree with these. Where you disagree, explain your arguments.

Arguments in favour

1 The jobs replaced by computers are the rather mundane ones. People are free to do more interesting tasks.
2 Higher productivity enables people to work fewer hours and yet have the same standard of living. A greater amount of leisure time will improve people's quality of life.
3 Other countries make use of IT. If we did not, our goods and services would become uncompetitive and there would be even more unemployment.
4 There are many things that would be impossible without the use of IT. Air-traffic control, credit cards and space travel are just some examples.
5 New jobs are being created by the introduction of information technology, such as programming and network managing.

Arguments against

1 Life without IT is slower and less stressful.
2 Computers are cheaper than people, so if a job can be done by a computer then it will be, leading to even higher unemployment.
3 The new jobs being created by the use of IT are only for highly skilled and qualified people.
4 The people who did the boring, repetitive jobs now done by computers no longer have jobs.
5 The storage of personal data held on computers has eroded people's privacy.

6 The gap will be widened between those countries able to afford the new technologies and those that can not.

Changing employment patterns

With the introduction of computer-controlled technology employment patterns have changed considerably. Changes include the following:

1 Many of the manual tasks, such as assembly work and paintspraying in factories, are now being performed by robots.

2 Many industrial processes operate 24 hours a day and are continually being monitored and controlled by computers.

3 There are fewer paper-based systems in offices. Some jobs, such as filing clerks, no longer exist. New jobs involving computers have been created.

4 More and more people work from home, with the advantage of no travelling and the freedom of being able to live in any part of the country (or the world for that matter).

5 Computers are sometimes used to monitor the performance of their users. For instance, in supermarkets they can tell the management about the number of customers dealt with per hour or how many items are passed through the scanner in a day. Order entry clerks and airline booking clerks can have their work similarly monitored.

6 There is a continual need to retrain people, who no longer spend year after year doing the same job.

Reduced number of manual jobs

The opportunity to work from home

De-skilling or even elimination of some office jobs

THE EFFECT ON THE INDIVIDUAL

Increased unemployment

The creation of new and interesting jobs

The opportunity to work for yourself

The need to continually update skills

Figure 19.2 *The effect of IT on the individual*

Environmental, ethical, moral and social issues raised by IT

Environmental issues

Reduced energy consumption

Computers now control many of the heating systems in offices and factories, so it is possible for only the rooms that are being used to be heated. This can save huge amounts of energy.

Reduced wastage in industrial processes

There are many process control systems used in our factories, and because these are more accurate, there is less wastage, thus saving valuable resources.

Saving trees

The use of the electronic office and EDI has led to paper being almost eliminated in many offices and this means that fewer trees need to be felled, so not only are the trees saved, but the energy that went into the making of the paper is also saved.

Reducing car pollution

Teleworking (working at home using information technology) means that some people no longer have to travel to the office to work. This reduces petrol consumption and pollution by cars.

Ethical, moral and social issues

Software theft

It could be said that the use of personal computers has made many users into thieves. How many people could honestly say that all the software on their hard disks has been purchased by them? As you can see from the Copyright, Designs and Patents Act 1989, it is a criminal offence to copy or steal software.

Email

Viruses

Working from home (teleworking)

Chat: you can make friends with people around the world and learn about different cultures

Censorship of certain material

Books and newspapers waste paper

You can work from anywhere

Surfing the net can waste time

Information is more likely to be up-to-date

Sites set up by criminals part people from their money

Hacking

Vast amounts of information can be accessed from anywhere in the world

Figure 19.3 *Global network issues*

Hacking

Hacking means gaining illegal access to someone else's computer system. Many people see this type of thing as a challenge and not as an illegal activity.

Privacy

As more and more information is held there is more chance of some of it being incorrect. Your private life is becoming less and less private.

Job losses

Is it right to develop new systems in the knowledge that staff will inevitably be made redundant? Should we put shareholders' dividends and profits before people? These are difficult questions and ones which need to be addressed. Everyone has their own opinion on this. What is yours?

Things to do

1 It has been suggested that motorists might be charged for their use of roads by having a system which identifies each car. When a car passes over a sensor in the road, a central computer will record that car's entry into a charge zone. One of the side effects of this is that a record could be kept of every car's movements. Discuss some of the social implications of such a system, giving reasons why certain groups of people may be for or against the system.

2 There is an ongoing debate that many people would like to see the introduction of an identity card that everyone would be required to carry. Write a short paragraph explaining, and giving your reasons, whether or not you are in favour of the introduction of this card.

3 Information technology has replaced or changed many jobs.
   (a) Give the names of **two** types of job that have been replaced by IT.
   (b) Some jobs have changed their nature due to the introduction of IT. Name **two** jobs where this has happened.
   (c) With the creation of the information superhighway, some jobs are in danger of being lost. Name **two** of these jobs.

4 The advertisement in Figure 19.4 appeared in newspapers during the early days of computing, when many businesses were being computerised for the first time. Naturally, many people felt that their jobs could be in jeopardy and the aim of this advertisement was to explain how, in the long term, the use of computers would benefit mankind.
   (a) The list below shows some negative aspects of computerisation. For each item in the list try to present a positive aspect. For instance someone may say that the use of a word processor de-skills the job of a typist. The positive aspect to this might be that, because the word processor is easy to use, everyone can produce high quality, accurately typed documents.
   (i) Computers lead to unemployment and are therefore a bad thing.
   (ii) Some computers are able to report on the number of keystrokes made per hour (particularly in supermarket point-of-sale terminals), so computers can make the employees slaves to their machines.
   (iii) People need to be retrained, sometimes against their will.
   (iv) There might be a reduction in the amount of overtime available.
   (v) All the information held about people invades privacy.
   (vi) Computers can be very impersonal.

(b) Write a report outlining some of the advantages of the use of information technology. Try to contrast the way jobs were done before the introduction of the new technology with the way they are done now.

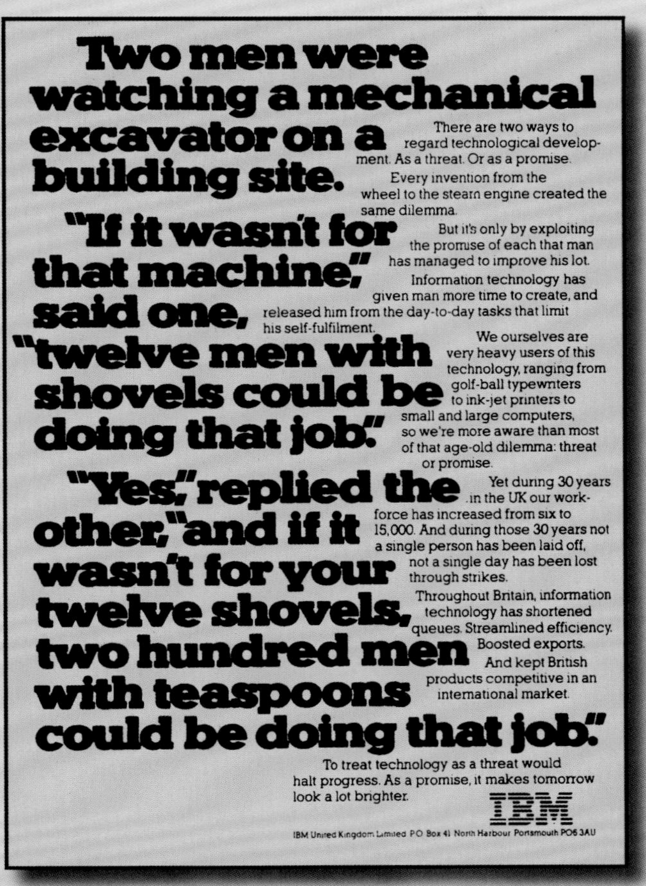

Two men were watching a mechanical excavator on a building site.

"If it wasn't for that machine," said one, "twelve men with shovels could be doing that job."

"Yes," replied the other, "and if it wasn't for your twelve shovels, two hundred men with teaspoons could be doing that job."

There are two ways to regard technological development. As a threat. Or as a promise.

Every invention from the wheel to the steam engine created the same dilemma.

But it's only by exploiting the promise of each that man has managed to improve his lot.

Information technology has given man more time to create, and released him from the day-to-day tasks that limit his self-fulfilment.

We ourselves are very heavy users of this technology, ranging from golf-ball typewriters to ink-jet printers to small and large computers, so we're more aware than most of that age-old dilemma: threat or promise.

Yet during 30 years in the UK our work-force has increased from six to 15,000. And during those 30 years not a single person has been laid off, not a single day has been lost through strikes.

Throughout Britain, information technology has shortened queues. Streamlined efficiency. Boosted exports. And kept British products competitive in an international market.

To treat technology as a threat would halt progress. As a promise, it makes tomorrow look a lot brighter.

IBM

IBM United Kingdom Limited P.O. Box 41, North Harbour, Portsmouth PO6 3AU

▲ **Figure 19.4**

When people think of computers they usually think of them being used in offices for administrative purposes. There are other things that computers can do: they can be used to control things. In this chapter we will look at how computers can be used to control devices.

Robots

We have all seen robots in science-fiction films. The robots can usually talk, walk, reason with humans and occasionally go berserk. The robots in these films are far removed from the robots actually being used in factories.

Robots are used in factories because they can reduce labour costs and improve the quality of the finished products.

Robots on the move

When robots start to move from place to place there are several problems to solve.

1 How are robots able to navigate themselves?
2 How do robots avoid colliding with each other and with other objects?
3 How is the power provided?

How to solve these problems

To allow robots to navigate themselves, tracks are provided which are set into the floor and the robots follow these. This type of system is used in factories, where movable robots are used to move materials around the production line, and also in warehouses where robotic forklift trucks move goods. The robots also keep a record of the distance they have travelled and the angles they have turned through, so that they always know their exact position.

What would happen if a person stood in the way of one of these moving robots or another robot dropped something in its way? On each robot there is an ultrasonic detector which emits a beam of infrared radiation. If anything gets in the way of the beam, the robot just stops.

Power is usually provided by batteries. When the batteries need recharging, the robot automatically goes to a place where the batteries can be recharged.

▲
Figure 20.1

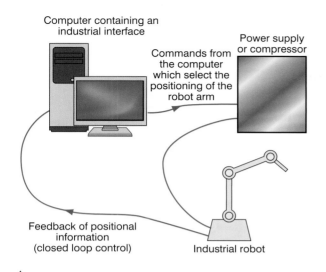

Figure 20.2 *A robot arm being controlled by a microcomputer*

Figure 20.3 *When developing robots, some practical difficulties have to be solved*

Computers in control

Using sensors

Sensors are used to detect various physical quantities, such as temperature, pressure, sound and light. The sensors are connected to a computer through an interface, and with special software the physical quantities can be displayed in a variety of ways on a computer screen.

Figure 20.5 shows a selection of sensors. We will now look at each one, together with examples of how they can be used.

Mercury tilt switch

If a device is tilted or moved, a blob of mercury in the switch touches the contacts and completes a circuit. Such a switch can be used in a pinball machine to detect whether someone is tilting the machine. It could also be used to trigger an alarm in a vending machine.

Light sensor

A light sensor has many uses. For instance, it can be used to detect low light levels so that street lighting is turned on. It could also be used to detect the light reflected from a barcode.

Push switch

You might find a push switch being used to turn on the interior light inside a car when the door is opened. You could also use one for detecting when a fridge door is opened, so that the light is then switched on.

Temperature sensor

One of the most common sensors is a temperature sensor. These are used, for example, in central heating systems to keep the temperature of a house constant.

Sound sensor

Environmental health officers could use sound sensors to record the level of sound coming from shops, clubs or houses where loud music is being played.

Proximity sensor

A proximity sensor is made in two halves. If the halves are moved away from each other then a signal is activated. You often see these sensors on windows, so that if the window is opened the two halves of the sensor are separated and an alarm is activated.

Position sensor

A position sensor detects the angle of a spindle. It could be used to feed back the position of a robot arm.

143

▲
Figure 20.4

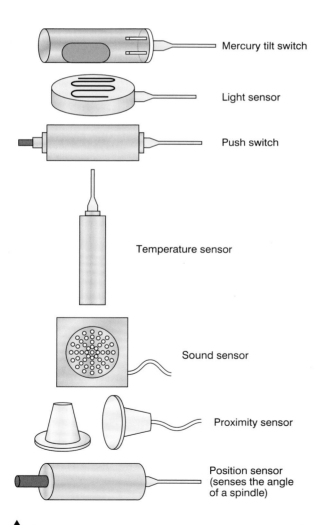

▲
Figure 20.5 *Input sensors*

pH sensor

A pH sensor is used to find out how basic or acidic a solution is.

Humidity sensor

A humidity sensor is used to determine the amount of moisture present (in the air or perhaps in soil).

Questions

1 Give the name, with reasons, of the sensor you would use to:
   (a) detect the temperature of the air inside a greenhouse
   (b) find out whether a pinball machine has been tilted by a player
   (c) detect whether a refrigerator door has been opened
   (d) measure the loudness of the music coming from a boutique
   (e) determine if a cup of tea has cooled sufficiently to enable a person to drink it
   (f) determine whether a solution is acidic or basic
   (g) measure the water content of the air in an art gallery
   (h) determine whether a pot plant needs watering
   (i) find out if a box on a conveyor belt has passed a certain point
   (j) determine whether the street lights should be switched on.

Interfaces: what are they and why are they needed?

An interface is the name given to the hardware and associated software needed to compensate for the difference in operating characteristics (e.g. speeds, codes) of the peripheral units and the computer. Figure 20.6 shows an interface used to connect sensors to the computer. Sensors (a maximum of four) can be linked to the interface box which is then connected to the computer. The software is then loaded and the computer knows to which sensors it is connected.

▲
Figure 20.6 *The interface connects the sensors to the computer*

Figure 20.7 shows the positions of a typical stepper motor. The rotor can be turned through a certain angle from, say, position 1,1 to 2,2 and so on. Pulses sent from the computer instruct the motor to turn through the required angle. Stepper motors can also be speeded up or slowed down and operated in forward or reverse direction. To connect a stepper motor to a computer, we use a buffer. Stepper motors are used in robot arms.

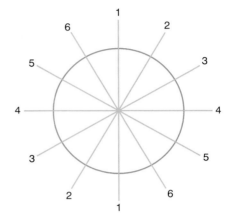

▲
Figure 20.7 *Positions of a stepper motor*

Buffers

The speed of data transfer of a device connected to a computer may be different to that of the computer. Usually a special store area, called a buffer, is used to hold data temporarily to compensate for any difference in speeds.

Actuators

Actuators are hardware devices, such as motors, which react according to signals given to them by computers. An actuator motor, for example, would be used to open a window in a greenhouse when it gets too hot.

Stepper motor

A stepper motor, as the name suggests, is a motor which turns in a series of small steps. Stepper motors generally look fatter than ordinary motors and have several wires coming out of them.

Using sensors in hospitals

The medical condition of a patient in an intensive care unit can be continually monitored using sensors connected to the patient. Respiration, blood pressure, temperature and electrical activity of the heart and pulse can all be measured by the sensors. A computer is used to continually monitor the results from the sensors, and if the patient's condition changes suddenly or values exceed given thresholds then an alarm sounds to alert medical staff.

Questions

1 What advantages are there in using computers to monitor the condition of seriously ill patients?

2 Are there any disadvantages?

The importance of feedback

A computer can be used to control a robot arm. If we wanted the robot arm to move through a certain angle we can give an instruction to a special motor that moves small steps at a time. When the command has been issued the arm will move to the required position. If there is an object in the way of the arm, it will stop. The problem is that if this happens it will assume that it has reached its desired position. The computer can no longer be sure of its position.

What is needed is a way of the arm relaying its actual position back to the computer. It can do this by making use of sensors. The sensors continually send data about the position of the arm back to the computer. If the robot arm is not in the correct position then remedial action can be taken to put it in the correct position. Here, output from the system directly affects the input. Such a system is said to use feedback.

Example of process control

Here is a simple example of process control. In a chemical process a container is filled with water to a certain level and heated up to a temperature of 70 °C.

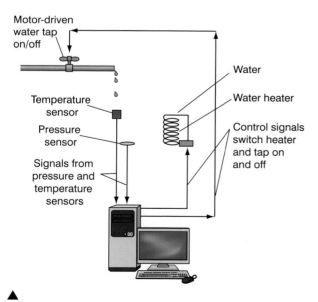

▲ **Figure 20.8** *Using a computer to control a chemical process*

The computer issues a control signal to the motorised tap, instructing it to turn the tap on and let the water into the container. As the water enters and the level rises, the water pressure is continually fed back to the computer. As soon as the pressure reaches a certain value the water is up to the correct level. A control signal is sent back to the tap to turn the water off. At the same time a signal is fed back to the computer from the temperature sensor. If the temperature of the water is less than 70 °C, a control signal is sent to the heater to turn it on. The temperature is continually measured and sent back to the computer, which compares the temperature with its set level (i.e. 70 °C). At soon as the temperature reaches this level, a control is issued to the heater to turn it off. At any time when the temperature drops below 70 °C, the heater is switched on again so that the temperature remains constant at 70 °C.

Process control

Computers are used throughout the manufacturing industry for the control of many industrial processes. They are able to monitor and control a process automatically. Like robots, they also make use of feedback.

Process control is used in nuclear power stations, oil refineries and in the chemical industry. Various sensors are used to relay electronic signals back to computers. Such sensors include devices that measure temperatures, pressures and liquid flow rates. Because these systems operate in real time, they are able to respond instantly to variations in these quantities and make slight adjustments to the controls.

The advantages of computer control include the following:

1 Computers are able to respond instantly to changes in conditions.
2 Fewer staff are needed, so costs are reduced, making the final product cheaper.
3 The system can keep working 24 hours per day, 365 days a year.

4 Some processes are dangerous. Keeping people away from these processes can help prevent accidents.

5 It is easy for a manufacturer to change a product by reprogramming a computer.

The disadvantages of computer control are as follows:

1 Fewer people are needed to do a job, so this leads to unemployment.

2 Computers tend to be expensive to introduce initially.

Pseudocode

Pseudocode is useful for writing instructions before these are translated into a language that the computer can understand. With pseudocode you can express the logical flow of a program in ordinary words. Many control languages use a language similar to pseudocode.

Using pseudocode you start at the highest level by writing a list of the tasks that the program must perform. You can then refine the program by making it more structured. Let us now look at a task you should be familiar with: washing the dishes.

The first level could be a simple description of the task, such as:

    wash the dishes

This could then be broken down into the sub-tasks like this:

    collect dishes
    take to the sink
    fill sink
    add small amount of washing-up liquid
    wash dishes
    put on drainer to dry
    dry hands
    dry dishes with a cloth
    put dishes away

Each of these sub-tasks could be broken down even further. For instance, 'fill sink' could be broken down in the following way:

    put in plug
    turn on hot tap
    turn off hot tap
    if water too hot

    turn on cold tap
    turn off cold tap

If you look at the above list carefully you will see that it probably does not represent the way you would actually fill the sink. For example there is nothing that tells you when you should turn off the hot or cold taps. Also it does not cover the situation where the sink is about to overflow. We need to refine this program to take into account these situations. Here is the final attempt:

    IF water in sink
    pull out plug
    wait for water to drain away
    ENDIF
    put in plug
    turn hot tap half on
    turn cold tap half on
    DO UNTIL water is deep enough
    IF water too hot
    turn down hot tap
    turn up cold tap
    ENDIF
    IF water too cold
    turn down cold tap
    turn up hot tap
    ENDIF
    ENDO

Even the above could be broken down further, but it is in sufficient detail as a general program. However, if a robot were to be washing the dishes it would need to have a lot more information. For instance, the part of the above program for turning on the hot tap could be broken down into the following:

    move arm to position above hot tap
    lower hand until it touches tap
    get hold of tap
    turn tap anticlockwise
    rotate tap for half a turn
    release tap
    move arm away from tap

Breaking down a large complex task into its smaller, more manageable parts is called the top-down approach. We used the same approach when we drew structure diagrams in Chapter 12.

Computers in greenhouses

For successful growing of plants it is necessary to give them the correct environment and to keep this environment constant. In particular, the temperature and humidity (the amount of moisture) in the air must be kept constant. Sensors are used to record the humidity; signals from these sensors are sent to a computer. If the humidity falls then the computer will operate a motor to close any open windows and then switch on a pump for a certain period that will spray water as a fine mist inside the greenhouse. An increase in humidity (i.e. too much moisture in the air) will cause the windows to open to assist in ventilation and drying out the air.

The temperature may be controlled in the following way. If the greenhouse gets too hot, the windows are opened. If it gets too cold, the windows are closed and a heater is switched on. Plants grow much faster with such careful control of conditions.

The inputs and outputs of the system are as follows:

Inputs

humidity – analogue signal
temperature – analogue signal.

Outputs

windows – digital signal (either open or closed)
heater – digital signal (either on or off)
pump for water spray – digital signal (either on or off).

In practice, the control could be much more complicated than this. For example, we could have windows which opened by small amounts depending on the temperature and the humidity.

Computers and safety of cars

Many new cars are fitted with a braking system called ABS (antilock brake system). ABS uses sensors to detect the rotational speed of each wheel when the brakes are applied. The speed of each wheel is relayed

Questions

The greenhouse in Figure 20.9 is used to grow delicate plants and must be kept at a constant temperature of 24–28 °C throughout the year. If it gets too hot, the glass panel is opened by a motor. If it gets too cold, the glass panel is closed.

You now have to write some pseudocode which will do the following:

- start with the window closed

- wait for the temperature to rise above 28 °C

- produce a sound (e.g. a buzz) and then open the window to allow the cooler air in

- wait for the temperature to fall below 24 °C

- produce a sound (e.g. a buzz) and close the window.

It is decided that this system would be incapable of maintaining the temperature in the winter, so a heater needs to be included. Decide on the series of steps that the system would take and write a new piece of pseudocode for the control program.

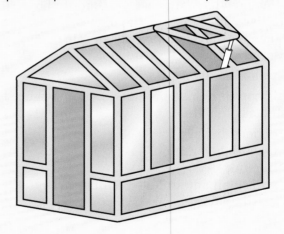

▲
Figure 20.9

to the computer. If the wheels start to lock, the computer sends a signal which eases the pressure on the brakes at each wheel. This prevents the wheels from locking and sliding out of control. Using ABS, a driver is able to control the car more safely during braking.

Navigation systems

GPS stands for Global Positioning System, which is the system that uses the signals from several satellites to obtain the exact position of any object (e.g. aircraft, ship, car) on the Earth's surface. Many cars are equipped with satellite navigation systems which use GPS so that the driver can locate their position on a map on a small screen inside the car. The driver can then use the system to obtain directions to their destination. Satellite navigation systems give the directions (turn left, turn right, etc.) on a screen, as well as giving verbal directions using voice synthesis as you approach junctions and turns. People use hand-held satellite positioning systems when walking in unpopulated areas such as mountains or deserts. Satellite navigation is a feature on some mobile phones.

The benefits of navigation systems include:

- You can tell the emergency services your exact whereabouts if there is an emergency.
- They are safer as the person is not trying to read directions from a map whilst they are driving.
- The system could save your life if you were lost in a desert.
- Less fuel is used because you can travel straight to the destination without getting lost.

The drawbacks of navigation systems are:

- Satellite navigation systems in cars may be stolen.
- New roads may be built or routes changed that the system will not know about.
- The systems can often send you along unsuitable roads.
- Sometimes the satellite signal is blocked by tall buildings or mountains.
- Backup maps still need to be kept in case the satellite navigation system breaks down.

▲ **Figure 20.10** *Satellite navigation systems are built into many new cars*

Data logging

Data are often collected automatically over a period of time and then processed at a later date. You may have seen pressure sensors which look like thick wires placed across the road to record the volume of traffic passing. If you follow these sensors they lead to a black box which is usually padlocked to a lamp post to prevent it from being stolen. This box, called a data logger, records data about the volume of traffic passing. The alternative way of recording these data would be to use humans to do it manually. This is clearly expensive and not the most exciting of jobs.

There are two main types of data loggers: those which need to be connected to the computer all the time and those which do not.

Data loggers with permanent computer connections

These data loggers take readings and then send them to the computer via a wire or an electronic signal. The computer can either process the readings at once to produce a graph or store them on disk for processing at a later date. These data loggers are ideal for experiments in the laboratory, but suitable ones for use in the field are too expensive for schools to use.

Data loggers with temporary computer connections

These data loggers are ideal for monitoring environmental conditions over a period of time in the field. As with all data loggers, the time intervals (the time between each reading) and the period over which the logging takes place can be varied.

The readings are stored by the data logger, then loaded into the computer at a later date where they can be processed and displayed. Because they are used in remote places, these data loggers need their own power supply.

Data logging has many advantages:

1 it can be performed 24 hours per day, 365 days per year if necessary
2 it is possible for processing to be carried out immediately if the data logger can send the data in the form of a radio signal to the main computer.

Questions

You have been concerned about the road where you live being used by lorries, vans and cars as a short cut to avoid a busy junction. You have persuaded local residents to sign a petition which has been sent to your local council.

The council has said that it will monitor the situation and place a data logger on the road for two weeks.

1 Explain what a data logger is.
2 To monitor the flow of traffic you got together with the other residents to stand at the side of the road and to count the number of certain types of vehicles travelling along the road between 10 and 11 in the morning.
   (a) What advantages does the data logger have over your manual method?
   (b) What methods of display could be used to present the data from the data logger?

Things to do

1 (a) A computer program is used to control a robot, which is moving and stacking boxes in a warehouse. The program uses commands to control its movements
   FORWARD steps
   BACK steps
   RIGHT angle
   LEFT angle
   UP steps
   DOWN steps

▲ **Figure 20.11**

For example,
   FORWARD 50   moves the robot forward 50 steps in a straight line.
   RIGHT 45   turns the robot 45° to the right.
   UP 2   raises the forks 2 steps.

The robot is found to be dropping the boxes in the wrong place.
Give two different mistakes in the program that could be causing this.
(b) Following a nasty accident, the robot has to be adapted to stop if it meets an unexpected obstacle in its path. What changes would need to be made to the robot design?

2 In Figure 20.12 the heating of water in a tank is under the control of a microprocessor. Cold water enters the tank via valve 1. It is heated to a set temperature and leaves the tank via valve 2.
  (a) Describe how feedback could be used in the system.
  (b) (i) Where should an analogue-to-digital converter be placed in the system? Draw your answer on the diagram.
     (ii) Why is an analogue-to-digital converter necessary?

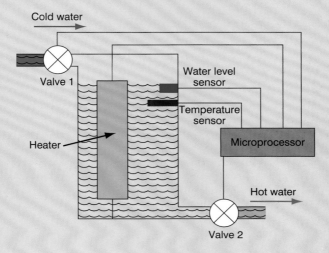

▲
Figure 20.12

3 (a) A washing machine is designed to wash, rinse and spin for predetermined times regardless of whether the washing is clean or not. Is this an open-loop or closed-loop control system?
  (b) A central heating system is continually monitoring the temperature of a room. If it is too cold, the heating is switched on. When the room gets too hot the system switches the heater off. Is this open-loop or closed-loop control?
  (c) Traffic lights may either use closed-loop or open-loop control. Using traffic lights as an example, explain the difference between open-loop and closed-loop control.

4 Computer systems are now being used in hospitals as part of life-support systems.
  (a) Blood pressure is a human physical response suitable for monitoring by computer. Suggest two others.
  (b) Give three reasons why computers are used in life-support systems.
  (c) Give three tasks for which human medical staff are more suitable than computers.

5 A car park entrance (shown in Figure 20.13) is controlled by a microprocessor.
When a car approaches the barrier a ticket is produced, which the driver takes. The barrier then opens, and the light changes from red to green. When the car has passed, the light changes to red and the barrier comes down.
  (a) Describe a suitable sensor for detecting the approaching car.
  (b) List the steps involved in carrying out this process, using suitable instructions.
  (c) What information needs to be on the ticket?
  (d) Give two ways in which this can be encoded in machine-readable form.

Things to do

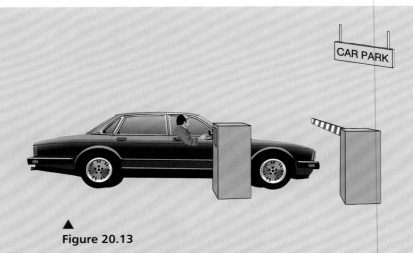

▲
Figure 20.13

6 The table below shows a number of different situations. Fill in the boxes to show the time intervals between logging and the overall period of logging.

Situation	Sensor	Time interval	Period of logging
Collecting data on seasonal temperature variations for weather records	Heat		
Collecting data about the temperature change which takes place when ice is added to a beaker of water	Heat		

7 The greenhouse shown in Figure 20.14 must be kept at a temperature between 24 °C and 28 °C throughout the year. It has been decided to use a computer-controlled system. Produce an outline design for the system that is required.

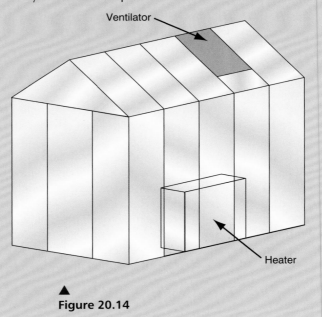

Ventilator

Heater

▲
Figure 20.14

8 A diagram of a refrigerator is shown in Figure 20.15.
   (a) What quantity does the sensor measure?
   (b) A refrigerator makes use of feedback. Explain what feedback means and say why it is necessary to have it in the refrigerator.
   (c) A control program is stored on the chip. Write down a series of instructions which will help keep the refrigerator at a constant temperature.
   (d) When the door of the refrigerator is opened a light comes on. Examine your fridge at home and see if you can find out how this sensor works.
   (e) Insurance companies pay out large sums of money each year to people who have ruined food by leaving the door slightly open. Design a system which could help prevent this problem.

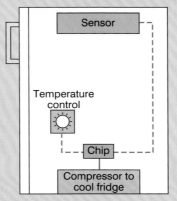

▲ **Figure 20.15** *Refrigerator*

21 Computers and Your Health

The problems

There are many health problems that can occur when you are working with computers for long periods. Repetitive strain injury (RSI), backache, eye strain, headaches and skin rashes are conditions which can occur. By using various devices, correct posture and good working practices, these conditions can be prevented. Figure 21.1 shows some things you ought to pay attention to when working with VDUs.

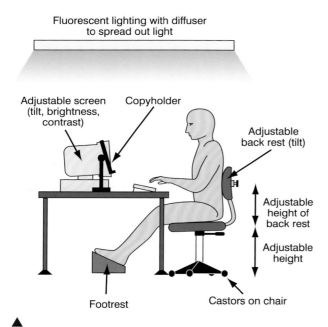

▲ **Figure 21.1** *What you need to work efficiently at a computer*

Repetitive strain injury (RSI)

RSI is caused by the joints in the fingers constantly being pounded by typing at high speed. RSI causes pain in the joints and can cause long-term disability. Good keyboard design, a well-positioned keyboard, a good typing technique and frequent breaks can help prevent RSI from occurring. You can also buy wrist guards which ease fatigue when you are using a keyboard for long periods.

Eye strain

In a study of VDU operators, it was found that nearly 70 per cent suffered some form of eye problem, such as eye strain, irritated eyes or blurred vision. However, eye strain is fairly common in other types of close work. One way of avoiding eye strain is to look at a distant object now and again (ask your physics or biology teacher to explain why this helps). Regular computer users should have regular eye checks.

Reproductive hazards

There have been some stories in the newspapers regarding abnormal births in pregnant women who have been using VDUs for long periods. VDUs, like a lot of other electrical appliances, give out radiation when they are working. Most of this radiation is given out from the back and the sides of the VDUs. A large amount of research has been done on this and at the moment there is little evidence that VDUs do any damage.

▲ **Figure 21.2** *There are lots of scare stories concerning radiation from VDUs. There is no real evidence though, so you need not worry*

▲
Figure 21.3

Protecting the workforce

Because of the various health problems that can occur with incorrect computer use, there are now laws which require employers to provide the following:

- **Inspections** – Desks, chairs, computers and so on should be inspected to make sure that they reach the required standard.
- **Training** – Employees should have training on health and safety matters.
- **Job design** – The job should be designed so that the worker has periodic breaks or changes of activity when using computers.
- **Eye tests** – For computer users there should be regular free eye tests, with glasses provided if necessary, at the employer's expense.

The law also lays down some minimum requirements for computer systems and furniture. All new furniture and equipment bought must meet these standards:

- **Display screens** – These must have a stable picture with no flicker. Brightness, contrast, tilt and swivel must be easily adjustable. There must be no reflection off the screen.

- **Keyboard** – This must be separate from the screen and tiltable. Keyboards should be easy to use and the surface should be matt to avoid glare. There must be sufficient space for people to change position.
- **Desks** – Desks must be large enough to accommodate the computer and any paperwork and must not reflect too much light. An adjustable document holder should be provided so as to avoid uncomfortable head movements.
- **Chair** – This must be adjustable and comfortable, and allow easy freedom of movement. A foot rest must be available on request.
- **Lights** – There must be no glare or reflections on the computer screen. Windows must have adjustable coverings.
- **Noise** – This should not be loud enough to distract attention and disturb speech.
- **Software** – This must be easy to use and appropriate to the user's needs and experience.
- **Other matters** – Heat, humidity and radiation emissions must be kept at adequate levels.

Things to consider when designing an office

1 Single pendant lamps (like the ones you have in your house) should be avoided since they produce glare on the screen. Instead, fluorescent tubes with diffusers (plastic covers) which spread out the light should be used.
2 Carpets made of synthetic fibre should be avoided. These cause static electricity which can destroy data stored on magnetic disks.
3 Windows should have adjustable blinds on them to avoid sunlight producing glare on the screen.
4 Cables should not be left trailing across the floor.
5 Ample sockets should be fitted so that it is not necessary to use multiple sockets, which could be dangerous.

▲
Figure 21.4

1 Figure 21.4 shows all sorts of poor working practices and bad equipment. How many can you spot? Write a list and say what needs to be done to put them right.

2 There are various products for sale in computer catalogues which are aimed at the 'computer safety market'. Look at these catalogues and write a brief report stating what devices are available and how much they cost.

3 You have been asked to look at the equipment and the working conditions in your school or college's computer rooms. Some of the things you should look at are:
   - whether sockets have too many plugs in them
   - whether carpets are made of synthetic fibre
   - whether document holders are provided
   - whether there are adjustable blinds on the windows
   - whether wires trail across the floor.

(a) Your task is to complete this list of things to look for. After you have completed your list, design a suitable document which can be filled in when you look around the room. This document should be word-processed.

(b) Look around the computer room and fill in the document.

(c) Prepare a report which gives a summary of what you have found, making any recommendations where necessary.

Investigations

Soo, Grabbitt and Runn is a partnership of lawyers. The original partners are now retiring and new partners have come into the business. The new partners wish to get rid of the firm's old-fashioned image and would like to improve efficiency. They would like to make the main office open plan. Each of the five partners in the firm has to have his or her own office, since the firm's clients would like privacy when discussing personal matters. The accounting system is to be computerised and all the letters and forms, both sent out and received, are to be recorded on the system. The use of a local area network (LAN) will enable both office staff and the lawyers to view client information via their own terminals.

There are various problems with the existing office:

- the office chairs do not have castors and are non-adjustable

- the carpet is made of nylon and staff frequently complain of getting electric shocks

- the main lighting is from single lights hanging from the ceiling, which causes uneven illumination

- the partners have curtains on their windows which frequently have to be closed because of the sunlight coming in

- each partner has a highly polished oak desk; staff in the open-plan office have shiny-topped desks

- the three computers in use at the moment have keyboards and VDUs in one unit.

You have been asked to help plan the installation of the new information system. Figure 21.5 shows the layout of the office at the moment. You do not need to get involved in the actual dimensions of the office since this would make the project far too complicated.

1 Prepare a report, using word-processing software, making some preliminary recommendations concerning new office furniture and equipment. Your report should identify the factors to be considered when deciding the location and layout of the various terminals in the main office.

2 Obtain, from equipment and office furniture suppliers, prices for the equipment you have suggested and detail your costs using an appropriate software package.

3 The partners prefer to have their desks in the positions marked on the plan, but you think that, with the introduction of the terminals, some of these positions are unsuitable. Write short memos to the partners concerned explaining why the positions of their desks should be changed.

For the whole of the office, design your best possible layout. A diagram should be drawn, either by hand or using a suitable software package, showing the positions of the main pieces of equipment, desks and so on. Also include a report outlining the reasons behind your proposed arrangement.

Staffing and equipment information

Staffing

5 partners
1 lawyer
2 trainee lawyers
1 office manager (in charge of administrative/secretarial staff)
1 senior secretary
2 junior secretaries
1 general/filing clerk
1 receptionist

Equipment

5 terminals (1 for each partner)
1 terminal for the lawyer
2 terminals for the trainee lawyers
1 terminal for the office manager

All the secretarial staff have terminals, which they mainly use for word processing. Staff without terminals still have a desk.

2 laser printers (connected to the network)
1 document scanner (used to scan documents into the system)

1 fax machine   1 photocopier
1 drinks machine   1 typewriter

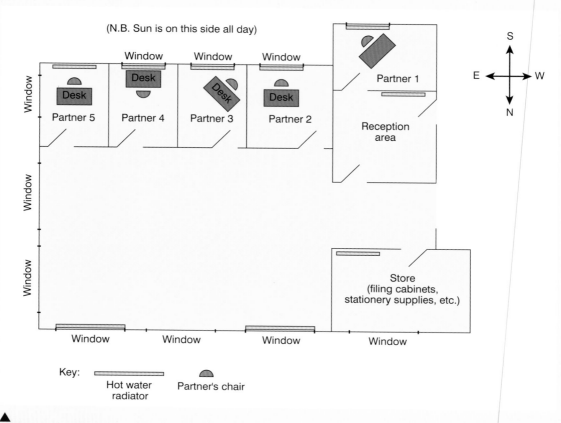

Figure 21.5 *Office plan for Soo, Grabbitt and Runn*

Equipment and facilities in an electronic office

Fax

A fax machine is rather like a long-distance photocopier, where you put the document into the fax machine at one end and a copy comes out of a fax machine at the other end. The original is first scanned with a beam of light and then converted into electronic signals that can be passed along the telephone lines. The copy is printed out at the other end on the recipient's machine.

Faxes are particularly useful since drawings can be transferred. Also, because a fax is really a picture of the document, letters or contracts which include a signature may be sent and this is useful to lawyers. If you have a fax/modem then you can send faxes from your computer without the need to print out and then scan them.

Electronic mail (email)

With electronic mail, data or messages can be sent electronically via the telephone network or other data networks and via a central computer. Electronic mail has advantages of speed and economy (there is no need for stamps, envelopes, etc.). With electronic mail both sender and recipient can store the letters or documents on disk for future reference.

Electronic mail is used extensively by companies that have networks for their internal mail. The wider use of electronic mail is hindered because not everyone has the facilities.

Electronic data interchange (EDI)

EDI is the method by which different companies' computers automatically exchange data. Large food retailers use this method. When stores are running low on a certain item, an order is automatically issued and sent electronically to the supplier's computer where it is dealt with. Payment for the goods is made electronically from the retailer to the supplier via their bank accounts. This all happens without any paperwork.

Videoconferencing

Videoconferencing allows meetings to be conducted between people who can see each other, but without them having to be in the same room or even in the same geographical area. Videoconferencing systems are often used on the TV news to enable a news reporter to interview people in other countries.

Using videoconferencing, people at the 'virtual' meeting can see and speak to each other by making use of web cameras and microphones and special videoconferencing software. They are also able to share documents, presentations, etc.

Questions

1 How would the following make use of a fax machine? For each one, say how the fax machine would be useful:
   (a) a lawyer
   (b) an accountant
   (c) an architect
   (d) an engineer.

2 A document can also be sent using electronic mail. A lawyer needs to send a copy of a contract which has been signed by a client to a bank. It is important that the client's signature is on the copy. What problem is there in using electronic mail?

Advantages

- Employees experience less stress as they do not have the stresses of travelling to meetings.
- More time can be spent with your family as there is less time spent away from home.
- Saves money as businesses does not have to spend money on travelling expenses, hotel rooms, meals and so on.
- Improvement in the productivity of employees, as they are not wasting time travelling to meetings.
- Meetings do not have to be planned well in advance, so they can be called at short notice.
- Better for the environment as the carbon footprint is reduced because of the reduction in journeys to meetings.

Disadvantages

- It is expensive to buy the specialist hardware and software needed for videoconferencing.
- The image and sound quality can be poor unless very high-speed broadband is used.
- Some people enjoy the experience of travelling to new places and meeting others face to face.
- There may be things such as an actual product that cannot be passed around at a meeting using videoconferencing.

E-commerce

E-commerce is the selling of goods or services over the internet, as opposed to using traditional methods such as buying goods or services from shops or trading using the telephone.

Most companies have their own websites. In some cases the websites are simply to make people more aware of their business and for advertising. Other companies use the internet for e-commerce where customers can make online orders for goods and services.

Some advantages of e-commerce to companies are:

- It is cheaper – there is no requirement for shops on the high street which require high rentals.
- Fewer staff are needed. Much of the administrative work is done by the customer (e.g. checking the price, checking availability, typing in the order).
- A company can operate 24 hours per day, 365 days per year.
- It can reach lots of different countries.
- It can locate its warehouses anywhere in the world.

Some advantages to the customers are:

- Goods are generally cheaper than in shops on the high street.
- They can shop around other internet shops without leaving home, to make sure they are getting the best deal.
- Goods are delivered straight to the customer's house – there is no need to collect them.
- Goods can be ordered from anywhere in the world without going there.

Some disadvantages to customers are:

- Poorer people may not be able to afford the equipment and ISP cost to connect to the internet.
- You need some ICT skills to use the internet.
- You usually need a credit card to make online purchases. If you are poor, or a bad credit risk, then getting a credit card is not easy.
- Many people are wary about typing in their personal details and credit card number because they think that hackers can get at the information.
- If things go wrong, for example the goods arrive damaged, then you have the chore of posting the goods back.

Digital telephones

Digital telephones are used for modern landline phones as well as mobile phones. Digital telephones have many more facilities than the older analogue phones. They make it possible to:

- send and receive text messages

- make phone calls
- take digital photographs
- take short video clips
- surf the internet
- watch live TV
- send and receive email
- download and listen to music
- download and play games
- send picture messages
- play videos
- use GPS (as a satellite navigation system).

Mobile phones

There has been a huge change in the way that people communicate with each other. The use of mobile phones means that people can be contacted anywhere, at any place and any time. The use of text messaging means that you can still contact people if they are busy and do not answer the phone.

Here are some situations that could be helped by the use of mobile phones:

- Your train is delayed and someone is waiting at the station to pick you up. You need to ring them to tell them you will be late.
- There has been a serious accident along a quiet country road. You need to contact the emergency services.
- Your car has broken down. You need to ring for help.

Advantages

- Personal security – you feel safer if you need to contact someone in an emergency situation.
- You can access the internet from the latest phones if you can get a signal.
- People who are constantly on the move can be contacted by their base (e.g. lorry drivers, repair staff, company reps/ salespersons).
- It removes the difficulty of trying to find a public telephone that works.
- It can avoid the need to make expensive telephone calls from a hotel phone.
- You can send and receive email.
- You can send and receive text messages.

Disadvantages

- People forget to turn their phones off during concerts, lectures and whilst in libraries. The rings can be offputting to others.
- People can become so dependent on their phones that they use them for no real purpose.
- They can be a nuisance in public places (restaurants, bars, trains, service stations etc.)
- People can be contacted at any time, even when it is inconvenient.
- People try to use phones in cars without hands-free kit, which is very dangerous and can lead to accidents.
- Use of mobile phones can be very expensive.

Telecommuting

As our cities become more congested and polluted, people will start to look at alternative ways of working. Consider the insurance company we looked at earlier. In this company everything was done electronically. Using networks it would be possible for a worker at home to access all this information. Many companies are considering allowing staff to work at home.

There has been much concern in the media about the general move for many people from employed status to self-employment or contract work. From a company's point of view, the increasing use of IT is providing more and more rapid changes, making competition more intense and producing pressure to reduce the workforce. From an employee's point of view, the reducing cost and increasing power of telecommunications, computer equipment and software are making self-employment a more viable option.

There are some disadvantages in teleconferencing and telecommuting:

- while computer hardware is cheaper than it was, it is still expensive
- telecommunication costs are high
- people like personal contact.

Questions

You have been asked by the insurance company we looked at earlier to work from home. The company will install and pay for all the necessary equipment in your home.

1   What advantages might there be in your being able to work from home rather than travel into a central office each day?

2   Are there any disadvantages in working from home? Explain what they are.

3   There are also some advantages to the insurance company of this way of working. What are they?

Test Yourself

Using the words in the list below, copy out and complete sentences **A** to **E**, underlining the words you have inserted. The words may be used more than once.

document   fax   data interchange
teleconferencing   telecommuting

A A machine which is a bit like a long-distance photocopier is called a _____ .

B _____ image processing involves using a scanner to scan the documents into the system so that the original paperwork may be disposed of.

C Electronic _____ _____ uses computers automatically to issue orders and pay for them.

D _____ enables conferences to be organised without the people involved leaving their homes or offices.

E Staying at home and working using computers and telecommunications equipment is called _____ .

Things to do

1 Draw a diagram of a paper-based office and include on your diagram the usual areas, such as:
   - photocopier and print room (containing a photocopier and a duplicating machine)
   - filing room (containing filing cabinets and a microfilm reader)
   - typing area (containing manual typewriters)
   - accounts area (containing typewriters and calculators)
   - post room (containing addressing machines, postage meter, sorting racks for incoming mail, telex and telephone switchboard).

2 Now draw a diagram of the office after it has been converted into an electronic office.

3 With the introduction of electronic offices, some people's jobs will change, while others may even disappear. With reference to the following list, say how each job might change and state which, if any, of the jobs will remain the same:
   - filing clerk
   - copy typist
   - shorthand typist
   - secretary
   - post-room clerk
   - manager
   - accounts clerk.

4 An ordinary telephone which has no special features can be used only to dial numbers and receive incoming calls. Investigate the latest phones and explain the features that are now available.

5 There has been a great increase in the use of systems involving communication between computers.

   Describe a system which makes use of a communication network.

23 Simulations
Almost as Good as the Real Thing

Modelling

A model consists of a set of equations which describe the behaviour of a process or object. In a computer model we use the computer to solve these equations so that we can carry out a simulation. Performing a simulation therefore means actually using the model to see what happens in certain situations.

3D modelling

3D models are often set up by architects and design engineers to see what a finished building or product will look like before it is built or produced. For instance, a large supermarket uses CAD (computer-aided design) and 3D models to produce three-dimensional views of stores and can show the effects of varying light sources, intensity of colour and different finishes of materials. A large supermarket also uses 3D modelling to look at the way a new store will blend into an existing main street. 3D models are also used to plan the outside of stores.

Modelling inflation

Suppose you are planning for the future and would like some money for when you stop working. In other words you need a pension. A pension is a sum of money you get each week when you retire from work. Everyone has to think about this sooner or later, but how much might you need? Suppose you are earning $500 per week now, what will you be earning just before you retire? The answer is you do not know. However, if you are arranging a pension, you need to have an idea of how much you are going to need.

So you need a model. Let us design a model to determine how much a 23-year-old person who earned $500 per week in 2010 would be earning in 2050, the year before they were due to retire.

There are various constraints to our model.

1 No one knows what the percentage rate of inflation will be over the next 40 years. We could look at the past rates of inflation over, say, the last 20 years (you should be able to get these figures from the library or your economics teacher) and use an average value, or you could use another value.

2 To make things simpler, we have to assume that the person does not get promoted and his wage increases only in line with inflation. When you have got used to the model you might try increasing the wage at some point in the future.

3 Our worker's wages may rise faster than the rate of inflation. Some occupations have done well over the last 20 years, while others have fallen behind. Is it possible to take these factors into account?

Questions

1 The first five years can be calculated manually, assuming that the inflation stays at a constant rate of 5 per cent per year. Before you attempt this, we will look at how to do this for the first couple of years.

We will fill in a table with these column headings:

End of year   Wage

To work out how $500 would need to change in order to keep pace with inflation we perform the following calculations. We find 5 per cent of $500 in the following way:

$$5/100 \times \$500 = \$25$$

This is the amount by which the weekly wage would need to grow. Hence, the new weekly wage at the end of year 1

$$= \$500 + \$25$$
$$= \$525$$

We can add these to the table like this:

End of year	Wage
1	$525

We then repeat the process using this new wage:

$$5 \text{ per cent of } \$525 = 5/100 \times \$525$$
$$= \$26.25$$

Hence,
at the end of year 2, weekly wage

$$= \$525 + \$26.25$$
$$= \$551.25$$

You can start to build up the table like this:

End of year	Wage
1	$525
2	$551.25

You next have to complete the table for the first five years by repeating the processes outlined above. Good mathematicians will be able to do these calculations using a faster method than that shown above. If you want to know more, ask your mathematics teacher.

2 Obviously, for this type of repetitive calculation, a spreadsheet would be ideal. Prepare a model using a spreadsheet and find out how much the person would need to earn in 2050 just to keep pace with inflation.

3 Try to refine your model so that it better reflects reality. For instance, collect some inflation figures and see if 5 per cent seems about right.

Games

Many computer games are simulations. For instance, when you play a football game on your computer you are simulating a real game. Some games simulate in an exciting way the running of a business. For example, one game requires you to build rides that will attract the public. The more entertaining your rides are, the more people will come to your theme park.

Flight simulators are very popular on home computers, so if you fancy landing a jet on an aircraft carrier, you can buy a package to realise your dreams. These simulations either run in non-real time, where things happen slower than they would do in real life, or in real time, where things happen at the real speed. Although visually they resemble the real thing, only a genuine flight simulator gives the movements and feel of actually flying an aircraft.

Expert systems

Expert systems are ICT systems that use artificial intelligence to make decisions based on data supplied in the form of answers to questions. This means that the system is able to respond in the way that a human expert in the field would to come to a conclusion. A good expert system is one that can match the performance of a human expert in the field.

The three components of an expert system

Expert systems consist of the following components:

- Knowledge base – a huge organised set of knowledge about a particular subject. It contains facts and also judgemental knowledge, which gives it the ability to make a good guess, like a human expert.
- Inference engine – a set of rules on which to base decisions. Most of these rules have the 'if–then' structure. It is the part of the expert system that does the reasoning by manipulating and using the knowledge in the knowledge base. There is usually a way of phrasing a question to the system or a way of searching for information using a search engine.
- User interface – the user interface presents questions and information to the operator and also receives answers from the operator.

Creating a new expert system

Here are the steps taken when creating a new expert system:

- Potential users of the system are interviewed to find out what is required from the desired expert system.
- Experts are consulted and asked to supply data about their expertise.
- The knowledge base is created using the information collected from the experts.
- Rules connecting the knowledge are identified.
- The rules are used to create the inference engine.
- The user interface is created which allows the user to enter data as input from various sources. The output screens are also created.
- Testing is undertaken to ensure that the expert system is producing the same results as a human expert in the field.
- The system is evaluated and improvements are made to the system before it goes live.

Why and where expert systems are used

Expert systems can be used for all sorts of applications and here are some of them.

Medical diagnosis

There are many different types of blood infections. If the correct antibiotic is given, the infection will clear up. The trouble is matching the correct antibiotic to the infection. This is where the expert system comes in. The expert system can be used by a less-experienced doctor to make a correct diagnosis without having to waste time growing a culture, which could take several days, by which time the patient could be dead.

Prospecting for minerals and oil

Using geological information, an expert system can use the information to determine the most likely places to choose for further exploration. This reduces the cost of mineral or oil exploration because highly paid and very experienced geologists do not need to be paid to interpret the data as the expert system can do this.

For giving tax advice to individuals and companies

Tax is complex and a lot of expertise is needed in order to give the correct advice. This is where expert systems come in. They are able to store a huge amount of data and they can ask the user a series of questions and come up with expert advice on how to pay less tax.

Car engine fault diagnosis

Modern car engines are very complex and when they go wrong it is hard for engineers to know what the problem is. Using an expert system created by the car manufacturer, the engineers can be guided through a series of tests until the exact fault is identified.

The advantages and disadvantages of expert systems

There are advantages and disadvantages of expert systems and these are outlined here.

Advantages of expert systems:

- More expertise than a single expert – many experts can be used to create the data and the rules, so the expert system is a result of not one but many experts.
- Always asks a question that a human expert may forget to ask.
- Fewer mistakes – human experts may forget, but expert systems do not.
- Less time to train – it is easy to copy an expert system, but it takes many years to train a human expert.
- Cheaper – it is cheaper to use an expert system than a human expert because human experts demand high wages.

Disadvantages of expert systems:

- They lack common sense – humans have common sense, so they are able to decide whether an answer is sensible or ridiculous. Human experts can make judgements based on their life experiences, and not just on a limited set of rules, as is the case with computer systems.

- Lack senses – the expert system can only react to information entered by the user. Human experts have many senses that they can use to make judgements. For example a person describing a type of pain might use body language as well, which would not be detected by an expert system.
- The system relies on the rules being correct – mistakes could be made that make the system inaccurate.

▲
Figure 23.1 *Expert systems can use geological data to decide where best to find minerals such as copper, aluminium and gold.*

▲
Figure 23.2 *Expert systems enable doctors to make a more accurate medical diagnosis*

Simulations

When most people think of simulators they think of flight simulators, but there are other types of simulation. Simulations are useful, for example, in experiments that would be too difficult, too dangerous or too costly to carry out.

Examples of simulations include:

- experiments in chemistry
- nuclear physics experiments
- airline training
- queues at petrol filling stations
- traffic light systems
- queues at supermarket checkouts.

When new bridges or buildings are being designed by engineers, they can simulate the construction by using the computer to calculate the stresses at various points and discover the safest construction without having to build it first. Simulations are usually performed to avoid the expense or danger of making mistakes.

Flight simulators

Airlines find it very expensive to tie up aircraft for the training of pilots, so they use simulators instead. In addition, all manner of dangerous flying conditions, some of which the pilot would be very unlikely to experience, can be simulated. A landing simulation with ice on the runway, thick fog and only one of the four engines working would really test the pilot's ability.

Flight simulators like the one shown in Figure 23.3 enable pilots to experience turbulence, snowstorms, thunderstorms, fog and air pockets, as well as landing at different airports throughout the world, without leaving the ground.

If you look at Figure 23.4 you can see that a flight simulator is a windowless capsule that looks like a spacecraft. The hydraulically controlled struts (i.e. the legs) can propel the machine in six directions, simulating the pitch and roll of a real plane. In helicopter simulators a vibrating pilot's seat is used to add reality; and in fighter plane simulators the seat has air pumped into it to simulate the 'g' forces when the pilot performs tight turns.

The scene out of the 'windows' is as realistic as the behaviour of the plane. When a particular airport is chosen the scene looks identical to the surroundings of that particular airport.

▲
Figure 23.3 *Inside a flight simulator*

▲
Figure 23.4 *Flight simulator viewed from the outside*

Virtual reality

Virtual reality is being used to help understand how the human heart works. The heart beats once every second, but when it stops there are four minutes before you die. Researchers need to understand what happens when a heart dies. To do this, the scientists have used a computer program to model the heart when it starts to go wrong. They produce a model of the heart in 3D using a computer. To do this takes a huge amount of computer power. To model just ten seconds of the heart time takes six months of the scientists' time. To understand what happens when the heart fails they need to know what is happening over the full four minutes. Once the 3D model of the heart has been produced, the surgeons can feed in the patient details to the computer and they can then work out the best treatment.

Another use for virtual reality is to give medical students some idea of what it is like to be exhausted due to a serious medical condition. When patients undergo chemotherapy for cancer treatment it makes them extremely tired. To get an idea of what this is like, the students sit in a chair with foot pedals and they wear a head-mounted virtual reality headset. Through the headset they can see the layout of a typical house. If the doorbell goes then they use the pedals to move around the room to answer it. The pedals are made hard to move and this gives the medical student an idea of how hard it is to do simple things. The image in the headset can also be made blurred, to give the student the impression of dizziness. It is hoped that the system will make doctors more aware of the problems that some patients face.

Inputs and outputs in virtual reality systems

Inputs to a virtual reality system include:

- special gloves with sensors to allow you to pick up virtual objects
- a mouse which allows you to point to where you would like to view an object.

Outputs from a virtual reality system include:

- 3D view of the surroundings using a headset or series of computer screens

- movement using electric motors to simulate turns, acceleration, deceleration and so on.
- sound effects from loudspeakers
- simulated smells.

Uses for virtual reality include:

- medical training (e.g. dental procedures, surgical procedures)
- teaching subjects in schools such as history
- training soldiers in battlefield techniques
- virtual tours of properties, hotels and places of interest
- investigating problems in chemical or nuclear plants
- viewing insides and outsides of buildings before they are built.

▲ **Figure 23.5** *The virtual reality headset is like wearing a wrap-around screen*

An example IT task

A predator/prey model

Suppose that we wanted to protect the vegetables in a greenhouse against attack by greenfly or some other pest. We could either use pesticides, or use a 'natural' method by introducing a predator of the greenfly, namely the ladybird. To find out the optimum number of ladybirds to introduce, we have to understand something about how the predator (the ladybird) and the prey (the greenfly) reproduce. With no control over their numbers, the greenfly would multiply at an alarming rate and eventually destroy all of the crop. On the other hand, it is hard to eliminate all the greenfly and, if we did this, the ladybirds would all starve to death. The optimum state is when the population of the greenfly has reached equilibrium, where the numbers of greenfly are constant. When this occurs the ladybirds will have enough to eat and the damage to the crop will be minimal.

When setting up this model you need to decide on the inputs to the system.

What are the inputs?

We can divide the inputs into two:

- inputs for the predators (i.e. the ladybirds)
- inputs for the prey (i.e. the greenfly).

The inputs for the predators will be:

- the number of ladybirds at the start of the year
- the breeding rate (factor by which they increase each month)
- the number of greenfly each ladybird eats each month.

The inputs for the prey will be:

- the number of greenfly at the start of the year
- the breeding rate (factor by which they increase each month).

We now need to design a spreadsheet model. We will use three columns:

Start of month	Number of ladybirds	Number of greenfly

Let us first look at the situation for the first month, January. The situation will be as follows:

Start of month	Number of ladybirds	Number of greenfly
Jan	10	100

At the start of February the following will happen. The number of ladybirds will increase by a factor of 1.5, so there will now be 15 of them. The greenfly will breed, increasing their population by a factor of 4, making their number 400. However, during January some of them will be eaten. If we assume that the 10 ladybirds at the start eat 30 greenfly in the month, then 300 greenfly would be eaten, making a total of 100. So at the start of February, we will have 15 ladybirds and 100 greenfly, as shown in the table:

Start of month	Number of ladybirds	Number of greenfly
Jan	10	100
Feb	15	100

Problems with the model

The above model is too simple. It does not take account of the following areas.

1 The breeding rates of the ladybirds and the greenfly will not stay the same throughout the year. The rates will probably increase in the warmer months. We really need to alter the breeding rates for the summer months and make them different from the winter months.

2 If there is not enough food for the ladybirds to eat, they will die.

3 We also need to incorporate a death rate for the ladybirds into our model. To make it simpler, you could assume that the greenfly will remain alive provided that they do not get eaten by the ladybirds.

Questions

1 Produce a revised model taking the above into account.

2 You have been asked to extend this model for the whole of the 12 months. Do this using a spreadsheet and make sure that you link the cells using formulae.

Things to do

1 Write down one reason why computerised simulation is better than using a manual simulation for each of the following situations:
(a) a simulation to find out how many checkouts will be needed at a new supermarket
(b) an experiment to find out the best temperature for carrying out a chemical process.

2 You can use spreadsheet software to make a computer model.
(a) Give an example of an investigation for which you would use a spreadsheet package to make a computer model.
(b) Describe how you would set up the model on the spreadsheet.
(c) Explain why you would use the computer model instead of creating the real thing.

3 (a) Give one advantage of using a computer model to study the relationship between hunting animals and their prey.
(b) Give two reasons why your teacher may prefer to use a simulation rather than a school trip to an African jungle.
(c) What software package would you use to display the data collected?

4 Flight simulators are used to train airline pilots.
(a) Describe what a flight simulator is.
(b) What advantages are there in using such a flight simulator rather than using a real aircraft?

5 A local council wants to know if it should redesign a road junction. It has three options – leave it as it is, put in a set of traffic lights or construct a roundabout.
(a) Explain how a computer model could be useful to the council.
(b) What data would be required for the model?
(c) For each item of data above, describe how the council could collect the data.
(d) What other variables might be used in the model?

1 A certain type of bacterium increases its numbers at a rate of 20 per cent per hour. If there are 100 bacteria at the start of the day, produce a model showing how the population will have grown over each hour in the day.

2 This task is suitable only for students who are very good at maths.

The iterative formula for finding the cube root of a number n is given by

$$a_{n+1} = 1/3 \ (2a_n + N/an^2)$$

Produce a spreadsheet where you can put in a number n, and the computer simulates the iterative process and comes up with the answer correct to five decimal places. Test your model using the following numbers: 27, 50, 1480 and 3600.

Some ideas for models and simulations

1 Explain the effect of pollution on a river system.

2 Collect data from a science experiment and then use the data from the results to find the relationship between the variables.

3 Look at the heat supply and the heat loss from a house.

IT Tasks

Task 1

The depreciation of cars

You have been asked by a car dealer to produce a model of the depreciation of cars. You will need to consider the following when building or refining your model.

- Is the depreciation the same for each year or do cars depreciate more in the early years?

- Do some cars depreciate more than others? How can this be built into the model?

You could try comparing the values in your model with values obtained from a car price guide which you can obtain from any newsagent.

You could produce a series of graphs showing how the price varies over a number of years.

Finally, produce a report on your model/simulation.

Task 2

Dangerous situations

Simulations are often performed using computers where the real situation would be too costly or dangerous to perform any other way. Investigate such situations and produce a brief report outlining your findings.

Programs, Representation of Algorithms and Documentation

What is a computer program?

A computer program is a set of instructions written in a computer language that the computer can understand and which can solve a particular problem.

The main requirements of a programming language

There are many different types of programming language. These requirements are common to all programming languages:

- They must allow the manipulation of data of various types (e.g. letters, numbers, calculations) and structures.
- They must control the input and output.
- They must provide selection, repetition and subprogram communication.

Top-down design

Top-down design provides a method of producing computer programs or systems. These are the main features of top-down design:

- The program is broken down into parts or modules.
- The parts or modules are broken down into more parts or modules.
- Soon each part or module is easy to produce because it contains enough detail.

Breaking problems into smaller parts makes it clear what needs to be done. At each stage of refinement the problem becomes less complex and easier to work out.

Top-down design has a number of advantages:

- It is easier to update and understand.
- It is easier to remove bugs in programs (i.e. easier to debug).
- It allows several programmers to work on a task as the task is broken down into several modules.

- It may be possible to reuse parts of the solution.

Pseudocode

Pseudocode is an outline of a program, written as a series of instructions using simple English sentences. These English sentences can easily be changed by a programmer into programming statements.

There are no real formatting or syntax rules with pseudocode, so it is quick and easy to write, as you will see in the following example.

Input and output

Read means that the system will take some values which it will use as the input for the processing to produce the output. Read is used with variable names like this:

Read Name (this means that a name is entered (Name is used as the variable))
Read Mark (a mark is entered and assigned the variable Mark)

Once data have been processed it is necessary to display the results, or the output as it is called. Print used with a variable name is used to produce the output. Here are some examples:

Print Total (this outputs the value of the variable called Total)
Print Name (this outputs the variable called Name)

Pseudocode structures

In order to create pseudocode to help solve problems it is necessary to learn about the structures that the pseudocode can have.

Sequence structure

In the sequence structure the processing steps are carried out one after the other.

The instructions are carried out in sequence unless a selection or loop is encountered.

Selection structure

The selection structure is also known as the decision structure. It is used when a decision or comparison has to be made. It shows a condition from which the decision is based and a set of actions to be taken if the condition is true, and a set of actions to be taken if the decision is false.

For...to...next loops

For...to...next loops are used when you want to perform the sequence of instructions in the loop a set number of times. This type of loop is sometimes called a counting loop because it counts how many times the instructions inside the loop have been carried out.

Here is an example of a For...to...next loop:

```
Total = 0
For N = 1 to 10
    Read number
    Total = Total + number
Next N
Print Total
```

The above pseudocode contains a sequence of instructions inside the loop (i.e. the steps between the For...to...Next instructions). The steps inside the loop allow a user to input a number and then it adds this number to the total, which starts off at zero. This is done a total of 10 times, which means that 10 numbers are added up as the user enters them.

When the loop has been repeated 10 times it moves onto the step outside the loop, which results in the final total of all 10 numbers being output.

Example of a problem solved by a For...to...next loop

A routine is required where you input 50 numbers and the number of negative numbers are counted and then the result is output.

Here is an example of pseudocode that will do this:

```
negnumber = 0
For N = 1 to 50
    Input number
    If number < 0 then negnumber =
    negnumber + 1
Next N
Output negnumber
```

If...then...else...endif

The following pseudocode shows the If...then...else...endif selection structure.

```
If student is full_time Then
    add 1 to full_time_count
Else
    add 1 to part_time_count
EndIf
```

Testing a condition

In selection or conditional statements comparisons can be tested using the following:

```
= (Equals)
> (Greater than)
< (Less than)
>= (Greater than or equal to)
<= (Less than or equal to)
<> (Is not equal to)
```

Here is a section of pseudocode making use of If...then...else where a condition is tested:

```
<space>
If age >= 17
    Display 'You can drive a car'
Else
    Display 'You are too young to drive a
    car'
Endif
```

Repeat...until

The sequence of instructions inside the loop is always performed at least once. This is because the test is performed after the sequence of instructions has been carried out. Each time the instructions inside the loop are performed, the condition is tested and if the condition is false the loop repeats. If the condition is true, the loop ends.

Here is a section of pseudocode that adds up a series of numbers until the total exceeds 100.

```
Total = 0
Repeat
Read number
Total = Total + number
Until Total >= 100
Print Total
```

Case of...otherwise...endcase

Case of... is used when there are multiple options from which to choose. Here is an example section of pseudocode that uses Case of...

```
Case grade of
    0 to 20 Display 'Grade E'
    21 to 35 Display 'Grade D'
    36 to 45 Display 'Grade C'
    46 to 60 Display 'Grade B'
    60+ Display 'Grade A'
Endcase
```

While...do...endwhile

This structure is used when you do not know how many times the steps inside a loop need to be performed. At the start of the loop there is a condition that is tested and this is used to either end the loop or continue carrying out the instructions inside the loop.

```
Do While Total < 100
    Read item_name
    Display item_name
    Total = Total + 1
EndDo
```

In this section of pseudocode, the set of instructions in the loop (i.e. between the Do While and EndDo) are repeated until the total is 100.

Example showing how the pseudocode is created for a problem

The cost of making an item depends on how many parts are in the item.

A company makes three different items and the cost of making these items is shown in the following calculations:

Item A: Item cost = parts cost × 2.5
Item B: Item cost = parts cost × 3.5
Item C: Item cost = parts cost × 4.5
The company makes 500 items per day.

Write an algorithm using pseudocode that will:

- input the item type and the parts cost of each item
- output the item cost
- calculate the mean item cost per day if 500 items are made each day.

A suitable algorithm that will do the above is shown here:

```
Total cost = 0
For N = 1 to 500
    Input item_type, parts_cost
        If item_type = A then item_cost =
        parts_cost × 2.5
        If item_type = B then item_cost =
        parts_cost × 3.5
        If item_type = C then item_cost =
        parts_cost × 4.5
        Else print error
    total_cost = total_cost + item_cost
    Print item_cost
Next N
average_cost = total_cost/500
Print average_cost
```

Here are the main points of this algorithm:

- If you are keeping a running total you should set the total to zero outside the loop at the start.
- The items steps inside the For...Next loop are repeated 500 times.
- The system needs a user to input the item_type (i.e. A, B or C) and on the basis of what is typed it will be multiplied by 2.5, 3.5 or 4.5.
- Notice the important step which will print that an error has occurred if the item_type entered is not A, B or C.
- A running total is then created which adds up the item costs each time the algorithm goes around the loop.
- Once the algorithm has allowed the entry of 500 items, the loop is exited and the algorithm will then use the total_cost, which will now be the total cost of all the items, to calculate the mean, which is then printed.

Flowcharts

Flowcharts provide another way of showing an algorithm visually rather than by using pseudocode.

Figure 24.1 shows how either a digital or analogue temperature sensor can be used to control the temperature inside a room.

Example

Produce a flowchart that will display the number of integers entered using the keyboard and will also add up all the numbers entered and display the final total. The flowchart should end when the number 0 is entered (Figure 24.2).

Answer

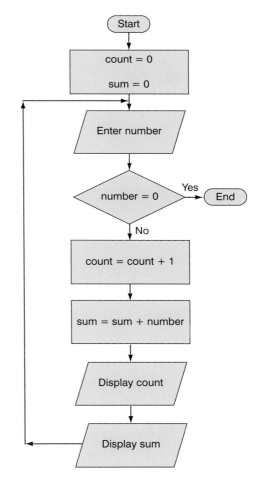

▲
Figure 24.2 *Flowchart 2*

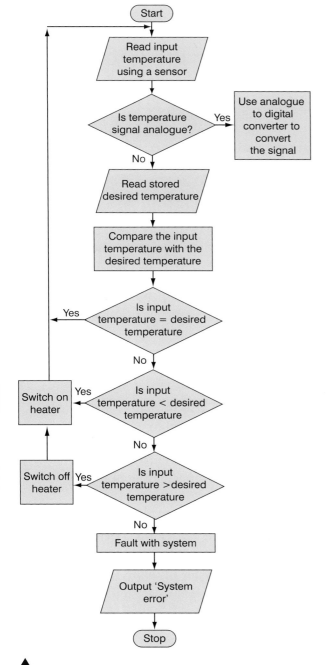

▲
Figure 24.1 *Flowchart 1*

Dry runs

Once you have drawn a flowchart or produced pseudocode you need to check it for errors and this is best done using a dry run. A dry run is a check to make sure that the logic is correct and no steps have been left out.

Test data are used as input for the pseudocode or flowchart. The steps are obeyed in turn and the values of the variables are recorded in a table as they change. The output is also recorded in the table, which is called a trace table.

Trace tables

Trace tables are used to test algorithms, to make sure that there are no errors in the logic of the algorithm. The results are displayed in a table that includes rows and columns. The columns show each variable and the rows show the numbers put into the algorithm.

Example of a dry run

Look very carefully at Figure 24.3.

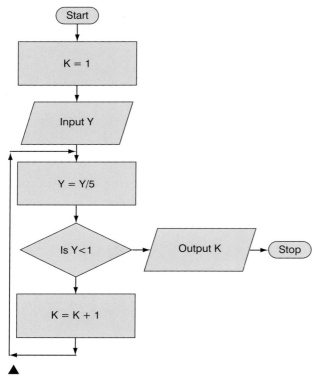

▲
Figure 24.3 *Flowchart 3*

To perform the dry run and complete the trace table, an input value is needed for the variable Y. Here the value 125 is to be used as the input value.

To keep track of the changes made we record the values as they change, in a table like the one in Figure 24.4.

Figure 24.4
▼

K	Y
1	125
2	25
3	5
4	1
5	0.2 (i.e. 1/5)

The output from this flowchart is 4.

Test data for use with algorithms

Testing strategies

Algorithms need to be thoroughly tested to make sure they work correctly. They are tested with real/live data that are typical of the data that could be entered by a user.

Testing strategies often make use of a test plan. A test plan is a detailed list of the tests that are to be conducted on the system when it has been developed to check that it is working properly. These test plans should be comprehensive. A good way of making sure that they are comprehensive is to make sure that:

- tests are numbered
- each test has clearly specified date
- the reason for the test is stated
- the expected result is stated.

Space should be left for:

- the actual result and/or comment on the result
- a page number reference to where the hard-copy evidence can be found.

Testing using normal, abnormal (unacceptable) and extreme data

Testing should always be performed with the following three types of data:

- Normal data – data that should pass the validation checks.
- Abnormal data – data that are unacceptable and that should be rejected by the validation check. If data are

rejected then an error message will need to be displayed explaining why they are being rejected.

- Extreme data – data on the borderline of what the system will accept. For example, if a range check specifies that a number from one to five is entered (including one and five) then extreme data used would be the numbers one and five.

Here is a test plan to test a spreadsheet for analysing the marks in an examination. A mark is input next to each candidate's name. The mark is a percentage and can be in the range 0 per cent to 100 per cent. In this exam, half marks are possible.

The 'Actual result' column would be filled in when the test mark was entered. If the expected result and the actual results are all the same then the validation checks are doing their job. If the two do not agree, then the validation checks will need to be modified and retested.

Figure 24.5
▼

Test no.	Test mark entered	Purpose of test	Expected result	Actual result
1	45.5	Test typical data	Accept	
2	100	Test extreme data	Accept	
3	0	Test extreme data	Accept	
4	123	Test abnormal data	Reject and error message	
5	−3	Test abnormal data	Reject and error message	
6	45D	Test abnormal data	Reject and error message	

Things to do

1 A farmer has a total of 100 animals on his farm. Each animal has a tag with a unique code attached to the animal's ear. The code consists of four numbers, with the first number in the code used to identify the type of animal according to the following:

1 = sheep

2 = goat

3 = cow

4 = camel

For example, for the code 1642, the 1 identifies that the animal is a sheep and the code 3782 identifies that the animal is a cow.

Write an algorithm using pseudocode or otherwise, that:

- inputs the codes for all 100 animals

- validates the input code

- calculates how many of each animal there is on the farm

- outputs the four totals of each animal.

2 Study Figure 24.6.

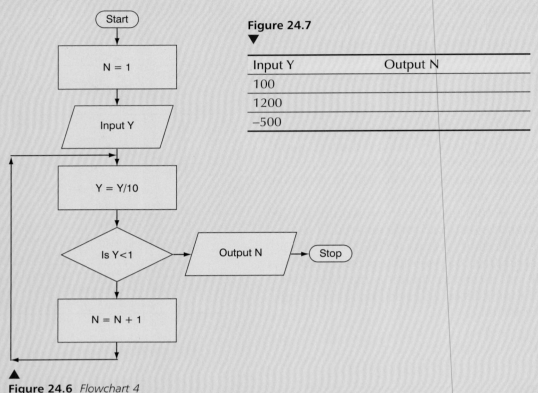

Figure 24.7
▼

Input Y	Output N
100	
1200	
−500	

▲
Figure 24.6 *Flowchart 4*

Complete the table (Figure 24.7) by entering the outputs from the flowchart for the three inputs shown.

3 Produce a flowchart that will display the number of integers entered at the keyboard and their sum. The flowchart should end when the number 0 is entered.

4 Produce a flowchart for the following:

LG Plastics wants you to produce a flowchart that will allow employees to enter their salary, status (part-time or full-time) and hours worked. If employees are part-time and have worked for 40 hours they are given a bonus equal to 10 per cent of their salary and are promoted to full-time. The flowchart should output the bonus and the status.

5 Write pseudocode that will read and find the average of three numbers entered using the keyboard.

6 Write the pseudocode that reads a student's mark and then outputs the appropriate grade according to the data in Figure 24.8.

Figure 24.8
▼

Mark	Grade
85–100	A*
75–84	A
65–74	B
60–64	C
50–59	D
0–49	E

Computer Applications

CCTV cameras

Electronic security cameras have helped cut down violent crime and robberies in many of our city centres. Sometimes these cameras are visible and act as a deterrent, whereas others are hidden and are used during police surveillance. Although most people feel safer in city centres with the use of these cameras, some people feel that they are an infringement of privacy. Cameras are also used for traffic control at busy junctions and on motorways.

▲
Figure 25.1 *A CCTV camera*

▲
Figure 25.2 *The police often use hidden cameras*

Information technology in the supermarket

Tesco is the largest food retailer in the UK. It used to have many small shops on every high street, but the company has been concentrating on the development of huge new units called superstores. Each superstore stocks over 14,000 food lines and has a sales area of over 2,300 square metres.

The laser scanning system (barcode reading system)

Most large stores now use barcode readers, which are commonly called laser scanners, to input product details into the computer system. The objectives of the scanning system are to improve the service to customers and to increase company productivity and profits. Figure 25.3 shows the scanning system used to scan in a barcode.

The scanning system uses a laser beam to read the barcode on the goods. The bars contain the same information as the numeric code at the bottom of the barcode without the likely inaccuracies of typing the number in. As the barcode is passed across the scanner this number is read and the price and description of the goods are obtained from the computer, the sale registered and an itemised receipt produced.

▲ **Figure 25.3** *Using a barcode reader at a point of sale terminal*

Benefits of the system to the customers

There are numerous benefits to customers, including the following.

1 With the old system, prices were entered into the cash register manually. With the scanning system this is done automatically, which eliminates typing errors, so accurate pricing is assured.
2 The scanning till is estimated to be 15 per cent more efficient, so customers will spend less time waiting to be served.
3 Produce such as loose tomatoes are weighed at the checkout, so customers no longer have to queue twice (once at the pricing point and again at the checkout).
4 Customers using a debit card can withdraw cash from any checkout.

5 More promotions may be offered, such as 'buy two and get one free' (multisaver).
6 An itemised receipt is produced. This receipt includes detailed information about what has been bought.

Benefits of the system to the company

Some benefits are easily quantified, but others are more difficult.

1 Checkout accuracy is improved. There are no longer any operator errors and fraud is limited, since in the past it was possible to key in a lower price and pocket the money.
2 Throughput is faster and more efficient. There is, on average, a 15 per cent saving in time to register the goods in a shopping trolley.
3 Customer service can be improved. New services, such as loyalty cards and multisavers, ensure customer loyalty.
4 Productivity is increased. There is no need to price each individual article, as in the past. Prices are included on the edges of the shelves next to the articles. Weighing and pricing at the checkouts eliminates the need for separate pricing points.
5 Sales information from the checkout is used to create the orders for stock replacement.
6 Stock levels can be reduced. More efficient stock control means less money is tied up in stock and there is less likelihood of running out of certain items on the sales floor.
7 Wastage is also reduced. Perishable goods such as fresh meat and salads can be ordered accurately using the sales information obtained from the checkout.
8 Promotional analysis and sales analysis are improved. Scanning data can be used to assess the effectiveness of special promotions and can provide important information about the sales of certain goods.

The barcoding system

Figure 25.4 shows a barcode from a tin of baked beans. The number at the bottom is called the European Article Number (EAN); a number is allocated to all product

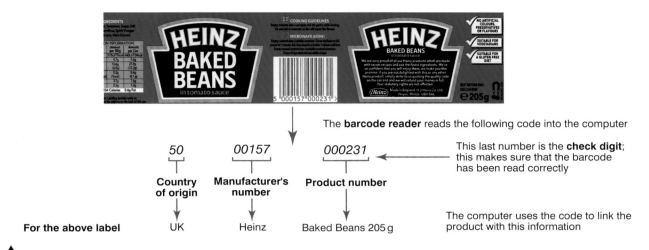

Figure 25.4 *How a computer uses a barcode*

manufacturers by the Article Number Association. The system works as follows:

- the first two digits represent the country where the goods are produced
- the next five digits identify the manufacturer of the goods
- the following five numbers identify the product
- the final number is a check digit and is used to check that the other 12 numbers have been entered correctly.

EFTPOS and the use of debit cards

EFTPOS stands for electronic funds transfer at point of sale and is the method used by many stores to transfer money from customers' credit card companies or debit cards directly to the store's bank account. A debit card is rather like a cheque, since the money comes straight out of the bank account. However, there is no limit to the amount you can spend using one of these cards, provided that you have the money in your account. This is in contrast to cheques, where there is a limit to the value of the cheque that is covered by the guarantee card.

Using checkout information for planning bakery production

Sales information from checkouts is used by in-store bakeries to plan the production for the same day for the next week. This reduces wastage and means stores are less likely to run out of bread.

Sales-based ordering

Sales-based ordering is the automatic reordering of goods from the warehouse using the sales information from the checkouts. If, for example, 200 tins of baked beans are sold from a certain store in one day, then 200 tins will automatically be reordered and delivered to the store the following day from one of the distribution centres.

The large articulated vehicles that deliver goods to supermarkets are specially constructed: they have compartments which can be kept at different temperatures, so, for instance, chilled food, frozen food and other types of food which do not need cooling may be carried in the same vehicle.

Stock control

All ordering is performed by computer. There are fast electronic communication lines between the shops, the distribution centres and the head office. There are also direct links to the major suppliers, which means that orders can go straight through to production lines. One advantage of this is that stock arrives just in time, before sale, so it is always fresh. Another advantage of this system is that money does not need to be tied up in stock and can be used for more productive purposes.

Electronic data interchange (EDI)

Electronic data interchange is a method of speeding up the transfer of orders to suppliers. Using EDI eliminates the need for paperwork, since the ordering is done by data being transferred between the supplier's computer and the store's computer. This system is less expensive and faster than sending the orders by phone, post or fax, and cuts out errors, such as lost or wrongly printed orders. Stores can send information to suppliers regarding sales forecasts and information about stock levels so that they may plan their production appropriately.

Once an electronic order has been placed, the electronic invoice is generated automatically by the supplier's computer. This is sent back and checked by the store computer before payment is made.

Designing store layouts using CAD

It is no longer necessary to use drawing boards for planning new stores and redesigning existing ones. Instead, computer-aided design (CAD) is used and this has reduced the time taken to plan new stores. A databank holds designs and plans from many stores and these may be adapted for new stores. CAD is also able to show three-dimensional views of the stores; colours, lighting and different finishes of material can be altered simply with a mouse.

When a new store is to be placed in a town high street, photographs of the existing shops in the street can be used in conjunction with CAD to see what the street will look like with the storefront in place.

CAD is also used to design warehouse layouts, the roads and the surrounding areas around the distribution centres. This is important since the company needs to make sure that there is ample room for the large articulated vehicles to turn round.

Warehouse systems

Computers are used in the warehouse to monitor complex stock control procedures and make the best use of space, time and labour. Like all areas of retailing, better operating methods need to be found to ensure the store's continued success. As with all the other systems, paperwork has been eliminated wherever possible, so the thick binders containing stock items are replaced by computer terminals. In fact, these terminals can be found mounted on forklift trucks; they give the operators information regarding the movement of the pallets so that they may be moved quickly and efficiently. If some stock goes out of the warehouse then a slot is available for the new stock arriving and notification of this is obtained from the terminal. Efficient use of the available space means that the trucks have to travel shorter distances and the whole process is therefore faster.

The computer system also monitors where each forklift truck is situated in the warehouse so that a particular job can be given to the truck best able to complete it in the least amount of time.

Electronic mail

With conventional methods of communication there are many problems, such as lost post, unanswered telephones, engaged fax machines, people not at their desks. To try to contact someone urgently during office hours can be more difficult than you think. Electronic mail eliminates many of these problems.

A commonly used system uses a series of standard forms, so memos, letters, reports and so on all have a set format. Advantages to the store of using electronic mail include:

1 The recipient does not need to be there when the message is sent; he or she can receive mail at any terminal connected to the system. Compare this with a telephone call, where someone needs to be available to answer the call.
2 People can be sure that the messages are received.

3 It is possible to send mail to a department or a group of people. Anyone in the company can send mail to a whole department without knowing anyone in the department by name.

4 The electronic mail system is used as a company information and notice board. Members of staff can find out about the latest job vacancies and appointments, and look at the latest share price.

5 Electronic mail can be sent to the major suppliers, thus speeding up orders and so on.

IT and the music industry

MIDI (musical instrument digital interface)

A musical instrument digital interface (MIDI) allows communication between a musical instrument and a computer. This means that when a musician plays an instrument, MIDI interface will convert the analogue signal from the instrument into a digital format that the computer can store and edit. It is also possible for the computer to issue signals back to an instrument such as a keyboard so that it can play the music back.

▲ **Figure 25.5** *Producing music has been made much easier with the use of ICT systems*

Creating music

ICT can help musicians create their own music by the use of these technologies.

Sequencers (multitrack recording studios)

Sequencers are hardware or software used to create and manage electronic music, and include the following devices:

- Drum machines – musical instruments that simulate the sound of a drum and sometimes other percussion instruments. Drum machines are sequencers because they create and manage the drum beats.
- Music workstations – electronic equipment that allows a musician to create electronic music. Music workstations consist of the usual computer, but with a large screen with all the controls, such as knobs, sliders, buttons and sampling information. Some music workstations make use of touch screens.

Notators (music composition software)

A notator is software that allows you to compose your own music. Notes can be entered into the computer in a variety of ways, including:

- a keyboard
- a MIDI system
- scanning a piece of music on paper using a scanner.

When the notes have been entered, the musician can experiment by changing notes, loudness, tempo and so on. The main advantage is that the notator allows the musician to experiment and to find the combination of notes that sounds best. The notator can also be used to create the music for individual musical instruments which can then be played together to produce the final piece of music.

Sound wave editors

Sound wave editors are software that allows the editing of sound waves. Using the software, sound waves can:

- be edited

- be cut, copied and pasted
- have effects like echo, amplification and noise reduction applied.

▲ **Figure 25.6** *A modern recording studio is full of technology*

IT and the TV/video industry

Computer-generated graphics

Computer-generated graphics are images designed by graphic artists that are used for logos, commercials and news inserts during television or video transmissions. The artists use systems similar to a painting package produced for microcomputers. Some of the more sophisticated graphics systems allow artists to produce three-dimensional images.

Special effects

Sometimes when watching the television you see images manipulated in some way to produce special effects. These may be produced with digital video signals, since each pixel (dot of light) on the screen can be moved individually. Using a computer with special software it is possible to change the shape of a picture to, say, a circle or hexagon. You can also zoom into the image, rotate it and even manipulate several different images on the screen at the same time.

Animation

In the past, to produce animation, it was necessary to draw a series of images, each one differing slightly as the movement proceeds. A picture was taken of each diagram (frame) and then the series of frames played back. This process is tediously slow and requires whole teams of artists, so the final piece of animation or cartoon is very expensive.

Individual frames can be created using graphics software. A start frame and an end frame are produced. The software then produces the animation between these two frames automatically. The computer has to be told about the rate at which the intermediate images are to be produced. Because the number of frames is often quite large, powerful computers with large hard disk capacities are used for this type of work.

Information technology and medicine

All hospitals make use of information technology and, because of the diverse nature of the work that hospitals do, the computer has many quite different uses.

Organ transplants

Computers are very good for looking at and comparing lists. When a person dies and

▲ **Figure 25.7**

their organs are donated, the computer can be used to match and identify a patient to receive them. This needs to be done extremely quickly and this is why computers are essential (Figure 25.7).

Computers are used to diagnose many illnesses. Often the information is fed directly into the computer from machines attached to the patient, such as electrocardiographs, which measure the heartbeat, and body scanners.

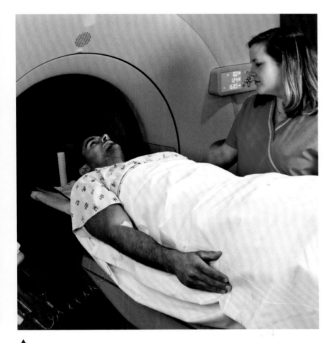

▲ **Figure 25.8** *Using a body scanner with computer diagnosis*

Computers can be used to locate tumours at an early stage when they cannot be easily and surely detected by other means. Body scanners send rays into the body (Figure 25.8) and these are picked up by a detector. Signals from the detector are analysed by the computer and converted to a digital form which can then be displayed as a picture on a television screen (Figure 25.9). On screen the tumour appears as a dark patch.

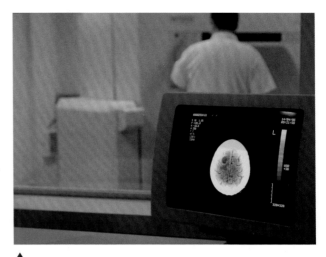

▲ **Figure 25.9** *Information from the body scanner is used, here, to build up a picture of the human brain in sections. Any tumours can thus be precisely located*

Monitoring hospital patients (sensors: analogue and digital)

There are many measurements that need to be recorded for a hospital patient. In order to free up time from medical staff, this routine recording of data can be performed automatically using sensors.

Sensors are devices that can be used to detect physical, chemical and biological signals and provide a method of measuring and recording them using processors or computers.

There are two different types of sensor:

- Analogue sensors are used to measure an analogue quantity, which is a quantity that can have an almost infinite set of values, such as temperature, pressure.
- Digital sensors can detect digital quantities. For example, a switch can only have two positions (on and off, or 0 and 1) and so can be represented as a digital quantity.

If an analogue sensor is connected to a computer, then the signal it produces will need to be converted into a digital signal before it can be processed or stored by the computer. The reason for this is that computers are nearly always only capable of processing and storing digital signals.

Sensors are used in medicine to measure the following:

- temperature
- blood pressure
- central venous pressure (to determine the amount of blood returning to the heart and the capacity of the heart to pump blood into the arteries)
- pulse
- blood gases (e.g. concentration of dissolved oxygen)
- blood sugar
- brain activity
- electrical activity of the heart (ECG, or electrocardiogram)
- intracranial pressure (pressure inside the skull)
- breakdown of gases from a patient's breath
- respiratory rate.

Sensors can be used to monitor patients but as well as the data being used by a computer to assess whether the condition of the patient is worsening and to alert the medical staff, the data can also be used to control medical equipment that takes over the function of some of the organs of the patient.

Life support systems use the data from sensors to control medical equipment that assists or replaces important bodily functions

and so enables a patient to live who otherwise might not survive.

Data from sensors can be used to control:

- respiration – a ventilator is a machine that pumps air in and out of the patient's lungs
- excretion
- heart function – machines can take over some of the functions of the heart
- kidney function – dialysis machines are used when kidneys fail to function correctly
- intravenous drips containing fluids.

Advantages of using sensors for patient monitoring

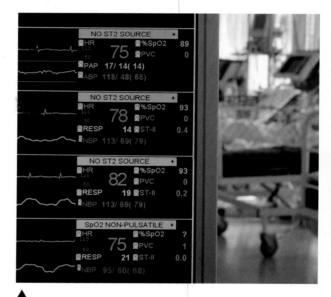

▲ **Figure 25.11** *Patient monitoring in an intensive care unit*

There are many advantages in using sensors and ICT systems for patient monitoring, including:

- Measurements are never forgotten to be taken as they are taken automatically.
- Real-time monitoring – patient's vital readings are taken in real time which is much better than taking readings every so often by staff. If any measurements fall outside the acceptable range, an alarm sounds to alert medical staff.
- It frees up medical staff from taking routine measurements, allowing them to focus on administration of drugs and so on.

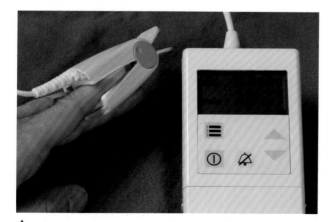

▲ **Figure 25.10** *This sensor is being used to measure the amount of dissolved oxygen in a patient's blood*

- Reduces costs – one member of staff can be responsible for more patients in intensive care units.
- Trends in the patient's condition can be detected – the side-by-side graphs on the screen make it easy for doctors to spot trends in the patient's condition.
- Readings are more accurate – sensors produce more accurate readings than people, who can make mistakes when taking readings.

Keeping patients' records

Computers can be used to provide a complete, accurate, up-to-date and readily available source of information about patients' health. Records of patients are usually kept for the duration of their lives, so in the past a large amount of space was taken up by paperwork. There were also problems in locating a particular patient's file – especially if, say, the patient moved about the country a great deal.

Most hospitals now store patients' records on magnetic tapes or disks. The information can be found immediately by the computer. There are terminals at certain places in the hospital where doctors or nurses can find details of a particular patient very quickly.

Inpatients' records are probably best kept on magnetic disk. This method allows quicker access because it is a random access storage medium. These records will be needed much more often than the outpatient records. Outpatient records contain a large quantity of information that may only be used, say, a couple of times in a patient's lifetime. So these records can be stored on magnetic tape which has a slower access time.

New data can be added to the patient's records by keying this into the computer via a terminal. Thus the patient's record can be kept up-to-date with the latest information about his or her condition or circumstances. Doctors and nurses used to spend about 30 per cent of their time processing information in files, but now this has been vastly reduced because of the introduction of computers.

One problem with using a computer in this way is that very confidential information is kept about the patient. Obviously, many patients would not like this information to be seen by just anyone. One way round this problem is to introduce a code or password, which the user needs to type into the computer before he or she can gain access to the patients' files. Another way, used in some of the extremely complicated systems, is to allow the terminals only a certain amount of necessary information for different users. So, a nurse could obtain some information, and a doctor would be able to get further details.

Information technology and banking

Banks were one of the first business organisations to use computers and this experience has meant that they have always been at the forefront of any new technology. Banks make use of a variety of systems and many of these have already been encountered. If you need any information on the following aspects of banking, then you should refer to the index. To help you locate this information, here is a list of topics that are covered elsewhere in the book.

MICR (magnetic ink character recognition)
EFTPOS (electronic funds transfer at point of sale)
EDI (electronic data interchange)
Credit card use
EFT (electronic fund transfer)
Credit card fraud
Smart cards

Some aspects of banking which have not been covered elsewhere are detailed below.

Cheque clearing

Suppose Jane, who lives in the UK, wants to buy a portable colour television from Comet Electrics and pay by cheque. Jane banks with Lloyds and Comet Electrics banks with Barclays. Figure 25.12 shows what happens to the cheque, from when it is given to Comet Electrics to when the money is subtracted (debited) from Jane's account and added (credited) to Comet Electrics' account. This process is called **cheque clearing** and,

1   Jane writes out a cheque for £240 made payable to Comet Electrics.

2   Comet Electrics pay the cheque into their Barclays branch.

3   Barclays Bank types in the amount of the cheque in magnetic ink characters so that it can be read at the clearing house using MICR.

4   All cheques, including this one, are sent to a bank in London called a clearing house. Here, all the cheques are sorted into bank sorting code numbers.

▲
Figure 25.12 The process of cheque clearing

5   The details of all the transactions (items of business) are sent on magnetic disk to the Bank of England from the clearing house. The Bank of England transfers the £240 from Lloyds Bank to Barclays Bank.

6   The cheque is sent from the clearing house to Jane's branch of Lloyds Bank, identified by a sorting code number, where the amount is deducted from her account.

7   Barclays Bank receives notification that the cheque has been cleared and credits Comet Electrics' account with £240.

8   The whole process of cheque clearing takes a minimum of three days.

because of the large number of cheques cleared each day, computers are used for nearly all of the process. As more people set up systems to take money automatically from their account for the payment of bills, and the purchase of goods is performed using credit/debit cards, the use of cheques will eventually be phased out.

Bankers' Automated Clearing Services (BACS)

Bankers' Automated Clearing Services Ltd was set up in the UK by the larger banks to deal with standing orders and direct debit payments. It is situated in Edgware, north-west of London.

As well as processing transactions that take place in this country, BACS also houses the Swift computer for the UK which deals with international payments.

The BACS service is used to pay two-thirds of all monthly salaries directly into employees' accounts. It is also used to pay regular bills and payments such as pensions, council tax, mortgages and loan repayments.

The BACS computers keep a diary of all the payments to be made. These payments are made and are transferred between the banks on magnetic tape. The fact that not many people have heard of BACS shows the system's reliability and success.

ATM (automated teller machines)

ATMs are the 'hole in the wall' cash dispensers which many people use when the bank is not open or when they do not want to queue inside.

Here are some of the things you can do using an ATM:

- get cash out
- find out the balance in your account
- change your PIN (personal identification number)
- make deposits (i.e. put cash, cheques or both into your account)
- obtain a mini statement listing your recent transactions (i.e. money in and out of your account).

How the system works

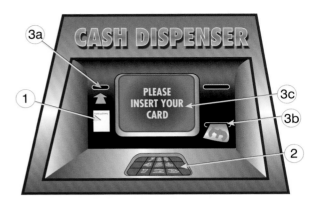

1 The customer is given step-by-step instructions on how to operate the cash-dispensing machine.
2 The keyboard (input device). The customer types information in here, including the customer's secret number (PIN).
3 a This is where the customer inserts the plastic card. The card must be inserted the right way round.
  b From here, the amount of money the customer has keyed in is released.
  c This is the VDU screen where messages appear, such as 'Enter personal number'. The screen gives instructions to the customer.

▲
Figure 25.13 *Using an ATM*

Benefits to the banks of using ATMs

There are some benefits to the banks from the use of ATMs, including:

- Staff are freed from performing routine transactions so that more profitable sales-orientated work can be done.
- Fewer staff are needed since the computer does much of the routine work.
- A 24-hour-a-day service is provided to satisfy their customers' demands.
- The system makes it impossible for a customer to withdraw funds from their account unless they have the money in their account.

Benefits to the customer of using ATMs

- Some customers prefer the anonymous nature of the machine since it cannot think you have stolen the cheque book or that you are spending too much.
- It is possible to use the service 24 hours per day – ideal for those people who work irregular hours.

- It is possible to park near the dispenser in the evening, so getting cash is a lot quicker.
- There are fewer queues since the transactions performed by the ATM are a lot faster.

Traffic control systems

Computerised traffic control systems are a feature of all large towns and cities. Their purpose is to keep the traffic moving, particularly during the morning and evening rush hours.

The main aims of a traffic control system are:

- to improve traffic flow
- to reduce accidents caused by driver frustration (e.g. changing lanes frequently)
- to make sure that delays in a journey are kept to a minimum
- to reduce the pollution caused by the exhaust fumes from stationary or slow-moving traffic
- to reduce the amount of fuel used by drivers (cars use fuel inefficiently when crawling along).

Traffic lights need to be set to a sequence that can be varied throughout the day. During the morning rush hour the lights can be set on green longer for those main routes into the town and in the evening the lights are on green longer for the routes out of town.

One system called SCOOT does not work with a set sequence for the lights. Instead the traffic lights are sequenced to try to keep the number of lights on red to a minimum. Sensors in the roads are used to detect the frequency of the vehicles on either side of a junction and these are used as the inputs to the computer system. The data from these sensors are sent to the computer using either wire-based or fibre-optic cables. The computer then analyses the data and sends signals back to the lights that amend the traffic signal timings and the offset between the sets of lights.

In an emergency the system is able to give emergency vehicles an uninterrupted path through a system of linked traffic lights.

It does this by giving a green signal to the emergency vehicle as it reaches each set of lights along the route.

Car park management systems

Car park management systems are computer-controlled systems that direct vehicles round town centres to car parks with available space. The special signs tell motorists how many spaces are available in each car park by working out how many vehicles have arrived and how many have left. These signs, which operate in real time, reduce congestion by getting the cars into the nearest available car park without them having to drive around from one car park to another.

Vehicle speeding systems and red light cameras

Vehicle speeding systems consist of sensors to detect the vehicle speed and a camera that takes a picture of the speeding vehicle with the speed superimposed on the photograph. Using the registration number, the Police National Computer (PNC) is used to obtain the name and address of the registered keeper of the vehicle so that appropriate action can be taken.

Red light cameras detect and photograph those vehicles that have jumped traffic lights.

Figure 25.14 shows a vehicle passing through a red light detected using a red light system.

Weather forecasting

The Traffic Control Centre also has several remote weather stations which collect data about the weather and relay the data back to the centre using modems and telephone lines. The physical quantities measured by the system include the following:

- wind speed
- humidity
- air temperature
- ground temperature.

The data from the weather station are also passed to the Meteorological Office (weather centre) for the production of weather forecasts. The data can also be used to

▲
Figure 25.14 *Jumping the lights*

predict the likelihood of black ice on the road surface. When the weather system shows that there could be black ice forming overnight, an ice alert goes out, which means that the gritting teams who put salt and grit on the road can be sent out.

There is another important type of sensor that is able to detect the amount of salt on the road surface. For instance, if a road has been gritted the previous night, and it has not rained or snowed, there may well be enough salt left on the road to avoid the need for further gritting. The whole system saves both overtime money paid to the gritting teams and the cost of the grit used.

Pollution monitoring

Local authorities often have to monitor air pollution in their areas. Most of them do this remotely and they have sensors which monitor the main polluting gases (nitrous oxides and sulphur dioxide) situated at the busiest junctions. The data from these are used to monitor the air quality and also used by the Meteorological Office to record air quality information for the region as a whole. Again, modems and telephone cables are used to transfer the data to the authority's technical department where the traffic control system centre is situated.

Virtual learning environments (VLE)

A virtual learning environment (VLE) is a set of teaching and learning tools, including computers and the internet, which is used to improve the learning process for students.

Here are some of the things you are likely to find in a VLE:

- curriculum material that the teacher has uploaded for the students (e.g. notes, slides from presentations, multimedia material such as quizzes)
- discussion forums or bulletin boards, so learners can post messages and teachers and other learners can reply to them
- file space for students to store their own work
- internet links to outside resources such as exam board material, revision websites.
- chat rooms so students can enter and chat about their work or teachers can hold tutorials
- messaging so that students can see if other students or teachers are online to ask them a question or talk about their work
- online assessment where the students can take assessments which can be marked by the computer.

How teachers can use a VLE

- Teachers can upload teaching material so that students can get on with the work independently.
- Students can complete work and submit it to their teachers so that they can mark it and return it to the student digitally.
- Teachers can set online quizzes/assessments for the students to complete which are marked automatically and the marks are transferred to the teacher automatically.
- Teachers can answer student questions on the forums.
- Teachers can hold revision tutorials using chat rooms.

Advantages of a VLE

- Learning is not restricted to a particular place (i.e. the classroom) as material can be accessed from anywhere using the internet.

- Learning is not restricted to a particular time as students can access all the materials at any time.
- They can repeat the material many times that helps them revise.
- The multimedia material will help present the material in a more interesting way.

Disadvantages of a VLE

- The VLE software is expensive.
- Training is needed to take advantage of what a VLE has to offer, and the time and finance to do this may not be available.
- It could seriously disadvantage those students who do not have internet access at home.
- Time is needed for the teachers to upload content to the VLE.

Virtual reality in training

Training dentists using virtual reality

Virtual reality is used in dentistry for training dentists. A realistic 3D mouth is shown on the screen in real time and the student can hold a tool that simulates the real tool used for a certain procedure. This tool allows the student to feel the same sensations as they would experience if they used the same tool on a real mouth.

The system is used for training and it is possible to train students in a variety of dental procedures, such as removing plaque from teeth.

Figure 25.15 *A 3D virtual dentistry simulator training system*

▼

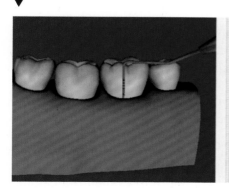 

There is also a mode where the instructor leads the student. By holding onto the dental tool the student can experience the same sensations and movements needed to complete a certain dental procedure.

Advantages of the system

- Students can try the procedures many times until they get them right.
- There is the option for the instructor to test the trainee on each procedure.
- The students can access the system using the internet and can therefore practise in their own time.
- The system could eliminate the need to practise on real patients or model mouths.
- It is less expensive than using real patients with real equipment.

Disadvantages of the system

- The system does not have the interaction between a real patient and the dentist (i.e. talking to the patient).
- Only a limited number of dental procedures are available.
- The feeling of the tools for the student dentist may not be the same as with real instruments.

Virtual reality used to train employees in the operation of nuclear/chemical plants

Nuclear and chemical plants need highly trained staff to operate them. They need to be able to react quickly to a whole range of dangerous situations.

Virtual reality is used to ensure that staff operating these plants are competent in all the systems, such as:

- control of the processes
- safety
- environmental protection.

Using virtual reality ensures that:

- staff are trained to a high degree of competency
- staff are tested at regular intervals to check they are competent in dealing with any situation.

▶

Figure 25.16 *Virtual reality can be used to train staff on what to do if there is a fire at an oil refinery like this one*

Advantages

- Lower cost as instructors are not needed to train staff.
- Dangerous situations can be simulated using virtual reality that would be too dangerous to create in real life.

Disadvantages

- Virtual reality systems are very expensive to create.
- Virtual reality systems do not always mimic the real situation exactly.

Applications of ICT in libraries

Most libraries are computerised and the systems usually make use of barcodes and a relational database.

Each member is given a unique member number which acts as the primary key in the members table of the database. Rather than type this number, the number is coded in the form of a barcode. This is faster and more accurate than typing it in.

Books are also barcoded with a unique number and when they are borrowed the member's ticket barcode is scanned, along with the barcodes of all the books that have

been borrowed. On their return the books are scanned, thus telling the computer that the borrower has returned the books.

If books are not returned by the due date, the system will issue a reminder automatically which can be sent by post or by email.

Figure 25.17 *Library systems issue a library card to members which contains a barcode or magnetic stripe, or both as on this card*

▼

The book table can be used to locate a specific book and to find out whether it is on the shelf or has been borrowed. Books can be reserved using the system, so when the book arrives back it is kept aside rather than put back on the shelf.

Modern security systems

Modern security systems make use of the latest developments in ICT. For example many access systems to rooms and buildings make use of biometric methods, such as iris or fingerprint recognition. These systems make use of a unique property of the human body: the pattern of blood vessels on the back of the eyes in the case of iris recognition, or the pattern on the fingers in the case of fingerprint recognition.

Passports

Passports are very important documents as they allow the holder of the passport access to other countries. Passports are sometimes forged so it is important for staff to check that the person using the passport is genuine. Information about the passport holder is encrypted in the chip and only the passport control staff with the special reader can read this information.

The passports held by the residents of certain countries contain a chip and/or a loop circuit.

The reader is able to read the information in the loop or chip and this is used to check that the holder of the passport is the correct holder.

▲
Figure 25.18 *This passport contains a small chip along with a loop circuit*

26 The Internet

Internet service provider (ISP)

Unless you are from a large company or organisation which can have a file server permanently connected to the internet, you will have to use the services of an internet service provider (ISP). The ISP provides a permanent connection to the internet. When you log on your modem dials the number of the ISP, and when your password has been validated you are allowed access to their file server. As well as providing a connection to the internet, ISPs provide a lot of content of their own. Figure 26.1 shows just some of the things a typical ISP provides.

The internet can be described as a network of networks. Once you connect your computer to the internet you become part of the network known as the internet. The huge amount of content on the internet means it is the first place most people look when trying to find information about something.

Using the internet, data can be rapidly transferred around the world. This can cause problems. If an untrue story about a well-known person is placed on the internet, it is difficult or even impossible to determine who put it there. Once it is on the internet many people all over the world can read it and believe that it is true.

The global nature of the internet means that information about atrocities, human rights violations (people locked up by governments for no justifiable reason) and so on can be passed around the world quickly. It is much harder for oppressive regimes to keep secrets. Actions by groups of countries (such as the United Nations) can then be taken to put pressure on these countries.

▲ **Figure 26.1** *The signing-on screen for the internet service provider Virgin Media*

World Wide Web (WWW)

The World Wide Web (WWW) is a part of the internet where graphics, sound, video and animation are used, as well as text. The word used for this mix of media is hypertext. Special hypertext links are built into the World Wide Web that allow the user to move around by clicking with a mouse on words or graphics on the screen. Special software, called browser software, is needed to take full advantage of the World Wide Web.

Websites

All organisations, including schools and colleges, are reaping the benefits of having their own websites. Basically, a website allows communication between the organisation and the outside world. For commercial organisations it allows potential customers to learn about the organisation, its products or services. Some websites allow the user to place electronic orders. The cost of conducting business on the web is low compared with other, more traditional methods.

Websites can be written using Hypertext Markup Language (HTML), which is easy to use, and you can get instructions on how to create a website online from your internet service provider. Most websites include a counter to count the number of visitors to the site. This is a measure of how useful other people have found the site. When you make up your own website, it is stored on space allocated to you by your ISP.

Website hosts

When you connect up your home computer to the internet you need two things: a modem and a means of connecting to an internet service provider. This ISP has a computer permanently connected to the internet, so when you log on with them, they provide the mechanism for getting you on the internet.

Many large companies who are not internet service providers also need a computer permanently connected to the web so that they can send email and files to other sites. They may also use the computer as a website host so that they can provide details of their goods and services to anyone interested. Additionally, these people may decide to place online orders.

Questions

In what ways is it cheaper to conduct business over the internet?

Why would it be useful for a school to have its prospectus on a website? What other information might a school put on a website?

Electronic mail

Electronic mail (email) is a method of sending messages from one terminal to another via a communications link. There are various providers of electronic mail, including internet information service providers. Many people are confused about how electronic mail works. To communicate using electronic mail, you first have to have an email address of your own and you must, of course, also know the email address of the person to whom you wish to send a message. You can then write your message using email software. Next you need to use your communications software and modem to connect to a service provider's file server. Once you are connected you can transmit your message.

The message is then placed in a mail box on a main computer. As soon as the person to whom you have sent the message logs onto the system, they can access their mailbox and read any letters that have been sent. One of the advantages of electronic mail is that the same message can be sent to many different people at the same time, simply by referring to their email addresses.

Obviously you cannot send mail in this way to a person who is not a subscriber to one of the electronic mail systems.

Questions

1 A lot of people think that when you send a message by electronic mail it automatically pops up on the screen. In fact it is stored in a mailbox on a file server.

  (a) Why can you not simply send the message to the other person's computer where it could be stored on their disk drive?

  (b) Many people get fed up with all the junk mail that they get in their mailboxes when they subscribe to electronic mail services.

    (i) What is meant by 'junk mail'?

    (ii) Which feature of electronic mail makes it easier for suppliers to advertise their products and services?

2 Someone says that eventually electronic mail will replace the postal service. Do you think this is likely? Write a paragraph to support your opinion.

Replying to an email

When you receive email you will notice that there is a button to click for your reply. Once this is clicked all you have to do is type your reply, as the email address is automatically added. You can also return the message that was sent to you so that your reply is set in context, and the receiver does not have to look for their original letter.

Address book

Internet service providers have a feature called an address book for managing your email addresses. In the address book are the names and email addresses of all the people to whom you are likely to send email. Instead of having to type in the address when writing an email, you just click on the email address or addresses in the address book.

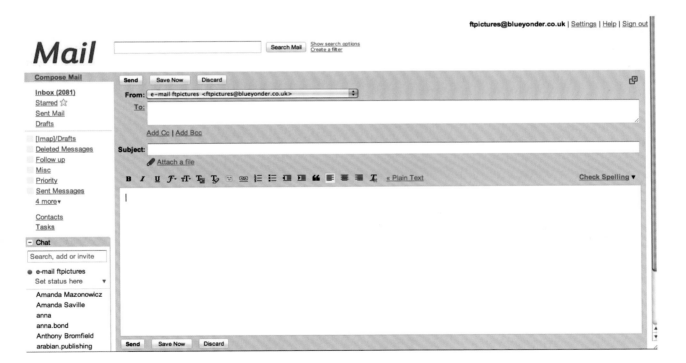

▲ **Figure 26.2** *The email preparation screen from Virgin Media. Notice that you can format the text (bold, italics, etc.). Notice also that there is an address book of 'contacts' and you can attach files using the 'Attachments' button*

Mailing lists

Mailing lists are lists of people and their email addresses. They are used when a copy of an email needs to be distributed to people in a particular group. For example, if you were working as part of a team and needed to send each member the same email you could set up a mailing list. Every time you needed to send the members of the team email, you could use the list which would save time.

File attachments

You can attach files to emails. For example you could attach a file containing a photograph of yourself obtained from a digital camera, a piece of clip art, a picture that you have scanned in or a long document. You can, in fact, attach anything that can be stored in a file.

You can attach more than one file to an email, so if you had six photographs to send, they could all be attached and sent with a single email.

Before you attach a file you must first prepare an email explaining the purpose of your email and giving some information about the files that you are attaching (what their purpose is, what file format they are in, etc.).

Once the email message has been completed, you click on the file attachment button and select the file you want to send. A box will appear to allow you to select the drive, folder and eventually the file that you want to send.

If you want to send more than one file, repeat the file attachment process. Usually, if there is more than one file to send the files will be compressed to reduce the time taken to send them.

How they work

Here is how file attachments to emails work:

1 The organisation you use as your ISP gets the email message you sent.
2 The email address on this message is looked at to find the ISP.
3 The email and attachment are sent to this ISP.
4 The person the email was intended for logs onto their ISP to see if there is email for them.
5 They see the email in their inbox and then download the email and file attachment onto their own computer.

Problems in using file attachments

There are a number of problems in using file attachments. Here are the main ones:

- You are usually restricted by your ISP to the size of file that can be sent as a file attachment.
- File attachments are frequently sources of viruses, so people can be reluctant to open them.
- File attachments are often compressed and the recipient may not have suitable software to decompress and view the file.

Is email private?

Email is not as private as ordinary mail. With ordinary mail you can usually tell if the envelope has been opened and stuck down again but it is impossible to tell if somebody has read your email. Because of the way email is distributed over the internet it is possible for others to copy, forge or intercept messages. You should never divulge passwords or credit card details in email, even if the request for the information looks official.

Advantages and disadvantages of using email

In many countries now, more emails are sent than traditional letters. There are advantages and disadvantages to using email instead of traditional letters.

Advantages

1 It is very fast, as mail is sent immediately and a reply can be returned as soon as the receiver checks their email. Ordinary post takes several days.
2 Emails lack the formal structure of a letter, so they are quicker to write.
3 You can attach a copy of the sender's

email to your reply, saving them having to search for the original message.

4 Email is cheaper than a letter. No stamp, envelope or paper are needed. There is also a time saving, so this makes email cheaper. Even if an email is sent across the world it costs no more than a local email.

5 The sender does not have to go out to a post box.

6 You do not have to waste time shopping for stamps, envelopes and paper.

Disadvantages

1 Not everyone has the equipment to send and receive email. However, with internet access from televisions, landline phones and mobile phones, most people will soon have access in some way.

2 Junk mail is a problem. You can waste time looking through emails that are just adverts.

3 Emails are not as secure as traditional letters.

4 The system relies on people checking their email regularly.

5 Older people may feel left out because they consider themselves too old to learn to use computers.

6 The equipment to send and receive email is quite expensive compared to traditional methods.

Aspects of the internet

In this section we will be looking at some internet terms and other aspects of the internet.

Web browser

A web browser is a program that allows access to the World Wide Web (WWW).

Web server

A web server is a computer that contains the information that users of the internet can access using their web browser. A web server needs to be connected to the internet at all times, so that users are able to access the information at any time. The web servers

Questions

1 Explain how each of the following can make using email services easier.
 (a) Address book.
 (b) Mailing lists.

2 Some emails are sent with a file attachment.
 (a) What is meant by a file attachment?
 (b) Give an example of a data file that you might attach to an email.

3 A company is thinking of setting up a system to allow its employees to send email both within the company and also externally to its customers.
 (a) Describe briefly the steps involved in the sending of an email message.
 (b) Describe three advantages of sending emails rather than sending letters by the traditional post.
 (c) Describe two disadvantages of sending email.

of internet service providers contain many websites. If you develop your own website, it will usually be stored on the web server of your internet service provider.

Communication features common to net software

No matter which web browser you use, some features are common to them all. Here are some of the main ones.

The ability to store links (Favourites, Favourite places or Bookmarks)

When you surf the World Wide Web you quickly move from one web page to another. On each web page there are links to other web pages, and when you click on these they take you to a different web page, which may be on the same site or a different one. If you want to go back to a site, it is hard to remember the links you took to get there. By noting a web page in your favourites list, you are storing its name and web address so that you can return to it at a later date. When you add a site to your list of favourites, you are creating a short cut to the site.

History

A history list shows all the sites/pages that you have visited in the sequence you visited them. This is useful if you want to go back to a previous site during a surfing session. History lists can also tell you the sites that others have visited.

▲
Figure 26.3 *History allows you to view the sites that you have recently visited*

Navigation

Browsers show a toolbar containing buttons that you use to move around sites and perform certain actions, a typical example of which is shown in Figure 26.4.

These buttons would typically include:

- **Back** – go back to the previous page
- **Forward** – jump forward to the next page
- **Refresh** (also called reload) – refresh the contents of the page
- **Home** – return to the page that you use as your home page (i.e. your starting point) or the page that your internet service provider uses as their home page
- **Stop** – stop trying to load the page.

▲
Figure 26.5 *Here are buttons (from left to right) for back, forward, refresh, home and stop*

Cache (sometimes referred to as temporary pages)

This is a storage area on your hard drive where some text and images from web pages are stored so that they load quickly when they are revisited by you.

Finding your way around the internet

There are three ways to find your way around the internet:

1 **By typing in the web address**.
   If you know the web address of a website, then simply type it in. Web addresses are everywhere; you can find them in magazines, advertisements and even on the side of planes. Web addresses look like this:

   www.nelsonthornes.com

2 **By 'surfing' the internet**.
   Surfing the internet means rapidly moving from one web page or website to another until you find something of interest. In doing this you are making use of hypertext links. The hypertext links are in the form of either underlined text or text in a different colour. When you move your mouse pointer over a hypertext link it changes shape (usually into a hand). On double-clicking the right mouse button, you will be taken to the new site or page.

3 **By using a special program called a search engine**.
   A search engine can be used to search for information on a certain subject.

▲
Figure 26.4 *An internet browser toolbar*

You simply enter keywords or subject names, and the program will search for those sites with information containing your keywords. As there is so much information on the internet, finding what you want can be quite difficult. If you are careful and specific in choosing your keywords, you have more chance of getting what you want. There are a number of search engines in use, including:

Google	http://www.google.com
Alta Vista	http://www.altavista.com
Yahoo!	http://www.yahoo.com
Lycos	http://www.lycos.com

Features of common internet services

Here are some of the main features of internet services.

World Wide Web (WWW)

The World Wide Web is the multimedia branch of the internet. Using the web, the user is able to view text, graphics, video and sounds. You can use the web to access computers all round the world and search and view the information stored on these computers. You can also download files stored on other computers.

The World Wide Web consists of a huge number of web pages. Web pages are grouped together to form websites. The user is able to use links called hyperlinks to move between web pages or websites.

Hacking

Hacking means gaining access to a computer system illegally; the people who do this are called hackers. The internet has made it possible for a determined individual to gain access to an organisation's computer systems without leaving their home. Despite security measures to prevent illegal access, organisations still have problems with hackers. As the main motivation for hacking is to 'beat the system', the more secure a computer system is, the more determined the hackers are to get into it.

It is possible to deter hackers using the following:

- usernames and passwords
- firewalls.

Spam

Spam is email that a computer user has not asked for, and it causes problems because it wastes user's time deciding whether to delete it or whether it should be looked at first. Luckily there is software called a spam filter that will remove spam automatically.

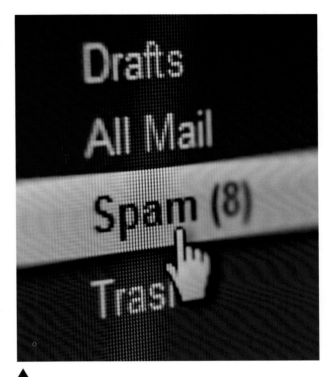

▲ **Figure 26.6** *Email software often contains a spam filter which keeps the spam in a separate folder so that it can be deleted in one go*

Spyware

Spyware is software that is put onto a computer without the owner's knowledge and consent. The purpose of spyware is to monitor use of the internet. Spyware is a problem because it:

- can monitor your keystrokes so it can be used to record usernames and passwords, which means that you could have your identity stolen and the details used to commit fraud

- can record your web browsing history, thus invading your privacy
- can cause your computer to crash unexpectedly as the spyware program contains errors (i.e. bugs)
- causes your computer to run slowly as the spyware runs at the same time as your other programs are running
- causes a security breach as some spyware has been known to switch off the antivirus software.

To remove spyware you should:

- install antivirus software as this often checks and removes spyware
- install anti-spyware software that will detect and remove spyware
- perform routine scans for spyware.

Cookies

A cookie is a small text file which is downloaded automatically when you visit certain websites. The owner of the website can use the cookie to find out if you have visited the website before and also what the user looked at whilst on the website. The owner of the website can see how effective their website is and determine the sorts of things the user is interested in so that they can suggest products and services.

The main objection to cookies is that they erode privacy and in most cases this monitoring is done without our knowledge and permission.

Phishing

Phishing means fraudulently trying to get people to reveal usernames, passwords, credit card details, account numbers and so on by pretending you are a bank, credit card company, tax office or similar.

Emails are sent to you supposedly but not actually from a bank, building society, credit card company and so on. They usually say that there has been a problem with your account and ask you to reveal information such as passwords and account details.

Under no circumstances should you reveal this information. If you do then these details will be used to commit fraud.

Pharming

Pharming involves a hacker accessing a computer illegally to deposit malicious programming code. Any users who try to access a website which has been stored on the computer will be directed automatically by the malicious code to a bogus website and not the website they wanted. The website they are directed to looks almost the same as the real website. In many cases the fake or bogus website is used to obtain passwords or banking details so that these can be used fraudulently.

Modern developments in the use of the internet

In this section you will be looking at some of the modern uses of the internet.

Wikis – a wiki is a web page that can be viewed and modified by anyone who has web browser software. Using web browser software allows you to change the content of a web page. You have probably used the online encyclopaedia Wikipedia. This encyclopaedia has been created by ordinary people and anyone can add material or delete material from it. You may think this is bad idea, but if someone posts incorrect information then there are plenty of people around who will view it and correct it.

Social networking websites – these are virtual communities of people who communicate about a particular subject or interest or just make friends with each other. Members of these sites create their own profiles with information about themselves, such as hobbies, likes and dislikes. You have to ensure that you do not reveal too much information about yourself as others view this information. Social networking websites enable members to communicate using instant messaging, email, a type of blog and even voice or videoconferencing.

The main social networking websites are:

- Facebook
- MySpace
- Twitter.

Blogs/web logs – these are online diaries of events or journals usually organised in date order. Blogs can be about anything. Groups, singers and celebrities have blogs, which let people know about their lives and what they are doing. Blogs are also used by politicians and for collecting public opinion about certain topics.

Digital media sharing websites – these websites allow anyone to upload their videos and digital images to a website, which allows others to access the media. In this way material can be shared by others. The main advantage of these sites is that you do not have to take up storage on your own computer and it is easy to direct people to the site if they want to view your photographs. Examples of such sites include YouTube for video clips and flickr mainly for photographs.

Web browsers – this is the software that you use to search for information stored on the internet. You are able to choose which web browser you use.

Search engines – this is software that finds information on websites on the internet based on input criteria. You type in a keyword or phrase and the search engine locates websites containing those keywords or phrases.

Download – download means the transfer of a file or program from the internet to the user's own computer or portable device (e.g. mobile phone, PDA).

Upload – this is the transfer of a file or program from the user's computer to a remote computer where that file or program is then stored.

ISP – this is the organisation that provides you with your connection to the internet. When you log onto the internet, you are connecting to your internet service provider which then connects you to the internet.

Tagging – tagging is done in order to find content later. For example if you stored a photograph on a digital media sharing website then you (and others if you allow it) can search for pictures of a person by name. Suppose you tagged a photograph with the text 'Ahmed at his sister's wedding', then at a later date you could look at all the pictures of 'Ahmed' and this one, along with any others stored, will come up.

Podcasts – these are digital media files that can be audio or video. They are released in episodes so that you can be fed them automatically when you connect to the service. This method is called web syndication. They are useful sources of current affairs information.

Bit streaming – it is the process of sending a continuous stream of bits representing data over a communication path. The bits are sent serially, which means they are sent one at a time.

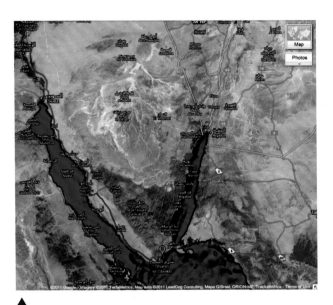

▲ **Figure 26.7** *This is a combination of an aerial photograph and a road map*

Satellite maps – using a combination of the internet and satellites it is possible to view either stored or live images of buildings, roads, gardens and so on anywhere in the world. Satellites are used to take photographs of the area as they pass over the Earth and they relay them back to Earth, where they are stored, joined together and then posted on the internet. It is possible to use a combination of an aerial photograph and a traditional road map so you can know exactly what you are looking at. There are many uses for this, such as:

- You can view a house and the surrounding area you are thinking of buying or renting before you view it yourself.
- You can see what roads really look like so you can check they are suitable for your vehicle.
- You can look for a landmark such as a nice beach and then find out where exactly it is.

Online maps are available on the internet and these can be used to:

- locate a road or street if you know the postcode
- produce a set of driving directions from one place to another
- work out the distance between two points or how much time it will take for the journey.

You can see a picture of the location or route superimposed on a map on the screen (Figure 26.7).

Chat rooms

You will probably have used chat rooms. They are an ideal way of talking to people from around the world without leaving your home. They are not without some danger and you should never divulge any personal details until you are sure about the person you are talking to. Do not be too trusting and be very careful about arranging to meet someone face to face, as people are not always what they seem in chat rooms.

Services over the internet, such as radio, video and music

It is now possible to hear a radio programme over the internet, provided that your computer is equipped with a sound card and speakers. Some music sites can transmit music to your computer and this is useful if you want to listen to a sample track from a new CD before deciding whether to buy it.

Some artists have their concerts distributed live over the internet. With video, pictures as well as music can be sent, so watching a concert using the internet is just like watching it on television.

Advantages and disadvantages of the internet as a source of information

Advantages

- You can access the internet from anywhere and a huge amount of information is provided to you from all over the world. The use of laptops and internet access using televisions and mobile phones means that users can also access the internet in a non-traditional setting.
- Information is up to date. By the time books are written, edited and printed the information they contain can be out of date. Information on the internet can be continually updated. However, you do still need to make sure that any information you use is up to date and accurate.
- Multimedia can be used. Information can be presented in the most interesting way possible, using video clips, animation, sound and so on.
- You can access huge amounts of information. Encyclopaedias, dictionaries, newspapers, magazines and many research papers are available on the internet. You do not even need to leave your house to access them.
- Search engines are available to help you find the information you are looking for. Searching in traditional books is very slow; using a search engine and the internet makes browsing very easy.
- Using email you can access experts all over the world on certain subjects. If you have a question about something on a website you can send an email to its author and they can send you their reply using email.

Disadvantages

- The equipment and connection needed are relatively expensive. Computers, modems (or ISDN adapters), telephone and/or internet service provider (ISP) costs must all be met. The costs, however, are decreasing quite rapidly.

- You need some knowledge to perform searches successfully. If searches are constructed incorrectly, then you will get either no information or too much, most of it irrelevant.

E-commerce
What is e-commerce?

E-commerce is selling goods or service over the internet, as opposed to using traditional methods such as buying goods or services from shops or trading using the telephone.

How could it change the way we shop?

More and more people are able to access the internet via their computers, special television sets, telephones or mobile phones. All these users will now be able to take advantage of e-commerce to buy their goods and services cheaper and more efficiently than before. As well as needing the hardware and software to access the internet, the user also needs a credit card to pay for purchases. One problem is that well-off people will be able to take advantage of the savings, whereas those who are not able to afford access to the internet or have no credit card will lose out.

The battle for customers: shopping traditionally or shopping using e-commerce

In the battle for customers e-commerce means some businesses will lose out while others gain business.

Losers

- Some traditional shops may have to close, resulting in a loss of jobs.
- Companies that fail to get involved in e-commerce will see lower profits.
- Shopping as a leisure activity may go into decline as goods are bought online.
- City centres may become deserted as shops close down.
- The gap between richer and poorer members of society may widen as the richer take advantage of the savings made by shopping online.
- Society in general may lose, as more people choose to interact with computers rather than people.

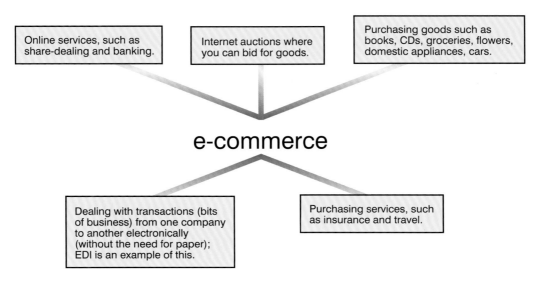

Online services, such as share-dealing and banking.

Internet auctions where you can bid for goods.

Purchasing goods such as books, CDs, groceries, flowers, domestic appliances, cars.

e-commerce

Dealing with transactions (bits of business) from one company to another electronically (without the need for paper); EDI is an example of this.

Purchasing services, such as insurance and travel.

▲
Figure 26.8 *Some of the things you can do using e-commerce*

Winners

- E-commerce sites have made some people wealthy as they become 'dot com' millionaires.
- If many goods are delivered straight to customers' homes, there is a huge increase in the number of staff employed by the delivery/postal companies.
- Those people employed to set up websites, such as programmers will be in great demand.
- Criminals may more easily take advantage of anyone off their guard when divulging credit card details.
- People with mobility problems (e.g. the elderly or disabled) will be able to shop more successfully from their homes.
- The users of e-commerce sites could find it hard to decide whether a site is a reputable one.

Advantages of shopping online

Shopping online has many advantages over more traditional ways of shopping, including the following:

1 Online catalogues can be viewed. Products can be searched for by a large number of criteria. You could search for a book according to author's name, ISBN (international standard book number) or subject.
2 There is a much bigger choice of products. internet bookshops have huge stocks of books compared to a local bookshop.
3 Product reviews can be obtained before you buy. For example, you can see what previous buyers say about a book before you buy.
4 Orders can be placed on the internet at any time of the day or night, on any day of the year.
5 You can buy software over the internet and receive it by downloading it. This can be easier than having to order it by post or by visiting a shop.
6 Goods or services are usually cheaper on the internet. Organisations find it cheaper to use the internet as they do not need as many staff or expensive premises, and some of these savings can be passed to the customer.
7 There are programs that can search for the best price for a certain product. For example they could be used to find the cheapest flight from a range of airlines. There are also programs to find the cheapest domestic appliances.
8 Once the customer has placed an initial order, the customer details, such as name, address and credit card details, are stored and therefore need not be re-entered. This makes shopping online very fast. Supermarkets that deliver to the home also keep a shopping list of items that you order regularly, so you need only make changes to this list.
9 You can buy goods from anywhere in the world.

Test Yourself

Using the words in the list below, copy out and complete sections **A** to **G** underlining the words you have inserted. The words may be used more than once.

**internet   electronic mail   web servers
internet service provider   e-commerce
web browser   website**

A A company whose file server is permanently connected to the internet and which you can use to gain access to the internet is called an

_____ _____ _____.

B The World Wide Web is the multimedia part of the _____.

C Most companies and organisations have a _____ where outsiders can access details about the company or organisation.

D A short, to-the-point message that is transmitted electronically from one computer to another is called _____ _____.

E A program that allows access to the World Wide Web is called a _____ _____.

F Some computers are permanently connected to the internet and you can connect to the internet via them. These computers are called _____

_____.

G Conducting business electronically over the internet is called _____.

Things to do

1 The merger of the internet, television and computers is a powerful combination.

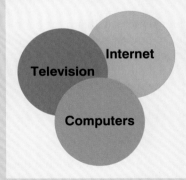

Television   Internet   Computers

(a) We are seeing telephone, television and computer technology coming together. Using interactive digital television you will be able to do a lot more than simply watch television programmes.
Describe two services that are (or will be) available using interactive digital television.

(b) Mobile phones can now do more than simply connect you to another phone for a conversation. Describe two of these services.

2 The internet is a useful resource and there are many people who would not be without it. However, it is not without its problems. You have been asked to produce a five-minute talk about the dangers of the internet. To do this you have decided to write down a bulleted list of the problems and then go through each one briefly. You should mention at least five problems and what steps can be taken, if any, to solve or minimise each one.

3 Many schools choose to communicate using a variety of methods, including post, email and telephone. The headteacher of a school wishes to communicate with:

(a) staff

(b) pupils

(c) the examination board.

For each of the above groups, give the advantages and disadvantages of using post, email and telephone as a means of contact.

4 E-commerce is very popular and it is now possible to buy almost anything over the internet. All you need to order goods or services using the internet is a computer/TV/phone connected to the internet and a credit card for making the payment. Here are some e-commerce sites for you to look at:

(a) www.cd-wow.com – a company that sells chart CDs.

(b) www.amazon.com – the largest book supplier in the world (they sell lots of other things as well).

(c) www.lastminute.com – a site for booking last-minute holidays, flights, hotels, etc.

(d) www.easyjet.com – a site for booking flights.

For each site write a short paragraph explaining what you were able to do using the site. Also say whether you found the site easy to use.

(e) Give three advantages of using e-commerce sites like these (rather than shops) for the purchase of products or services.

5 No matter which internet service provider you use, there are some features that they all have. For example they all allow the user to send and receive email.

Choose three features, other than email, and for each one describe how it is useful. (To help you with this question, you could look at what is provided on the opening screen of your internet service provider.)

6 E-commerce is set to change the way that most people shop.

(a) Give two advantages of buying goods over the internet.

(b) Give two disadvantages of buying goods over the internet.

(c) Some organisations will benefit by the use of e-commerce, while others will not.

(i) Give the names of two types of organisation that would benefit by the use of e-commerce.

(ii) Give the names of two organisations that are likely to lose out from the growth of e-commerce.

7 A parent is thinking of buying a computer to help her children (aged 7, 9 and 12) with their homework. She wants the children to access the internet. If you were the parent of these children, describe three worries you would have in allowing complete and unsupervised access to the internet.

8 Not all the material on the internet is reliable. You are trying to search for information to help you with homework. Describe two steps that you could take to check the accuracy of the material you are using off the internet.

IT Tasks

Task 1

For this task you will need to get together with a few other people in your class. You need about three or four in your team and each team member will have to find out about the facilities offered by a particular ISP. It will therefore help you if all your team members have access to the internet via a different ISP.

Each person should list and briefly explain the main facilities offered by their ISP.

Once everyone has made their own list your teacher will photocopy your team's lists and each team member will be given a complete set back.

Task 2

For this task you will be working on your own.

Using the lists from Task 1, identify and write down those items in your lists that appear more than once. This will provide a list of common features.

Task 3

For each of the common features in your list, write a short paragraph explaining how the feature helps an internet user.

Investigations

'The internet causes more problems than it solves.'

Although the internet is a great help and many people enjoy all the useful benefits it brings, there are some problems associated with it. What is your opinion about the above statement?

You are going to contribute to a class discussion about the above. Before you do this you will need to jot down a few opinions so that you can join in the discussion.

Here are a few things you might like to think about in addition to your own ideas:

- the opportunity to make friends with people from all over the world

- a way of buying products and services without leaving the house

- access to a huge store of information on every subject imaginable

- contact with people sharing the same interests as you.

Remember, you must include the negative things as well as the positive ones.

Logic Gates and Circuits

Electronic pulses

Data and instructions are both stored by the computer as the binary digits 0 and 1. Computers are able to process data in the form of pulse trains of voltage, with a low-voltage pulse representing 0 and a higher-voltage pulse representing 1.

Logic gates

Electronic pulses can be made to follow sets of rules if they are passed through certain components. These components act like electronic switches and are called logic gates. When pulses enter a logic gate, the output depends on the type of logic gate being used and the combination of pulses input.

There are two ways of representing logic gates and both ways are shown in Figure 27.1.

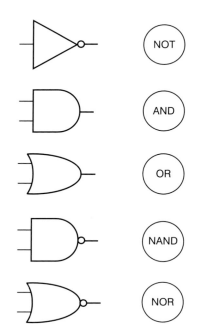

▲
Figure 27.1

The AND gate

AND gates can have two or more inputs, but they only have one output. If all the inputs are 1 then the output will be 1, but any other combination of inputs will give an output of 0 (Figure 27.2).

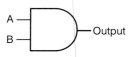

▲
Figure 27.2

A truth table shows all the possible inputs along with their corresponding output.

To draw the truth table for the AND gate we must first write down all the possible combinations that the inputs A and B can have. For a logic gate with two inputs the number of possible combinations will be four. For a three-input logic gate, there will be eight possible inputs. You will not be asked about logic gates with more than three inputs in the examination.

The truth table for a two-input AND gate is shown in Figure 27.3.

Inputs		Output
A	B	
1	1	1
1	0	0
0	1	0
0	0	0

▲
Figure 27.3

With an AND gate with three inputs (i.e. A, B and C) there are eight possible combinations of input and the only one that will give an output of 1 is when all three inputs are 1.

The truth table for a three-input AND gate is shown in Figure 27.4.

Inputs			Output
A	B	C	
1	1	1	1
0	0	0	0
1	0	0	0
0	1	0	0
0	0	1	0
1	1	0	0
1	0	1	0
0	1	1	0

Figure 27.4

The OR gate

OR gates can have two or more inputs, but for the examination you only need to know about OR gates with two or three inputs. If one or more of the inputs are 1 then the output will be 1. This means that only if all of the inputs are 0 will the output be 0 (Figure 27.5).

Figure 27.5

The truth table for a two-input OR gate is shown in Figure 27.6.

Inputs		Output
A	B	
1	1	1
1	0	1
0	1	1
0	0	0

Figure 27.6

The truth table for a three-input OR gate is shown in Figure 27.7.

Inputs			Output
A	B	C	
1	1	1	1
0	0	0	0
1	0	0	1
0	1	0	1
0	0	1	1
1	1	0	1
1	0	1	1
0	1	1	1

Figure 27.7

The NOT gate

Unlike the other gates, the NOT gate only ever has a single input and output. The NOT gate has the effect of making the output the opposite of the input. So if the input is 0, then the output is 1 and vice versa (Figure 27.8).

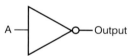

Figure 27.8

There is only ever one truth table for a NOT table, as shown in Figure 27.9.

Input	Output
A	
1	0
0	1

Figure 27.9

The NAND gate

The NAND gate operates as an AND gate followed by a NOT gate. To complete the truth table for a NAND gate you must follow the input first through the AND gate and then through the NOT gate (Figure 27.10).

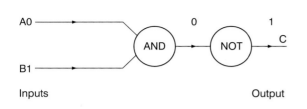

Inputs   Output

▲
Figure 27.10

When working out the outputs for combinations of logic gates, it is best to write down in pencil the inputs and how they change on going to the right for each combination of input. They can be rubbed out and another combination of inputs put in.

For example suppose we want to find out what happens when the inputs A=0 and B=1 go through the NAND gate. First we can work out what happens when they go through the AND gate. 0 and 1 through an AND gate gives a 0. So this 0 is the input going into the NOT gate. A 0 going into a NOT gate gives an output of 1. You can follow these steps for the other inputs and then complete the truth table.

Notice that we can keep track of the intermediate steps by putting these into the truth table shown in Figure 27.11.

Inputs		AND	NOT	Output
A	B			
1	1	1	0	0
1	0	0	1	1
0	1	0	1	1
0	0	0	1	1

▲
Figure 27.11

With practice, you will not need to fill in the extra columns. You will be able to just put the input and output in the table.

We do not draw these two gates because a NAND gate has its own symbol (Figure 27.12).

▲
Figure 27.12

The NOR gate

The NOR gate is formed by combining an OR gate with a NOT gate. Again we can work through the combination in two steps. First we work out the inputs and outputs for the OR gate. These are now the inputs for the NOT gate. The second step is working out the output of putting these inputs through the NOT gate. The truth table for a two-input NOR gate is as shown in Figure 27.13.

Inputs		Output
A	B	
1	1	0
1	0	0
0	1	0
0	0	1

▲
Figure 27.13

A NOR gate has the symbol shown in Figure 27.14.

▲
Figure 27.14

Important note

Sometimes, instead of using the symbols here, we can simply use a circle with the name of the gate inside. However, you do still need to remember the shape of the symbols as both of these representations are needed for the syllabus.

Questions

1 Figure 27.15 is a truth table of an AND gate. Copy and fill in the missing parts.

Inputs		Output
0	1	0

Figure 27.15

2 Which column, A, B, C or D, of the truth table in Figure 27.16 describes the output of the logic gate shown in Figure 27.17?

X	Y	A	B	C	D
0	0	0	0	0	1
0	1	0	1	1	0
1	0	0	1	1	0
1	1	1	0	1	0

Figure 27.16

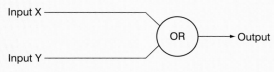

Figure 27.17

3 Fill in the truth tables for the following logic circuits.

(a)

Inputs		Output
A	B	C
1	0	
0	0	
0	1	
1	1	

Figure 27.18

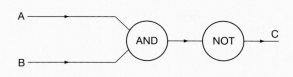

Figure 27.19

(b)

Inputs		Output
A	B	C
1	0	
0	0	
0	1	
1	1	

Figure 27.20

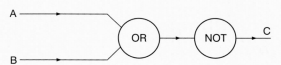

Figure 27.21

(c)

Inputs			Output
A	B	C	D
1	1	1	
0	0	0	
1	0	0	
1	0	1	
1	1	0	
0	0	1	
0	1	0	
0	1	1	

Figure 27.22

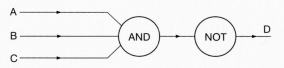

Figure 27.23

213

Questions

(d)

Inputs			Output
A	B	C	D
1	1	1	
0	0	0	
1	0	0	
1	0	1	
1	1	0	
0	0	1	
0	1	1	

Figure 27.24

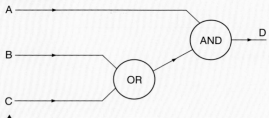
Figure 27.25

4 Figure 27.26 shows the input and output for the illustrated logic circuit in Figure 27.27. On a copy of Figure 27.27, write in the circles the names of the gates that are represented.

Inputs		Output
A	B	C
0	0	1
0	1	1
1	0	1
1	1	0

Figure 27.26

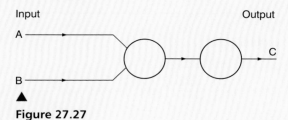
Figure 27.27

5 Write down the truth tables for the combinations of logic gates shown in Figures 27.28–27.32.

(a)

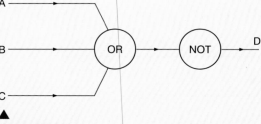
Figure 27.28

(b)

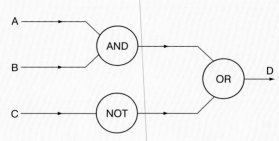
Figure 27.29

(c)

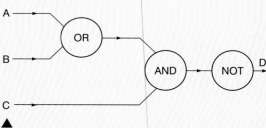
Figure 27.30

Questions

(d)

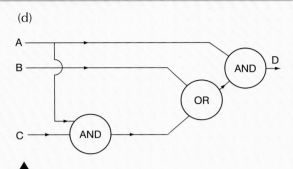

▲
Figure 27.31

(e)

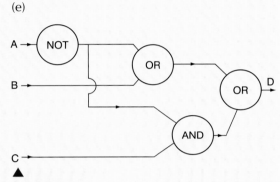

▲
Figure 27.32

6 (a) Draw a truth table that represents a NOT gate.

(b) Copy and complete Figure 27.33 for the network shown in Figure 27.34.

A	B	C	D	E
0	0	0		
0	0	1		
0	1	0		
0	1	1		
1	0	0		
1	1	0		
1	1	1		

▲
Figure 27.33

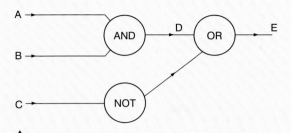

▲
Figure 27.34

(c) Draw a suitable logic diagram for Figure 27.35.

A	B	C
0	0	1
0	1	1
1	0	0
1	1	1

▲
Figure 27.35

(d) How could three NOT gates and one OR gate be arranged to produce the same output as one AND gate?

7 Using the circuits in Figure 27.36, complete a copy of Figure 27.37 for the output at X, Y and Z given the inputs A, B, C.

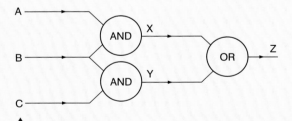

▲
Figure 27.36

Questions

A	B	C	X	Y	Z
0	0	0			
0	0	1			
0	1	0			
0	1	1			
1	0	0			
1	0	1			
1	1	0			
1	1	1			

▲
Figure 27.37

8 The output from the logic diagram Figure 27.38 is which **one** of the following?

A   logic 0

B   logic 0 and logic 1

C   logic 1

D   nothing at all

E   logic 1 or logic 0

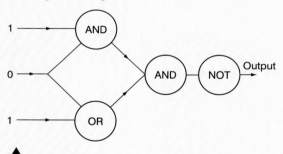

▲
Figure 27.38

9 (a)   Construct the truth table for the logic diagram Figure 27.39.

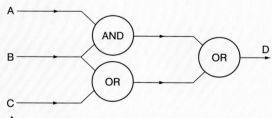

▲
Figure 27.39

(b) Which of the inputs has no effect on the final output?

10 Complete truth tables for the circuits in Figures 27.40 and 27.41.

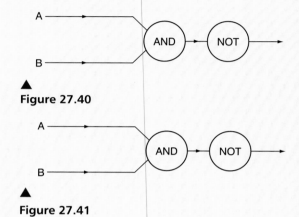

▲
Figure 27.40

▲
Figure 27.41

11 (a) Describe briefly the function of AND, OR and NOT gates.

(b) Copy and complete Figures 27.42–27.44 for each of the outputs X, Y and Z shown in Figure 27.45.

A	B	Output X
0	0	
0	1	
1	0	
1	1	

▲
Figure 27.42

A	B	Output Y
0	0	
0	1	
1	0	
1	1	

▲
Figure 27.43

Questions

A	B	Output Z
0	0	
0	1	
1	0	
1	1	

▲
Figure 27.44

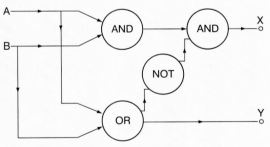

▲
Figure 27.45

12 Using the circuit shown in Figure 27.46, complete a copy of Figure 27.47 for the outputs R, S, T, X and Y.

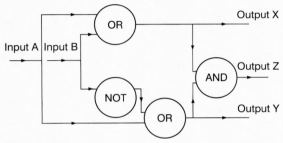

▲
Figure 27.46

A	B	R	S	T	X	Y
0	0					
0	1					
1	0					
1	1					

▲
Figure 27.47

13 Copy and complete a truth table for the logic circuit in Figure 27.48.

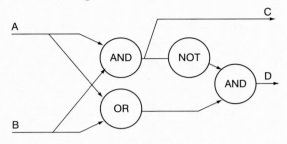

▲
Figure 27.48

14 Construct a truth table for the outputs at C and D for the circuit in Figure 27.49.

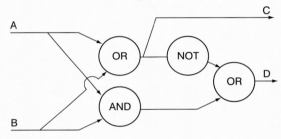

▲
Figure 27.49

Designing simple logic circuits

Any problem that has sets of conditions that have yes or no answers can be described using logic diagrams. First, we have to decide what the inputs and outputs are.

You saw in the last section that there are three main types of logic gate, with two additional gates. These gates can be combined and we can write a statement to describe how they work. Take the following written statement as an example:

If A AND B are on AND if C is on then the lights will be on.

If you work though the written statement you can see that there needs to be an AND gate between the two inputs A and B and then the output from these two gates is connected to another AND gate with another input C (Figure 27.50).

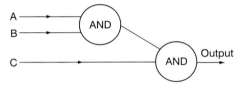

▲ **Figure 27.50**

Example 1

A hire purchase company will only lend money to a person who is a homeowner and in full-time employment. Draw a logic diagram and a truth table to satisfy these conditions.

To work this out, first decide what symbols you are going to use and write them down, along with what they mean.

For this example we could use the following symbols:

F = full-time employment
H = homeowner
L = loan
F and H will be the inputs and L will be the output.
If F = 1 this means that the person has full-time employment, but if F = 0 this means they do not have full-time employment.
L = 1 means a loan is given and L = 0 means no loan is given.

Now we can see that for the loan to be given, a person must own their home and be in full-

time employment. Any other combination will result in the hire purchase company not granting the money.

Now we can draw the logic diagram for this (Figure 27.51).

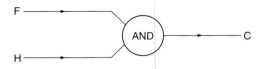

▲ **Figure 27.51**

The truth table is as shown in Figure 27.52.

A	B	Output C
1	0	0
0	1	0
0	0	0
1	1	1

▲ **Figure 27.52**

Example 2

The government will give grants to new companies provided they are in an area of high unemployment or are able to take on young school leavers. In addition to this they must be an engineering company.

Draw a logic diagram and truth table to reflect these facts.

We can show the first part of this question using an OR gate. However, first we must decide on a code:

U = area of high unemployment
Y = able to take on school leavers
E = engineering company
G = obtains government grant

We will also need to use an AND gate for the second part of the question. This will give us the logic diagram Figure 27.53, and we can now draw the truth table.

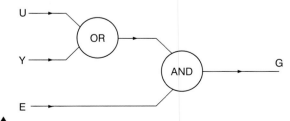

▲ **Figure 27.53**

Questions

1 Draw logic circuits to represent each of the following expressions:

(a) (A AND NOT B) or C

(b) A AND (B OR NOT C)

2 Draw logic circuits for the following expressions:

(a) A OR B OR C

(b) A AND B AND C

(c) (X OR Y) AND Z

(d) (X AND Y) OR Z

(e) (A OR B) AND (C OR D)

3 A finance company will grant a loan to applicants who have a bank account or are married house owners.

(a) Using the following codes:

B = bank account

H = house owner

S = single

L = loan:

draw a truth table to determine those who qualify for a loan.

(b) From the truth table, or otherwise, construct a logic diagram to satisfy the above condition.

4 A bank uses a double security system, based on key-operated switches. The manager, the chief cashier and his deputy each have a key. The door to the vaults can be opened by using any two of the three keys, but the door to the strongroom can only be opened if the vault door is open and all three keys are used to operate the strongroom lock.

Design and sketch a logic circuit to satisfy the above conditions, using standard logic elements. Ensure that your diagram is fully annotated.

28 Word Processing and Word-processing Exercises

Word-processing packages are the most popular type of computer software. For many people a word-processing package is the only software they use. It is hard to think of a single job where some use for word processing could not be found.

Many people now type their own documents directly into a computer rather than give them to a typist. This saves time if people can type quickly. Because the text is stored in memory once it is typed, people can alter their text before finally saving and printing (Figure 28.1).

Now even printing letters is becoming out of date, because electronic mail is often used to send word-processed documents in electronic form from one place to another. There is no need for an envelope or a stamp and the recipient may store the letter on disk for future reference, thus saving valuable storage space.

Hardware and software for word processing

The most common hardware arrangement is:

- a microcomputer
- a high quality printer (a laser or inkjet printer)
- a mouse (necessary if the word processor uses Microsoft®Windows® or the Macintosh® operating system)
- a keyboard.

Apart from the operating system, the only software needed is a word-processing package. This can be a separate package which just does word processing, or part of an integrated package where word processing is only one part of the complete package.

You can also use special voice recognition software to dictate straight into a word processor.

Notes prepared beforehand   Thoughts and ideas keyed in directly

▲ **Figure 28.1** *Typing your thoughts directly into the word processor saves time, but it is not quite as easy as working from notes*

The advantages of word processing

Word processing has several advantages compared with typing.

1 Much more professional results can be obtained by everyone and not just those who are experienced typists, because typing mistakes are easily altered on the screen before printing out.

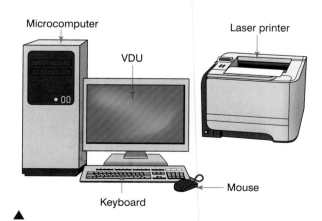

Microcomputer   Laser printer

VDU

Mouse

Keyboard

▲ **Figure 28.2** *A typical word-processing system*

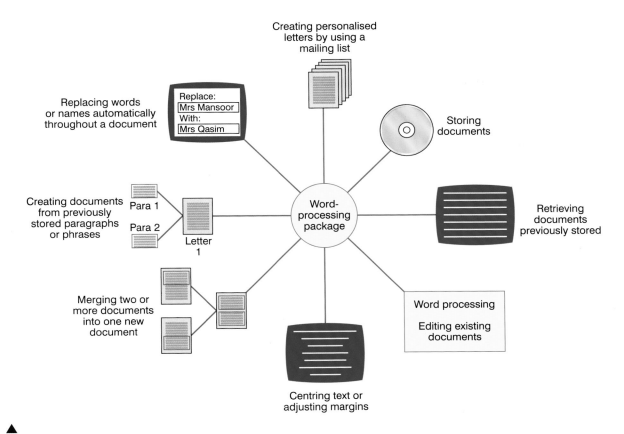

Replacing words or names automatically throughout a document

Replace:
Mrs Mansoor
With:
Mrs Qasim

Creating personalised letters by using a mailing list

Storing documents

Creating documents from previously stored paragraphs or phrases

Para 1
Para 2
Letter 1

Word-processing package

Retrieving documents previously stored

Word processing

Editing existing documents

Merging two or more documents into one new document

Centring text or adjusting margins

Figure 28.3 *Some of the things you might find in a typical word-processing package*

2 Fewer resources are used, provided that material is carefully proofread on the screen before finally printing. Since we can edit and correct mistakes before printing, this reduces the amount of paper used. Most large companies now send all their internal letters and memos using electronic mail. The widespread use of electronic mail will help to conserve valuable resources.

3 More people are able to produce their own documents rather than pass them to someone else to type. This can save both time and money.

4 More word processors are becoming like simple desktop publishing packages. These extra facilities enable people to produce notices, posters, tickets and so on with very little training.

What can you do with word-processing software?

Wordprocessing software is software that is able to store, edit and manipulate text. All word-processing software allows you to enter text, then edit and rearrange it before storing it and printing it out. Some word processors are WYSIWYG (what you see is what you get). This means that you are able to see on the screen exactly what the page will look like when it is printed out.

Most word processors allow you to change the fonts (type styles and sizes). Figure 28.3 shows some of the things you might find in a typical word-processing package.

Spell checkers

Nearly all word processors have a dictionary against which the words in a document can be compared to check their spelling. Most allow you to add words to the dictionary, which is useful if you use special terms in subjects such as law or medicine. It is important to note that spell checking a document will not remove all the errors. For instance, if you intended to type 'the' and typed 'he' instead, the spell checker will not detect this since 'he' as a word is spelt correctly. After using a spell checker it is still necessary to proofread a document.

Thesaurus

A thesaurus is useful for creative writing (perhaps for English coursework). It allows you to highlight a word in a document and the computer lists words with similar meanings (called synonyms) (Figure 28.4).

▲
Figure 28.4

Mail merge

Mail merging involves combining a list, say, of names and addresses, with a typed letter, so that a series of similar letters is produced, each addressed to a different person. The list is either created using the word processor or by importing data from a database of names and addresses. The letter is typed, using the word processor, with blanks where the data from the list are to be inserted.

Indexing

Indexing allows you to highlight words that you would like to use in an index. The word processor keeps a record of the words and creates an index when instructed to.

Macros

Macros allow you to produce a sequence of keystrokes automatically so that, for example, you can just press one key or a combination of keys and have your name and address printed at the top of the page. You can also insert dates just by pressing a couple of keys. Macros are very useful for things that need to be done repetitively.

Grammar checkers

Some of the more sophisticated word processors have a feature called a grammar checker. This is useful if your English is not so good. If the word processor you use does not have this facility, then you can buy a separate grammar-checking package to use with it. Figure 28.5 shows a grammar checker being used. Because of the complexities of the English language, grammar checkers do have their limitations. As yet they find only a few faults and do tend to provide an incorrect analysis of the grammar of writing. You need to exercise care when using them.

Other features found in most word-processing packages

Here are just some of the many features you will find as part of a professional word-processing package such as Microsoft® Word.

Print preview – using the print preview you can see the whole page (as a smaller version) before you print it out. This can save time and paper.

Templates and wizards – here the framework of the document (fonts, sizes, headings, etc.) is laid out for you. You do not need to worry about the layout. All you have to do is supply the text.

Save in different file formats – this means you can transfer your word-processed material to almost any other package.

Figure 28.5 *The text above contains a grammatical error. The grammar checker on this word processor is able to find it and suggest how it could be corrected*

Word count – this counts the number of words in a document or part of a document. This is useful if you have to write essays or coursework of a certain number of words.

Online help – you can search for help by entering a keyword or by selecting a topic from a list. Good online help is particularly important as a lot of software is supplied without manuals.

Drawing tools – these tools allow you to produce arrows, shapes, boxes and so on, without having to use a special graphics package.

Zooming in and out – particularly useful if you have difficulty seeing small text on the screen.

Tables – rather than use a spreadsheet, you can use the tables function in the word processor. If there are numbers in the tables you can even perform simple calculations on them.

Ability to import clip art/other files – documents can be made much more attractive by importing pictures (clip art) or photographs from pre-stored files.

Using a word processor to compile email

Many people use word-processing software to prepare and edit email. Word-processing software is used for the following reasons:

- You can spell check your email before sending it.
- You can check your grammar using the grammar checker.

Although most emails can be written using the software supplied by the internet service provider, this usually provides only basic editing facilities.

The email address of the person to whom the email is being sent, e.g. MQasim8768@aol.com

Insert a suitable title

The email address of anyone who is to be sent a copy of the email

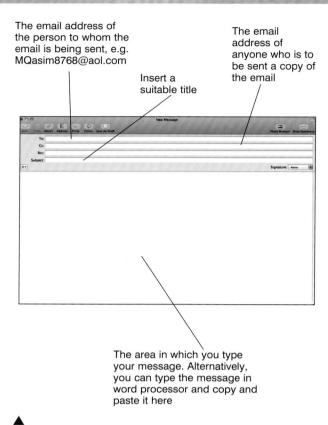

The area in which you type your message. Alternatively, you can type the message in word processor and copy and paste it here

Figure 28.6 *How to compose a typical email message*

The steps for sending a typical email are as follows:

1 Log onto your internet service provider.
2 Obtain the email address of the person you are sending the email to. Notice the address book where you can store all your email addresses.
3 Put in the CC window the email addresses of anyone else who may need to see the email. They will be sent a copy automatically, as well as the main recipient.
4 Give your email a suitable title that indicates to the receiver what its contents are.
5 Type in your email or import it from another package.
6 You can attach files to your email. You could send a multi-page document, a spreadsheet or drawing prepared using CAD as a file. The user at the other end needs to have the applications software to use the data files you have sent to them.
7 Click the 'Send' button' to send your email.

Questions

1 Find out how to do each of the following tasks using your word processor. Write down for future reference how you would perform each task.

(a) how to load the word-processing software
(b) how to edit a document
(c) how to alter the margins
(d) how to do special text effects, such as:

- bold type
- underlining
- italics

(e) how to centre text
(f) how to insert a line
(g) how to produce a temporary indent
(h) how to save text
(i) how to load previously saved work
(j) how to move blocks of text around (called block moves or cut and paste)
(k) how to print a document.

2 This question concerns the more advanced features of word processors.

Find out how to do each of the following using your word processor and write down for future reference how you would perform each task.

(a) how to spell check a document
(b) how to use the thesaurus
(c) how to use the search and replace facility
(d) how to use macros
(e) how to use mail merging.

Test Yourself

Using the words in the list below, copy out and complete sentences **A** to **F**, underlining the words you have inserted. The words may be used more than once.

word processor   DTP   high   electronic mail

grammar   spell checker

A The most commonly used piece of software is the_____ _____.

B With a word processor, you can type in a letter and then send it directly to another part of the country or even the world, using _____ _____.

C One of the main advantages of word processing is that an inexperienced typist is able to produce _____ quality documents.

D Many word processors now contain features you would normally find only in _____ packages.

E The most useful advanced feature on the word processor is the _____ _____, which is used to check the spelling of an entire document after it has been typed.

F The more advanced word processors have _____ checkers, where you can check that the structure of the English is correct.

Things to do

1 (a)   What does a word processor consist of?
  (b)   As a document is being typed, where is it stored?
  (c)   Why is it always advisable to save your document before printing it and not the other way round?
  (d)   The minutes of a meeting have been typed on a word processor and stored on a disk. The draft copy shows one mistake. In the middle of a long paragraph, the word 'the' has been typed in twice. Describe briefly how the operator would correct the minutes.

2 A friend of yours has never used a word processor before. Explain to her what advantages word processors have over conventional typewriters. Give at least four advantages.

3 You have just loaded the 'Quickword' word processor and the menu shown in Figure 28.7 appears on the screen. You want to retrieve a previously saved document, make a couple of alterations and finally produce a printout. Write down the order in which the commands should be used.

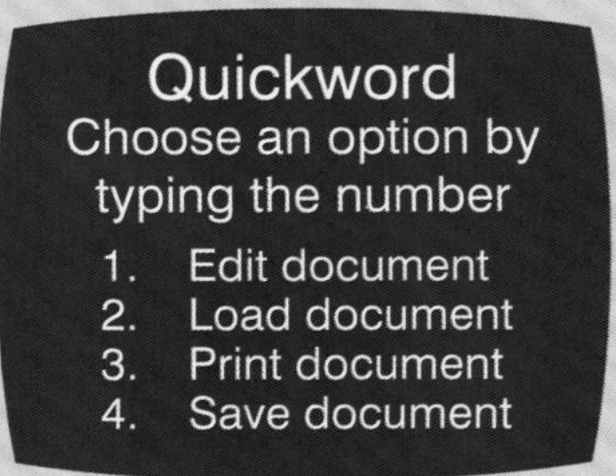

Quickword
Choose an option by typing the number

1.   Edit document
2.   Load document
3.   Print document
4.   Save document

▶ **Figure 28.7**

IT Tasks

Task 1

Load your word-processing software and type in the following text, making sure that you do not press the return or enter key at the end of a line unless you want to leave blank lines between paragraphs.

> When you first start to use the word processor you may find it hard to think up what you are going to say and have to write it down first. This does destroy the point of the word processor (i.e. it is supposed to save time). Try to type in your work directly and remember that the beauty of the word processor is its ability to let you change things around.
>
> Also, beginners often correct their mistakes as they go along, whereas high-speed typists will probably not know they have made the mistake until they carefully read through their document (proofread) afterwards.

(a) Proofread the above document and correct any errors that you spot.
(b) Save your document.
(c) Print the document.

Task 2

Type the following letter into your word processor.

> Dear Mr Kawael,
>
> This is just the chance you have been waiting for. You have been specially selected to enter our prize draw. Just imagine the difference our $100,000 first prize would make to your lifestyle. Or if you do not win the first prize, imagine the envy of your neighbours when a brand new Ferrari sports car appears on the Kawael drive.
>
> All you have to do, Mr Kawael, to enter our new competition is to purchase a copy of *Your Rights as a Consumer*. This useful book looks at all matters related to consumer problems and deals with such things as your rights when taking goods back, problems with credit and how to deal with shoddy home repairs. In fact nearly every problem you could encounter is mentioned in this invaluable book.
>
> All you have to do, Mr Kawael, is return the enclosed entry form. You do not need to send any money. The book will be sent to you, together with the invoice for $39.95. If you do not wish to purchase the book, simply return the postage paid package within 14 days and you will still be entered for our prize draw. If you reply within 7 days then you could win a cash bonus of $20,000. Can you afford not to reply, Mr Kawael?

(a) Proofread the document by carefully comparing it with the original. If there are any errors, correct them.
(b) Save and then print a copy of the document.
(c) Highlight *Your Rights as a Consumer* using bold print.
(d) Underline 'You do not need to send any money'.
(e) Search for and then replace all occurrences of 'Mr Kawael' with 'Mrs Ho'. (You must use the word processor's search and replace facility to do this.)
(f) Search for and then replace all occurrences of $20,000 with $10,000.
(g) Start a new paragraph for the sentence starting 'If you reply within 7 days' by leaving a blank line.
(h) Save the revised document.
(i) Print the final document.

Task 3

You have been asked to produce a slip to explain a special deal that a company which manufactures calculators has given your school. The slip is to be photocopied and one is to be given to each student in the school (there are 1,600 students in the school). Because the school wants to save paper and photocopying charges, it would like to copy this document three times, if possible, onto an A4 page.

Type in the following text:

SPECIAL OFFER

Here is a very special offer to all our students. We have managed to negotiate a special price on a CASIO 6543 scientific calculator which we recommend to all our students. This calculator is the cheapest on the market at only $13.50 and has all the features of calculators costing twice as much.

It is easy to get a calculator. Just fill in the form and return it with payment (cash or cheque payable to Green Hill PTA) to the school secretary, who will supply your son/daughter with the calculator.

Name ....   Form ....

Number of calculators you wish to buy ....

Signature of parent/guardian ....

(a) Try to make this advert as appealing as you can by the use of bold type, italics, underlining and different fonts.
(b) Copy this document to see if it will fit on an A4 page three times.
(c) When you are happy with it, save and print the page.

IT Tasks

Task 4

Load your word processor and type in the following document.

Curriculum vitae

A curriculum vitae is used to tell people about yourself and what you have done with your life so far. By reading it, another person is able to get an impression of you by the personal details and experience you have put down. CVs are normally attached to a letter of application for a job. A CV should include what your achievements have been to date and an outline of your qualifications (or exams taken if you are still awaiting the results). A CV is very important, so you need to take time to produce a good one.

It is best to produce a list of the things you need to include and then produce a first draft. Ask another person to read through it. Your English teacher may check it for spelling mistakes and grammatical errors. You should then produce the final version.

Make sure that you leave plenty of space between the various items and that it is no longer than about two sides of A4 size paper.

Make sure that you include such things as qualifications, what interested you at school, any work experience, any positions of authority you have held, details of hobbies and sports played. Remember, the purpose of the CV is to sell yourself.

(a) Type in the document exactly as it appears above.
(b) Proofread the document by looking at it carefully on the screen and checking that it compares exactly with what was written above.
(c) Save your file using a suitable name.
(d) Print out a copy of the file.

Task 5

In task 4 you typed in a passage about CVs. Now you are going to design one of your own. Imagine that you are applying for a college place or a job and have been asked to supply a CV. Produce your CV using word-processing software.

IT Tasks

Task 6

Your maths teacher would like you to investigate how to type equations into the word processor. He would like to be able to use the word processor to produce a worksheet on Pythagoras's theorem. As well as the equations, he would like you to investigate the possibility of including labelled diagrams of triangles in the worksheet. He has handed you the following handwritten sample of part of the worksheet.

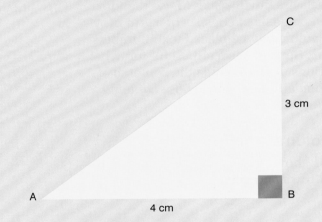

Using Pythagoras's theorem

$$AC^2 \quad = AB^2 + BC^2$$
$$AC^2 \quad = 4^2 + 3^2$$
$$AC^2 \quad = 16 + 9$$
$$AC^2 \quad = 25$$
$$AC^2 \quad = 25$$
$$AC \quad = \sqrt{25}$$
$$\quad = 5\ cm$$

Figure 28.8

Design and produce a worksheet which could be used by the mathematics teacher to teach Pythagoras's theorem. Your worksheet should look appealing and not too cluttered. Try to import labelled diagrams of the triangles into the document.

The mathematics teacher shows your efforts to the chemistry teacher, who is very impressed. She would now like you to find out about doing similar worksheets containing chemical equations. Although she is familiar with the simple functions of the word processor, she has no idea how to import diagrams or how to produce the equations. She has asked you to produce a guide for her, along with a couple of examples of what can be done.

The chemistry teacher supplies you with the following equation as an example of a typical chemical equation.

$$H_2SO4 + 2NaOH = Na_2SO4 + 2H_2O$$

Task 7

Using the tabular features of your word processor, produce a copy of your school or college timetable.

Task 8

Investigate the mail merge facility on your word processor.

29 Spreadsheets and Spreadsheet Exercises

What is a spreadsheet?

Spreadsheets are much easier to use than to explain. A spreadsheet consists of a grid of cells into which may be placed text, numbers or formulae. Spreadsheets are useful for 'what if' calculations. If you change the contents of one cell, then all those cells whose contents depend on it will change as well.

Rows, columns and cells

Figure 29.1 shows a spreadsheet grid with its horizontal rows and vertical columns.

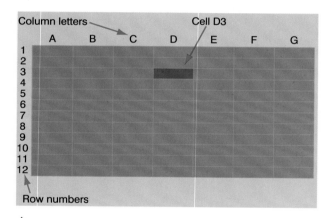

Figure 29.1 *Spreadsheet grid*

This small figure can show only part of a spreadsheet. Spreadsheets are frequently very large and only a small part of the sheet can be viewed on the screen at any one time. It is rather like looking at the sheet through a movable window, as in Figure 29.2.

Spreadsheets are made up of cells, each of which has its own address. For instance, the intersection of column D with row 3 will give a cell with the address D3.

All spreadsheets can total columns or rows of numbers. To do this, you type a formula into the cell where you want the total to be displayed. This formula must state which is the first cell in the series that is to be added up and which is the last.

CASH FLOW ANALYSIS FOR J HUGHES MARKET GARDENER

APR	MAY	JUN	JUL	AUG	SEP	OCT	NOV	DEC	JAN	FEB	MAR
245.31	303.58	458.31	683.92	647.84	609.72	648.67	560.98	758.42	858.90	680.40	416.84
120.00	120.00	120.00	120.00	120.00	120.00	120.00	120.00	120.00	120.00	120.00	120.00
115.00	115.00	115.00	115.00	115.00	115.00	115.00	115.00	115.00	115.00	115.00	115.00
480.31	538.58	693.31	918.92	882.84	844.72	883.67	795.98	993.42	1093.90	915.40	651.84
80.00	80.00	80.00	918.92	882.84	844.72	883.67		85.00	85.00	85.00
40.00	12.00	0.00						48.28	84.30	126.00
240.00	0.00	0.00	80.00	80.00	80.00	85.00	85.00	12.00	25.62	12.80
8.62	4.84	3.00	0.00	0.00	0.00	0.00	0.00	25.60	17.23	14.00
12.00	13.00	10.00	0.00	0.00	0.00	286.30	15.00	14.85	13.23	12.50
54.84	54.84	54.00	0.00	0.00	0.00	286.30	15.00	54.84	54.84	54.84
40.00	15.00	2.00	3.22	3.41	4.84	5.26	6.00	1.85	0.00	0.00
32.00	10.80	0.00						2.64	15.70	0.00
85.00	0.00	0.00	10.54	8.21	7.54	14.80	28.50	18.50	20.00	45.00
18.00	18.00	18.00	54.84	54.84	54.84	54.84	54.84	18.00	18.00	18.00
12.00	125.00	0.00	2.50	1.80	0.00	0.00	12.00	0.00	0.00	0.00
14.00	5.00	0.00						0.00	0.00	0.00
25.00	0.00	0.00	0.00	0.00	0.00	0.00	0.00	27.00	0.00	1.80
120.00	120.00	120.00	120.00	120.00	120.00	120.00	120.00	120.00	120.00	120.00	120.00
781.46	45848	289.10	286.26	285.22	584.20	339.34	300.38	411.44	428.56	453.92	490.00
-301.15	80.10	404.21	632.66	597.62	260.552	544.33	495.60	581.98	665.34	461.48	161.84
0.00	-221.05	484.31	1036.87	1230.28	858.14	804.85	1039.93	1077.58	1247.32	1126.82	623.32

▲
Figure 29.2 *Looking at a spreadsheet through a 'window'*

What can you put into a cell?

You can put in:

1 words (titles, row headings, column headings, etc.)
2 numbers (ordinary numbers, currency, dates, etc.)
3 formulae (used to perform calculations with the numbers).

Figure 29.3 shows a Microsoft® Excel® worksheet.

Entering data correctly

There are two common mistakes that people make when using spreadsheets.

Entering numbers as text

When people first start using spreadsheets, they like to be able to centre the data when they type them in. They soon find that they can do this by pressing the space bar several times before they type in the data.

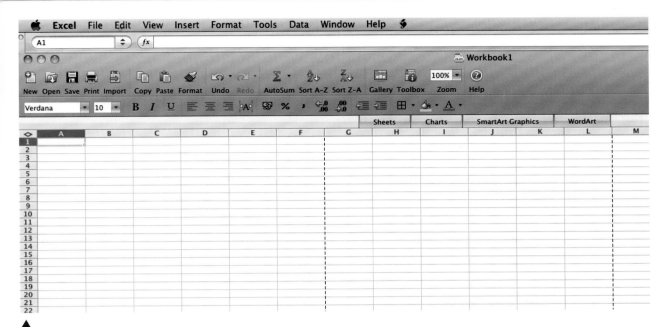

Figure 29.3 *The opening screen of Microsoft® Excel®*

If a number is typed in after the space bar has been pressed then the number will be treated like text and it will be impossible to use this number in calculations. Most spreadsheets have a function which will move the cell contents to the right, left or centre. It is best to get all the data typed in and then change the position of the data in the cells.

Referring a formula to its own cell

Suppose we wanted to add up the data in the cells C1 to C7 and put the total in C8. If we typed in =sum(C1:C8) then we are using the cell where the formula is, which is not allowed. Instead we need to type:

= sum(C1:C7)

Here is a sample spreadsheet:

	A	B	C	D
1	Expenses			
2	Phone	152.80		
3	Electricity	262.40		
4	Gas	189.00		
5	Stationery	76.00		
6	Postage	101.00		
7	Car expenses	896.00		
8	Total			

To calculate the total and put it into cell B8 we could move the cursor to this cell and then type in a formula like this:

+B2+B3+B4+B5+B6+B7

This is tedious, especially if we had to find the total of 100 cells, and there is a quicker command =sum(B2:B7) which adds up all the cells from B2 to B7 inclusive. These formulae may not work with your particular spreadsheet. Unfortunately not all spreadsheets are the same, so you will need to ask your teacher how to enter formulae if the above does not work.

If we change the electricity cost from 262.40 to 362.40, then as soon as we enter it, the spreadsheet automatically recalculates the new total (see Figure 29.4).

Let the spreadsheet do the work for you

When using spreadsheets for the first time many people reach for the calculator to do the calculations, or even do them in their heads. This defeats the object of the spreadsheet. It means that if you change one of the cells, then you will possibly have to recalculate many other cells. If there had

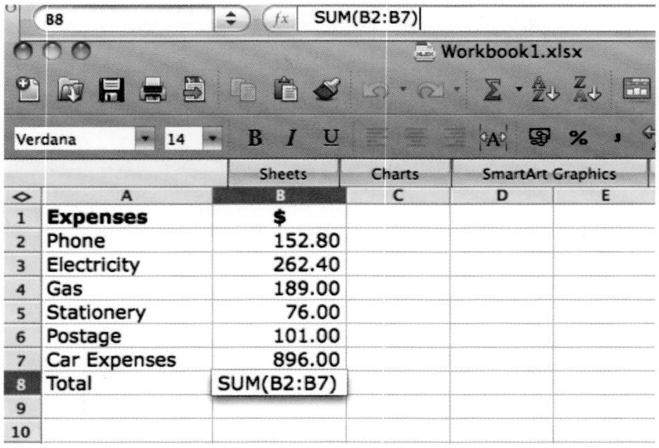

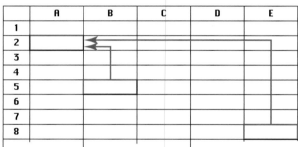

Figure 29.4 *Adding up data in Microsoft® Excel®*

been a formula, then the spreadsheet would have done all this work for you.

Also, the spreadsheet will always arrive at the correct answer, provided that you have given it the correct formula, of course.

Cell referencing

There are two ways of making a reference to another cell in a spreadsheet: using relative referencing or using absolute referencing. This is particularly important when you copy or move cells. An absolute reference always refers to the same cell on the spreadsheet. A relative reference, however, always refers to a cell which is a certain number of columns and rows away from the current cell. This means that when the current cell is moved or copied to a new position, the cell to which the reference is made will also change position.

This is best seen by referring to Figures 29.5 and 29.6.

You do not need to do anything to change cell references into relative cell references, since they are this by default. Relative cell references are useful because the spreadsheet can adjust the formulae automatically when the formulae are copied to other cells. If you need to refer to a particular value in a certain cell (such as an interest rate or tax rate), then you need to make any references to it absolute; this is done by putting a dollar sign in front of the column and row number.

For example the relative cell reference C4 could be converted to an absolute cell reference by inserting the dollar sign as follows: $C$4.

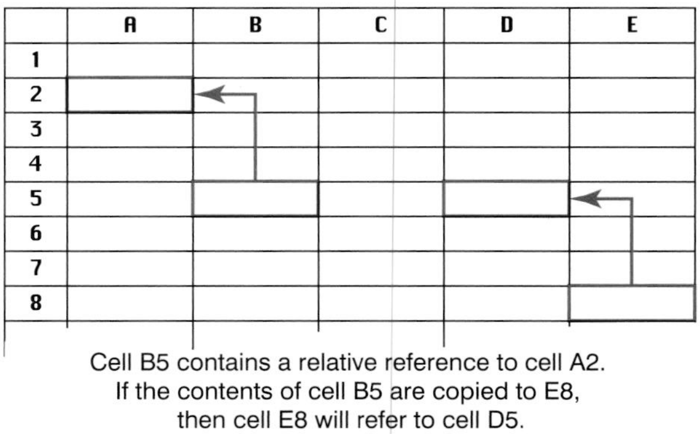

Cell B5 contains a relative reference to cell A2. If the contents of cell B5 are copied to E8, then cell E8 will refer to cell D5.

Figure 29.5 *Relative references in a spreadsheet*

If cell B5 had an absolute reference to cell A2, then if the contents of cell B5 are copied to E8, cell E8 will still refer to cell A2.

Figure 29.6 *Absolute references in a spreadsheet*

Some of the many features of spreadsheets

Spreadsheets can do many things besides performing simple arithmetic such as adding up columns of numbers. In this chapter we look at some of the more advanced and more powerful features of spreadsheets. Here are just some of the many more powerful features you will find as part of a typical spreadsheet package:

- **Borders** – you can add borders around the whole of your spreadsheet or just around certain parts.

- **Spell checkers** – you can check the spelling of text, just like with a word processor.
- **Print preview** – you can see what the spreadsheet looks like on the page before wasting paper.
- **Formatting** – this includes the font, font size, style (bold, italic, underline, etc.) and the alignment (centre, right, left and justified).
- **The use of colour** – this is useful if the material in the spreadsheet is to be presented to other people.
- **Autofill** – you can get the spreadsheet to automatically enter data such as the months of the year or days of the week. You can also start from a certain value and go up to another value in steps (e.g. 10 to 100 in steps of 5).
- **Multiple sheets** – sheets relating to the same project can be kept together.
- **Import data from other packages** – you could create a company logo in a graphics package and insert it into a spreadsheet.
- **Macros** – you can create a series of commands that a spreadsheet can perform automatically.

Tips for building a spreadsheet

1 Start with a title saying what the spreadsheet does. Also include the date.
2 Fill in the column and row headings.
3 Fill in the data, leaving blanks where the results of calculations need to go.
4 Fill in the formulae and copy them where necessary.

Mathematical operators

The table below shows some of the mathematical operators that can be used in a typical spreadsheet such as Microsoft® Excel®:

Operator	Use	Example
+	Addition	A1+B1
–	Subtraction	B2–C2
*	Multiplication	A1*C6
/	Division	A1/B1
%	Percentage	30%

The use of most of these operators is obvious, but let us look at how the percentage operator works by following an example.

A salesperson is paid commission on what they sell. They get 10 per cent commission on all their sales.

We can set up this information about commission as a spreadsheet in the following way:

▲ Figure 29.7

Note that the spreadsheet, when it multiplies the cells B1 and B2 together, automatically knows that it is working with percentages.

Using conditions in spreadsheets

Most spreadsheets, including Microsoft® Excel®, have a function called IF. The IF function tests a condition and then chooses between two actions, based on whether the condition is true or false. This sounds complicated, so we will look at a simple example.

Example

Set up the following spreadsheet, showing the marks obtained in an examination by ten students. The pass mark for the examination was 50 per cent. The teacher wants the spreadsheet to show automatically those pupils who have passed and those who have failed.

We use the following statement in cell B4:
=IF(B4>=50,"Pass","Fail") This examines the value in cell B4 to see if it is greater than or equal to 50. If it is then 'Pass' is displayed, and if it isn't 'Fail' is displayed.

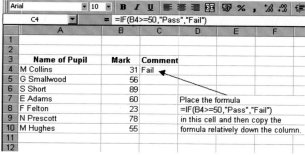

Figure 29.8

Once the condition has been placed in cell B4 it can be copied relatively for all the other marks.

Questions

The idea of the following spreadsheet is to model a stock control system. Once the quantity in stock falls below a certain level, called the minimum reorder level, a message appears which says 'Reorder'. If the quantity in stock is above the reorder level, then the message 'OK' appears. These messages are to appear in column G in this spreadsheet.

	C	D	E	
1	Qty in Stock	Min order Qty	Min reorder level	Price e
2	12	5	10	
3	15	5	7	
4	20	10	15	
5	10	5	5	
6	26	10	10	
7	30	15	10	
8	45	20	10	

▲
Figure 29.9

1 Your task is to set out the spreadsheet as shown and then include a condition that will enable one or other of the two messages to appear.

2 Once you have done this, can you improve the appearance of the spreadsheet?

Printing spreadsheets

Spreadsheets can be quite large, so there can be problems printing them out. Usually we want to fit the sheet across the width of the page. The better spreadsheet packages are able to do this by adjusting the size of the type. It is also possible to use condensed print.

Printing may be done in either portrait or landscape formats, as shown in Figure 29.7.

Questions

1 Find out how each of the following is done using your spreadsheet, and write down for future reference how you perform each task:
   (a) how to edit a cell
   (b) how to insert a row or column (this is useful if you forget to put one in)
   (c) how to widen a column (the column width is usually set at nine characters, but you can set it to another value)
   (d) how to position the text or numbers in each cell; for instance, you may wish to centre the contents of a group of cells
   (e) how to enter a formula
   (f) how to copy a cell; cells may be copied absolutely or relatively
   (g) how to load a spreadsheet (it must have been previously saved)
   (h) how to underline, make bold and italicise text (some spreadsheets do not have this facility)
   (i) how to save a spreadsheet
   (j) how to print out a spreadsheet; you can either print part of a spreadsheet by specifying a certain range or you can print out the whole sheet.

2 This question is about writing formulae for your particular spreadsheet. Not all spreadsheets use the same commands and you have to construct formulae differently for some spreadsheets. Your teacher will tell you how you should construct a formula.

Write down the formula you would put in a cell to do the following:
   (a) add cells B3, D7 and E11 together
   (b) multiply cells B3 and C3 together
   (c) subtract cell D3 from cell C3
   (d) find 5 per cent of cell D4
   (e) divide cell A2 by cell B4
   (f) find 17.5 per cent of cell A4
   (g) add all the cells from cell A5 to F5 inclusive
   (h) find the average of cells from A3 to G3 inclusive
   (i) add cells A3 and B3, and then divide this total by cell E5.

Graphs

All spreadsheets enable you to produce graphs and charts like the ones shown in Figure 29.8.

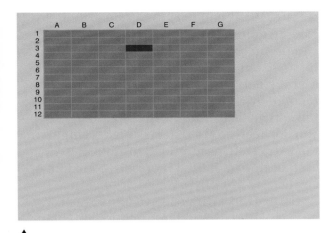

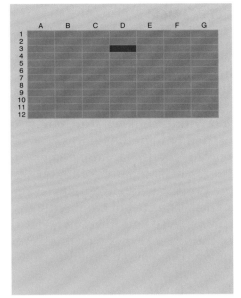

▲

Figure 29.10 *Printing a worksheet in landscape mode (above) and in portrait mode (right)*

Figure 29.11 *All these graphs are produced from this simple table of half-yearly sales figures*

▼

Half-yearly Sales

Month	Sales
Jan	1250
Feb	3400
Mar	980
Apr	1200
May	3178
June	4329

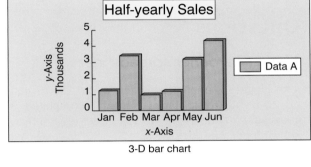

3-D bar chart

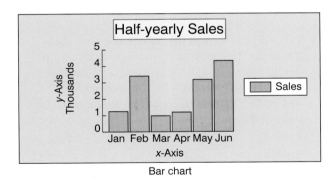

Bar chart

Pie chart

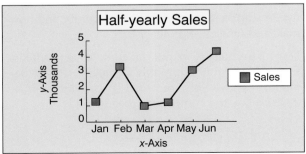

Line graph

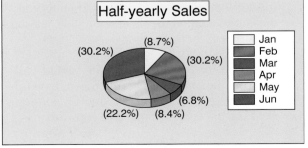

3D pie chart

Business decisions

Julia, the sales manager of a company, can use a spreadsheet to help make business decisions. She sets up a spreadsheet which includes all the income (money coming into the business) and costs or expenditure (money going out of the business). A series of formulae is used to total the figures and work out the profit (profit = total income – total expenses). The company could, on the basis of the profit, decide to employ more salespersons. The cost of employing them will be an expense and this will need to be added to the expenses. The profits will now go down because the expenses are greater. What happens to the sales though? Having more people selling the goods should increase the sales and therefore the income, but by how much? Julia reckons that the extra sales staff should increase the income by about 10 per cent, so she adjusts the spreadsheet and the profit alters. The spreadsheet shows that it is worth employing the extra staff, assuming that Julia's assumption about the increase in income is correct.

Spreadsheets are used in all types of businesses to provide information on which to base decisions. After word processors, spreadsheets are the most common type of software.

Questions

Market gardener spreadsheet

John Hughes is unemployed and would like to start his own business. Having recently completed a course in horticulture, he decides to set up as a market gardener. His uncle owns a large garage and next to this is a field which his uncle also owns. He agrees to rent the field to John at a rent of £80 per month. John decides that he will grow a variety of vegetables on the land, which he will sell to customers who come into his uncle's garage.

John realises that his first year's trading will be tough and he needs to make sure that he has enough money coming in each month to pay his overheads. To make sure of this he sits down and writes a list of all his income and likely expenditure.

1 Figure 29.9 shows the data you have to type in. Make sure that you include the title of the spreadsheet, along with the date. Then type in the information on the sheet accurately, leaving blank spaces for the missing data.

2 Put in a formula in the column for April to work out the total income. Add this column up manually to check that your formula is correct. Now use the copy command to copy this formula relatively so that all the totals for the months are filled in.

3 Using a suitable formula, find the total expenditure for each of the months.

4 Calculate the profit, using a formula to subtract the total expenditure from the total income.

5 We will now look at the cumulative total for the profit. This represents the money that John would have left at the end of each month. He would need this money to continue trading. Remember that his trade will be seasonal, so he will need some money to tide him over the slack periods.

In April, he will make a cumulative loss of £300.15. In May he makes a small profit of £80.10, which is added to the loss in April, reducing the cumulative loss. In June he starts to make a profit and now makes a cumulative profit.

Using a formula, work out the cumulative profit/loss for April and then copy this formula for the other months to give you your final spreadsheet. Figure 29.10 shows the completed spreadsheet.

2011 to 2012	CASH FLOW ANALYSIS FOR J HUGHES MARKET GARDENER											
INCOME	APR	MAY	JUN	JUL	AUG	SEP	OCT	NOV	DEC	JAN	FEB	MAR
Sales	245.31	303.58	458.31	683.92	647.84	609.72	648.67	560.98	758.42	858.90	680.40	416.84
Rent Allowance	120.00	120.00	120.00	120.00	120.00	120.00	120.00	120.00	120.00	120.00	120.00	120.00
Grant	115.00	115.00	115.00	115.00	115.00	115.00	115.00	115.00	115.00	115.00	115.00	115.00
Total Income												
EXPENDITURE												
Rent	80.00	80.00	80.00	80.00	80.00	85.00	85.00	85.00	85.00	85.00	85.00	85.00
Heating	40.00	12.00	0.00	0.00	0.00	0.00	0.00	0.00	0.00	48.28	84.30	126.00
Fertilisers	240.00	0.00	0.00	0.00	0.00	286.30	15.00	0.00	86.00	12.00	25.62	12.80
Lighting	8.62	4.84	3.22	3.41	4.84	5.26	6.00	7.84	26.80	25.60	17.23	14.00
Petrol	12.00	13.00	10.54	8.21	7.54	14.80	28.50	12.90	16.40	14.85	13.23	12.56
Loan	54.84	54.84	54.84	54.84	54.84	54.84	54.84	54.84	54.84	54.84	54.84	54.84
Seeds	40.00	15.00	2.50	1.80	0.00	0.00	12.00	1.80	4.40	1.85	0.00	0.00
Gro-bags	32.00	10.80	0.00	0.00	0.00	0.00	0.00	0.00	0.00	2.64	15.70	0.00
Compost	85.00	0.00	0.00	0.00	0.00	0.00	0.00	0.00	0.00	18.50	20.00	45.00
Van hire	18.00	18.00	18.00	18.00	18.00	18.00	18.00	18.00	18.00	18.00	18.00	18.00
Equipment	12.00	125.00	0.00	0.00	0.00	0.00	0.00	0.00	0.00	0.00	0.00	0.00
Seed trays	14.00	5.00	0.00	0.00	0.00	0.00	0.00	0.00	0.00	0.00	0.00	0.00
Boxes	25.00	0.00	0.00	0.00	0.00	0.00	0.00	0.00	0.00	27.00	0.00	1.80
Wages	120.00	120.00	120.00	120.00	120.00	120.00	120.00	120.00	120.00	120.00	120.00	120.00
TOTAL EXPENDITURE												
PROFIT/LOSS												
CUMULATIVE PROFIT/LOSS												

Figure 29.12 *Blank 'market gardener' template*

2011 to 2012	CASH FLOW ANALYSIS FOR J HUGHES MARKET GARDENER											
INCOME	APR	MAY	JUN	JUL	AUG	SEP	OCT	NOV	DEC	JAN	FEB	MAR
Sales	245.31	303.58	458.31	683.92	647.84	609.72	648.67	560.98	758.42	858.90	680.40	416.84
Rent Allowance	120.00	120.00	120.00	120.00	120.00	120.00	120.00	120.00	120.00	120.00	120.00	120.00
Grant	115.00	115.00	115.00	115.00	115.00	115.00	115.00	115.00	115.00	115.00	115.00	115.00
Total Income	480.31	538.58	693.31	918.92	882.84	844.72	883.67	795.98	993.42	1093.90	915.40	651.84
EXPENDITURE												
Rent	80.00	80.00	80.00	80.00	80.00	85.00	85.00	85.00	85.00	85.00	85.00	85.00
Heating	40.00	12.00	0.00	0.00	0.00	0.00	0.00	0.00	0.00	48.28	84.30	126.00
Fertilisers	240.00	0.00	0.00	0.00	0.00	286.30	15.00	0.00	86.00	12.00	25.62	12.80
Lighting	8.62	4.84	3.22	3.41	4.84	5.26	6.00	7.84	26.80	25.60	17.23	14.00
Petrol	12.00	13.00	10.54	8.21	7.54	14.80	28.50	12.90	16.40	14.85	13.23	12.56
Loan	54.84	54.84	54.84	54.84	54.84	54.84	54.84	54.84	54.84	54.84	54.84	54.84
Seeds	40.00	15.00	2.50	1.80	0.00	0.00	12.00	1.80	4.40	1.85	0.00	0.00
Gro-bags	32.00	10.80	0.00	0.00	0.00	0.00	0.00	0.00	0.00	2.64	15.70	0.00
Compost	85.00	0.00	0.00	0.00	0.00	0.00	0.00	0.00	0.00	18.50	20.00	45.00
Van hire	18.00	18.00	18.00	18.00	18.00	18.00	18.00	18.00	18.00	18.00	18.00	18.00
Equipment	12.00	125.00	0.00	0.00	0.00	0.00	0.00	0.00	0.00	0.00	0.00	0.00
Seed trays	14.00	5.00	0.00	0.00	0.00	0.00	0.00	0.00	0.00	0.00	0.00	0.00
Boxes	25.00	0.00	0.00	0.00	0.00	0.00	0.00	0.00	0.00	27.00	0.00	1.80
Wages	120.00	120.00	120.00	120.00	120.00	120.00	120.00	120.00	120.00	120.00	120.00	120.00
TOTAL EXPENDITURE	781.46	45848	289.10	286.26	285.22	584.20	339.34	300.38	411.44	428.56	453.92	490.00
PROFIT/LOSS	−301.15	80.10	404.21	632.66	597.62	260.552	544.33	495.60	581.98	665.34	461.48	161.84
CUMULATIVE PROFIT/LOSS	−301.15	−221.05	183.16	815.82	1413.44	1673.96	2218.29	2713.89	3295.87	3961.21	4422.69	4584.53

Figure 29.13 *The completed worksheet. Check that yours is the same as this*

Finding the maximum volume of a box made from a sheet of metal

Varipack is a company that makes metal boxes from sheet metal for various customers. An open box (i.e. one without a lid) is to be made out of a rectangular sheet of metal by cutting out squares of metal from each corner, bending the sides up and then welding the joins. Figure 29.14 shows how this is done.

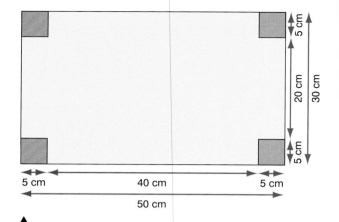

▲ **Figure 29.15** *Working out the dimensions of the box from the corner size*

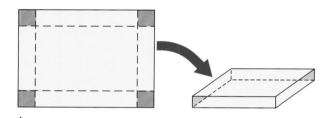

▲ **Figure 29.14** *Cutting out squares from each corner and then folding along the dotted lines makes the box*

If we had a sheet of metal 50 cm by 30 cm and cut out squares of 5 cm from each corner, we can work out the length, width and height of the box in the following way.

The length of the box will be $50 - 2 \times 5 = 40$ cm, the width will be $30 - 2 \times 5 = 20$ cm and the height of the box is the same as the corner size, that is 5 cm.

The volume of this box is calculated using the formula:

volume = length × width × height

so:

volume = $40 \times 20 \times 5 = 4,000$ cm^3

There are many different-sized boxes that could be made out of this sheet of metal. Varipack wants to know what size corners to cut out, to make the volume of the resulting box as large as possible.

To do this we can use a spreadsheet with the following formulae:

length of box = 30 − 2 × corner size
width of box = 20 − 2 × corner size
height of box = corner size

To start off, we can produce a spreadsheet using corner sizes from 1 cm to 10 cm in

	A	B	C	D	E	F
1	Spreadsheet 1 to determine the rough corner size to give the maximum volume.					
2						
3						
4	Corner Size	Length of box	Width of box	Volume of box		
5	1	28	18	504		
6	2	26	16	832		
7	3	24	4	1008		
8	4	22	12	1056		
9	5	20	10	1000		
10	6	18	8	864		
11	7	16	6	672		
12	8	14	4	448		
13	9	12	2	216		
14	10	10	0	0		
15						
16	Spreadsheet 2 to determine a more accurate corner size to give the maximum volume					
17						
18	Corner Size	Length of box	Width of box	Volume of box		
19	3.50	23.00	13.00	1046.50		
20	3.60	22.80	12.80	1050.62		
21	3.70	22.60	12.60	1053.61		
22	3.80	22.40	12.40	1055.49		
23	3.90	22.20	12.20	1056.28		
24	4.00	22.00	12.00	1056.00		
25	4.10	21.80	11.80	1054.68		
26	4.20	21.60	11.60	1052.35		
27	4.30	21.40	11.40	1049.03		
28	4.40	21.20	11.20	1044.74		
29	4.50	21.00	11.00	1039.50		

▲ **Figure 29.16** *Using a spreadsheet to work out the corner size that gives the maximum volume*

steps of 1 cm. We cannot have a corner size greater than 10 cm, since this would make the width of this box zero.

From this first spreadsheet, we see that the maximum volume occurs when the corner size is 4 cm. We need to set up a spreadsheet to get a more accurate value for the corner size. We will now investigate from 3.5 cm to 4.5 cm in steps of 0.1 cm (i.e. 1 mm).

We now find that the corner size to give us the maximum volume is 3.9 cm. If we wanted to we could investigate either side of this figure to get an even more accurate value. You may like to do this. Also, try using the graph-plotting facility to plot the volume on the y-axis and the corner size on the x-axis for the three spreadsheets.

Lookup tables

We came across lookup tables as a form of validation check in Chapter 7. Lookup tables work in the following way. You type in a unique number (such as a product number, stock number, employee number) and, provided that the number is one which is stored, the details will automatically be displayed.

Creating a lookup table using the spreadsheet Microsoft® Excel®

We can set up an example of a lookup table as follows. First we need to enter a table of data (see Figure 29.17). Cells A11 to D14 consist of a table of data. In this example the

item number is to be keyed in and the price and the item name should automatically appear. Here is what you have to do to set up this lookup table.

1 First we will enter the data into the empty table. The column headings are typed in and then the data are entered into cells A11 to D14.

2 The text (item number, price and item) is entered into cells A3, A4 and A5 respectively.

3 In cell B4 we type the following: =VLOOKUP(B3,A12:D14,4,FALSE)

4 We will now try to understand what this means. B3 is where the data are entered to match a value held in the table of data. For example 1001 is entered into cell B3 and this command tells the computer to look at the first column of the table until a match is found. We also have to tell the spreadsheet the range of the data it has to look through, and this is the part A12:D14 which is where the table is. It then needs the '4' to tell that the data that need to be filled in are in column 4. If the user enters an item number for which there is no match, it will produce the message 'N/A error' in the cell because the match is FALSE.

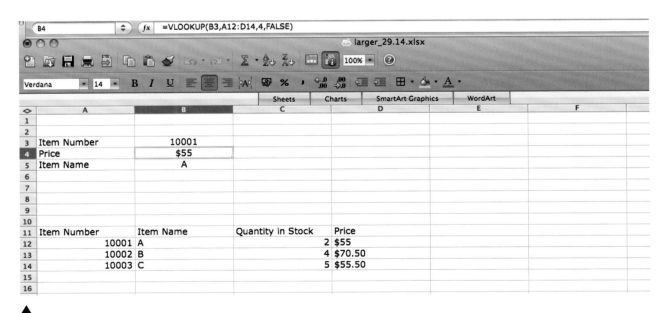

Figure 29.14 *A simple lookup table*

5 In cell B5 type:
=VLOOKUP(B3,A12:D14,2,FALSE).
Here the 2 in the second column is there because the data that need to go in cell B5 are in the second column of the table.

6 You can now test your spreadsheet by entering item numbers that are in the table. You also need to test it to see what happens if an item number that is not in the table is entered.

IT Tasks

Task 1

Produce your own lookup table

For this task you have to produce a lookup table using a spreadsheet to satisfy the following requirements.

A mail order computer hardware company keeps the price list shown below as a table.

The company's managers want to be able to put this table on a computer and be able to type in a product code so that the spreadsheet automatically displays the product code, product description and price.

You have to produce a lookup table and provide evidence to show that it works.

Here is the table of data for you to use.

Product code	Product description	Price
3501	TB-Western Digital USB hard drive	$80.00
3502	Flip video HD camcorder	$149.99
3503	LG Electronics i-Tunes server	$120.99
3504	Seagate TV media player	$90.00
3505	Kingston 16 GB SOHC flash card	$47.50
3506	Samsung 10.2 Mpix digital camera	$120.75
3507	HP wireless mouse for desktop computer	$30.00
3508	HP wireless mouse for laptop computer	$2850.00
3509	HP wireless full-size keyboard	$78.99
3510	3G broadband router	$102.44

Producing a lookup table using a spreadsheet for calculating commission from a table of commission values

This lookup table calculates commission for salespersons based on the values of the sales they make. There are different rates of commission based on the amount of sales. The table with the commission rates is included at the bottom of the spreadsheet (see Figure 29.15). In cell C4 the following formula is placed =VLOOKUP(B4,$A$15:$B$19,2)*B4.

This formula uses the data in cell B4 and tries to find a match with the table in cells A15 to D19. If no match is found, the spreadsheet finds the value in the table that is the next lowest value. In cell B4 the value is 780. Since there is no value of 780 in the table, the next lower value 500 in the table is found. The commission rate in the second column that goes with this is 8 per cent. This commission rate is then multiplied by cell B4 (i.e. the sales) to give the commission.

Figure 29.18 shows what the spreadsheet looks like with the first formula put in cell C4.

The formula is then copied down so that commissions can be calculated for all the other salespersons.

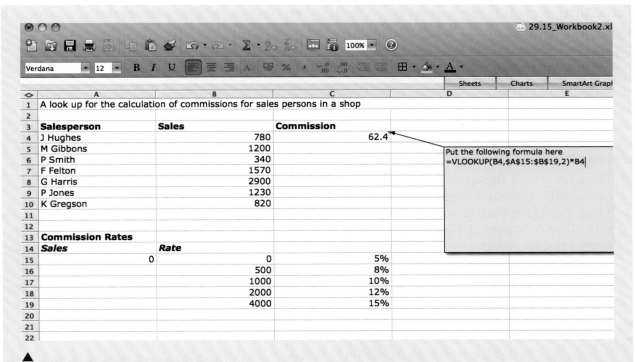

Figure 29.18 *Using a lookup table*

Task 2

Using a lookup table, work out the interest received on a certain amount of money invested in a bank account.

Here is a problem that can be solved using the lookup feature in a spreadsheet.

A bank offers the following interest rates, which vary depending on the amount of money invested.

Amount	Annual rate of interest
$1–999	3.5%
$1,000–4,999	4.5%
$5,000–9,999	5.5%
$10,000–19,999	6.0%
$20,000–49,999	6.5%
$50,000 and over	7.0%

The bank wants to be able to type in an amount of money to be invested. The system should then display the correct interest rate and the amount of interest the sum of money will earn over the year.

You have been asked to design a spreadsheet to solve this problem. Produce a fully documented spreadsheet to do this, and as part of the documentation provide evidence to show how you have approached the problem.

Creating a database using a spreadsheet such as Microsoft® Excel®

You can create a database using a spreadsheet and use many of the powerful functions in the spreadsheet and the ability of the spreadsheet to produce many different kinds of graphs.

To create a database in Microsoft® Excel® this is all you have to remember:

1 The first row in the spreadsheet needs to contain the field headings.
2 The records are then placed directly below this. (Do not leave any blank lines as this causes the spreadsheet to think that it has reached the end of the database.)

When you have created your database you can do the following with the data:

- You can sort the data into any order.
- You can extract data which match certain criteria (i.e. you can perform searches for specific data).
- You can use the calculating ability of the spreadsheet.
- You can easily generate subtotals.

- You can produce graphs and charts to illustrate features of the data.

You will need to ask your teacher, use the online help or consult a user guide or book to find out how to create and use a database.

Presenting data held in your spreadsheet

The table shown in Figure 29.19 contains data concerning the sales at a garden centre in the various departments for the four seasons of the year. As it is, it is quite boring.

	Spring	Summer	Autumn	Winter
Seasonal	9800	14500	15600	21900
Plants	21800	36900	14500	2800
Tools	8900	12700	6400	3900
Compost/Fertiliser	10900	12300	6100	1900

▲

Figure 29.19 *A breakdown of garden centre sales by type and season*

We can improve this greatly by presenting the information both in a table and graphically, and we can also add colour. The new version is shown in Figure 29.20. Which do you prefer?

It is not too difficult to be able to produce work like this. Your teacher or a reference book

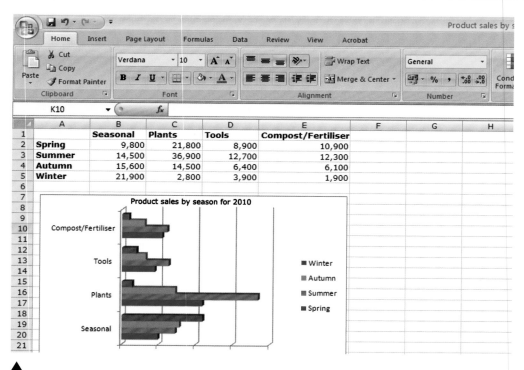

▲

Figure 29.20 *Improved presentation of the data in Figure 29.19*

will be able to show you how to improve the appearance of the data in your spreadsheets.

Formatting a spreadsheet improves its appearance. However, you need to consider the use to which the spreadsheet is to be put. If you are the only person who will see it, it is probably not worth the trouble of improving its appearance too much. If others are to see it you will need to present it in the most interesting way you can.

Testing a spreadsheet

Whenever you produce a spreadsheet it needs to be thoroughly tested before any of the values taken from the spreadsheet are relied on. There is a variety of errors that can occur, including:

- making a mistake during the construction of a formula
- using absolute rather than relative cell references or vice versa
- making reference to the wrong cell.

In order to discover these mistakes it is necessary to test your solution. There are several ways to do this:

- you can work out the results manually and compare these with those values calculated from the spreadsheet

- you can print out all the formulae and use this to check that they refer to the correct cells
- you can show it to a user for checking and evaluation; they may spot things you have missed.

Documenting your spreadsheet

Frequently, the person who has to use a spreadsheet is not the same person who created it, so it is always important to document any spreadsheets you produce. If you decide to use a spreadsheet to solve a problem in your project, you will have to fully document it. The minimum documentation should include:

1 a printout of the final spreadsheet showing the data
2 a printout of the spreadsheet with the formulae in each cell displayed
3 a user guide to the spreadsheet; the origins of the data (i.e. where it comes from) and how to produce the output (printouts, graphs, etc.) should be mentioned
4 any handwritten annotations (these are little notes) on the printouts explaining how the spreadsheet works.

Things to do

1 The spreadsheet below shows data on agriculture in the UK.
(a) Which cell would you use to put the total agricultural area?
(b) What formula would you put in that cell?

	A	B	C	D	E
1	Country	Agriculture	%	%	%
2	Name	Area	Grass	Arable	Fruit & Veg
3	England				
4	Wales				
5	Scotland				
6	Ireland				
7					
8					

▲
Figure 29.21

(c) The spreadsheet has the ability to produce the following types of graph:
Bar   Line   Pie   Scatter

Which one would be most suitable for showing:
(i) the proportions of grass, arable and fruit & veg for England?
(ii) a comparison between the agricultural areas of the four countries?
(d) If you want to add similar data for other countries, where could you find that data?

2 Sabina and Noel have set up in business making bird tables. They make two types: 'Cottage' and 'Mansion'. The wood for Cottage costs $8.80 and for Mansion $11.80. The cost of fittings (screws, nails, etc.) for each is $1.20. The Cottage model takes 2.6 hours to make, whilst the Mansion takes 3.1 hours to make. Sabina and Noel would like to pay themselves $5 per hour. They hope to sell 20 of each type at a profit of 30 per cent. Find out, using a spreadsheet, how much they should sell each model for.

3 Sometimes spreadsheets are used for things that do not include calculations. For instance, it is possible to show the lines that make up the columns and rows, and this can be useful if you want to draw tables. Some word-processing packages can be used to do this, but sometimes it is easier to use a spreadsheet.

Using a spreadsheet, produce a copy of your school timetable and print it out. Evaluate the use of the spreadsheet for this task, stating the problems and limitations you encountered.

4 Investigate a variety of spreadsheet packages and, using the spreadsheet's matrix to help you, design a page that a magazine reader could use to compare the various features.

5 A friend of yours says, 'Spreadsheets are a waste of money because they can not do anything that you cannot do with a pen, paper and calculator'.
(a) Can you think of any functions included in spreadsheet packages which would take a long time using the manual method? Write them down.
(b) Give as many advantages of the use of spreadsheets as you can think of.

Task 1

1 Load your spreadsheet package.
2 Enter the following data into the spreadsheet. You may need to widen the column for the package names.

	A	B	C	D	E	F	G
1	Monthly sales of software for a computer shop						
2	Package	Net Price	Tax	Total Price	Number Sold	Total	
3	PageMaker	394			4		
4	Clipper	292			3		
5	Symphony	385			1		
6	Info Publisher	145			12		
7	AutoSketch	61			3		
8	Floorplan	129			2		
9	AutoCAD	373			10		
10	DBase 5	245			28		
11	Lotus 1-2-3	247			52		
12	CorelDraw!	415			27		
13	WordPerfect	214			58		
14	Wordstar	227			42		
15	Grammatik	33			12		
16	Excel	219			28		
17	Visual Basic	193			15		
18	Paradox	275			41		

Figure 29.22

Skills Building

3 To work out the tax at 17.5 per cent, we can use a formula in cell C3. To calculate 17.5 per cent of the net price we can use the formula tax = net price × 17.5/100. To enter the formula into the spreadsheet at cell C3 we have to adapt the formula to read: +B3*17.5/100. When the formula is entered, the tax is put automatically into the cell. The next formula is placed in cell C4 and would be =B4*17.5/100. In fact it would be very tedious to do this all the way down the column, so there is a way of copying the original formula, taking into account the slight change in cell positions. This is called replicating (or copying) a formula relatively. Find out how to do this for your spreadsheet package and complete the column.

4 We now need to add the tax to the net price to give the total price. The formula =B3+C3 is placed in cell D3. This formula is then copied relatively down the column.

5 To work out the total amount, we multiply the total price by the number of items sold. Do this by placing the correct formula in cell F3 and copy this formula relatively down the column.

6 Save your spreadsheet, calling it MSALES.

7 Print your spreadsheet, trying to get all of it on a single page if you can.

Task 2

Last year Jordan Kung kept a record of his finances using a spreadsheet package. Figure 29.23 shows what his spreadsheet looked like at the end of the year.

	A	B	C	D	E	F	G	H	I	J
1	Month	Wage	Rent	Electric	Gas	Phone	Food	Car	Clothes	Hols
2	Jan	850	120	134.76			129.34	138.12	86.21	30
3	Feb	850	120			45.23	135.98	125.34	23.78	30
4	Mar	856	120		189.23		78.21	128	12.98	25
5	Apr	857	120				200.76	134	48.99	45
6	May	912	120	287.02			100.23	187.98	201.99	70
7	June	908	120			23.39	78.34	143.98	100.23	100
8	July	945	120		103.67		176.19	125.9	10.99	100
9	Aug	965	120				123.53	145.65	34.99	80
10	Sept	965	120	120.98			123.76	154.65	76.45	30
11	Oct	1000	120			56.99	109.01	200.07	230.12	10
12	Nov	987	120		100.05		165.45	167.95	201.76	10
13	Dec	1200	120				250.45	140.98	300.34	10

▲
Figure 29.23

1 Start off with the heading 'Jordan Kung's income and expenses for the last year'. Type in the data exactly as they appear in Figure 29.23.

2 In the next empty column insert the heading 'Expenses'. Expenses are the total amount of money that Jordan is spending each month. In this column total the January expenses on the January row.

3 Replicate this formula relatively down the column for February to December.

4 Using a formula, deduct the expenses for January from the wages for January and put this in the next empty column, under the column heading 'Balance'. This is the amount of money he had left.

5 Replicate this formula down the column for February to December.

6 Calculate the total income, expenditure and balance for the whole year. Put these in a suitable position on the spreadsheet.

7 Save your spreadsheet using a suitable filename.

8 Print your spreadsheet.

Task 3

The table shown in Figure 29.24 shows the number of calories you burn up when you do certain activities.

Activity	Men	Women
Moderate cycling	256	192
Hard cycling	660	507
Domestic work	200	153
Ironing	160	120
Rowing	800	600
Moderate running	592	444
Hard running	900	692
Squash	600	461
Moderate swimming	300	200
Hard swimming	640	480
Tennis	448	336
Moderate walking	224	168

▲

Figure 29.24   *Number of calories burnt when you do certain activities*

1 Enter this table into a spreadsheet (you will need to widen some of the columns).

2 Design a form to give to your friends to record the time spent doing the various activities during the day.

3 Design a method by which the spreadsheet could be used to work out the calories burnt per day by each of your friends.

4 Explain carefully, using printouts where appropriate, how you solved this problem. Mention any things you tried before you arrived at the final solution and explain why you discounted them.

30 Desktop Publishing

With the aid of desktop publishing software, people can produce high quality documents without having to go to a typesetter. This can save time and money.

Desktop publishing (DTP) can be used to produce pages that combine text and graphics (photographs and line drawings) for books, magazines, posters and leaflets. Different typefaces (fonts) can be used to add interest and diagrams can be added, with the text flowing around them. Photographs can be scanned in and their size adjusted so that they fit in a particular position on a page. The only real limit is your own imagination.

Figure 30.1 shows examples of a poster and a brochure that have been produced using DTP. Figure 30.2 shows the types of document you can use desktop publishing for.

▲ **Figure 30.1** *Just two examples of DTP documents*

Equipment needed

The computer

To work effectively with DTP packages you need a computer with a high specification, ideally with the largest amount of RAM (random-access memory) and the highest-capacity hard disk that can be afforded. DTP files consisting of text and pictures take up a lot of disk space. Ideally either a PC or an Apple® Macintosh® computer is used.

A mouse

The mouse is one of the most important tools in desktop publishing. The mouse is moved around on the desk and transmits the movement of your hand and fingers to the computer. Buttons on the mouse are pressed in order to make selections.

Desktop publishing software

There is a variety of software available. If you require only simple features, then you may

▲ **Figure 30.2** *Some of the documents you can produce using DTP*

be able to buy a word-processing package which contains them. The more features you require, the more likely you are to need to buy specialist desktop publishing software.

The visual display unit

The monitor should be the largest that you can afford (usually a 17-, 19- or 21-inch screen) in order to avoid eye strain. You often have to work with two pages on the screen at once, so the text can be quite small and difficult to read.

The printer

Either an inkjet printer (cheaper) or a laser printer could be used to output DTP documents. For really high quality a colour laser printer can be used.

The scanner

If you want to incorporate your own photographs or hand drawings into your documents, you will need to use a scanner to scan them in. Flatbed scanners are the most popular type of scanner and most are able to capture colour images. The quality of the scanned image depends on the resolution (in dots per inch) of the scan.

▲
Figure 30.3 *A flatbed scanner*

Digital cameras

Digital cameras are able to take photographs and store the image on a disk in the camera. You do not need a film and there are no developing costs. Instead the image can be directly transferred to the computer. It can then be altered, sized and incorporated into a DTP prepared document.

Some features of desktop publishing

Figure 30.4 shows some of the features of DTP.

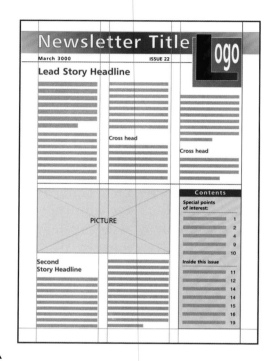

▲
Figure 30.4 *Some of the features of DTP*

Columns

In word processors you work in pages, but in DTP you will need to be able to work in both pages and columns. A look at a newspaper or magazine will show you how common the column format is.

Frame layout

Many DTP packages use a frame-based system of layout. Here, text and graphics are placed in boxes called frames, which can be moved and repositioned around the pages. Other packages are not frame-based.

Embedded graphics

It is possible to place drawings and pictures in position and then to flow the text around them, as shown in Figure 30.5.

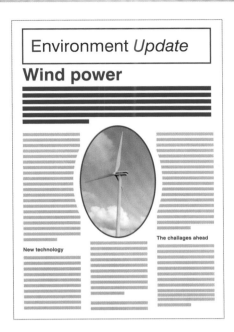

▲
Figure 30.5 *Notice how the text flows around the photograph on this page*

Templates

Templates are used to record certain properties of a document, such as its page size, margins, headers (the space at the top) and footers (the space at the bottom). Templates usually also include styles and any standard text that will be included in all documents to be based on them.

Style sheets

Style sheets are used to help make the main text, headings and subheadings consistent. When you are choosing the fonts and type sizes for a DTP document, you can highlight each paragraph or heading in turn and select the typeface and size. However, if a document is to be consistent it is better and faster to set up style sheets and then apply styles to the text.

Scaleable fonts

There are many fonts available in DTP packages and sometimes it is difficult to choose which one to use. It really depends on the type of document you are designing. Some fonts would not be used for business documents, but could be ideal for invitations

to an 18th birthday party. A huge range of sizes is usually available for each font, varying from the very small to the very large. Font sizes are measured in points. One point is 1/72 of an inch.

Advantages of desktop publishing

Here are just a few of the advantages of DTP, for preparing books, magazines, posters and leaflets, compared with word processing alone.

1 You have much more control over the way the text is laid out compared with an ordinary word processor, especially over the formatting and arrangement of text.
2 DTP can be used to bring lots of different files together on the same document.
3 DTP may be used to produce the output in a certain way so that the material can be professionally printed, if required. This is usually done if you want to print a large number of copies of your document. If your work is going to be output professionally, then you will need to make sure that you use one of the major DTP packages, such as Adobe® InDesign®, QuarkXPress, Adobe® PageMaker® or Microsoft® Publisher.

When to use a DTP package

Modern packages are so full of features that it is difficult to choose software. Word processors have some DTP facilities, and some graphics packages can be used to produce simple posters and leaflets. For a simple poster, like the one shown in Figure 30.6, you will probably find that a graphics package is the easiest one to use.

As far as your coursework is concerned, you need to decide which type of package to use. You have to give reasons why you choose a type of software for a particular job (e.g. why you might choose a DTP rather than a word-processing or graphics package). The reason could simply be that the task could not be performed with the other two, or it could be that you found the DTP package was better suited to the job.

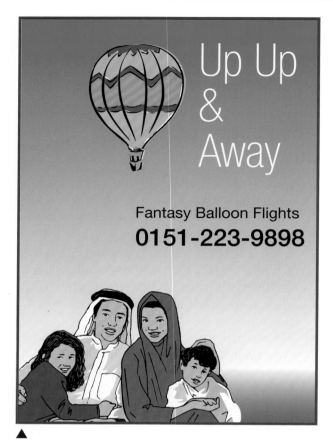

▲
Figure 30.6 *Poster designed using a graphics package*

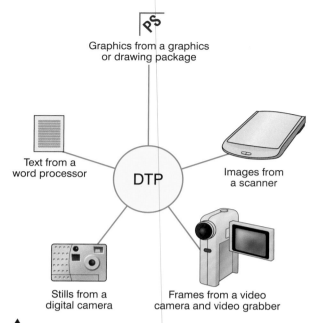

▲
Figure 30.7 *DTP acts as an integrator, bringing lots of different files together*

Graphics from a graphics or drawing package

Text from a word processor

DTP

Images from a scanner

Stills from a digital camera

Frames from a video camera and video grabber

DTP acts as an integrator, because with this software you can bring many different files together into the same document. You can bring in text from a word processor, graphics from a painting or drawing package, images from a scanner, frames from a video grabber and stills from a camera. Figure 30.7 illustrates this.

Basic techniques used in DTP

Here is a list of some of the basic techniques used in desktop publishing.

Page setup

The first step in preparing a DTP document is often to specify the size of the pages and whether they are to be in portrait or landscape format (see Figure 30.8). The second step in setting up the page is to decide on the number of columns.

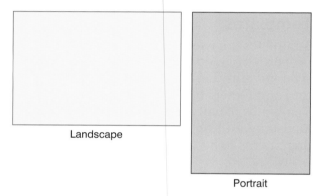

Landscape

Portrait

▲
Figure 30.8 *Pages arranged in landscape and portrait formats*

The column guides make the text word-wrap to the columns automatically. It is rather like word processing in a single column. Figure 30.9 shows snaking, where, once one column is filled, the text automatically flows to the top of the next column.

Typing text

Most DTP packages allow you to type text directly into them, but you may find it easier to use a word processor to do your typing and then import the files into the DTP package.

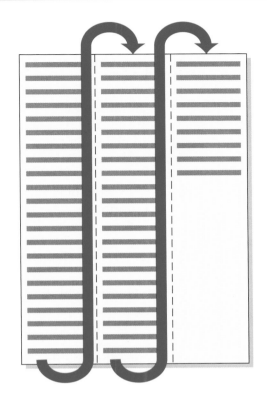

▲
Figure 30.9 *Snaking using three newspaper-style columns*

Word processors tend to have more facilities, such as spell checkers and thesauruses, and they are often quicker to type into.

Placing text
When you import text you can decide in which of the columns the text should be placed.

Placing graphics
When you import graphics you need to decide on the graphics you will be using and their position on the page. It is possible to place a blank area around a graphic so that the text cannot flow too close to the drawing or photograph.

Sizing and cropping graphics
Cropping means removing part of a picture by cutting off and discarding the part that is not needed. For instance, in a photograph of a group of people scanned in with a scanner, you might want to include only one of the people. You could crop the picture and leave

just the required part. This part could then be resized to fit the space available.

Drawing lines and boxes
You can make your text stand out more by placing it in a box. Sometimes it is possible to choose different designs for the box and to have shading around the box, for instance.

Summary of the main features of a DTP package

The size of the font can be altered to make parts of, say, an advert stand out.

The **font** *style* **can** *be* ***varied*** to add more interest

You can add some appropriate clip art or photographs to make it more attractive.

You can use frames to vary the layout.

- You can add bullets
- to list your points.

You can add a border to make your design stand out:

You can add **colour** to produce an eye-catching look.

You can use a pre-stored design and just alter it slightly. This way you will have a professional design.

You can use a spell checker to check that your advert contains no embarrassing spelling errors.

▲
Figure 30.10

Your DTP package might also have a grammar checker to ensure there are no grammatical errors.

Glossary of terms used in desktop publishing

Bold text Text in heavy type.
Bullet A symbol placed before a paragraph in a list to make the paragraph stand out.
Clip art A library of artwork from which you can choose to put into your documents.

Clipboard A temporary storage place for text, frames or pictures which have been cut or copied.
Crop Select part of the image and discard the rest.
Cut Remove an area containing text or a picture and place it on the clipboard.
Font A complete set of characters of the same design/style; it will be available in a range of sizes.
Frame A rectangular box in which you can place text, pictures or graphics.
Header The line of text included at the top of every page.
Import To load text or pictures created by a different package.
Italics Text that slants to the right; the characters are a different shape.
Justified Text that is aligned with the right and left margins.
Kerning The process of adjusting the spacing between the characters.
Leader This is usually a row of dots to guide the reader across the page, for example, in a table of contents.
Paste The process of inserting the contents of the clipboard into a document.
Template The master page and paragraph styles for a given document.
TIFF A special file format used for images.
WYSIWYG Stands for 'what you see is what you get'. You see on the screen exactly what will be printed out.

Things to do

1 (a) With DTP packages, text can be imported from a word-processing package.
  (i) What does the abbreviation DTP stand for?
  (ii) Explain, in simple terms, what the above sentence means.
 (b) Pupils in your school are going to produce a school newsletter which will be produced using desktop publishing.
  (i) Give three items of hardware which they might use apart from the computer (i.e. apart from the CPU, keyboard, VDU and mouse).
  (ii) Give reasons for your choices in (b)(i).

2 Why is it important to use a large VDU if you are working on DTP packages all the time?

3 Describe fully the features which would be desirable in a desktop publishing package for it to be used to prepare a high quality school prospectus. State clearly why each of the features is necessary.

Importing text into a DTP package

Here is a piece of text which you should type into your word processor exactly as it appears here.

Basically, a DTP package in its simplest form allows you to deal with graphics and text at the same time. Usually a DTP package has some word-processing and graphics facilities, but they are never as comprehensive as the facilities in the separate packages. Some DTP packages may contain a spell checker. This is very useful to make sure that you do not produce posters with spelling mistakes that everyone else spots except you.

A feature of a DTP package is its ability to import text from a word-processing package. Using your DTP package, import the text you have just typed into your word processor.

Choosing the right font

Selecting the right font is very important in DTP work. For each of the following, choose a suitable font and then use your DTP package to type the relevant sentence in the font you have chosen:

- an invitation to a party
- a poster for a disco to be held in your school hall
- an advertisement for a new restaurant
- a menu for a wedding
- an advertisement for a new car
- an invitation to a festival in your local town or village.

DTP skills

Here is a series of tasks you may need to carry out when doing project work in IT or other subjects:

- select pictures or photographs from a CD-ROM and place them in separate files
- type in the text to go with the artwork on your word processor
- load the pictures into your DTP package and adjust them if necessary
- load the text from the word processor and make it flow around the artwork.

Try to do the above tasks using the software and hardware you have available.

Skills Building

IT Tasks

Task 1

Take a look at a leaflet or poster. Look at it from the DTP point of view (choose one that is not too complicated).
- How many different fonts have been used and why have they been selected?
- How many sizes of type have been used?
- Does the text flow around any diagrams or photographs?
- Has any clip art been used?

Task 2

Your company is a rapidly expanding mail order company that sells aquarium equipment from adverts placed in specialist fish-keeping magazines. You have been asked to investigate desktop publishing for your company and produce a report on its value.

In your report you should include the following, along with any other material you think is important:
- what DTP is (is it hardware or software or a combination of the two?)
- the minimum equipment for running DTP
- any additional equipment which might be useful (e.g. scanners)
- how DTP is different from a sophisticated word-processing package such as Microsoft® Word
- what an average DTP package can do
- what packages are available, how much they cost, which one you think is the best and why.

Task 3

Your local police station wants to crack down on crime. It wishes to draw people's attention to crime prevention. The police have asked you to produce some fact sheets and posters with hard-hitting messages on crime prevention. To help you with this you could try to get hold of crime statistics and incorporate these into your material.

Task 4

The information technology coordinator in your school has been asked by the headteacher to run an 'Introduction to Computers' course on a Tuesday evening. The course is to start on Tuesday 12 September between 6 p.m. and 9 p.m. and will run for 30 weeks. The cost of the course is $100.

The course is practically based and covers:
- word processing
- databases
- spreadsheets
- graphics
- desktop publishing.

You have been asked to produce a desktop-published leaflet that can be placed in local libraries, supermarkets and so on, advertising the course.

All the essential course information needs to be included and it is decided that a map showing where the school is should also be included.

31 Databases

Before looking at this chapter it would be a good idea to refresh your memory on the contents of Chapter 8: 'How Data Are Stored', where some of the database concepts and terms are explained. In particular you should understand the terms *file*, *record* and *field*, and you should be able to design a record.

Creating a database

Before creating a database, you first have to give some thought to its structure. To help you, here is a list of steps which should be taken.

1 Decide which fields you need and write them down as a list. Then put your list into order of importance, with the most important field at the top (the most important field is usually the key field).
2 Give each field a suitable fieldname. The fieldnames do not have to be the same as in step 1 and you will probably want to abbreviate the longer ones. Make sure that, when you are describing your system, you mention what the various abbreviations mean. Also, try not to make the fieldnames too long, since they may have to be typed in when you are performing searches.
3 Decide on the field types. This is whether they are numeric, character, date or logical fields.
4 Decide on the field lengths. A sample of the data you are going to put into the database will reveal how many characters long each field needs to be.

Sometimes you will need several databases. For instance, for a system to be used in a video library there would be three:

- a member database to hold all the members' details, such as name and address

- a video database to hold details of the videos kept by the library, such as title and price
- a rental database to hold the details of the rentals, such as the video number, member's number and date borrowed.

We will now look at a problem and see how we can design a database to provide a solution to the problem.

The problem

Widgets Ltd is a small manufacturing company employing around 40 staff. The company has its head office in the local town and this is where most of the administration work is done. At the head office there is a personnel department which keeps information on all the staff. At the moment, although other departments make use of computers, the personnel department still keeps manual records of all staff in a series of filing cabinets.

There are various problems with the manual system:

- files can take a long time to find, especially if someone has put them back in the wrong place
- to answer questions such as 'How many women do we employ under 20 years old?' would involve looking at every file and then calculating everyone's age from their date of birth; doing this could take a long time
- files need to be kept about ex-employees in case they want a reference in the future.

The filing cabinets are taking up more and more space.

Research

A questionnaire has been sent to all the members of the personnel department, asking them about the sort of information that they frequently need to know about the employees.

Interviews with the staff who will be using the system and the results of a questionnaire filled in by staff revealed that the following information was necessary for each member of staff:

- surname
- forename
- title
- first line of address
- second line of address
- third line of address
- postcode
- home phone number
- date of birth
- date the member of staff started with the company
- job department the staff member is in (i.e. production, sales, accounts)
- job grade (each job is given a grade from 1 to 5: grade 1 is the highest level of responsibility)
- job salary (how much each staff member earns per year before deductions)
- job hours (how many hours per week each staff member is contracted to work)
- days off work sick so far this year
- National Insurance number
- holidays total (the number of days of holiday entitlement)
- holidays taken (number of days taken this year).

We now need to decide on the fieldnames that we are going to use for the above and the type of data that will be in each field, that is numeric, character (sometimes called text) and so on, and also the number of characters or numbers in each field.

Questions

What would be the best way of determining the width of the fields for the above data?

After careful examination of the manual records to make sure that the field lengths are adequate and the type of field is correct, the following structure was developed.

Num	Field Name	Field Type	Width	Dec
1	EMPLOYEE_NO	Character	4	0
2	SURNAME	Character	30	
3	FORENAME	Character	20	
4	TITLE	Character	4	
5	ADD1	Character	30	
6	ADD2	Character	30	
7	ADD3	Character	30	
8	PCODE	Character	9	
9	HPHONE	Character	13	
10	DOB	Date	6	
11	START_DATE	Date	6	
12	JOB_DEPT	Character	10	
13	JOB_GRADE	Numeric	10	
14	JOB_SALARY	Numeric	8	2
15	JOB_HOURS	Numeric	2	0
16	DAYS_SICK	Numeric	3	1
17	NAT_INS_NO	Character	1	5
18	HOLS_TOTAL	Numeric	2	1
19	HOLS_TAKEN	Numeric	2	1

▲

Figure 31.1 *Database structure*

At this stage it is not too important to get the structure exactly right, since in our example a database program is being used where it is possible to go back and change the structure even after data have been entered. Ask your teacher if you can do this with the database software you are using.

IT Tasks

Task 1

1 Load your database program.
2 Create a new database, calling it 'Person'.
3 Set up the structure set out in the table in Figure 31.1.
4 Save your structure.
5 Print a copy of your structure.

Putting data into the database

Once the structure has been set up, the data may be put into the database. This usually involves typing the data in using the keyboard, but this is not the only method. If the equipment is available, you could scan data in.

Widgets Ltd has decided to type the data in. Figure 31.2 is a list of some of the employees.

N.B. You need to decide on the format of the data you are going to type in. It is probably best to use capital letters for the start of a word and then small letters for the rest of the word.

IT Tasks

Task 2

Produce a list of all the records in the database and verify them by checking that they are identical to the list in Figure 31.2. Make the corrections if necessary.

EMPLOYEE_NO	0001	0002	0003
SURNAME	Gregson	Dawkins	Prescott
FORENAME	Margaret	Steven	Simon
TITLE	Miss	Mr	Dr
ADD1	12 Wood Lane	3 River Road	The Verlands
ADD2	West Derby	Aintree	Warren Road
ADD3	Liverpool	Liverpool	Liverpool
PCODE	L13 8BQ	L9 4HG	L23 3ED
HPHONE	0151-252-3542	0151-525-0999	0151-924-0008
DOB	12/12/51	01/03/56	01/07/64
START_DATE	01/03/81	03/09/03	05/05/98
JOB_DEPT	Production	Sales	Production
JOB_GRADE	2	3	1
JOB_SALARY	14800	12300	28500
JOB_HOURS	35	35	35
DAYS_SICK	0	03	07
NAT_INS_NO	YY432512D	YY346523E	FX208974R
HOLS_TOTAL	28	28	30
HOLS_TAKEN	09	07	21

EMPLOYEE_NO	0004	0005	0006
SURNAME	McGinley	Ahmed	Johnston
FORENAME	Stuart	John	Mark
TITLE	Mr	Mr	Mr
ADD1	3 Robin Close	12 Moor Lane	5 Forrest Court
ADD2	West Derby	Waterloo	Crosby
ADD3	Liverpool	Liverpool	Liverpool
PCODE	L13 9MM	L22 6RT	L23 5RR
HPHONE	0151-252-6875	0151-928-8732	0151-924-7865
DOB	12/04/75	12/05/80	01/02/79
START_DATE	07/01/96	12/11/08	10/12/88
JOB_DEPT	Production	Sales	Accounts
JOB_GRADE	5	3	4
JOB_SALARY	4800	6700	7100
JOB_HOURS	40	40	40
DAYS_SICK	14	21	05
NAT_INS_NO	SD453623G	GH346512Y	HJ901834K
HOLS_TOTAL	28	28	28
HOLS_TAKEN	05	10	26

EMPLOYEE_NO	0007	0008	0009
SURNAME	Hughes	Sumner	George
FORENAME	Julie	Suzanne	Julie
TITLE	Mrs	Miss	Mrs
ADD1	5 Orchard Hey	2 Ocean View	The Coach Hse
ADD2	Maghull	Blundellsands	Hesketh Bank
ADD3	Liverpool	Liverpool	Southport
PCODE	L31 8AF	L23 8TT	PR8 9YT
HPHONE	0151-520-8100	0151-931-6534	01704-12776
DOB	03/07/70	26/10/79	07/01/75
START_DATE	09/10/96	03/06/02	02/08/95
JOB_DEPT	Admin	Admin	Accounts
JOB_GRADE	2	5	1
JOB_SALARY	14500	6300	20500
JOB_HOURS	35	40	35
DAYS_SICK	01	0	08
NAT_INS_NO	YY872322P	TT765323U	FF983203P
HOLS_TOTAL	35	28	35
HOLS_TAKEN	20	06	23

EMPLOYEE_NO	0010	0011	0012
SURNAME	Murphy	Davies	Jones
FORENAME	Sean	Paul	Samantha
TITLE	Mr	Mr	Miss
ADD1	12 Bewley Road	12 King Street	54 Moor Drive
ADD2	Kirkby	Wavertree	Hesketh Bank
ADD3	Liverpool	Liverpool	Southport
PCODE	L13 7YY	L17 8UU	PR5 9YU
HPHONE	0151-531-9089	0151-342-7765	01704-34223
DOB	01/02/65	30/12/63	25/02/50
START_DATE	09/03/02	23/11/85	23/05/76
JOB_DEPT	Sales	Production	Sales
JOB_GRADE	3	4	1
JOB_SALARY	12300	18000	28900
JOB_HOURS	30	35	35
DAYS_SICK	12	09	0
NAT_INS_NO	WW769000T	RR600004T	YY454672K
HOLS_TOTAL	28	35	35
HOLS_TAKEN	10	21	24

EMPLOYEE_NO	0013	0014	0015
SURNAME	Flynn	Jones	Jones
FORENAME	James	Debbie	Julie
TITLE	Mr	Ms	Miss
ADD1	2 Copy Lane	5 Bellair Ave	5 Bellair Ave
ADD2	Maghull	Aintree	Aintree
ADD3	Liverpool	Liverpool	Liverpool
PCODE	L31 9KJ	L9 7HH	L9 7HH
HPHONE	0151-531-0009	0151-534-4566	0151-534-4566
DOB	12/11/60	27/09/80	30/01/83
START_DATE	09/12/86	12/12/07	03/04/04
JOB_DEPT	Production	Marketing	Admin
JOB_GRADE	2	2	3
JOB_SALARY	19000	21000	14500
JOB_HOURS	40	35	35
DAYS_SICK	12	03	08
NAT_INS_NO	TT231276F	RT900078Y	RO679797G
HOLS_TOTAL	28	35	28
HOLS_TAKEN	13	28	14

▲
Figure 31.2

EMPLOYEE_NO	0016	0017	0018
SURNAME	Dewer	Stephenson	Ho
FORENAME	Alison	Carl	Michael
TITLE	Miss	Mr	Mr
ADD1	5 Cobley Court	4 Moor Drive	6 Pit Street
ADD2	Wavertree	Crosby	Everton
ADD3	Liverpool	Liverpool	Liverpool
PCODE	L24 6FT	L23 6HH	L12 6TT
HPHONE	0151-675-8900	0151-924-5565	0151-253-9000
DOB	03/11/77	01/08/80	30/09/58
START_DATE	01/05/91	04/09/05	23/08/86
JOB_DEPT	Sales	Admin	Accounts
JOB_GRADE	5	4	5
JOB_SALARY	3400	5200	2800
JOB_HOURS	25	25	15
DAYS_SICK	02	02	03
NAT_INS_NO	YY909076G	HH897678R	GG878789U
HOLS_TOTAL	20	20	15
HOLS_TAKEN	17	08	07

EMPLOYEE_NO	0025	0026	0027
SURNAME	Sinnot	Jones	Rowlands
FORENAME	Jackie	Gareth	Julie
TITLE	Mrs	Mr	Miss
ADD1	23 Osbert Road	2 Firs Close	3 Blandford Rd
ADD2	Blundellsands	Formby	Ainsdale
ADD3	Liverpool	Liverpool	Southport
PCODE	L23 8GY	L34 5TR	PR4 5DS
HPHONE	0151-924-7322	01704-98899	01704-11223
DOB	01/11/57	27/08/68	30/09/69
START_DATE	12/02/89	12/12/01	12/12/01
JOB_DEPT	Production	Sales	Admin
JOB_GRADE	2	4	2
JOB_SALARY	4700	14500	17000
JOB_HOURS	15	40	35
DAYS_SICK	0	07	10
NAT_INS_NO	TH435200T	YY767678R	FT090976R
HOLS_TOTAL	12	35	35
HOLS_TAKEN	03	12	10

EMPLOYEE_NO	0019	0020	0021
SURNAME	Johnston	Stuart	John
FORENAME	Mark	South	Jones
TITLE	Mr	Mr	Mr
ADD1	5 Hart Street	5 Fir Crescent	4 South Road
ADD2	Formby	Southport	Waterloo
ADD3	Merseyside	Merseyside	Liverpool
PCODE	L45 8MM	L34 5TT	L22 6GG
HPHONE	01704-45464	01704-67738	0151-928-0088
DOB	31/01/55	09/01/53	03/05/85
START_DATE	02/09/79	02/09/79	01/02/08
JOB_DEPT	Production	Production	Sales
JOB_GRADE	2	2	5
JOB_SALARY	18700	19000	3900
JOB_HOURS	35	35	27
DAYS_SICK	10	09	10
NAT_INS_NO	WW352920R	YY875658T	HJ870020G
HOLS_TOTAL	28	28	28
HOLS_TAKEN	14	09	10

EMPLOYEE_NO	0028	0029	0030
SURNAME	Doyle	Doyle	Smith
FORENAME	Norma	Ruth	Tony
TITLE	Mrs	Miss	Mr
ADD1	5 Trevor Drive	5 Trevor Drive	4 Bridge Road
ADD2	Crosby	Crosby	Waterloo
ADD3	Liverpool	Liverpool	Liverpool
PCODE	L23 6GT	L23 6GT	L22 6GG
HPHONE	0151-924-8989	0151-924-8989	0151-924-8767
DOB	02/05/72	03/10/80	01/02/57
START_DATE	03/01/91	18/09/97	05/05/04
JOB_DEPT	Sales	Production	Admin
JOB_GRADE	5	3	5
JOB_SALARY	5900	6500	7800
JOB_HOURS	25	30	30
DAYS_SICK	0	0	9
NAT_INS_NO	GG902323R	HJ880213F	DE562376S
HOLS_TOTAL	15	25	35
HOLS_TAKEN	10	12	13

EMPLOYEE_NO	0022	0023	0024
SURNAME	Wong	Owens	Hughes
FORENAME	Christine	Susan	Stephen
TITLE	Miss	Mrs	Mr
ADD1	23a Devon Close	54 Wood Street	5 Rotten Row
ADD2	Walton	Aintree	Southport
ADD3	Liverpool	Liverpool	Merseyside
PCODE	L14 6TR	L9 8HY	L65 6YY
HPHONE	0151-525-3123	0151-523-0099	01704-78222
DOB	12/07/79	25/09/49	15/09/56
START_DATE	03/06/99	09/06/98	07/07/79
JOB_DEPT	Sales	Marketing	Accounts
JOB_GRADE	3	1	1
JOB_SALARY	15000	29000	38000
JOB_HOURS	35	35	28
DAYS_SICK	09	01	08
NAT_INS_NO	GS676799K	WW780367F	GG566658L
HOLS_TOTAL	35	35	40
HOLS_TAKEN	23	30	12

EMPLOYEE_NO	0031	0032	0033
SURNAME	Snell	Peat	Farley
FORENAME	Peter	Fred	John
TITLE	Mr	Mr	Mr
ADD1	2 The Close	5 Geraints Way	2 Channel View
ADD2	Seaforth	Waterloo	Thornton
ADD3	Liverpool	Liverpool	Liverpool
PCODE	L21 5RR	L22 6RD	L18 5FF
HPHONE	0151-931-2121	0151-928-0078	0151-924-7923
DOB	19/03/59	13/12/70	01/04/77
START_DATE	17/04/81	15/05/02	12/12/04
JOB_DEPT	Production	Marketing	Production
JOB_GRADE	2	2	2
JOB_SALARY	16000	14800	16300
JOB_HOURS	40	35	40
DAYS_SICK	03	09	10
NAT_INS_NO	RR234237T	QQ545454Y	TG090988T
HOLS_TOTAL	35	35	35
HOLS_TAKEN	12	21	18

▲

Figure 31.2 *cont.*

EMPLOYEE_NO	0034	0035	0036	EMPLOYEE_NO	0037	0038	0039
SURNAME	Jackson	Low	Crowther	SURNAME	Jenkins	Pauling	Smith
FORENAME	Roy	Jane	Louise	FORENAME	Sheila	Jenny	Carol
TITLE	Mr	Mrs	Ms	TITLE	Mrs	Mrs	Ms
ADD1	3 Crane Street	5 Hart Street	45 Park Lane	ADD1	2 Cobham Road	3 Belham Road	32 The Byway
ADD2	Wavertree	Seaforth	Kirkby	ADD2	West Derby	Thornton	Crosby
ADD3	Liverpool	Liverpool	Liverpool	ADD3	Liverpool	Liverpool	Liverpool
PCODE	L13 5FD	L21 5RE	L31 4AS	PCODE	L13 8HU	L23 6TH	L23 4FR
HPHONE				HPHONE	0151-252-3409	0151-924-6512	0151-924-0071
DOB	12/12/64	16/01/75	12/09/86	DOB	30/09/60	27/02/61	29/04/71
START_DATE	15/01/05	17/01/05	08/05/05	START_DATE	12/10/81	13/12/85	10/02/03
JOB_DEPT	Production	Sales	Admin	JOB_DEPT	Personnel	Marketing	Production
JOB_GRADE	3	4	4	JOB_GRADE	1	2	1
JOB_SALARY	12300	8900	9550	JOB_SALARY	20500	17500	23000
JOB_HOURS	35	35	35	JOB_HOURS	35	35	35
DAYS_SICK	0	0	03	DAYS_SICK	4	0	0
NAT_INS_NO	YY354323C	CC676741V	FR566643D	NAT_INS_NO	FF342345R	HK090945R	JH890148F
HOLS_TOTAL	28	35	28	HOLS_TOTAL	28	28	28
HOLS_TAKEN	12	05	00	HOLS_TAKEN	28	15	28

Figure 31.2 *cont.*

Data verification

Data verification is a pre-input check to make sure that what is on a form is exactly what goes into the database. For the personnel database it is a question of proofreading each record on the screen to check that it is exactly the same as what is on the form.

Data validation

Validation checks are checks that the database performs to make sure that the data are allowable. Databases will not allow you to put letters into a field which you have specified as numeric. Validation is performed by the actual database software.

Questions

A person tries to type a number into a field that has been specified as a character field. Will the computer accept it?

Using the database

Queries

Performing a query is sometimes referred to as searching or interrogating a database. Basically this involves extracting information from the database. For instance, you could make a request of the database to list the details of all personnel over a certain age. Suppose we do not want a list of every field in the database, but only a list of surnames and addresses, we could issue a command such as:

LIST SURNAME, ADD1, ADD2, ADD3, PCODE

Notice the list of the required fields is after the LIST command.

IT Tasks

Task 3

Write commands that would enable you to list the following fields (if your database commands are different, then use them):
1 a list of surnames, job departments and salaries for all employees
2 a list of surnames, their holiday totals and their holidays taken
3 a list of all employees' surnames, forenames and home telephone numbers.

Using search conditions

You may not want all the specified fields for each person to be listed. For example you may just need the details on people in a certain department.

Suppose you wanted the surnames and salaries of the personnel in the production department. We could use a command similar to this:

LIST SURNAME, JOB_SALARY FOR JOB_ DEPT = "Production"

Or you might want to list the employee number, surname and job department for all employees earning over $15,000. You could use a command like this:

LIST EMPLOYEE_NO, SURNAME, JOB_ DEPT FOR JOB_SALARY > 15000

Note that > is the symbol meaning greater than.

IT Tasks

Task 4

Write commands to perform the following searches and check that they work by producing a printout from the personnel database:
(a) the employee number, surname and department of staff working under 20 hours
(b) the names and addresses of all staff in the sales department
(c) the names and addresses of all the male employees (note you will need to think about how to do this)
(d) the surname, job department and grade of all the staff who have taken no time off sick
(e) the names, job departments and dates of birth of all staff who joined the company after 1/1/86.

Combining conditions

You can combine conditions using AND, OR and NOT. If you wanted to search the database for members of the production department who earned over $20,000 you could issue a command similar to the following:

LIST SURNAME, JOB_SALARY, NAT_ INS_NO FOR JOB_DEPT ="Production". AND. JOB_SALARY >20000

If you wanted a list including people in the production department earning $20,000 exactly you would replace the last part >20000 by =20000.

Notice also that JOB_SALARY is a numeric field and you do not put inverted commas around the number. Inverted commas are placed only around character fields.

Adding new records to the database

Following expansion of the company, three new employees have been taken on. Add information about these to the database (this process of adding records to an existing database is called appending the database).

EMPLOYEE_NO	0040	0041	0042
SURNAME	Kent	Marshall	Hall
FORENAME	Colin	John	Peter
TITLE	Mr	Mr	Mr
ADD1	3 Hall Road	10 The Close	5 Bows Lane
ADD2	Seaforth	Thornton	Crosby
ADD3	Liverpool	Liverpool	Liverpool
PCODE	L20 9YU	L23 6RT	L23 5FD
HPHONE	0151-928-0087	0151-924-4546	0151-924-8976
DOB	30/09/79	20/10/83	21/09/87
START_DATE	22/04/09	12/05/09	13/05/09
JOB_DEPT	Production	Admin	Personnel
JOB_GRADE	5	4	5
JOB_SALARY	$9000	$11000	$8500
JOB_HOURS	40	35	35
DAYS_SICK	0	0	0
NAT_INS_NO	FR232355H	GF802023F	HJ651023L
HOLS_TOTAL	28	28	28
HOLS_TAKEN	0	0	0

Deleting records

Julie Hughes and Steven Dawkins have left the company, so their records need removing from the database. Perform this task and then explain how you did it.

Amending the database

Following the annual review of staff performance, the following staff have been promoted:

- Suzanne Sumner is now grade 3 and has a new salary of $8,500
- Sean Murphy is now grade 2 and has a new salary of $14,700
- Margaret Gregson is now grade 1 and has a new salary of $17,800.

Also, the following amendments need to be made to staff records:

- Miss Margaret Gregson now becomes Mrs Margaret Hewitt
- John Ahmed has moved to the following address: 15 Forefield Road, Aintree, Liverpool, L9 7ET Phone 0151-546-2111.

It is the end of the month, so the holiday and days off sick records need amending. The following people have been sick or taken days off.

	Holidays taken this month	Days off sick this month
Sean Murphy	1	2
Margaret Gregson	5	
Simon Prescott	7	
Mark Johnston	2	
Stuart McGinley	1	3

Make all of the above amendments to your database.

Questions

How can the personnel department be sure that the personnel records are up to date?

Sorting and indexing

Sorting

Suppose we want to sort the personnel database into alphabetical order according to SURNAME. We could use the SORT command. With the SORT command a new file is produced which has the same contents as the original file but in a different order. Using the SORT command is quick, but has the disadvantage that a new file is produced which takes up as much disk space as the original. Performing several sorts using a large database could mean that you could run out of disk space.

Using SORT you can usually sort on only one field. To sort a file into alphabetical order according to SURNAME you can use a command similar to this:

SORT ON SURNAME TO S1

SURNAME is the field we are sorting and S1 is the filename we are giving to the new sorted database.

IT Tasks

Task 5

Using the personnel database, do the following:

1 Sort the file into alphabetical order according to SURNAME. Produce a printout showing the fields SURNAME and EMPLOYEE_NO to check that the sort has taken place.
2 Sort the file according to JOB_SALARY, with the personnel earning the most money at the start of the file (it is possible to sort in ascending or descending order; in this case it should be in descending order).

Indexing

Each record in a database is given a record number by the computer. This is not the same as the EMPLOYEE_NO. The record number is used to produce an index. Let us look at the first five records of the file.

Record number	SURNAME	FORENAME
1	Gregson	Margaret
2	Dawkins	Steven
3	Prescott	Simon
4	McGinley	Stuart
5	Ahmed	John

If these were to be placed in alphabetical order according to SURNAME, the record numbers would need to be in the order 5, 2, 1, 4, 3. These record numbers are contained in an index, and when displaying or printing out the list the computer uses this index to put things in the correct order. Indexing has the advantage that it does not eat up disk space, since only the index and the original database need storing.

Not all databases have an index facility. Check with your teacher to see if yours has.

You can index on a main, primary field, and then have another, secondary index. So you could have employees in departmental order and then in alphabetical order of surname within each department.

IT Tasks

Task 6

Produce a list of personnel in alphabetical order according to surname:
(a) using a SORT
(b) using an INDEX, if your database can do this.

Forms and screens

Forms, or screen designs as they are often called, are used to allow the user to type data into the system. You can design boxes on the screen where the user can type in the data.

Reports

Reports are summaries of the data held on a database. They have a date and title, and contain neat columns of data. Reports are usually printed on paper.

Labels

Some databases allow you to print names and addresses from your database on self-adhesive labels to be used for mailshots. Some systems also allow the production of barcodes from the data in the database.

Comma-separated variables

The file shown below, consisting of names and addresses, has been typed into a word processor. Each of the items of data enclosed between quotes and separated by commas can be transferred directly to a database and

the items correspond to the fields in the database. We can therefore export the data from the word processor and import it into the database.

"Stephen","Doyle","12 Bancroft Rd", "Crosby","Liverpool","L23 4ER"
"Norma","Prescott","3 Forest Rd", "Formby","Merseyside","L31 OBQ"
"Jim","Jones","3 Foregarden Ave", "Waterloo","Liverpool","L22 4RR"
"Frank","Moor","123 Edge Lane", "Prescott","Merseyside","L13 5SE"

Comma-separated variables (sometimes called comma-delimited variables) are often used for merging data from a database into the gaps in a standard letter. This is called a mail merge.

If you are using an integrated package (i.e. one with a database, spreadsheet and word processor all in one), you will find the transfer of the data between the modules a lot easier.

Creating an information system using a database

The problem

To create an information system we must start with a problem to be solved. It may be that there is a manual system that needs replacing, or it may be that an existing computer system is inadequate and needs improvement. For either of these, the processes involved in the design and implementation of a system are the same. It is very important to make a careful choice of the problem to be solved. If it is too ambitious then it will be hard to satisfy the assessment objectives, and if it is too simple then all the objectives will probably not be met.

Always choose a topic that interests you or something you can find information about easily. Use friends or relatives to come up with problems they might encounter in their jobs. Often the better projects are real projects that have been developed for an actual problem.

Make sure that the school or college has the equipment available to enable you to perform your project and that you will have enough time to complete it.

Initially you will be asked for a statement of the problem. Before stating what the problem is, it is best to write a short passage on the background of the organisation involved.

Research

If you are basing your project around an actual company or organisation, you will need to find out about what it does and how it is done. The best way to do this is to produce a questionnaire (word-processed, of course) and send it to your contact in the organisation concerned. When you get this back, read it carefully and write down a list of interview questions which come to light from the questionnaire.

Try to arrange to see the potential users of your system.

Description of the existing system

1 The existing system

A description of the existing system, along with its strengths and weaknesses, should be included. Any manual documents should be copied and diagrams should be drawn to illustrate the flow of paperwork for the administrative procedures.

2 User requirements

The users will be more familiar with the problem to be solved than you will be, so it is important to ask them about the input, output and processing. Since you will be regarded as being more knowledgeable about what is technically possible, you should be able to make suggestions.

3 Constraints

The usual constraints of time and money always apply. Too much time may be needed to develop the new system or project. The user will need to be convinced that the benefits of the new system outweigh the costs of its introduction. For instance the large volume of data that would need to be keyed in might prohibit the use of a large database. Alternative input methods, such as barcoding and OCR, could be looked into as an alternative to keying in.

4 The social implications of a new system

An appreciation of the effect of the new system on the workforce should be considered. Many employees will be naturally sceptical about a new system. You will need to have some answers to their fears.

System design

Bearing in mind the constraints, an alternative to the original system should be developed that will do as many of the things suggested by the user and yourself as possible. Sometimes there may be several ways of solving the problem. Remember that the best solution to a particular problem is not always the one that is chosen and that the choice is nearly always a compromise.

When designing your system you need to mention the following.

- Explain how the proposed system works, using diagrams rather than text wherever possible. The diagrams should include systems flowcharts and structure diagrams.
- Hardware and software requirements should be outlined, with reasons for their choice.
- Show how features have been designed. For instance, with a database you would need to mention how you arrived at the structure, or with a spreadsheet you would mention how the format you have adopted was arrived at.
- Input and output need to be considered. Here you should look at the most appropriate form for the input and output. Methods of data capture can be included, along with the reasons for their choice.
- Information is needed about the choice of storage media, along with justification.

Implementation

You need to give information about the implementation of a system, including:

- the method of implementation, along with the reason for its choice (e.g. step-by-step, parallel running)
- how existing files are to be changed to the new file format, including how data will be keyed in (or the use of alternative methods such as OCR)
- how the new hardware and software are to be installed
- how the people who will be using the new system will be trained
- how the new system will be maintained – what needs to be done and how often in order to keep the system up to date
- the social effects of the implementation of your system.

Documenting the system

Two levels of documentation are needed: one for the user and the other for the technical specialists.

User documentation

This should include:

- input and output formats
- sample runs to show the output
- error messages and what to do when things go wrong (e.g. data are sent to the printer without it being switched on)
- brief limitations of the system.

Technical documentation

This should include:

- the purpose of the system
- the requirements of the system
- the input and output formats
- the method of solution
- the further development potential (how the system could be improved or any extras which could be added on).

Questions

1 Debbie, an information technology manager, says, 'It's no use having a computerised database unless it is properly maintained.'
   (a) What does she mean by 'properly maintained'?
   (b) What sort of tasks would be involved in maintaining the database?

2 In the 'personnel' database, we did not record a person's age, but instead recorded their date of birth (DOB). Why is the age not included?

3 Take a look at your parents' car insurance details to see what information is held.

   Suppose a mistake was made by someone in the insurance company's office while keying the information in. What could be the consequences of such an error?

Things to do

1 Jane, who is a dentist, would like to install a computer system in order to provide information regarding her patients' teeth, their appointments, their treatment and how much their treatment costs.

   She decides to buy a PC with a 1,500GB hard disk and a laser printer.
   (a) What type of application software should she buy? Give reasons for your choice or choices.
   (b) Describe how the system could be used to handle the information for the various uses she has. Also mention the output she could expect from such a system.
   (c) What advantages are there in using an off-the-shelf application package rather than a tailor-made programmed package? What disadvantages might there be?
   (d) Give a possible advantage of the new system to each of the following groups of people:
   - receptionists
   - nurses
   - dentists
   - patients.
   (e) What possible disadvantage might there be in using the new system?

2 A company of estate agents, with a main branch in one town and several branches in nearby towns, is planning to change from a manual system to a computerised one.
  (a) The company plans to set up a computer file with details of houses that are for sale. This file will store the name of the owner, the address, the phone number and type for each house. Suggest **four** other fields that might be included on the file.
  (b) Explain why some of the data in the fields in this file are stored in coded form.
  (c) The file will store details of several thousand houses. People interested in buying any house should be able to obtain a printout of the details by simply calling in at a branch of the company. What type of store would be needed for the file? Give **two** reasons for your choice.
  (d) Some of the fields in this file are of fixed length, others are of variable length.
    (i) Give **one** advantage of using fixed-length fields.
    (ii) Give **one** disadvantage of using fixed-length fields.
  (e) Describe the hardware the company will need to install in each of its branches and in the main office for the new computerised system.

3 A company sells general hardware. It stores details of stock in a database.

  For each item the database stores the following:
      Stock_no
      Description
      Location_code (aisle number)
      Supplier_code
      Reorder_quantity
      Minimum_stock_level
      Current_stock_level
      Lead_time (days)
      Date_of_last_delivery

  (a) The database can be accessed using a special query language
      (e.g. List Stock_no,Description,FOR Current_stock_level less than 50).
      Write down a query command which would print out the description for all the items that the company has more than 100 of in stock, with a Lead_time of less than 14 days.
  (b) The company cannot function without the database. Which backup procedures should be used for the database files?
  (c) The database file is very large. What method can be used to minimise storage requirements when archive copies are made?
  (d) To be able to produce orders to be sent to suppliers, an additional database file is issued.
    (i)   What file would this be?
    (ii) What type of information would it contain?
    (iii) Copy and fill in the table below to show the structure of this file.

Fieldname	Field type	Size

  (e) Describe, using any suitable method, the way in which the two files would be used to produce orders for all items where the Current_stock_level is below the Minimum_stock_level.

4 A film club hires films to members. The club uses separate database files to store details about:
  • films
  • members
  • films hired.

The table below shows **part** of the **FILMS** database file.

Film number	Film name	Film category	Rating	Hire charge
0123	Mermaids	Comedy	15	$2.00
0124	Lagaan	Drama	U	$2.50
0254	Star Wars	Adventure	U	$1.50
0361	Mad Max 2	Adventure	18	$2.00
0422	City Slickers	Comedy	15	$1.25
0744	Die Hard 2	Adventure	18	$1.50
0813	Friends	Comedy	15	$1.50

Write down the instructions or steps that you might use if you wanted the FILMS database to display a list of adventure films which are rated 18 and cost less than $2.00 to hire.

(a) Choose suitable items of information for the MEMBERS database file from the list below.

Address of the club   Film name   Member's name
Original cost of film   Film number   Name of club manager
Membership number   Date of birth   Film category
Hire date   Phone number   Length of hire

	ITEM1	ITEM2	ITEM3	ITEM4
FILMS HIRED FILE				

(b) When new members join the club they complete an application form. The form is used to enter information into the MEMBERS database file. Design a suitable form.

5 A company uses a computer to put buyers of second-hand cars in touch with people who are selling cars. It collects information from sellers by getting the sellers to complete a form. Buyers can then ring up and ask for a list of people who have the sort of car they want.
(a) Design a form for the input of information from a SELLER.
(b) Describe clearly the processes required to get a list (in price order) of all Ford Escort cars less than 5 years old in the price range $6,000 to $8,000.
(c) Explain why a manual card index might be better than a computer for a second-hand car dealer who usually has between 8 and 10 cars for sale.

IT Tasks

Task 7

You have been asked to design an information system for a DVD library. Assume that the library has around 2,000 members and 1,400 DVDs, and that, at present, it uses a manual system for recording details of members and DVDs.

It would be a good idea to arrange to visit a DVD library to see how such a system works. It might be hard to find a DVD library that uses a manual system, so try to find out how a manual school library system works, as the system will be similar.

IT Tasks

Task 8

Your local tourist board has decided to produce a database of attractions within a 20-mile radius of where you live. Some of the information they need would include:
- name of attraction
- location
- admission costs
- opening hours.

Design and produce a database to help them.

Task 9

You have been asked to write an article on database packages for inclusion in a computer magazine. The article is aimed at the 14–18 years age group. You need to outline what a database is and how useful it can be. Also, you need to outline some of the facilities of the more popular database packages so that the reader can choose one.

Task 10

Investigate and then develop and implement an information system centred around one of the following:
(a) a database of members of a health club
(b) a database of books held in a library
(c) a database of pupils in a school
(d) a database held by a mail order computer games company.

Task 11

Investigate and then develop a system to hold information about the prices of branded goods at different supermarkets. This could be used by prudent shoppers so that they can go to different supermarkets and buy just those goods that were cheaper than anywhere else.

Fully develop and document the system.

Using database software

Describe how you would perform the following, using the database software you are going to use:

(a) load the database
(b) create a new database and design the structure
(c) save the structure and print it out
(d) add records to the database
(e) save the database
(f) go back to the structure and make changes, such as delete a field and insert a new field
(g) go back to the database and
    (i) edit a record
    (ii) delete a record
(h) perform a simple search (searching on a single field)
(i) search on several fields using the logical operators (AND, OR and NOT)
(j) produce a report containing selected fields
(k) change the format of a report.

A car stock list

A large second-hand car company keeps details of all its cars in stock using a series of records held in a filing cabinet. It is decided that the data should be transferred to a database held on computer.

Here is part of the file:

Make	Model	Price	Year	Type	Mileage
Honda	Legend	$17,000	2009	Saloon	23,000
Ford	Focus	$9,800	2007	Estate	30,000
Chrysler	Sebring	$5,600	2006	Saloon	25,000
Audi	A4	$2,300	2009	Sports	65,000
Volvo	C70	$14,000	2010	Saloon	15,000
Peugeot	307	$3,900	2004	Saloon	27,000
Ford	Focus	$12,000	2009	Estate	13,000
Ford	Mondeo	$10,000	2008	Saloon	45,000
Porsche	911	$45,000	2009	Sports	30,500
BMW	325	$29,000	2009	Sports	23,000
Vauxhall	Corsa	$6,000	2010	Saloon	35,000
Fiat	500	$5,000	2010	Saloon	11,000
Volkswagen	Golf	$8,000	2009	Saloon	15,000
Ford	Focus	$11,950	2010	Estate	12,000
BMW	X5	$32,650	2010	Estate	8,000
BMW	X5	$34,500	2009	SUV	3,000
Suzuki	Swift	$7,999	2010	Saloon	13,000
Nissan	Micra	$3,600	2007	Saloon	45,000

Skills Building

Ford	C Max	$14,000	2009	MPV	24,000
Citroen	Picasso	$15,750	2008	MPV	36,000
Toyota	Yaris	$10,000	2009	Saloon	38,000

1 Load your database software.

2 Create a structure for your database file (use only character and numeric fields), with suitable widths. When you are happy with your structure, save it and print a copy.

3 Enter the above data, verify it by proofreading and then save and print a copy.

4 Reload your database and make the following amendments:
- the Nissan Micra for $3,600 is actually a Nissan Note
- the Citroen Picasso needs its price reducing to $14,995
- the Honda Legend is a 1998 model
- the BMW 325 needs its price reducing to $27,000.

Make these amendments and save and then print a copy of the database.

5 The following cars have come in, so they should be added to the database:

Nissan	Micra	$25,500	2003	Saloon	72,000
Ford	Mondeo	$3,560	2003	Saloon	55,000
Nissan	Primera	$3,995	2004	Saloon	4,000

Add them and then save the database.

6 The following cars have been sold so their details need deleting from the database.

Chrysler	Sebring	$5,600	2006	Saloon	25,000
Opel	Corsa	$6,000	2010	Saloon	35,000
Toyota	Yaris	$10,000	2009	Saloon	38,000

After deleting these records, save the database.

7 Sort the cars file
(a) alphabetically according to make, with the As at the top of the file
(b) numerically according to price, with the most expensive car at the top
(c) using an index (if your database has one) according to make and then, within this, according to price.

Produce a printout for each one to check that it has been sorted correctly.

8 Search for
(a) details of all cars costing less than $5,000
(b) details of all Ford cars costing less than $13,000
(c) details of all cars costing between $5,000 and $8,000
(d) details of all sports cars.

You should produce a printout to provide evidence that the search is correct.

32 Measurement and Control

Before reading this chapter you should look at Chapter 20, especially the section on pseudocode. In this chapter we will look at monitoring, data logging and using computers for control.

Turtle graphics

In this section we will look at how you can use a series of instructions to move a turtle around on the screen of a computer. As the turtle moves, it can be instructed to leave a line behind it showing its path.

Turtle graphics is just one of the features of a programming language called LOGO. Ask your teacher how to load the LOGO software and get the turtle to appear on the centre of the screen. We can now instruct the turtle to move and leave a line drawn behind it to show its path.

Moving the turtle

When the turtle is facing a certain way, it can move only in that direction. To move in another direction you have to turn the turtle before moving it.

Let us now look at some of the commands:

FORWARD 30 moves the turtle 30 units forward. How far this is depends on the screen you are using. Notice also that a line is not drawn showing its path.
BACKWARD 10 moves the turtle 10 units backward.
PENUP raises the pen and stops the line being drawn.
PENDOWN puts the pen down so that a line is drawn behind the turtle.

Turning the turtle

The turtle is made to turn by giving it a direction of turn (LEFT or RIGHT) and an angle of turn in degrees. The angle is

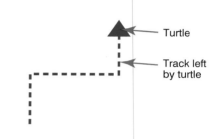

Figure 32.1 *With LOGO you control a moveable turtle*

measured from the line the turtle would take if it proceeded normally. Figure 32.1 helps explain this.

Here are some commands and explanations:

LEFT 90 turns the turtle to the left by 90 degrees.
RIGHT 90 turns the turtle to the right by 90 degrees.
CLEARSCREEN clears the screen.

Making a program

A program is a list of instructions arranged in a logical order that can be obeyed by a computer. We will now look at how to put some of the commands together that we have already learnt.

We can draw a square using the following program:

```
CLEARSCREEN
FORWARD 20
RIGHT 90
FORWARD 20
RIGHT 90
FORWARD 20
RIGHT 90
FORWARD 20
```

This method is tedious, so there is an easier way:

```
REPEAT 4 (FORWARD 20 RIGHT 90)
```

The above instruction tells LOGO to draw four lines, each 20 steps long, and to turn 90 degrees between lines.

Suppose we want to draw many squares. How do we do this?

Well, we can use what is called a procedure. This is a series of instructions to which we give a name. We can make up the procedure for the square like this:

TO SQUARE
REPEAT 4 (FORWARD 20 RIGHT 90)
END

Each time we refer to SQUARE it will repeat this section of program called a procedure. Sometimes what actually happens is not always what you think will happen. Take the following, for instance:

REPEAT 4 (SQUARE)

You might have expected this to draw the square and then go over it another three times. What actually happens is shown in Figure 32.2. Try to use the instructions with a piece of paper and pen, but when you do, remember that it is important to know in which direction the turtle is pointing. What you are actually doing is performing a DRY RUN. A DRY RUN means working through a program with a pen and paper to see if it produces the expected results.

Figure 32.2

Questions

1 See if you can work out, using pen, paper and a protractor, what happens in the following procedure.
TO PATTERN
FORWARD 50
RIGHT 150
FORWARD 60
RIGHT 100
FORWARD 30
RIGHT 90
END
Draw an accurate diagram of what you would see (assume that the pen is down).

2 Repeat the above pattern using the program:
REPEAT 20 (PATTERN)
Explain why it did not go over the drawing in the first question 20 times.

3 Write a LOGO program to draw an equilateral triangle on the screen with sides of length 50. (N.B. In an equilateral triangle, all the sides are the same length and all the angles are 60°.)

4 A polygon is a many-sided figure. All of the interior angles in a regular polygon are the same size and the sides are the same length. Write a series of programs to produce the following shapes:
(a) a square
(b) a pentagon (five sides)
(c) a hexagon (six sides)
(d) a heptagon (seven sides).

1 The following instructions will draw a shape.

REPEAT 4 [FORWARD 5 RIGHT 90]
(a) Show clearly on squared paper the shape drawn.
(b) Write a similar list of instructions to draw a rectangle with sides of length 4 and 6.

2 A robot is used to retrieve fuel rods from a nuclear reactor. To get the rod labelled X, the following instructions could be given:

FORWARD 3
TURN RIGHT
FORWARD 1
TAKE

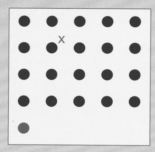

(a) The robot has an instruction (INPUT var) that allows numbers to be input into variables, which can then be used instead of the numbers indicated above. Write a program so that it will allow any rod to be retrieved. Make sure you clearly identify the use of your variables.
(b) Why would a robot be used for this job?

3 The pen on a graph plotter can be controlled by a computer using a simple set of commands which are stored as a program:

PEN UP
PEN DOWN
FORWARD x moves the pen forward x cm
RIGHT x turns x degrees to the right
LEFT x turns x degrees to the left
STOP

(a) You will need a protractor to measure the angles in the following program using the above commands:

PEN DOWN
FORWARD 10
RIGHT 90
FORWARD 10
RIGHT 90
FORWARD 10
RIGHT 90
FORWARD 10
STOP

Using a pen, paper, ruler and protractor, trace the shape that the plotter would draw using the above instructions.
(b) Write a program using the list of commands shown above to produce an equilateral triangle of side 15.

(c) So that a series of instructions can be repeated, there are the following commands: REPEAT n TIMES

....
....
....
....

AGAIN

The dotted lines are used to represent the lines of commands that are repeated.
Write a program to draw a regular hexagon with sides of length 10 like the one shown in the diagram, using the REPEAT command.

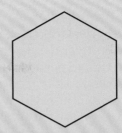

4 A computer can control a turtle on the screen. When the turtle moves it leaves a line on the screen. Some of the commands are:

FORWARD steps
BACK steps
RIGHT angle
LEFT angle

For example, FORWARD 50 moves the turtle forward 50 steps in a straight line. RIGHT 45 turns the turtle 45° to the right.
Here are the commands which are needed to draw the S shape.

FORWARD 50 LEFT 90
FORWARD 50 LEFT 90
FORWARD 100 RIGHT 90
FORWARD 100 RIGHT 90

The turtle starts from the position shown in the diagram.
Arrange these commands in the right order to draw the S shape.

Monitoring physical quantities (temperature, pressure, etc.) using a computer

Monitoring temperature

If we wanted to look at how coffee cools when placed in a polystyrene cup we could just use a stop watch and a thermometer and take a reading every minute over a period of an hour.

Doing it this way, we would need to sit with the whole apparatus for an hour and remember to take a reading of the thermometer every minute. Clearly this is tedious, even for one hour. If we needed to take more frequent readings over a longer period of time, we would probably give up.

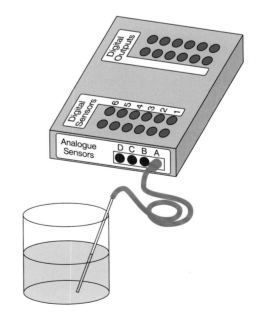

▲
Figure 32.3 *Analogue-to-digital conversion is necessary with a temperature sensor*

Help is at hand though in the form of data logging (see Chapter 14). Here we can use a computer (desktop or portable), an interface, suitable software and a temperature sensor to perform this experiment easily.

Once we have loaded the software and told the computer which sensors we have connected (some systems can do this automatically), we then need to tell the computer how frequently the measurements are to be made and over what period. We can then go away and do something else while the computer gets on with the job.

Most data loggers will record the data in the form of a table which can be imported into other software, such as spreadsheet or graphics packages for further work. You can usually display your readings graphically at the end of the experiment or while the experiment is taking place, since the readings are taken automatically by the sensor.

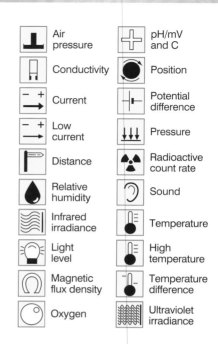

▲ **Figure 32.4** *The range of sensors available from Philip Harris Education, suppliers of data-logging systems, sensors and control equipment*

⊥	Air pressure	⊕	pH/mV and C
	Conductivity	⦿	Position
→	Current	⊣⊢	Potential difference
→	Low current	↓↓↓	Pressure
⌐	Distance	☢	Radioactive count rate
●	Relative humidity	⌒	Sound
≋	Infrared irradiance		Temperature
⌐	Light level		High temperature
⋒	Magnetic flux density		Temperature difference
⊙	Oxygen	▦	Ultraviolet irradiance

Logging

Logging interval

The logging interval is the frequency with which the individual readings are taken (i.e. per second, per minute, per hour, etc.). If you wanted to determine the average daily temperature you would probably choose to take a temperature measurement every hour. In one day you would have 24 separate measurements which could be added together and then divided by 24 to give the day's average.

Logging period

This is the time period over which the measurements take place. If you wanted to investigate the cooling of a cup of tea in different types of cup, you might choose a logging period of around one hour, since this would be near the time taken for the drink to cool to around room temperature.

▲ **Figure 32.5** *The uses of sensors are limited only by your imagination*

Advantages of data logging

Data logging can be used for recording data about fast events that would happen too quickly for you to take readings manually. It can also be used for very slow events where recording them manually would be tedious and time-consuming. Because the readings are taken automatically, accurate measurements are made without human error and exactly at the right time.

IT Tasks

Task 1

Data logging

Here is a variety of tasks you can perform using data-logging equipment. It is impossible to give exact instructions of how to use any particular piece of apparatus, because the instructions are different for different makes. This means you will have to find out from your teacher how to do the following:

1 Connect the sensor, interface and computer as instructed by your teacher.
2 Load the data-logging software (if necessary).
3 Specify how frequently the readings are taken (most packages allow you to vary this from about one ten-thousandth of a second to around 30 minutes).
4 Specify the total recording time (i.e. the total time over which the readings are taken). For most packages this can be from a fraction of a second to almost three weeks.
5 Display the data as a list on the screen.
6 Produce a display of the data plotted against time.
7 Save the data to disk for use later.
8 Plot the graph in real time, so that as a reading is taken it is automatically plotted on the screen.
9 Export the previously saved data into other software packages, such as spreadsheet or word-processing packages.

Task 2

Temperature variation of water

Use data-logging equipment to find out how the temperature of a glass beaker of boiling water varies with time when it is left to cool.

You will need to think about the following:
• how frequently the temperature reading needs to be taken and over what period
• what can be done to increase the time over which the water cools.

Try the experiment using different types of mug. Do tall, thin mugs keep the water hotter than short, fat mugs? Does the surface area in contact with the air matter? Try other, similar experiments.

Moisture content of soil
Monitor the change with time in the moisture content of the soil surrounding a house plant.
• What sensor or sensors will you use? (Hint: you will need to measure the moisture and any other physical properties on which the drying out of the soil depends.)
• How often does the data logger need to obtain a reading?
• Drying out is a slow process, so over what total time should the data logger operate? Why have you chosen this period?
• Explain exactly what you did and the reasons for doing it.

Conditions in a fish tank

Monitor the conditions in a tropical or marine fish tank over 24 hours.

You could use a variety of sensors, such as:
- light
- temperature
- pH
- oxygen.

In a tropical or marine fish tank the temperature should be kept constant using the heater and the thermostat. From your readings, how successful was this system in keeping the temperature constant? You could try plotting physical quantities against each other rather than against time. For example try plotting the amount of oxygen against the amount of light. Do they follow each other? Again, fully document your experiment, paying particular attention to the use of the data-logging equipment.

Wind chill factor

You may have heard the term wind chill factor being used by weather forecasters. We all know that, even on a warm day, it can feel a lot cooler if there is a wind.

One way of cooling a drink is to wrap a damp towel around the bottle and place it in a draughty place. The water evaporates and cools the bottle. Could we use this principle to make a device to give us a measure of the wind chill factor?

See what you can come up with and fully describe your solution.

Other examples of computer control

In this section we will look at how computers can be used to control devices and perform useful tasks.

Cold tea?

The problem

Make a system that warns you when your hot tea has cooled enough and is ready to drink. You should be able to cancel the alarm when you go to your drink.

Questions

- What temperature is the tea when it is cool enough to drink?
- What kind of a warning do you need?
- What will you use to tell the computer you have now received the warning and got your drink?

Solution

Tea at temperatures of around 55–70 °C might be suitable for drinking. A buzzer would give a suitable warning. The buzzer would continue until a push button is pressed to cancel the alarm. The sensors may be connected to the interface along with a special module which is used for control. The buzzer is connected as number 6 and the push switch as input 1. If the temperature is less than 70 °C the buzzer should be switched on. When the push button is pressed the buzzer stops. Using IF and WHEN, the computer tests the temperature and waits until the temperature condition is met.

Here is the control program:

```
WHEN TEMPERATURE IS
BELOW 70 THEN SWITCH ON 6
WHEN INPUT 1 IS ON
THEN SWITCH OFF 6
```

Here is another program that does the same thing:

```
REPEAT FOREVER
IF TEMPERATURE IS
BELOW 70 THEN SWITCH
ON 6
AGAIN
```

Alternatively, both solutions can be built as procedures to give the same results:

```
BUILD teaalarm
WHEN TEMPERATURE IS
BELOW 70 THEN SWITCH
ON 6
WHEN INPUT 1 IS ON
THEN SWITCH OFF 6
END
```

or

```
BUILD teatwo
REPEAT FOREVER
IF TEMPERATURE IS
BELOW 70 THEN SWITCH
ON 6
AGAIN
WHEN INPUT 1 IS ON
THEN SWITCH OFF 6
END
```

Further work

1 If the freezer breaks down you need to know if the food has started to thaw out.
2 You have just put a bottle of warm cola in the fridge. You need a cold drink and want to know as soon as it is ready to drink.

Make an alarm system.

Wake up

The problem

Make an alarm clock which switches on at dawn and switches off when you shout at it.

Questions

- How will the computer know if it is morning?
- How will the computer detect you have shouted at it?
- How loud do you need to shout to stop the alarm?
- What can you use to set the alarm?
- How could you tell that the alarm has been set?

Solution

The light sensor can measure the light level. When the light reaches a certain level the alarm will be switched on. A sound sensor is used to detect the voice. The sound level at which the alarm switches off should be set high enough so that it is not switched off by the alarm itself. Use the push switch to set the alarm and switch on a green light to indicate it is set. Connect the sound sensor and the module to the interface. Connect the light and sound sensors to the interface. The push switch is connected as input 1 and the green indicator lamp is connected as number 3.

Here is the control program. This program is written as a procedure.

```
BUILD alarm
REPEAT FOREVER
WHEN INPUT 1 IS ON
THEN SWITCH ON 3
WHEN LIGHT IS ABOVE 40
THEN SWITCH ON 6
WHEN SOUND IS ABOVE
80 THEN SWITCH OFF 6
SWITCH OFF 3
AGAIN
END
```

To make this procedure run, type the line below:

```
DO alarm
```

Further work

1 Make an alarm that tells you when you are playing your music too loud.
2 Make a burglar alarm that can be triggered by the noise level. The alarm sound can be on and off like a siren.

Shop

The problem

Make a buzzer for a shop that works when you go in and step on the doormat.

Questions

- What can you use to tell if the mat has been stepped on?
- What should the buzzer do – should it stay on all the time or should it switch off after a certain time?
- What should happen if another customer enters the shop?

Solution

Use a push switch to tell if the mat has been stepped on. If the push switch has been pressed, the buzzer should be switched on. The buzzer should stay on for a few seconds, then it should be switched off. Go back and check if the push switch has been pressed, in case another customer enters the shop. This will be repeated over and over. Connect the module to the interface. The buzzer is connected as number 6 and the push switch as input 1.

Here is the control program:

```
REPEAT FOREVER
WHEN INPUT 1 IS ON
THEN SWITCH ON 6
WAIT 20
SWITCH OFF 6
AGAIN
```

Alternatively, we can use a procedure called shop to do the same:

```
BUILD shop
REPEAT FOREVER
WHEN INPUT 1 IS ON
THEN SWITCH ON 6
WAIT 20
SWITCH OFF 6
AGAIN
END
```

To make this procedure run, type the line below:

```
DO shop
```

Further work

Make the buzzer produce an intermittent sound. As an alternative to the push switch it is possible to make a pressure 'switch' by attaching a near-flat balloon to a pressure sensor.

Use the same procedure as above, but replace the lines that read:

```
WHEN INPUT 1 IS ON
THEN SWITCH ON 6
```

with

```
WHEN PRESSURE IS
ABOVE 20 THEN SWITCH
ON 6
```

You may need to experiment with the value of the pressure to make the buzzer work in the way that you want.

Lighthouse

The problem

Make a flashing warning light for a lighthouse.

Questions

- Which colour will you use for the warning light? Give your reason.
- What should the warning light do?

Solution

Use a red light, LED number 1, as red is a good warning colour. The warning light should come on for a second, then go off for a second. This should repeat over and over. Connect the module to the universal interface.

Here is the control program:

```
REPEAT FOREVER
SWITCH ON 1
WAIT 5
SWITCH OFF 1
WAIT 5
AGAIN
```

Alternatively, you could build a procedure called flash to do the same thing:

```
BUILD flash
REPEAT FOREVER
SWITCH ON 1
WAIT 5
SWITCH OFF 1
WAIT 5
AGAIN
END
```

To run this procedure, type the line below:

```
DO flash
```

Further work

Use two flashing lights as the warning signal.

Go away

The problem

People keep ringing your door buzzer at night. Make a door buzzer that works only in the daytime.

Questions

- What will you use as a push button?
- How will the doorbell know whether it is night or day?
- What should the light level be for the door buzzer to work – above 60, above 40 or something else?

Should the buzzer work:

1 when it is pressed or the light level is low?
2 when it is pressed or the light level is high?
3 when it is pressed and the light level is low?
4 when it is pressed and the light level is high?

When should the door buzzer stop buzzing – when you stop pressing it, after a few seconds or when you answer the door?

Solution

Use the push switch as the door push button. Use a light sensor to find out whether it is night or day. Trial and error will determine the most suitable light level for the buzzer to work. The door buzzer should work only if two conditions are met: if the push switch has been pressed and if the light level is high. The buzzer should be switched off a few seconds

after the button has been pressed. Next go back and check if the push switch has been pressed again. This will be repeated forever.

Connect the light sensor and module to the universal interface. The buzzer is connected as number 6 and the push switch as input 1.

Here is the control program:

```
REPEAT FOREVER
IF LIGHT IS ABOVE 50
AND INPUT 1 IS ON THEN
SWITCH ON 6
WAIT 20
SWITCH OFF 6
AGAIN
```

Alternatively, you could use a procedure called buzzer:

```
BUILD buzzer
REPEAT FOREVER
IF LIGHT IS ABOVE 50
AND INPUT 1 IS ON THEN
SWITCH ON 6
WAIT 20
SWITCH OFF 6
AGAIN
END
```

Further work

Porch light

You want a light to come on at your front door whenever it is dark and switch off when it gets light. To save electricity, you also want to be able to switch the light off when you go to bed.

Welcome home

You want a light to come on at your front door when you arrive home at night. Obviously it does not come on during the day.

33 Modelling

Modelling a supermarket queue

In this example we will look at the problem of making a model of a supermarket queue. The way the model is written up is the same as that outlined before. When doing any coursework on modelling, make sure that you adopt a similar format.

Identifying the problem

Suppose we are opening a new supermarket. How do we decide how many tills or point-of-sale terminals to use? If the supermarket is part of a chain, then past experience may help us. But if this is our first supermarket we do not have any others to make a comparison with. Some other method will need to be used.

Analysing the situation

Why do we need to get it right?

If we do not get the number of tills right the consequences could be:

1 either we could buy too many POS terminals and thereby waste money
2 or we could buy too few and cause long queues, which might make the shoppers reluctant to shop at the store again.

What software do we need to use to perform this task?

Since we are trying to understand how a real system operates, we could use a spreadsheet. We do need to think carefully about the problem before we start trying to design the spreadsheet. We are going to construct a model of the queue using numbers.

We first need to decide:

1 the inputs to the system
2 the calculations that need to be performed on these numbers
3 the outputs from the system.

The advantage of constructing such a model is that we can make changes to the inputs and see what effects they have on the output. For example, the supermarket owner/manager can immediately see the effect of altering the number of tills on the lengths of queues and the average waiting times.

Figure 33.1
▼

What are the inputs to the supermarket model?

The inputs include:

1 how many people are waiting
2 how many POS terminals or tills there are
3 how long each person takes to be served. This will have to be an average time, since the time depends on the number of items the person is buying and the method of payment (e.g. credit card, debit card, cheque or cash).

Always produce the simplest model to start with. This will help you get a grasp of the problem and you can refine it later. Make sure that you include all your work if you are including a modelling/simulation project for your coursework.

Design

In this section we have to start designing our model. In this case we will be using a spreadsheet, so we can either design it straight onto the spreadsheet or plan it on paper first. If you are designing the model straight onto the spreadsheet, make sure that you know enough about the commands to move things around if you need to alter them.

In this problem we can have a heading and then divide the spreadsheet into two parts for the inputs and the outputs. Calculations are performed on the inputs to produce the outputs. Figure 33.2 shows the design.

	A	B	C	D	E	F	G
1							
2							
3	*Model of a supermarket queue*						
4							
5	Inputs						
6	Number of shoppers waiting						
7	Number of tills						
8	Time for a shopper to pass through a checkout						
9							
10							
11							
12	Outputs						
13	Average number of shoppers in each queue						
14	Time the last person in the queue has to wait						
15							
16							

▲ **Figure 33.2** *Design of the model*

Suppose that there are 40 shoppers waiting to pay for the goods and there are 20 checkouts. Let us also assume that, on average, it takes a shopper two minutes to pass through the checkout. We will have to assume that the shoppers will distribute themselves equally in the queues. We can then calculate the average number of shoppers in each queue using the formula:

$$\text{average number of shoppers in each queue} = \frac{\text{number of shoppers waiting}}{\text{number of tills}}$$

Using our figures we get:

$$\text{average number of shoppers in each queue} = \frac{40}{20} = 2$$

Now, the last shopper in each of these queues will have to wait a time which is given by the following formula:

time last person in queue has to wait = average time for a person to go through the checkout in minutes × average number of shoppers waiting in each queue

Using our figures we get:

time last person in each queue has to wait $= 2 \times 2 = 4$ mins

Now, the beauty of using a spreadsheet is the ease with which we can carry out the calculations. However, we must make sure that we link the outputs to the inputs using formulae.

Figure 33.3 shows the formulae that have to be used. You should be able to print your spreadsheet out showing any formulae placed in each cell. Produce this as evidence in your project.

Implementation

Implementation involves actually using the model. In other words we have to perform a simulation by putting in numbers to see what happens.

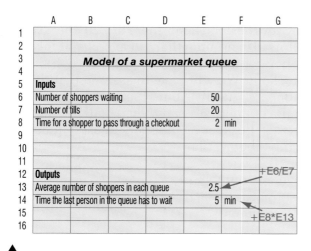

Figure 33.3 *Spreadsheet showing the inputs, outputs and the formulae used to calculate the outputs*

	A	B	C	D	E	F	G
1							
2							
3		*Model of a supermarket queue*					
4							
5	Inputs						
6	Number of shoppers waiting				50		
7	Number of tills				10		
8	Time for a shopper to pass through a checkout				2	min	
9							
10							
11							
12	Outputs						
13	Average number of shoppers in each queue				5		
14	Time the last person in the queue has to wait				10	min	
15							
16							

Figure 33.4 *Spreadsheet showing the effect of altering the number of tills*

Figure 33.4 shows the effect of altering the inputs to the system. Try to use the model you have created to explore the effect of changing the variables and rules and to test hypotheses.

Evaluation

We have to look carefully at the model we have produced. Maybe we could have made it better. Here we describe whether we are happy with the model, any improvements that could be made to it and whether it solves the problem that we started with.

Refinement

If the model is a good one, then no refinement is needed. If we need to alter the model in any way to reflect the real situation more accurately, then we need to say why and provide evidence of having done this, which would include printouts of the improved model. Obviously you could go on forever making changes and trying to get things right, but there has to be a point where you stop. Finally, perfection is impossible to achieve, especially if human behaviour is to be taken into account.

Questions

1 One of the assumptions used in the model was that queues consist of equal numbers of people. Does this always happen? Why not? What changes could be made to the model to reflect this?

2 Can you produce a better model of a supermarket queue than this? Remember that this is only an initial model. If you were submitting this as a piece of coursework you would need to refine it. See what you can do. Write up your report using the above headings and subheadings as a guide.

Break-even analysis

Beatbox is a new company set up by a brother and sister to manufacture small loudspeakers. They hope to sell the small speakers to people who want to attach their MP3/MP4 or CD players to them, or who need speakers for multimedia applications.

They realise that things will be hard to start with, so, to give themselves some light at the end of the tunnel, they would like to find out how many speakers they would need to sell to break even.

When a business is started, money has to be paid out for equipment, parts, premises and so on before the company starts making the products. So money goes out of the business, but there is none coming in. Once the product begins to be made and sold, the money starts coming back into the business. Eventually, when Beatbox has sold a certain number of loudspeakers, the company will break even. This point, called the break-even point, occurs when the money coming in from the sale of the loudspeakers balances the money that has been paid out. In other words the company is neither making a profit nor a loss. There will be a certain number of loudspeakers for which this will occur. Once past this point, the sale of the speakers will start to produce a profit.

Break-even analysis is important when starting a business, since the banks that lend the company money to start up will want to know when the borrower will start to make a profit.

In order to produce a model for break-even analysis, Beatbox needs to work out the fixed costs and the variable costs. The company's accountant tells the owners the following information.

Fixed costs

Fixed costs are any costs that do not depend on the number of loudspeakers sold. Fixed costs would include rent of buildings, rates, salaries and finance costs. It is important to note that fixed costs do not stay fixed forever. They are only fixed over the short term and over a certain range of production.

Variable costs

Variable costs are the costs that depend on the number of speakers produced. So the cost of the parts which make up the speakers and the electricity used would be classed as variable costs.

Beatbox has worked out the following figures:

fixed costs = $1,000
variable costs per speaker = $12.50
selling price per speaker = $18.00

Variable costs are the costs of making a certain number of speakers, and sales revenue is the money which comes in when the same number of speakers is sold. So:

$$\text{total cost of producing speakers} = \text{variable costs} + \text{fixed costs}$$

$$\text{variable costs} = \text{variable costs per speaker} \times \text{number of speakers}$$

$$\text{sales revenue} = \text{selling price per speaker} \times \text{number of speakers}$$

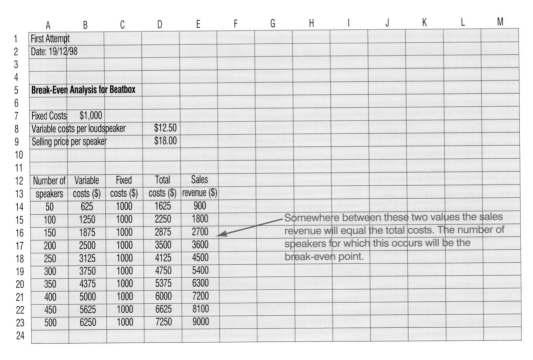

	A	B	C	D	E
1	First Attempt				
2	Date: 19/12/98				
3					
4					
5	Break-Even Analysis for Beatbox				
6					
7	Fixed Costs	$1,000			
8	Variable costs per loudspeaker			$12.50	
9	Selling price per speaker			$18.00	
10					
11					
12	Number of	Variable	Fixed	Total	Sales
13	speakers	costs ($)	costs ($)	costs ($)	revenue ($)
14	50	625	1000	1625	900
15	100	1250	1000	2250	1800
16	150	1875	1000	2875	2700
17	200	2500	1000	3500	3600
18	250	3125	1000	4125	4500
19	300	3750	1000	4750	5400
20	350	4375	1000	5375	6300
21	400	5000	1000	6000	7200
22	450	5625	1000	6625	8100
23	500	6250	1000	7250	9000
24					

Somewhere between these two values the sales revenue will equal the total costs. The number of speakers for which this occurs will be the break-even point.

Figure 33.5 *Spreadsheet showing the inputs, outputs and the formulae used to calculate the outputs*

We can now produce a table with the column headings shown below, using spreadsheet software.

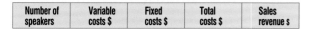

Number of speakers	Variable costs $	Fixed costs $	Total costs $	Sales revenue $

You will now perform a series of tasks which will determine the break-even point.

First attempt

The first attempt is used to obtain the very rough range that the break-even point could lie within.

In the first attempt to find the break-even point you can use numbers of speakers from 50 to 500, going up in steps of 50. Make sure that you key in all the information except that in the following columns: variable costs, total costs and sales revenue. You should work these out using suitable formulae and then copy them down the relevant columns. Check that your final model looks like the one in Figure 33.5.

The break-even point occurs where the sales revenue and the total costs are equal. As you can see, there is no such value on our spreadsheet, so we look for where the sales revenue goes from being smaller than the total costs to where it is greater. Looking at the spreadsheet you can see that this occurs between sales of 150 and 200 speakers. We need to investigate this region more closely to get a more accurate picture. We therefore produce a second spreadsheet just covering this area.

Second attempt

Produce another spreadsheet by altering the first one to go from 150 speakers to 250 speakers in steps of 10. Check with Figure 33.6 that you get the same values. It should reveal that the break-even point lies somewhere between 180 and 190 speakers.

Third attempt

Now repeat the process using the numbers of speakers from 180 to 190 in steps of one speaker.

What value do you get for the number of speakers to break even? What do you think you should do if it is not a whole number?

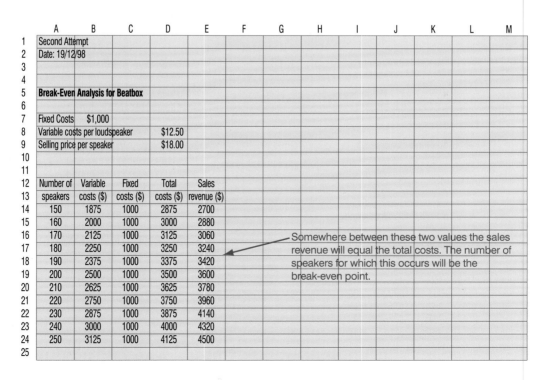

▲

Figure 33.6 *Second attempt at finding the break-even point*

Check that your spreadsheet looks like the one in Figure 33.7.

Finding the break-even point graphically

We can find the break-even point graphically by plotting the sales revenue and total costs against the number of speakers sold. You can do this either by using graph paper or by getting the computer to draw two line graphs like the one shown in Figure 33.8. The break-even point is where the two straight lines cross. The number of speakers sold to break even can be read from the graph.

	A	B	C	D	E
1	Third Attempt				
2	Date: 19/12/98				
3					
4					
5	Break-Even Analysis for Beatbox				
6					
7	Fixed Costs	$1,000			
8	Variable costs per loudspeaker			$12.50	
9	Selling price per speaker			$18.00	
10					
11					
12	Number of	Variable	Fixed	Total	Sales
13	speakers	costs ($)	costs ($)	costs ($)	revenue ($)
14	180	2250.00	1000	3250.00	3240
15	181	2262.50	1000	3262.50	3258
16	182	2275.00	1000	3275.00	3276
17	183	2287.50	1000	3287.50	3294
18	184	2300.00	1000	3300.00	3312
19	185	2312.50	1000	3312.50	3330
20	186	2325.00	1000	3325.00	3348
21	187	2337.50	1000	3337.50	3366
22	188	2350.00	1000	3350.00	3384
23	189	2362.50	1000	3362.50	3402
24	190	2375.00	1000	3375.00	3420
25					

▲ **Figure 33.7** *Third attempt at finding the break-even point*

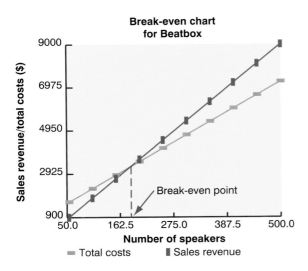

▲ **Figure 33.8** *Finding the break-even point graphically*

Test Yourself

John enjoys woodwork and has decided to make a bird table for his parents. The table he makes is seen by his neighbours, who ask him if he can make them one. Word travels around and before long John has a book full of orders. He even starts to get the odd order from a garden centre.

He would like to speed up the construction of the tables by using more power tools. He has $400 in the bank, which he spends on the latest woodworking equipment. His variable and fixed costs are:

fixed costs (woodworking equipment) = $400
variable costs = $15.00 per bird table
selling price = $25.00 per bird table

Using a spreadsheet, work out how many bird tables he would need to sell before he breaks even.

IT Tasks

Task 1

Use a spreadsheet to solve a pair of simultaneous equations, such as the pair:

$$3x + 4y = 25$$
$$3x + 2y = 17$$

There is a variety of ways you could approach this problem.
(a) You could use the spreadsheet to set up a table for each equation and then use each table to plot a graph. Where the two straight lines cross, the x and y coordinates will give the solution to the above pair of equations.
(b) You could develop a method on the spreadsheet using trial and error.
(c) You could use matrices. Some spreadsheets have a function where you can solve simultaneous equations. See if yours has and find out how to use it.

Task 2

Here is an equation to solve using a spreadsheet. Do not try to factorise it because it cannot be factorised.

$$x^2 - 8x - 6 = 0$$

Now, you can use the same method to solve a cubic equation. With cubic equations, there are three solutions. See if you can find all the solutions for the following cubic equation:

$$x^3 - 6x^2 + 3x + 10 = 0$$

To give you a clue, all the solutions lie somewhere between -2 and $+6$.

You may also like to plot the equations using a graphics, curve-sketching or spreadsheet package. Can you spot your solutions on the graph?

Task 3

Ayesha is 25 and lives at home with her parents. She is bored with her present job working in an office and would like a challenge. Her present job brings in $150 per week.

She has just seen an advertisement in her local newspaper advertising a training course to become a driving instructor. Fees for the tuition and final examination are $1,300. She can drive at the moment, but does not have her own car. She therefore needs to buy a car with dual controls. Ayesha sees a car she likes and with the dual controls it will cost her $8,000.

In order to get established, Ayesha reckons she will need to undercut the fees charged by the other driving schools. She therefore decides to charge $12 per hour. To attract customers, she decides to advertise in the local paper and this will cost $30 per week. Her mother, who is at home all day, will answer the phone calls and make bookings, and Ayesha will give her mother $20 per week for doing this.

Before giving up her job and going ahead with the venture she decides to work out how many hours she would need to work each week in order to break even. To do this she must work out her fixed and variable costs. This she has done and the following figures are obtained.

Fixed costs

Advertising in the local paper = $30.00 per week
Payment to her mother = $20.00 per week
Borrowing to buy the car and pay for tuition fees for course = $40.00 per week
Depreciation of the car = $80.00 per week

Variable costs

The only variable costs will be the running costs of the car. These include petrol, repairs and so on. She works out these variable costs to be 20 cents per mile. On average, in a one-hour lesson, she estimates that she will travel about 15 miles. Hence, the variable costs for one lesson will be 15×20 cents = $3.00.

Ayesha has asked for your help in making her decision.

You have your own computer and have told Ayesha that you will help her by making use of appropriate computer software.

1 Set up a model of the business and use your model to determine the number of lessons she would need to do each week in order to break even.
2 Suggest some improvements she might make and show them as printouts.
3 Write a brief report on the proposed business. Should she quit her job or stick with it? What do you think on the basis of your figures?

IT Tasks

Task 4

In mathematics you often come across equations such as:

$x^2 - x - 6 = 0$

We would normally solve this by factorisation like this:

$(x - 3)(x + 2) = 0$

giving values of $x = 3$ or -2.

Some equations are difficult to solve. For instance the quadratic equation:

$x^2 + 6x - 2 = 0$

has the solutions $x = 0.32$ or -6.32 to two decimal places, so we cannot solve it by simple factorisation. We could use a spreadsheet, however, and try various values of x in the equation to see if we can get zero.

Task 5

You are the promoter for a pop concert. You are going to organise a concert with a famous group or singer. You have certain overheads, such as the costs of the group or singer, as well as costs of rental of the hall, printing of tickets, security guards, refreshments, programmes and so on.

You are to produce a model of the business and simulate a variety of different situations, such as very few people turning up or a sell out concert.

Produce a report showing examples of your model and explain any assumptions you made in making your model. Give a conclusion explaining how closely your model mimics the real situation and outline any improvements you could make.

Task 6

In this task you will be required to solve a pair of equations simultaneously.

Here is the pair of equations:

$y = x^2 - 4x + 7$

$y = x + 1$

The first equation is called a quadratic equation and the second is called a linear equation. The solution to the simultaneous equation will be a value of x when put into either of the equations that will give the same value of y. There are two such values of x for which this will happen and you, using a spreadsheet model, will have to find them.

Task 7

Explore a model of traffic flow at a crossroads with traffic lights. Find out the best timing of the north–south and east–west lights to minimise the queues of traffic for particular rates of traffic flows in each direction. Produce a brief report, including at least one printout to support your conclusions.

Model a set of temporary traffic lights, one at each end of some road works 100 m long. Only one line of traffic can pass, so the lights must be set to allow safe passage of traffic. Investigate the effect of different lengths of time on green on the length of queues for particular rates of traffic flows. Produce a brief report, including printouts of your model and of the queue for different values of variables.

Task 8

You have been asked to produce a model for electricity usage in a house over a year. Quantity of electricity is measured in a unit called a kilowatt hour (written as kWh). A 1 kWh appliance, such as a one-bar electric fire, used for one hour would consume 1 kWh of electricity. Used for half an hour it would consume 0.5 kWh. If you are unsure how to calculate amounts of electricity from the power of an appliance and the time it is used, consult your physics teacher.

Things to think about:

- Design a document on which you could record the names of the appliances owned and their power consumption.
- Use this document to collect the information.
- Interview the people who use the appliance, find out how long they use it for each week or month and then use this figure to work out the daily usage. You need to do this because not every appliance will be used each day.
- You will need to find the cost of a 1 kWh unit of electricity.
- Design a spreadsheet to model the situation with suitable column and row headings.
- You will need to calculate the total cost per day and the total cost per year.

34 Graphics Packages

Graphics

Graphics is a word used for all types of artwork, including line diagrams, bitmap images (made up of lots of tiny dots), photographs, graphs and charts.

Graphics packages

For most of us, graphics packages can mean just a simple paint package where you can draw line diagrams, flood fill and produce a variety of shadings. You can also produce text in a variety of fonts and typefaces. These simple but very useful packages can be used as an alternative to specialist and more complicated desktop publishing packages. Producing diagrams is extremely difficult using a mouse, so some professional artwork is hand drawn and then scanned into a graphics package. A great deal of professional artwork is now drawn with software packages which do not use a mouse.

Some graphics packages allow you to scan a photograph or diagram directly into the computer so that you can subsequently manipulate it in some way. Using special equipment and software it is possible to capture pictures from a television screen or from a video camera. The extra equipment needed to do this is called a video grabber. Digital cameras are very popular because you do not need a film and there are no developing costs. You can simply capture the photographs from the camera and then manipulate the images on the computer screen.

If you need to use pictures you can use clip art.

Bitmap and vector graphics

There are two formats that a graphics file can have: it can represent the image as a bitmap or as a vector graphic.

A bitmap file represents each dot or pixel on the screen as a single bit of information in a file. If the pixel is in colour, then additional bits will need to be stored. Many paint packages create bitmapped images. One of the main disadvantages of bitmapped images is that they are difficult to change because they have to be altered a pixel at a time.

With vector graphics the lines are stored as equations inside the computer. They are expressed in vector format so they have a starting point, a length and a direction. The main advantage of vector graphics is that they are easy to change without any loss of resolution. With bitmapped graphics, if the image is enlarged, the number of pixels used stays the same. As a result of this the pixels move further apart and this makes the image look grainy. When a vector graphics image is enlarged, the number of pixels used to make up the image increases in proportion and the resolution stays the same.

CAD packages make use of vector graphics.

Clip art

For those without an artistic streak, the thought of having to draw pictures to be placed in an important document can bring on a cold sweat. Anyone who has tried to use a mouse to draw pictures using a paint or drawing package will know how hard it is. However, help is at hand with clip art. Clip art illustrations are copyright-free drawings which you can place in your documents. These documents could be word-processed, desktop-published or a diagram drawn using a graphics package. Some clip art is shown in Figure 34.1.

Because clip art is accurately pre-drawn, when imported into your documents it gives them a professional look. Disks containing clip art can be bought separately or as part

▲
Figure 34.2 *As well as importing clip art you can also import pre-stored photos*

▲
Figure 34.1 *Some holiday clip art*

of a graphics or DTP package. You can get special clip art packages and some have as many as one million images.

Presentation software

Pictures are able to communicate ideas and concepts to an audience much better than the written or spoken word alone. Presentations are used to sell products, services or just ideas to someone else. Good presentations use visual aids such as slides or transparencies on a projector. The visual aids are used to back up what the presenter is saying. Graphs are usually included in such presentations. If the work is displayed attractively, the audience will be more able to digest the key points.

While a projector is needed for a large audience, for smaller audiences a rolling slide show can be produced on the screen of a computer.

Multimedia (hypermedia) presentations

Multimedia is sometimes called hypermedia. Multimedia presentations are useful for training since students can see demonstrations on screen and can also interact with the software. It is hard to explain the capabilities of multimedia and you should look at different packages for yourself.

Colour

Colour printing is affordable if you use an inkjet printer, but colour laser printers are expensive to buy. When producing graphics you need to decide whether they are to be printed out. It you do not have a colour printer then there is no point in worrying about colour when planning your design on the screen. You will find that much clearer graphics are produced on black and white printers if you use black and white on the screen.

Computer-aided design

Computer-aided design, or CAD for short, is used by engineers, architects and so on to produce high quality technical drawings drawn to scale. The sorts of diagram produced by these packages include plans of houses, maps, circuit diagrams, engineering drawings and 3D plans of kitchens. Figure 34.5 shows a stairway design which has been produced using CAD.

Before computers were used, if a drawing needed a simple modification then it was often necessary to completely redraw it. Now, with the use of CAD software, modifications can be made at the press of a button.

Architects can produce a plan view of a building and then immediately view it in three dimensions and even rotate it to see what it looks like from different angles. The most popular CAD package is AutoCAD, which is quite expensive, so you are unlikely to see it in schools. There is a cut-down version available at a much lower price.

CAD images

▲
Figure 34.3

Figure 34.3 shows a ray-traced image and this is easily converted into a solid image which can be viewed from all angles by the computer.

▲ **Figure 34.4** *If you are artistic, then you can even produce graphic images like this one*

CAD software can be used to design electronic circuits as well as design the electrical wiring diagrams/plans for buildings.

Features of CAD software

Computer-aided design (CAD) software has the following features:

- There are banks of parts which can be added to a drawing without them having to be drawn separately.
- When adding components to a diagram each component added can have its cost added up and this allows a designer to work out the costs of the finished component.

Computer graphics

Using sophisticated graphics packages, the computer can be used to produce images like that shown in Figure 34.4.

Advantages of using CAD:

1 it saves a lot of time
2 it produces accurate scale diagrams
3 you can easily manipulate the images on the screen
4 you can produce drawings in 3D, which is especially useful for diagrams of kitchens, gardens, buildings and so on.
5 images can be saved on disk and retrieved at a later date
6 drawings can easily be scaled up and down.

Garden design software

Garden design software is one of the many specialist applications of design software and it allows gardeners to place their plants and features such as ponds, paths, terraces, and see what they would look like. Using this software you can view the garden in 3D and also from different angles. You can even see the garden in different seasons.

▲
Figure 34.5 *Stairway design produced using CAD software*

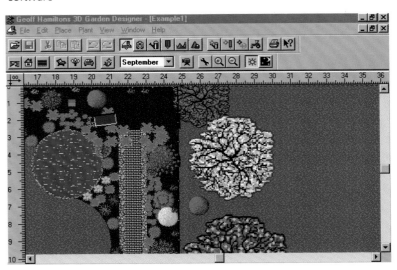

▲
Figure 34.6 *A plan view of the garden*

Screen shots taken from 'Geoff Hamilton's 3D Garden Design Software', published by Global Software Publishing

▲
Figure 34.7 *This shows one of the many 3D views of the same garden design*

293

1 (a) Explain what is meant by the abbreviation CAD.

(b) Give three advantages of using CAD against performing the same task manually.

2 A friend of your family knows of your interest in computers and has asked you your opinion regarding buying a multimedia computer system.

(a) What makes a multimedia system different from an ordinary computer system?

(b) Describe two of the multimedia packages that you have used.

3 Many people find it easier to use clip art than to use their own diagrams.

(a) Explain what is meant by clip art.

(b) Why is it easier to use clip art?

(c) What are the disadvantages of using clip art?

IT Tasks

Task 1

Pick one of the following and use any graphics, paint or other package to help you with your design.

1 Design a package that could be used to hold a single golf ball. You will need to design the shape of the package and design the net.

2 You have been asked by a fabric manufacturer to come up with a new design for a fabric. Use appropriate software to do this.

3 A friend of yours is a question master in a local pub quiz. He decides that it would be nice to include a page of flags of different countries of the world in the quiz. The idea is that each contestant will be given a sheet with the flags on and the contestant has to write the name of the country underneath. If you do not have access to a colour printer then you could try taking a photograph of the screen. You could find the designs of the flags with an atlas such as the World Atlas held on CD-ROM.

Task 2

Many companies use logos as part of their advertising. These logos are cleverly thought out and enable people to recognise the company or their products.

Choose a company which does not use a logo at the moment and design a logo for it using graphics software. You should include several designs, so that the company could choose between them. Also include a word-processed report outlining the ideas behind your logos.

Task 3

You have been asked by the teacher of a local primary school to produce diagrams of a series of objects that can be coloured in by the pupils. Underneath each diagram will be the name of the object in large print so that the pupils can be taught to read.

Using appropriate software, produce a series of suitable diagrams for this purpose. Remember that the diagrams will need to be quite large, otherwise they will be too difficult to colour in.

Task 4

Look through a selection of clip art for any connected with transport, using a drawing, painting or graphics package. The clip art should be grouped into the following:
- road: cars, bicycles, vans, lorries and motorbikes
- rail: locomotives and carriages
- air: balloons, gliders, spacecraft, jets and helicopters
- water: pleasure craft, ferries, tankers, yachts and freight ships.

Task 5

A teacher in a junior school has approached you for some help in designing a sheet to be used by pupils for explaining the names and properties of certain shapes. The shapes they would like you to include are as follows:
- rectangle
- square
- rhombus
- parallelogram
- kite
- trapezium
- right-angled triangle
- equilateral triangle
- isosceles triangle.

Remember, as well as drawing these shapes, you have to name them and write a small piece explaining their properties.

You could try doing a similar task involving 3D shapes, such as cuboids and cylinders.

Produce an attractive display of clip art images under each of the above headings. A small piece of text should be added about each one.

Task 6

Produce a heart shape for a greetings card using the LOGO programming language. Fully document your solution by providing explanations of the methods you used to try to solve the problem. Evidence of your work should be provided in the form of program listings and screen dumps onto a printer. Include all your work, including the parts that you rejected. Now try to use an art package to do the same thing. What functions in the drawing package did you use? Make comparisons between the two ways of solving the problem. Which one was the easiest to use? Again, fully document your solution.

IT Tasks

Task 7

This task requires a knowledge of chemistry.

Using suitable software, produce a selection of hazard symbols (see Figure 34.8).

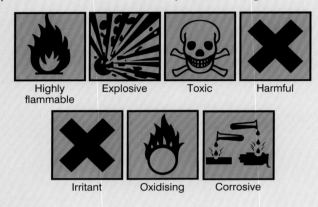

Highly flammable   Explosive   Toxic   Harmful

Irritant   Oxidising   Corrosive

▲
Figure 34.8

Task 8

Using a selection of clip art images and the cut, paste and copy facilities, come up with repeating designs for one of the following:
● birthday wrapping paper
● wallpaper.
● a printed fabric.

Task 9

Produce a garden design using a painting or other suitable package. Remember that certain plants are in bloom at different times of the year, so you could try to incorporate this fact in some way.

Task 10

A variety of diagrams can be used to describe a system, such as system flowcharts, structure diagrams and data flow diagrams. The diagrams make use of a variety of different-shaped boxes. Some graphics packages have these boxes included with them as clip art.

Find out if your graphics package has any of these shapes; if not, produce a selection and store each one in a separate file to be used later.

Finally, produce a systems flowchart (use Figure 12.13 on page 79 if you cannot make up one of your own) using your graphics package.

Task 11

You have decided to sell your home computer or games console. Use DTP software to produce an advert for the system you are selling which will be placed on a school or college notice board. Try to make your design as eye-catching as possible by using special text effects, boxes and graphics.

Task 12

Design and print a ticket for any one of the following:
- a disco
- a school concert
- a party for a special occasion
- a garden fete.

Task 13

You have been asked by your local hospital to draw people's attention to personal hygiene. You decide to produce a series of posters. The sorts of topics you might consider could include:
- washing hands after using the toilet
- keeping food covered while it is left out.

Any health or hygiene message can be used. Go for a catchy phrase to help get your message across.

Task 14

You have been asked by your history teacher to find out about one of the following events:
(a) the English Civil War
(b) the American Civil War
(c) the First World War
(d) man landing on the Moon for the first time.

Produce sample illustrations, such as photographs from encyclopaedias held on CD-ROMs, appropriate clip art, scanned artwork from a book or even a drawing you have produced yourself using a suitable package. In the chapter on desktop publishing (page 253) there is an exercise to incorporate these illustrations in the text.

You have been asked to produce a picture of a birthday cake like the one shown in Figure 34.9 using a drawing/paint package.

Happy
Birthday
Ayesha

▲
Figure 34.9

1 Load your software.
2 Draw a single candle with the flame at the top and save it to disk so that it can be copied as many times as you like.
3 Draw the rest of the cake.
4 Using suitable commands, copy and position the required number of candles on the top of the cake.
5 Select suitable fonts for the text and place the text in position on the diagram.
6 Save your design and then print it out.

Could you produce a better diagram of the cake shown? Have a go and print out your effort.

Skills Building

35 Exam Preparation

Revising

Most people think of revision as just reading notes and trying to remember them. This is true to some extent, but there are some ways of revising more effectively. We will look at several ways of revising and some of the likely questions you would want to ask about revision.

Where should you revise?

Choose a room where there will be no distractions. Work at a table or desk, make sure that there is a bright light on the table and that the room is warm. Some students like to work in a local library. This can be quite a good idea, but there can be distractions, such as people moving around. However, there will not be the other distractions that you may have at home, such as brothers, sisters, radios and TVs. Try to work in silence. Your revision will be a lot more effective and you will not need to revise for as long (Figure 35.1).

You should make a timetable and decide how long to revise for, then you will have earned your free time. Planned breaks in revision increase the amount of information you retain.

How often should you revise?

Revision should be a constant process throughout the years of your course (Figure 35.2). Try not to leave your revision to the last few weeks before the exam. Divide your work into topics and then revise a topic at a time. Do not move on to a new topic until you have mastered the old one. It is better to have a thorough knowledge of a few topics than a skimpy knowledge of the whole specification.

When is the best time to revise?

Most people are at their peak early in the morning. Near exam time try to get up earlier. If you are on holiday then early morning is an ideal time, because you will have fewer distractions from other people in the house. Early evening is a good time too, before you get tired.

▲ **Figure 35.1** *It is important to revise in the right surroundings*

299

▲
Figure 35.2

publications. If you cannot find them, ask the librarian in the reference section.

Near the time of the exam, check to see how much of the specification you have covered. Sometimes your teacher may not have time to cover the whole specification. If this happens, look at your specification to see which parts have been left out. You could then study the missing parts on your own. Having a set of past papers will enable you to see the way the exam is set out and familiarise yourself with the structure of the paper.

You can use the exam papers as an aid to your revision. Give yourself mock exams to see how your revision is going. Check your answers using this book or ask your teacher to have a look at them. Once you can answer most of the questions from the past papers, you will have nothing to fear about the actual exam.

What shall I revise?

Ideally it would be best if you could revise the whole specification. If you have difficulty with certain topics then you could leave them out, but you will need to know the other topics really well.

Obtain a copy of your specification either by asking your teacher or by sending off to the examination board for their price list.

Using the specification to guide you, make a revision checklist of all the topics you need to study and tick them off as you complete your revision of each topic.

Specification and past papers

It will help a lot if you get your own copy of the examination specification. Since there are many different examination boards, and sometimes different specifications even for the same subject with some examination boards, you should ask your teacher which board and specification you are following.

When you buy your own copy of the specification you will also be able to buy some copies of recent examination papers. You may also find that your local library or school library has copies of these

The exam

Before the exam

1 Collect the necessary equipment: two pens (in case one dries up), two pencils, a sharpener, a rubber, and a ruler. You may be allowed to use a flowchart template, but check first. You might not be able to use one with the names of the boxes on it.
2 Always take a watch into the exam. There will be a clock in the room, but if you are at the back you might not be able to see it.
3 Go to the toilet before the exam; this avoids the embarrassment of having to leave the room under supervision.
4 Check to see if you have to wear school uniform.

Things to check in the exam room

1 Check that you have the correct exam paper in front of you. Several different exams may be going on at the same time.
2 Check that there are no pages missing from the paper. It is not unknown for a page to be blank. If there is anything wrong with the paper, such as not being able to read the print, then you should ask for a new paper.

Use the knowledge you have built up during practical sessions

You will have built up your skills in using IT over a long period of time and will have been asked to demonstrate these skills.

Since many of the questions will be about actually doing certain tasks using IT, the greater your experience, the more knowledge you will have.

You should make sure that you demonstrate the experience you have gained when answering questions.

Even though you may have the knowledge, you might have difficulty answering questions. In the next section we will look at some important points when answering questions.

Answering questions

When answering examination questions it is important to know how much to write. You can sometimes tell this from the wording of the question. Here is a list of commonly used words that ask you to supply an answer.

At the top of the list only a single word or short group of connected words need be given. As you move down the list the amount of answer needed increases.

Simple answer required

Name
List
State
Give
Describe
Explain

More complex answer required (usually several sentences)

Use the mark scheme to help you

At the side of each section of an examination question there will be a number in brackets that tells you the number of marks for that part. Here is an example:

1(a) List the three main parts of the central processing unit (CPU).   (3)

There are three marks allocated for this part of the question, and because it says 'list' in the question this means that you only have to give a single word (or a few connected words) in answer.

A suitable answer would be:

Arithmetic and logic unit
Control unit
Main memory

Making sure that you understand the specialist terminology

There are many specialist terms used in IT. You may be asked about a specialist term in the exam. It is therefore important to be familiar with the meaning of these terms and also to be able to explain them to other people, including the examiner. You must be able to put these words into sentences.

Hints for the exam

The following list gives some hints on things you should do when actually taking the exam.

1 Always read the instructions on the front of the paper carefully. In particular, note the time you are allowed.
2 Time yourself. Do not spend too much time on a question that you can answer well at the expense of other questions.
3 Try to write neatly. The examiners have hundreds of scripts to mark and it is not worth risking annoying examiners by making them waste time deciphering an untidy script.
4 Only do what the question asks. If it asks for two reasons, make sure that you give two: not three or one. Always check that, in an answer to a question with two parts, you have not written similar answers to both parts. If you have, you will only obtain marks on one of them.
5 Use the mark scheme at the side of the questions as a guide to how much you should write. If there are, say, two marks, there must be two points you need to mention in order to get both marks.
6 After you have answered a question, read the question through again to make sure that you have not missed part of it out.

Things to do

A number of terms are shown below. For each term write a short sentence containing the words.
1 imported
2 encrypted
3 proofread
4 back-up copy
5 virus checker.

As with all examinations, you have to convince the examiner that you know the correct answer. If you know the correct answer but fail to express yourself clearly, the examiner will not be able to give you the marks. The examiner cannot guess what you meant to say.

Here is an example of an examination question:

Explain why accounts are prepared using a spreadsheet.

- You can correct mistakes easier by deleting or overwriting.
- The spreadsheet automatically recalculates totals when you change any of the figures and this saves you time.

Here is another examination question:

Name an application that uses MICR.

Here you are not expected to write a sentence.

If you had been asked to explain an application which uses MICR then you would have been expected to go into detail. You should use the marks allocated as a guide to how much to write.

Examination Questions

Here is a variety of recent examination questions covering material present on all the examination boards' syllabuses.

Chapter 1

1 CD-ROMs have become widely available.
   (a) Give two reasons why CD-ROMs help with learning. (2)
   (b) Give one disadvantage of using a CD-ROM in a classroom. (1)

2 (a) Give two reasons why CD-ROMs are used to store encyclopaedias. (2)
   (b) One type of information stored on a CD-ROM is text. Give two other types of information stored on a CD-ROM. (1)

Chapter 2

1 State two ways in which information technology can be used in the kitchen. (2)

2 Microprocessors are used to control many devices, such as washing machines.
   (a) What is a microprocessor? (2)
   (b) Name two different devices controlled by microprocessors. (2)
   (c) Give three different kinds of sensors that could be used in an automatic washing machine. (3)

3 There is now an increasing number of 'message pads' (PDAs) available in computer shops. These message pads use the screen for direct input. Data can either be entered by ordinary handwriting using a special stylus (or pen) or by pressing the keys of a 'simulated' keyboard.
   (a) (i) What is one advantage and one disadvantage of using ordinary handwriting as a means of data input? (4)
       (ii) How do the manufacturers attempt to overcome the disadvantage you have highlighted? (2)

(b) When a special connection kit is purchased, the PDA can be linked to an ordinary computer. Give two reasons why people might want to link their PDA to an ordinary computer. (4)

4 Special microwave ovens are now available for which you do not have to enter the power and the cooking time yourself.
   (a) Explain how such microwave ovens obtain the cooking power and time from the food packaging.
   (b) Explain why this system ensures that the food is always correctly cooked. (3)

5 Laptop computers have special requirements for their processors.
   State two desirable properties for the processors for laptop computers and for each one explain why the property is desirable. (2)

Chapter 3

1 Each piece of hardware in the table below is either an input, output or storage device. For each, put a tick in the correct box. As an example, a keyboard is an input device, so a tick is placed in the Input column.

Device	Input	Output	Storage
Keyboard	✔		
(a) Hard disk drive			
(b) Scanner			
(c) Speaker			
(d) Inkjet printer			
(e) CD-ROM drive			
(f) Heat sensor			
(g) Microphone			

(7)

2 You have been asked to choose a printer for the school office where an integrated package is being used. Explain four factors you would consider before making your choice. (3)

3 (a) Tick **four** boxes to show which of the following are **output** devices.

	Tick **four** boxes only
Dot-matrix printer	☐
Plotter	☐
Mouse	☐
CD-ROM	☐
Speaker	☐
Keyboard	☐
VDU	☐
ROM	☐
DTP package	☐

(4)

(b) Name **one** other output device, **not given** in the list above. (1)

(c) Name **two** input devices, **given** in the list above. (2)

(d) Name **one** other input device, **not given** in the list above. (1)

Chapter 4

1 Given below is a list of **nine** pieces of hardware.
(a) For each one, say if it is an **input device**, an **output device** or a **storage device**. The first one is done for you.

Hardware	Type of device
Keyboard	input
(i) Hard disk drive	....
(ii) Scanner	....
(iii) Mouse	....
(iv) Dot-matrix printer	....
(v) CD-ROM drive	....
(vi) Heat sensor	....
(vii) Inkjet printer	....
(viii) Concept keyboard	....
(ix) Optical disk drive	....

(9)

(b) A computer system has two types of memory, called RAM (random-access memory) and ROM (read-only memory). Give **one** example of the use of each of them. (2)

2 Most computer systems have immediate access store (IAS) and backing store.
(a) Give two limitations of immediate access store which make backing store necessary. (4)
(b) Explain how ROM differs from RAM. (2)

3 Which two of the following items are suitable for storing large amounts of data?

scanner   barcode   magnetic strip
CD-ROM   mouse   hard disk

4 A computer has two types of memory, RAM and ROM.
(a) (i) What does RAM stand for?
    (ii) What does ROM stand for? (2)
(b) Give two differences between RAM and ROM. (2)
(c) Give one use of RAM. (1)
(d) Give one use of ROM. (1)

5 Using examples, explain the following four computer terms:
(a) USB flash memory (1)
(b) HD card (1)
(c) MP4 player (1)
(d) Blu-ray disk (1)

Chapter 5

1 (a) Which three of the following tasks are carried out by all operating systems?
  A transferring data to a printer
  B allocating storage space on a disk
  C positioning text in a word-processing document
  D finding a database record
  E accepting keyboard input
  F adding colour to a drawing on screen. (3)

(b) Describe an additional task which would have to be carried out by a multi-user operating system. (2)
(c) What is a multitasking operating system? (3)

2 The design of the user interface of an application is very important. The two screens shown on page 305 are from a package which allows customers to choose and book a holiday.
(a) Describe three ways in which the user interface has been kept consistent in the two screen designs. (3)
(b) (i) In what ways does the design limit the choices a user can make? (2)
    (ii) Why has the package been designed in this way?
(c) Describe two changes you would make to the design which would make the interface easier for customers to use. Explain why these changes would help the user. (2)

(d) Sometimes holidays are fully booked for the dates required. A message is displayed on the screen to tell the user the holiday is not available.
   (i) Where on the screen should this message appear? (1)

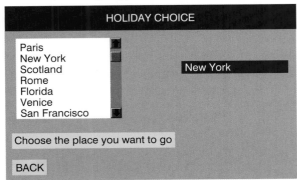

   (ii) Why is this position most suitable? (1)
   (iii) How could the user's attention be drawn to this message? (2)

3 Computers have become more user-friendly with the development of graphical user interfaces.
   (a) Give **four** features of a graphical user interface. (4)
   (b) Give **two** possible future developments to user interfaces. (2)

4 Ann has bought some new software. Give three items of documentation that came with it. (3)

5 An *operating system* is a program.
   (a) Name **two** tasks the operating system does. (2)
   (b) Name **one** operating system used by computers. (1)
   (c) Microcomputers can carry out *multitasking*. Give the meaning of the term multitasking. (1)

6 The tourist information office in a holiday resort wants an information system to allow people to find out about attractions in the area. The manager must decide whether to produce the system using an existing database package or to have a program written in a suitable computer language.
   (a) Give two advantages of producing this system using an existing database package. (2)
   (b) Give one advantage of writing a program for this application. (1)

7 Most computers have an icon-based graphical user interface (GUI).
   (a) What is an icon? (2)
   (b) Give two reasons why computers have this type of interface. (4)
   (c) What peripheral device is commonly used with this interface? (1)

8 (a) What is meant by a windows environment? (2)
   (b) Give two advantages of using a windows environment compared with a command-line environment. (2)

9 (a) Give **two advantages** to a company of buying an existing software package rather than having one specially written. (2)
   (b) Give **one disadvantage** to a company of buying an existing software package rather than having one specially written. (1)

10 The way in which a user interacts with computer software is important. A good human–computer interface makes software easy to use.

   Explain how the user makes choices in each of the following types of interface.
   (a) A graphical user interface (2)
   (b) A menu-driven user interface (2)
   (c) A command-driven interface (2)

11 Using examples, explain the following three computer terms:
   (a) Software (1)
   (b) Graphical user interface (1)
   (c) Multi-access (1)

12 Give **two** differences between high-level programming languages and low-level programming languages. (2)

Chapter 6

1 (a) Name two ways in which text can be input
to a computer. (2)

(b) Give one example where each of the
following is used:
(i) barcode reader (1)
(ii) magnetic ink character reader (MICR) (1)
(iii) optical mark reader (OMR). (1)

2 Data stored in a computer system is often coded.
(a) (i) Give two advantages of coding data. (4)
(ii) Give one disadvantage of coding data. (2)
(b) Give three considerations when designing
a coding system. (3)

Chapter 7

1 Last year a school stored all the examination
marks for year 7 on a computer. Each
examination had a maximum of 100 marks. At
the end of the year, some pupils' examination
marks were wrong when printed out. To try to
stop this happening again, the headteacher has
decided to use data validation.
(a) Explain what is meant by data validation. (3)
(b) Explain how each of the following methods of
data validation could be used in this situation.
(i) Presence check (2)
(ii) Range check (2)

2 The human resources department of the APEXAN
manufacturing company keeps a file of employee
records on a computer.

This is part of the file:

Employee number	Family name	First name	Sex	Number of years employed
0127	Ryan	Jean	F	15
2971	Hussain	Sabina	F	200
5234	Ryan	Pauline	F	5
1253	Mercadal	Jean	F	7
1074	Razaq	Fazal	M	11

(a) The contents of a field in one record cannot
be correct.
(i) Draw a circle around the error. (1)
(ii) Explain why the contents cannot be
correct. (1)
(iii) Tick one box to show the type of
validation check that could detect the
error.

	Tick **one** box
Check digit	☐
Range check	☐
Type check	☐
Table lookup	☐
Double entry verification	☐

(1)

(iv) Describe in full a validation check that
could detect this error. (4)

3 Explain why each of the following checks would
be used to validate the entry of data into the
record shown below:
Customer name: Miss Susan McGinn
Stock number: 4556216
Order quantity: 14

(a) Character or type check (2)
(b) Range check (2)
(c) Check digit (2)

4 Text prepared using a word processor can have
its spelling checked using a spell-checking facility.
When this is activated, each word in the prepared
text is checked against a dictionary of over
50,000 words.
(a) How can a spell checker confirm the
correct spelling of a word? (2)
(b) Certain rejected words may be correctly
spelt. Describe, with examples, two distinct
cases when this could occur and describe
how a spell checker could accommodate
such words for future reference. (4)

5 Tony studies business studies at Hightop School.
As part of his course, he collects data on
breakfast cereals eaten by students.
(a) Give **two** ways he could collect the data. (2)
(b) The software used by Tony to set up the
file allows him to validate the data. What
is validation? (1)
(c) A sample of Tony's file is shown below.

Student number	Form	Cereal
24	10A	Cornflakes
14	11C	Bran Flakes
21	10B	Rice Krispies

To ensure that every pupil's data are input, Tony
makes use of a hash total. Calculate the *hash
total* for the above sample. (1)

6 Data are to be keyed into a database. State **two** ways of verifying the data. (2)

7 A mail order electronics company uses a computerised stock control system in its warehouse.
(a) In order to find an item, a six-digit item code number has to be entered into the computer. Give **two** validation checks which could be used on this number. (2)
(b) Before the location of the item is displayed on the screen the database has to be searched. State the type of access to the hard disk which is required. (1)

8 (a) Personal data being entered into a police database must be verified. Explain why such data must be verified. (1)
(b) Describe two different methods that can be used to verify data. (2)

9 When a user creates a password to gain access to a network the password is verified.
(a) Explain why a new password should be verified. (1)
(b) Explain how the password is usually verified. (1)

Chapter 8

1 A school has computerised its library. Some of the information from the book file is shown in the table below.
(a) State how many *records* are shown. (1)
(b) State how many *fields* are shown. (1)
(c) Name the *key field*. (1)
(d) Why is a key field required? (1)
(e) The librarian wants the file *sorted* into *descending* order according to the *date of publication*. Complete the table in the next column to show the result of the sort.

Title	Date of publication
Computer Studies	2011

(f) Explain why the librarian would need to:
(i) *delete* a record from the book file (1)
(ii) *add* a record to the book file. (1)

2 (a) Define the following terms and give an example of each:
(i) verification (2)
(ii) validation. (2)
(b) Some of the files on a computer system have fixed-length fields while others have variable-length fields.
(i) Give one advantage of using fixed-length fields. (1)
(ii) Give one advantage of using variable-length fields. (1)
(iii) A variety of field types can be found in a database system, for example numeric field. Name two other types of field that could be found in a database. (2)
(c) Some of the fields within files are coded, for example, B-Boy, G-Girl. Give two advantages of coding data. (2)

3 Serial, sequential, indexed sequential and direct (random) are four methods of file organisation commonly used. Complete the table on page 308 to show which method can be used with magnetic tape and which method can be used with magnetic disk.

Accession No.	Title	Author	Publisher	Date of publication
1324	Computer Studies	Waites, N	BEP	2011
1333	Computing	Waites, N	BEP	2010
1325	Business GNVQ	Callaghan, P	BEP	2009
1272	Compilers	Mak, R	Wiley	2007
1174	Computer Graphics	Foley, J	Addison-Wesley	2004
1024	C Programming	Michie, D	Pelican	1989

Method	Magnetic tape	Magnetic disk
Serial	Yes	
Sequential		
Indexed sequential		
Direct (random)	Yes	

(6)

4 The following record structure for a datafile has been set up:

Field name	Field length	Field type	Key field
Name	30	Character	No
Address	25	Character	No
Membership number	6	Numeric	Yes
Telephone number	13	Alphanumeric	No
Date joined	8	Date	No

(a) How many fields does each record in this file contain? (1)

(b) Explain why only 'Membership number' is a key field. (2)

(c) Give one reason why it is important to specify the field type. (2)

5 A company which has been in existence for some time has accumulated a number of datafiles for its business. They are now considering replacing these datafiles with a database.

(a) Explain what is meant by a database. (3)

(b) Give two reasons why a database might be preferred to datafiles. (4)

A database management system (DBMS) is a program that provides an interface between the operating system and the user and simplifies access to the data.

(c) Give two other functions provided by the DBMS. (4)

Chapter 9

1 Tick **two** applications which use batch processing.

Monitoring a patient's heartbeat ☐
Producing electricity bills ☐
Air traffic control system ☐
Online cinema seat reservation system ☐
Clearing cheques ☐
Recording the temperature in an experiment ☐

(2)

2 Tick **two** applications which use real-time processing.

Printing examination certificates ☐
Calculating gas bills ☐
Central heating system ☐
Sending out reminders for overdue books ☐
Automatic pilot on an aeroplane ☐
Clearing cheques in a bank ☐

(2)

Chapter 10

1 An estate agent decides to store the pictures of the houses on the hard disk of the computer in a compressed form.

(a) Give two advantages of using compression in this situation. (2)

(b) Give one disadvantage of using compression in this situation. (1)

2 Sound, as most people hear it, is not capable of being stored or processed by a computer system in its natural form; it needs to be changed to a more suitable representation. An analogue to digital converter (ADC) performs this task.

(a) Using the axes below, draw a typical sound signal before and after conversion. (2)

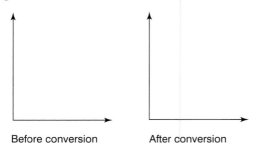

Before conversion   After conversion

Most modern computers have a speaker built into the system, but in some cases the quality of sound is poor.

(b) Explain how the sound quality could be dramatically improved by adding extra hardware. (3)

(c) Describe two applications where computer-generated sound might be used. (4)

3 Using examples, explain the following five computer terms:

(a) Interrupt (1)
(b) Polling system (1)
(c) Handshaking (1)
(d) Buffer (1)
(e) Checksum (1)

Chapter 11

1 The IT coordinator at Ballyhouse High School has a budget to spend on CD-ROMs. The school has five stand-alone CD systems in the library. Two of the systems are Mac-based and the others are PCs.

The following titles are available from a supplier's catalogue:

The Oxford English Dictionary of Quotations	PC only	£50
Hutchinson's Encyclopedia	PC only	£30
The Guinness Disk of Records	Mac/PC	£40
1000 Colour Clip Art images	Mac/PC	£90
Chess Coacher	Mac only	£25
Multimedia Space Encyclopaedia	PC only	£60
The Life, Time and Music of Mozart	Mac/PC	£30
A Hard Day's Night	Mac only	£30
Shakespeare Complete Works	Mac/PC	£40
Asterix Learn French	Mac only	£30
101 Games and Leisure Pursuits	PC only	£40
Musical Instruments	PC only	£30
The Sunday Times	Mac/PC	£100
Microsoft Art Gallery	Mac/PC	£40
The Tortoise and the Hare	Mac/PC	£40

The coordinator has been conducting a survey to find the most popular and relevant titles.

You have been invited to choose **four** titles for the library and say why each has been chosen. Give your choice and reasons. (8)

2 A kitchen company uses virtual reality for showing customers what their new kitchen will look like when it is installed in their home.
(a) Explain what is meant by virtual reality. (2)
(b) Explain two advantages of using virtual reality for this purpose. (2)

Chapter 12

1 The system flowchart below shows how a supermarket point-of-sale system works.

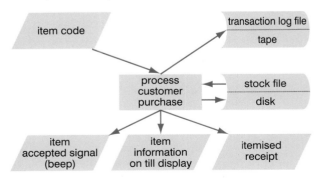

(a) How would the item code normally be input into the system? (2)
(b) Give two reasons why an item accepted signal is used in this situation rather than an item rejected signal. (2)
(c) These are the fields in the stock file:

> item code
> type
> description
> size
> quantity in stock
> minimum stock level
> reorder quantity
> supplier code

Which field in a stock record would be changed when an item is sold? (1)

SUPERSAVERS
High Street
Manchester
M50 9ZZ

20 June

To:
Bulk Grocery Supplies
Fax 0161 888 2740

Please deliver:

Type	Description	Size	Quantity
bargain brand	baked beans	450g	20 cases

(d) The stock file is also used by an automatic reordering system. This produces orders like the one shown above. Another file called the supplier file is used. Give three fields the supplier record will have to contain to allow the order to be produced.
(e) The transaction log file is kept on tape.
   (i) What data would be written to the transaction log file? (1)
   (ii) What is the purpose of this file? (1)

Chapter 13

1 A group of doctors in a medical centre wants to computerise their existing filing system. Analysis, design, implementation, testing and evaluation will all be stages in the production of their information systems.

At which of these stages does each of the following take place?
(a) Setting up a database of their patients

(b) Looking at which tasks to include in the new system
(c) Collecting information about how other doctors tackled this problem
(d) Producing a testing plan for the new system
(e) Planning the layout of a letter to the hospital
(f) Entering test data for the accounts spreadsheet
(g) Reviewing how well the patient database works
(h) Working out the record structure for the patients' database

2 When a new computerised system is suggested, a full analysis of user requirements has to be carried out. Describe the methods which can be used to find out about an existing system and what will be needed in the new system. Discuss the advantages and disadvantages of the methods used. (12)

3 During systems analysis it is important to find out as much as possible about the existing system. This is called fact finding.
(a) Describe four methods often used for fact finding. (8)
(b) Describe two activities carried out during the design stage of systems analysis. (4)
(c) Three methods that could be used to implement a new system are:
● direct
● phased
● parallel.
Explain each of these three methods. (6)

4 Jane is employed as a systems analyst by a software house. She has been asked to produce a computerised system for a holiday company. Describe briefly what is involved during the following stages of her work on the new system:
(a) analysis (2)
(b) design (2)
(c) implementation (2)
(d) maintenance. (2)

5 A video games shop has decided to use a spreadsheet to help with its finances. The tasks listed below have to be carried out during the development of this system:
A entering all the existing data for the income and expenditure of the shop
B working out the spreadsheet structure
C looking at the present system to see how it works
D finding out if the new system works
E setting up the spreadsheet

F reviewing how well the system works
G making a test plan.

Using the letters A to G from the list of tasks, answer the following questions.
(a) Which one of these takes place during the analysis stage?
(b) Which two of these take place during the design stage?
(c) Which one of these takes place during the testing stage?
(d) Which two of these take place during the implementation stage?
(e) Which one of these takes place during the evaluation stage?

6 A new system is to be introduced into a school for pupils to pay for their dinners using computer cards. Describe the steps taken in the analysis and design of this system.

7 A school is introducing a computerised system for attendance registers. Describe the main stages gone through before the system is operational.

8 A new computer system is to be produced to handle ticket sales for a sports stadium. The stages in production of this system include Analysis, Design, Implementation, Testing and Evaluation.

At which stage does each of the following tasks take place?
(a) Considering how well the system works
(b) Working out a testing plan
(c) Finding out how the present booking system works
(d) Deciding how to store the data
(e) Setting up the ticket sales database
(f) Finding out if it is possible to sell two tickets for one seat at an event

Chapter 14

1 Sensors can be attached to a computer system and used to collect data. In a geography investigation students are studying how temperature varies during the course of 24 hours. A sensor is connected to a computer to take readings.
(a) What do we call this method of data capture? (1)
(b) (i) What kind of sensor should be used? (1)
(ii) Why is this sensor needed? (1)
(c) (i) How often should a reading be taken? (1)
(ii) Why is this a suitable interval? (1)
(d) How could these data be presented in a report on the investigation? (1)

2 A computer at a regional weather centre gathers information from remote weather stations.

The computer at the regional weather centre contacts the computer at each remote weather station and downloads the information that has been recorded.

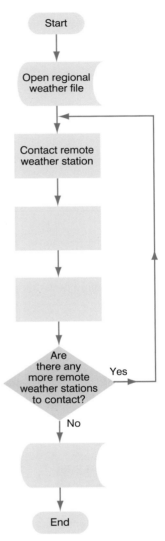

(a) Using terms from the following list, complete the flowchart to show what the computer at the regional weather centre does.
   Save regional weather file.
   Download information.
   Add information to regional weather file.

(b) Draw and label a diagram showing the computer at the regional weather centre communicating with the computer at a remote weather station using modems and the telephone network. (2)

(c) If the regional weather centre cannot contact a remote weather station, processing is halted and has to be restarted.
   (i) Tick **two** boxes to show why this is a shortcoming of the IT system.

	Tick **two** boxes
Information is not recorded at remote weather stations during the winter.	☐
Remote weather stations are solar-powered.	☐
Restarting the system wastes time as the same information may be collected from the same remote weather stations on several occasions.	☐
The information available is not collected if part of the system is faulty.	☐
The system cannot be restarted.	☐

(2)

   (ii) Using terms from the following list complete the two sentences below.

   monitoring and evaluation
   systems analysis and design
   systems investigation
   the holidays
   user training

   The shortcoming was built into the IT system during _____
   The shortcoming would be detected during _____

(2)

(d) Discuss the advantages and disadvantages of using this IT system. (6)

3 An automatic weather station is situated on the roof of a school and is connected to a computer in the classroom. The station has an anemometer to measure the speed of the wind.
(a) The computer cannot use the data directly from the anemometer.
   (i) Why is this the case?
   (ii) What device is needed to solve this problem? (2)
(b) Give two reasons why it is sensible to collect wind data in this way. (2)

Chapter 15

1 The ISDN (Integrated Services Digital Network) is now widely available.

(a) Describe **two** applications for ISDN. (6)

Three network configurations (topologies) commonly used are: **star**, **bus** and **ring**.

(b) Show the cabling configuration for each of these networks.

(i) **star**

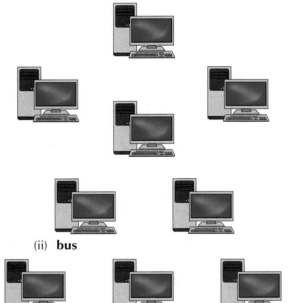

(ii) **bus**

(iii) **ring**

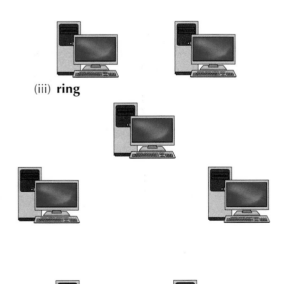

(c) Complete the table below to indicate a ring, bus or star network configuration as appropriate.

Network configuration	Advantage	Disadvantage
	Easy to add more stations without disrupting the network	The whole network goes down if the main cable fails at any point
	If one cable fails the other stations are not affected	Costly to install because of the length of cable required
	No dependence on a central computer or fileserver	Unuseable if a single station fails

(3)

(d) Apart from sharing resources, give **two other** benefits that a network of computers would provide. (4)

(e) Explain the following network terms:

(i) LAN

(ii) WAN.

(6)

2 The internet is a large worldwide network of linked computers. Give three different uses of the internet. (3)

3

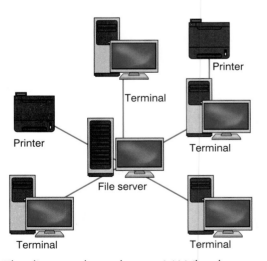

The diagram above shows a LAN (local area network) which is used in an office.

(a) Fill in the table to show **two** differences between this network and a WAN (wide area network).

	LAN	WAN
Difference 1		
Difference 2		

(4)

(b) Give **two** advantages to the **office staff** of having the network rather than the same number of separate computers. (2)

(c) Give **one** disadvantage to the **office staff** of having the network. (1)

4 Discuss the relative advantages and disadvantages of electronic mail (email) communication to communicate information around the world. (6)

5 Give **two** benefits of using a local area network. (2)

6 Computer networks often make use of either a star or ring configuration.
Eight computers are to be connected to form a network.
(a) Draw two diagrams: one diagram of the computers connected as a star and the other diagram showing them connected as a ring. (2)
(b) Outline the advantages and disadvantages of a star configuration. (4)
(c) Outline the advantages and disadvantages of a ring configuration. (4)

7 (a) Explain the differences between an intranet and the internet. (2)
(b) A company allows employees access to the company's intranet but not to the internet. Give two reasons for this. (2)

8 A company's management team is thinking of using a network in its business with all the computers being linked wirelessly.
(a) Explain two advantages of using a wireless link for the network. (2)
(b) Explain two disadvantages of using a wireless link for the network. (2)

(a) What is a computer virus? (2)
(b) Suggest how the virus may have got into Rashid's computer system. (2)
(c) How can Rashid remove the virus from his computer system? (1)
(d) What precautions can Rashid take to help prevent more viruses getting into his computer? (1)

2 Give **two** ways that data in a computer file can be protected from being seen by unauthorised people.

3 (a) Give one example of how a virus can affect a computer. (1)
(b) Give one way a virus can be removed. (1)

4 Newspapers often mention the terms *computer virus* and *computer hacking*.
(a) (i) What is a computer virus? (1)
(ii) How can a computer virus be detected and prevented? (2)
(b) (i) What is computer hacking? (1)
(ii) Give **one** way hacking can be prevented. (1)

5 Write down two ways in which you could prevent a computer virus affecting your machine. (2)

6 A school is going to buy a number of laptop computers for pupils to borrow and use at home. Give **two** problems that this may cause. (2)

7 In a medical centre, data about the patients are stored on the hard disk of the network file-server.
(a) Give **two** physical precautions that could be taken to keep the data secure. (2)
(b) Doctors need to see all the information about patients. Receptionists only need to see some of the information about patients.
Describe **one** way in which software could be used to restrict access to patient information. (2)

8 (a) Explain what is meant by a firewall. (2)
(b) Describe two uses for a firewall. (2)

Chapter 16

1 Rashid enjoys playing computer games. He often downloads demonstration versions of games from the World Wide Web. One day he discovers his computer system is producing lots of error messages. Several important data files have disappeared. His computer has a virus.

Chapter 17

1 (a) Describe two ways data protection laws try to protect individuals from the misuse of personal data held on computer. (2)

   (b) Other than the misuse of personal data, describe two ways in which information technology has created problems for the individual. (2)

2 'It is easier to misuse data when they are held in electronic form.' Discuss this statement. (4)

3 A life insurance company stores information about its customers on a large database.
   (a) Give **three** fields, other than **name** and **address**, which might be included in the file.
   (b) The insurance company, as a data user, must obey the rules set out in a Data Protection Act. Give **four** rules that data users must obey.
   (c) Give **two** rights a Data Protection Act gives to the customers.

4 Mrs Lee is a single mother with two children. She has recently returned to full-time education and is in the final year of a science degree. She has taken out student loans of $10,000. She regularly plays squash at the local sports centre. She does not have any credit cards. She rents a house from her local authority.
   (a) Using only the information given above, write down four facts about Mrs Lee which are likely to be stored in a computer database. (4)
   (b) Explain clearly the difference between information and data. (2)

5 A mail order company's computer system holds personal data about its customers.
   (a) The data held by the company must be registered under a Data Protection Act. Give **two** rights the Act gives to the customer. (2)
   (b) Personal information stored by a mail order company may be inaccurate. Give two examples of inaccuracies which could occur and, for each, describe a possible consequence for the customer. (4)
   (c) Tick **three** boxes to show which of the following have complete exemption from the UK's 1998 Data Protection Act.

	Tick **three** boxes
Word-processed documents	☐
Insurance companies	☐
A database of friends' names and addresses	☐
All police information, stored on a computer	☐
A database of doctors' patients	☐
Files stored on paper	☐

(3)

Chapter 18

1 (a) Name the UK Act of Parliament which is intended to protect software from being stolen or illegally copied. (2)
   (b) Explain the following terms:
       (i) hacking (3)
       (ii) virus. (3)

2 (a) Explain how the copyright law applies to computer software. (2)
   (b) What is meant by a hacker? (1)
   (c) What dangers do hackers present to other computer users? (2)

3 Some networks are protected against unauthorised access by using a smart card. The smart card is entered into a reader and then the user enters a PIN and is only allowed access if the PIN entered matches that encrypted and stored on the chip.
   (a) Give the meaning of PIN. (1)
   (b) Give two advantages of this system used to ensure the security of a network. (2)

4 (a) Describe two different ways in which data can be corrupted. (2)
   (b) For each of the ways described in part (a), describe what can be put in place to reduce the likelihood of the corruption of data. (2)

Chapter 19

1 The widespread use of IT has had a great impact on today's society. One benefit that the increased use of IT has brought is the creation of some new jobs.
   (a) Give **three examples of jobs** that have been created by the introduction of IT. (3)
   (b) Describe briefly **three other** possible benefits that this increased use in IT has brought. (3)

(c) Personal information, stored electronically, is potentially easier to misuse than that kept in paper files. Give **two** reasons why this is true.

(4)

2 Discuss the issues raised by the use of IT in society. Your answer should cover a number of different areas, taking into account the environmental, ethical, moral and social effects. You should highlight possible disadvantages as well as advantages.

(4)

3 Describe how computers might be misused, giving rise to legal and moral problems.

(4)

4 Explain the drawbacks of using robots in manufacturing cars.

(4)

Chapter 20

1 (a) What is a robot?

(2)

(b) Give two advantages of using robots for various tasks.

(4)

(c) Describe a situation where it would be almost impossible to do a particular task without a robot.

(2)

2 Sensors can be attached to a computer system and used to collect data. In a geography investigation students are studying how temperature varies during the course of 24 hours. A sensor is connected to a computer to take readings.

(a) What do we call this method of data capture?

(1)

(b) (i) What kind of sensor should be used? (1)
   (ii) Why is this sensor needed? (1)

(c) (i) How often should a reading be taken? (1)
   (ii) Why is this a suitable interval? (1)

(d) How could these data be presented in a report on the investigation?

(1)

3 A computer-controlled hopper is used to fill bottles. The bottles are placed on the conveyor which moves them under the hopper where they are filled.

The operator can use these instructions:

MOVE   Moves the conveyor one position
FILL   Opens the valve, fills the bottle and closes the valve
START Indicates the beginning of the program
END   Indicates the end of the program

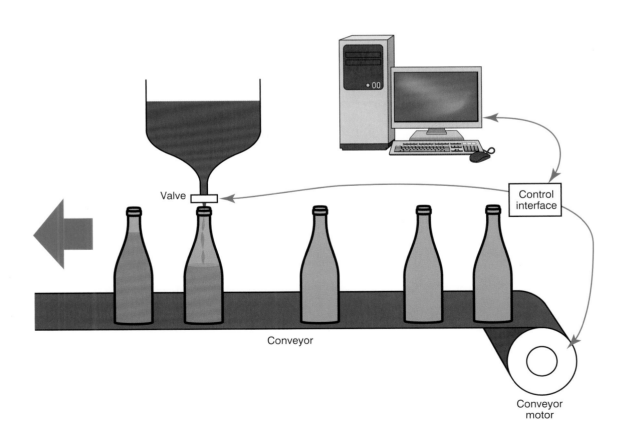

Valve

Control interface

Conveyor

Conveyor motor

(a) Write the instructions to fill these **three** bottles.
START
....
....
....
....
....
....
....
END

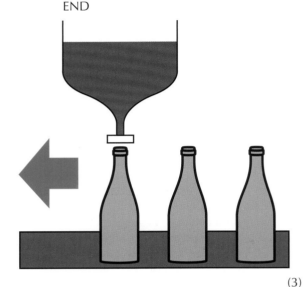

(3)

(b) (i) Explain why the computer system shown **cannot** be used to fill the bottles **automatically**. (1)

(ii) Describe the additional **hardware** needed so that the computer system could fill the bottles automatically. (2)

(iii) In this context, explain what is meant by **feedback**. (2)

(c) Tick **one** box to show the **type** of operating method used.

	Tick **one** box
Batch	☐
Library	☐
Joystick	☐
Realtime	☐
Serious	☐

(1)

(d) Discuss the advantages and disadvantages of automated manufacturing. (6)

4 A science class uses a computer to investigate the heat transfer through various materials. For this they need an interface, analogue sensors and a heater. The front of the material is heated and the sensors measure the heat at the front and at the back of the material.

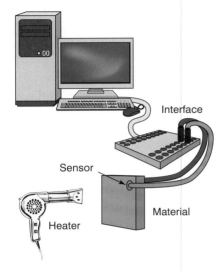

(a) Give two reasons why an interface is needed. (2)

(b) Explain the difference between an analogue signal and a digital signal. (3)

(c) Explain how the computer could be used to assist in plotting a graph showing the heat input and output over a period of time. (4)

5 Betterview prepares lenses for spectacles and contact lenses in their own laboratory. The conditions in the laboratory must be continuously monitored.

Humidity, temperature and dust must be kept constant to ensure that lenses are produced properly.

Conditions are computer-controlled.

(a) Explain how regular measurements of temperature could be recorded by the computer. (4)

(b) Explain how the computer controls the humidity, temperature and dust measurements to stay within certain limits. (4)

(c) The measurements of humidity, temperature and dust are stored regularly in a computer file. Describe how data that are stored in the computer could be processed to present and compare readings. (4)

(d) Describe TWO sensible analyses that could be performed on these stored data. (4)

6 A company breeds large numbers of fish for fish farms. The young fish will only grow if they have enough oxygen. A computer system is used to control the amount of oxygen in the tanks. Sensors in the tanks detect the amount of oxygen in the water. A pump connected to the computer system can be used to pump oxygen into the tanks.

Explain how **monitoring** and **feedback** can be used to make sure that the fish have enough oxygen.   (6)

7 A small buggy connected to a computer is placed in a maze. The buggy will travel through the maze and learn the correct path. State one sensor which should be attached to the buggy and describe how it would detect an obstacle.   (2)

8 A floor robot is placed at the entrance to a maze. It travels through the maze, reaching the exit, having made many wrong turns. The second time through the maze it travels directly to the exit without making a mistake.
Describe the features of the robot which enable it to do this.   (4)

9 Many vehicles are fitted with satellite navigation systems.
(a) Explain how the satellite navigation system (GPS) can find the exact position of the vehicle.   (2)
(b) Voice synthesis is used to issue instructions verbally to the driver. Explain what is meant by voice synthesis.   (1)
(c) Describe two advantages in drivers using satellite navigation systems.   (2)
(d) Describe two disadvantages in drivers using satellite navigation systems.   (2)

Chapter 21

1 The widespread use of computers has led to a reported increase in illnesses and health hazards associated with them. Some doctors are becoming worried by this development.

Describe one health hazard or illness specifically associated with using computers and suggest how it can be prevented.   (3)

2 A school secretary sits in front of a computer all day. Give two pieces of advice which should help prevent medical problems.   (2)

3 Computer monitors can be high, medium or low resolution and must conform to a certain standard to protect their users.

(a) The level of resolution is measured in pixels. What is a pixel?   (2)
(b) List and explain two potential dangers to people who use monitors.   (4)
(c) Explain one other health problem associated with the use of computers.   (2)

4 Describe two precautions which must be taken to ensure that a computer room is safe for pupils to use.   (2)

5 Describe some of the safety issues which must be considered when setting up a new computer room in a school.   (3)

6 Videoconferencing is used by many organisations and companies.
(a) Explain what is meant by videoconferencing.   (2)
(b) Describe two advantages in organisations using videoconferencing.   (2)
(c) Describe two disadvantages in organisations using videoconferencing.   (2)

7 There are many features of digital telephones that are useful to employees of an organisation who need to spend time away from the office. Give the names of three features of digital telephones and for each one explain why the feature is useful.   (3)

Chapter 22

1 A school has its own internal network which consists of terminals or computers linked to a file server. The network has other hardware devices linked to it which may be used by the pupils. It is not possible to access the internet from this network.
(a) Give **two** *other* hardware devices you would expect to find linked to this network.   (2)
(b) The school is considering producing an electronic newsletter on the internet, to advertise the school. The school has telephone lines and computer systems (*computer, disk drive and printer, word-processing, database and spreadsheet software*), but would need **additional** hardware and software to access the internet.
  (i) Give **one** extra hardware device the school must have in order to access the internet.   (1)
  (ii) Give **one** extra item of software the school must have in order to access the internet.   (1)

(iii) Give **one** advantage *to the school* of advertising on the internet. (1)

(iv) Give **one** disadvantage *to parents* of accessing an electronic newsletter on the internet. (1)

(c) Every day more and more uses are being found for the internet. Give **two** ways the internet could be used by the police to combat crime. (2)

2 A company has branches all over the world and uses videoconferencing to communicate with its employees.

(a) Describe videoconferencing. (2)

(b) Give two benefits to the company and its employees of using videoconferencing. (2)

3 One reason for the increase in popularity of teleconferencing is the potential for it to save companies substantial amounts of money.

(a) Explain the term teleconferencing. (3)

(b) Give two ways that teleconferencing could help to save money. (4)

(c) Apart from the computer system, name three items of hardware needed for teleconferencing. (3)

4 Many homes have access to the *internet*.

(a) What is the *internet*? (1)

(b) Users of the *internet* electronic mail service need a personal address, for example: info@wjec.co.uk. Once online, what are the main stages involved in sending a short electronic message? (3)

(c) Briefly describe **four** other, different services provided through the internet. (4)

(d) 'Traditional newspapers will be replaced by electronic editions.' Discuss why this is likely to happen. Explain the advantages and disadvantages of such a development. (11)

Chapter 23

1 An expert system can be used to give medical advice.

(a) Give **one** other example of an expert system. (1)

(b) Give **one** benefit of using this expert system. (1)

2 A spreadsheet is used to process data about the number of cars using two car parks over a year.

(a) Cell D3 shows how the most popular car park for January is calculated. After typing the formula in cell D3, describe a quick way of putting a similar formula into D4 to D14. (2)

	A	B	C	D
1	Month	Car park A	Car park B	Most popular car park
2				
3	January	120	145	if (B3>C3, 'A', 'B')
4	February	140	135	
5	March	174	201	
6	April	134	120	
7	May	167	130	
8	June	278	290	
9	July	290	315	
10	August	312	289	
11	September	216	290	
12	October	213	278	
13	November	126	178	
14	December	78	98	

(b) Describe how a chart or graph is created to show the use of car parks over a period of one year. (3)

(c) (i) Give one different situation which can be modelled using a computer. (1)

(ii) Give two reasons why a computer model would be useful in this case. (2)

3 A farmer uses insecticide to control insects that attack the crops. The farmer uses software to model the relationship between these three factors:
- the size of the insect population
- the volume of the insecticide used
- crop yield.

(a) Describe three other factors that could affect the relationship modelled. (3)

(b) The farmer describes one of the rules built into the model like this:
'As more insecticide is applied, more insects die.'

(i) Explain why the farmer's description is not always accurate. (2)

(ii) **T** is the total size of the insect population. **V** is the volume of insecticide used in litres. **N** is the number of insects killed. 1 litre of insecticide can kill 300 insects. Complete this table. Two rows have been done for you. (2)

T	V	N
1,300	4	1,200
800	1	
1,000	3	
700	3	700
400	2	

(iii) Using the terms from the following list, complete the sentence to show the exact rule built into the model.

T > V*300
T = V*300
N = V*300
N = T
N = V

    IF_____ THEN_____ ELSE_____ (3)

(c) Write down in words a **different** rule that would be built into this model. (2)

(d) Explain how you could compare the accuracy of a model. (2)

4 Expert systems are used in medicine to help diagnose illnesses.

(a) Explain what is meant by an expert system. (2)

(b) An expert system consists of three components. Name two of these components. (2)

(c) Give one benefit to the patient in using an expert system. (1)

(d) Give one benefit to the doctor in using an expert system. (1)

(e) Give one possible disadvantage in using this type of expert system. (1)

5 One example of where an expert system is used is to help doctors diagnose illnesses. Give one other use of an expert system. (1)

6 There are three parts to an expert system. One of the parts is the inference engine. Give the names of the other two parts. (2)

7 Describe the steps that are used when creating a new expert system. (6)

Chapter 24

1 Describe two advantages in using top-down design when developing computer programs. (2)

2 The algorithm shown below allows a user to enter 50 numbers and then outputs which number is the smallest.
```
10  smallest = 0
20  for N = 1 to 50
30  input number
40  if number < smallest then smallest = number
50  N = N + 1
60  next N
70  print smallest
```
There are three errors in this algorithm. State what each error is and describe what needs to be done to correct each error. (3)

3 The exchange rate between the US dollar (USD) and the Malaysian ringgit (MYR) changes daily. A user needs to exchange US dollars for Malaysian ringgits.

Produce an algorithm using pseudocode which allows the user to input the exchange rate for every day over a year (take it that one year is 365 days). The system should then output the following:
- The highest exchange rate
- The lowest exchange rate
- The average (mean) exchange rate. (5)

Chapter 25

1 Most banks now have automatic teller machines (ATMs) on the outside of their branches.

Banks issue customers with a plastic card so that they can use the ATM.

They also give customers personal identification numbers (PINs).

(a) Give the name of ONE data item that **must** be stored on the plastic card. (1)

(b) State the reason why each customer is given a PIN. (2)

(c) Give TWO benefits **to the bank** of this cash machine system. (2)

(d) Give TWO benefits **to the customer** of this cash machine system. (2)

(e) State ONE problem that the customer might find with using a cash machine. (2)

(f) Some bank customers can now carry out bank transactions from home. State ONE way in which a customer's home computer can be connected to the bank computer system to carry out bank transactions. (1)

(g) Ayesha is a customer who uses the home banking facilities. She wants to find out how much money she has in her bank account.

(i) When Ayesha accesses the bank system, a welcome screen appears. Part of the screen is shown on the next page.

Safe & Friendly Bank   Online Banking

Welcome to our customer home service
The date is 08/3/11

Please enter:

Name the TWO items that Ayesha will have to enter if she wants to use the home banking facility. (2)

(ii) The screen below then appears.

Safe & Friendly Bank   Online Banking

Name: Ayesha Qasim
Address: 178 Brierfield Avenue
         Newtown
         NT3 4DF

The following services are available to you:

A Balance enquiry
B Order new cheque book
C
D

Name TWO services that should appear on the menu for home banking services. (2)

(iii) Name a service that is not available through the Safe and Friendly Bank home banking system. (1)

(h) Give TWO advantages to a bank customer of using the home banking facility rather than visiting the bank. (2)

(i) Give TWO disadvantages to a bank customer of using the home banking facility rather than visiting the bank. (2)

2 A bank gives a cheque book and a cheque guarantee card to a customer who has a current account.

Anybank   45-83-21
23 High Street
Newtown
DG2 7QQ   *17 June 20**11***
Pay   *The Furniture Shop*   *only*
Three Hundred and twenty six pounds   £ 326-96
and 96 pence only   Miss P Smith
                Penny Smith

⑈100063   45 83 21   46075598

(a) Tick **two** boxes to show the information **printed** on a cheque before it is filled in.

Tick **two** boxes	
The bank's sort code	☐
The date the cheque is filled in	☐
Who is to be paid	☐
The amount to be paid	☐
The customer's account number	☐

(2)

(b) Tick **one** box to show how information on a cheque is **input** to a computer.

Tick **one** box	
Using CD-ROM	☐
Using voice recognition	☐
Using magnetic ink character recognition (MICR)	☐
Using a heat sensor	☐
Using mark sensing	☐

(2)

(c) (i) State one item of information that must be printed on a cheque after it has been filled in and **before** it is input to a computer. (1)

(ii) Explain why this must be done. (1)

(d) The cheque guarantee card can be used to withdraw money from a cashpoint or an automated teller machine (ATM).

(i) Write these steps in order to show what happens when money is withdrawn from a cashpoint.
Step 1: The amount of money is entered.
Step 2: The card is returned and the money is paid out.

Step 3: The personal identification number (PIN) is entered.
Step 4: The card is inserted. (1)

(ii) Explain why a PIN is entered. (1)

(iii) Using a term from the following list, complete the sentence.

actuator
barcode
hologram
graph plotter
magnetic stripe

The cashpoint reads information from the _____ on the cheque guarantee card. (1)

(iv) Describe **three** other tasks that can be done using ATMs. (3)

(e) Describe **three** other uses for a cheque guarantee card. (3)

3 Many supermarkets use a barcode system, as shown below.

(a) Give two items of data contained within a barcode. (2)

(b) Give one advantage to the customer of using a barcode system in the supermarket. (1)

(c) Give one reason why the price of a product is not included in a barcode. (1)

(d) Supermarket customers are allowed to pay for their shopping in several ways. Name four different ways they could pay for their shopping. (4)

(e) Many supermarkets and shops now encourage customers to have loyalty cards, as shown in the illustration below. Loyalty cards allow customers to earn points every time they spend money in the supermarket.

(i) Give **one** benefit *to the customer* of using such a loyalty card. (1)

(ii) Give **one** benefit *to the supermarket* in having a loyalty card scheme. (1)

4 Discuss the advantages and disadvantages of using information technology in shopping. (6)

5 A customer pays by electronic funds transfer (EFT) at the checkout of a supermarket.
(a) Give one item of data which is stored on the magnetic stripe of this card. (1)
(b) Describe what the EFT system does after the card has been swiped. (3)

6 Computers have changed the way that musicians write and produce music.
Describe two ways in which the use of computer hardware and software has changed the way music is written and produced. (2)

7 Sensors are used to monitor the condition of patients in a hospital intensive care unit.
(a) Sensors can either be digital or analogue. Explain the difference between digital and analogue data. (2)
(b) Sensors are used to take measurements. Give the names of three sensors that are likely to be used to monitor a patient's condition. (3)
(c) Give three advantages in using sensors to monitor a patient's condition. (3)

8 Virtual reality is used for training dentists. It instructs them how to do certain procedures on patients.
(a) Give two advantages in using virtual reality to train dentists. (2)
(b) Give two disadvantages in using virtual reality to train dentists. (2)

9 Virtual reality is used to train staff on health and safety in nuclear plants and chemical plants. Explain how virtual reality is used and explain what advantages and disadvantages it offers. (3)

Chapter 26

1 (a) The increasing use of IT at work and the development of global networks, such as the internet and the World Wide Web, have affected employment.

(i) Tick **three** boxes to show how some workers may be affected.

	Tick **three** boxes
More workers will be able to afford television	☐
Teleworking will be more widespread and more workers will work from home	☐
Workers will be paid in cash	☐
More workers will need IT skills	☐
Workers will need less education	☐
Some workers in the UK will compete or jobs with workers throughout the world	☐

(3)

(ii) Tick **three** boxes to show how some employers may be affected.

	Tick **three** boxes
Businesses will be virtual reality organisations	☐
Employers will use the World Wide Web for advertising	☐
Employers will train their workers using computer-based learning materials	☐
Employers will use email to communicate with their workers	☐
Employers will need to make sure that all their workers live locally	☐
Employers will need more reference books	☐

(3)

(b) State **three** ways in which help can be obtained using IT or global networks. (3)

(c) Using global networks, people can access a wide range of information.
Some people say that anyone should be able to put information on global networks, and that it should be available to everyone.

(i) Give three reasons for freedom of information on global networks. (3)
(ii) Give three reasons against freedom of information on global networks. (3)

2 Mohammed is working on some coursework at school and he wants to send a copy of his work to his home computer.
Describe the processes involved in sending a file attachment to his home computer. (4)

3 Arif and Ahmed are working on the same project and Arif needs to send Ahmed a file by attaching it to an email.

(a) Describe what happens to the file after Arif writes the email explaining what the file is about, attaches the file and then clicks on 'Send'. (2)
(b) There are a number of problems in sending file attachments to emails. Describe two of these possible problems. (2)

4 Using examples, explain the following five computer terms.

(a) spam (1)
(b) phishing (1)
(c) spyware (1)
(d) cookies (1)
(e) pharming (1)

5 A student needs to do some research on the internet using web browser software. Describe three features of web browser software that he would find useful when completing this research. (3)

6 It is possible to use aerial photographs to show houses and other buildings.

(a) The aerial photographs are sometimes superimposed on traditional maps showing road numbers/names. Give one use for this. (1)
(b) Online maps are available on the internet. Give one use for these online maps. (1)

7 Explain the difference between uploading a file and downloading a file. (1)

8 Using examples, explain the following five computer terms:

(a) ISP (1)
(b) podcast (1)
(c) wikis (1)
(d) search engine (1)
(e) web browser (1)

Chapter 27

1 Complete the truth table for the following logic network.

A	B	C	X
1	1	1	
1	1	0	
1	0	1	
0	1	1	
0	0	1	
0	1	0	
1	0	0	
0	0	0	

2 Here is a logic problem:

Access to a bank's safe (S) is obtained if the time lock (T) is OFF and the correct code light (C) is ON or the manager's code light M is ON and the time lock (T) is ON.

If access to the safe is allowed the output S = 1.

Draw the logic network for the above problem and complete the following truth table showing the output from the logic network.

T	C	M	S
1	1	1	
1	1	0	
1	0	1	
0	1	1	
0	0	1	
0	1	0	
1	0	0	
0	0	0	

Chapter 28

1 A secretary is writing a letter to a client using a word processor.
   (a) A letter can be made more attractive by including pictures and other graphic images. Tick two boxes to show how these can be input into a word processor.

	Tick **two** boxes
Line art can be drawn using a pencil	☐
Pictures can be copied from a clip art gallery	☐
Graphic images can be input using a scanner.	☐
Bar charts can be input using a flowchart	☐
Photographs can be scanned using a tracker ball	☐

(2)

   (b) Describe **two** other ways a word processor can be used to make a letter more attractive to a client. (2)
   (c) The secretary wants to send a personalised letter to several clients using mail merge. Describe what must be done **before** a mail merge can be run. (3)

2 A software company sends information to its customers by personalised letter. These letters are created using mail merging.
   (a) Describe the processes involved in mail merging. (3)
   (b) The company is considering using electronic mail to send information to its customers. Describe the process of sending and receiving electronic mail. (3)

3 You have a friend who wants to buy a word-processing package. He has asked for your advice. Assume that all word-processing packages will allow you to enter, edit, save and print text and change margins. Give four other features your friend might need in his new word-processing package. Explain why he might need each of the features. (4)

4 Office staff now use computers for word processing.
   (a) Text can be formatted when using a word processor. Give two examples of formatting. (3)
   (b) Give two advantages of using a word processor compared with using a manual typewriter. (2)
   (c) Give two ways in which office staff have been affected by the introduction of wordprocessors. (2)

Chapter 29

1 Fazal is a receptionist at one of the Betterview shops. He uses spreadsheet software to produce an appointment sheet for the opticians who work in his branch of Betterview. He makes one spreadsheet that contains details of the appointments for all three opticians.

   (a) Give **two** reasons why Betterview use spreadsheet software for this task. (2)

   (b) Appointments on a Monday are made from 10 a.m. to 4 p.m. An appointment lasts for 20 minutes. Each optician has a lunch break for 40 minutes. Design a suitable spreadsheet that Chris would use for the appointments on Monday. (6)

   (c) State **two** other tasks for which Betterview might use spreadsheet software. (2)

2 A group of friends who live in the north-east of England regularly go to pop concerts. Next year they are planning to go to five concerts. Not everyone wants to go to all of the concerts. Below is part of the spreadsheet that is used to work out the cost for each trip. This is produced once it is known how many people will be going to each concert and the cost of the tickets.

   (a) The travel cost for the car trip to Manchester was wrongly entered. The cost should have been **$35 not $30**. Which **cell** in the spreadsheet must be changed? (2)

   (b) Which **two other cells** would change automatically as a result of this change? (2)

   (c) What **formula** would be in the cell E5? (1)

   (d) Name **one** other cell, in another column, that contains a **different** formula. (1)

   (e) Last year the friends used a calculator to work out their costs. Give **three advantages** of using a spreadsheet like the one shown below, compared with their own manual method. (3)

3 A garden centre uses a spreadsheet to work out the cost of producing plants and how much they should be sold for. This spreadsheet is shown below.

   (a) Shade in the cell which shows the cost of compost for a lavender plant. (1)

   (b) The formula used to work out the selling price in G3 is
   =F3*1.5
   Write down the formula which is needed in each of the cells below.
   (i) I7
   (ii) F3 (2)

   (c) (i) Which cell would you change to find the effect on the profit of selling more pear trees? (1)
   (ii) Which cells would change as a result? (2)

	A	B	C	D	E	F	G
1	Group	Venue	Travel costs	No. of	Travel costs	Cost of	Total cost
2			for car	people in	for 1	1 concert	of trip for
3				the car	person	ticket	one person
4							
5	Kings of Leon	London	$60.00	4	$15.00	$20.00	$35.00
6	Beyonce	Birmingham	$40.00	4	$10.00	$18.00	$28.00
7	The Killers	Newcastle	$15.00	3	$5.00	$17.00	$22.00
8	Justin Bieber	Manchester	$30.00	2	$15.00	$15.00	$30.00
9	Ne-Yo	Glasgow	$40.00	2	$20.00	$15.00	$35.00

▲
Question 2

Question 3
▼

	A	B	C	D	E	F	G	H	I
1	Type of plant	Cost of pot ($)	Cost of compost ($)	Weeks to reach full size	Weekly cost of keeping plant	Total cost of plant	Selling price of plant	Number of plants sold	Total profit ($)
2	Rose	0.30	0.15	16	0.05	1.25	1.88	150	93.75
3	Pear Tree	0.70	0.75	52	0.05	4.05	6.08	75	151.88
4	Pansy	0.02	0.02	4	0.08	0.36	0.54	325	58.50
5	Lavender	0.08	0.10	12	0.04	0.66	0.99	125	41.25
6	Holly	0.15	0.20	16	0.04	0.99	1.49	147	72.77
7								Total profit	418.15

4 A keen music enthusiast hopes to purchase a new stereo music system. To help her choose the best of five different systems (A, B, C, D or E) she uses her computer. First she makes a list of the features of a system which are important to her. Following this she allocates a weighting to each feature, where a value of 9 is an extremely important feature and a value of 2 is less important. The completed list is shown below.

Feature	Weighting
Purchase cost	5
Control layout	7
Sound quality	9
Range of features	6
Ease of operation	5
Size of speakers	4
Remote control	9
Colour	2

She then ranks each system according to each of the above features and allocates a numerical score of either 5, 4, 3, 2 or 1, where 5 is the best and 1 is the worst.

The spreadsheet below was set up to model this situation:

(a) Which of the five systems would she purchase? (1)
(b) Which system is placed last? (1)
(c) What formula does cell E18 contain? (3)
(d) Which cells would need to be selected to produce the chart shown below? (2)
(e) (i) Suppose the music enthusiast changed her mind about the importance of the size of speakers and decided to award this feature a weighting of 9 instead of 4. Explain how the spreadsheet could quickly show the overall effect of this change. (3)
  (ii) Explain what effect this might have on her choice of system to purchase. (3)

	A	B	C	D	E	F	G	H
1								
2				*System Ranking where 5 = the best and 1 = the worst*				
3	**Feature**			A	B	C	D	E
4	Purchase cost			3	5	2	1	4
5	Control layout			4	5	2	1	3
6	Sound quality			4	3	5	1	2
7	Range of features			3	5	4	1	2
8	Ease of operation			4	5	3	1	2
9	Size of speakers			4	1	5	3	2
10	Remote control			1	3	5	4	2
11	Colour			2	5	3	4	1
12								
13				*Score obtained by each system*				
14	**Feature**		**Weighting**	A	B	C	D	E
15	Purchase cost		5	15	25	10	5	20
16	Control layout		7	28	35	14	7	21
17	Sound quality		9	36	27	45	9	18
18	Range of features		6	18	30	24	6	12
19	Ease of operation		5	20	25	15	5	10
20	Size of speakers		4	16	4	20	12	8
21	Remote control		9	9	27	45	36	18
22	Colour		2	4	10	6	8	2
23								
24				146	183	179	88	109

Question 4

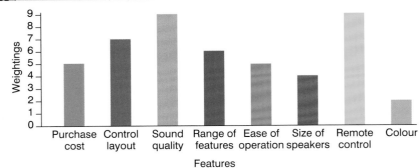

5 For the last 10 years a history teacher has used a manual typewriter to produce most of the worksheets. The history department is about to produce a new set of worksheets for year 7.

(a) Explain the advantages of using a desktop publishing (DTP) package for this task rather than the typewriter. (8)

(b) What arguments do you think the teacher could use for continuing to use a typewriter to produce the worksheets? (3)

Chapter 30

1 The Head of Drama has produced the outline shown below to advertise the school musical.

> Toptone School
> presents
> its
> Annual Musical
> 'Oh! What a Lovely War'
> Performances
> Thursday, Friday, Saturday
> 17th–19th July
> Tickets on sale in the school

The IT teacher has used his desktop publishing package to produce the poster shown:

Toptone School

**presents its
Annual Musical**

'Oh! What A Lovely War'
**Performances
Thursday, Friday, Saturday
17th–19th July
Tickets on sale in the school**

(a) Give four changes made to the original poster by the IT teacher. (4)

(b) Before printing out the final poster, the IT teacher used the spell-checker facility of the desktop publishing package.

(i) Why would the IT teacher use a spell checker? (1)

(ii) Describe how a spell-checker works. (2)

(c) In addition to word-processing and desktop publishing software the Head of Drama could use other software to help with the musical.

(i) Name **one** other *different* type of software which could be used to organise, administer or present the musical. (1)

(ii) What would this software be used for? (1)

2 A man has decided to sell all his golfing equipment. He plans to advertise the items he has for sale. He will put copies of his advert in the local shops and in the golf club. Below is a copy of the advert he has produced using a DTP package.

> FOR SALE – GOLF EQUIPMENT
> For sale FULL set of golf clubs, 10 irons, 4 woods and a putter.
> All clubs are in excellent condition and carry a well-known brand name.
> Also for sale golf trolley, umbrella, golf shoes (size 9) and 100 golf balls. $300 for a quick sale.
> Telephone Mustafa Kawael on 565656.

Describe **five different features** of a DTP package that he could use to improve the advert. Give a reason why each **feature** might be used (10)

3 You are producing a school magazine using a desktop publishing package. Compare alternative methods used to obtain pictures for inclusion in the magazine. (6)

4 An employment agency keeps a database of the jobs available.

This is part of the database.

Reference Number	Area	Job_Type	Employer	Pay ($ per year)
923	Carnforth	Driver	Zenco	11,200
145	Ireby	Sales Assistant	Wilson Clothing	9,000
14W	Fairbourne	Waiter	George Hotel	8,250
877	Sleaford	Waiter	Sleaford Hotel	7,500
402	Carnforth	Sales Assistant	Jean's Army Surplus	6,750
549	Ireby	Waiter	Three Crowns Hotel	8,500
267	Ireby	Driver	Xport	13,000

(a) (i) The **Reference_Number** 14W is incorrect. Tick **one** box to show a validation check that would detect this error.

	Tick **one** box
Reference_Number is not 549	☐
Reference_Number is alphabetic	☐
Reference_Number is alphanumeric	☐
Reference_Number is less than zero and bigger than 999	☐
Reference_Number is numeric	☐

(1)

(ii) Using a word from the list, complete the sentence.
bank
digit
range
type
field
The type of validation check that would detect this mistake is called a _____ check. (1)

(b) The **Job_Type** field is to be coded.
   (i) Design a suitable code for the jobs shown above. (1)
   (ii) Give three advantages in coding information. (3)

(c) Write down the **Reference_Number(s)** of the record(s) selected using the following search conditions.
Search condition 1: Pay is less than 8,000
Record(s) selected: _____

Search condition 2: Area is Sleaford OR Employer is Zenco
Record(s) selected: _____
Search condition 3: Area is Ireby AND Job_Type is NOT Waiter
Record(s) selected: _____ (3)

(d) Write down the **Reference_Numbers** in the order the records will be after they have been sorted into **descending** order on the **Pay** field. (3)

The database extract is shown again below.
   (i) Name the key field. (1)
   (ii) Write down the value of a valid key field for a record which is not shown above. (1)
   (iii) Explain why a key field is used. (1)

Reference Number	Area	Job_Type	Employer	Pay ($ per year)
923	Carnforth	Driver	Zenco	11,200
145	Ireby	Sales Assistant	Wilson Clothing	9,000
14W	Fairbourne	Waiter	George Hotel	8,250
877	Sleaford	Waiter	Sleaford Hotel	7,500
402	Carnforth	Sales Assistant	Jean's Army Surplus	6,750
549	Ireby	Waiter	Three Crowns Hotel	8,500
267	Ireby	Driver	Xport	13,000

Chapter 31

1 A pupil database contains two data files. The structure of the two files is shown below.

Pupils	Subjects
Pupil number	Subject code
Surname	Subject name
Forename	
Date of birth	
Address 1	
Address 2	
Address 3	
Contact phone number	
Home phone number	
Subject code 1	
Subject code 2	
Subject code 3	
Subject code 4	
Form	

(a) Why is it better to store the data in two separate files, rather than keeping it all in one file? (1)

(b) Why is date of birth stored rather than age? (1)

(c) To find all the pupils in the same form a search can be carried out. In this database package searches take the form

<fieldname><comparison><value>

A search for surname = 'Robinson' would find all pupils with the surname Robinson. Write down the search you would carry out to find all the pupils in the form called 7B. (3)

(d) The headteacher wants to be able to send personalised letters to the pupils' parent or guardian. What extra field would be needed to allow the letters to be produced? (1)

Chapter 32

1 A floor turtle can use the following instructions.

FORWARD *n*	Move *n* cm forward
BACKWARD *n*	Move *n* cm backwards
LEFT *t*	Turn left *t* degrees
RIGHT *t*	Turn right *t* degrees
PEN UP	Lift the pen off the paper
PEN DOWN	Place the pen on the paper

Write a set of instructions which makes the turtle draw the following shape. (4)

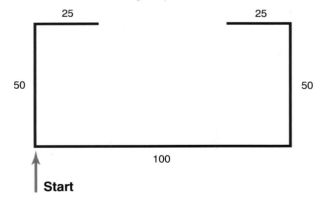

2 Simulators can be used to gain experience of driving cars at high speeds.

(a) Give **one** example of people who may need to use such a simulator as part of their job. (1)

(b) Give **two** reasons why a simulator would be used in this situation. (2)

(c) All simulators rely on rules built into the controlling software. Tick **three** boxes to show the rules that could reasonably be built into this driving simulator.

	Tick **three** boxes only
Motorway driving must be fast	☐
Cars take longer to stop on wet roads than on dry roads	☐
Cars over three years old must have a valid MOT certificate	☐
The faster a car is travelling, the greater the distance needed to stop	☐
Cars should stop at red traffic lights	☐
Younger drivers pay more for car insurance	☐

(3)

(d) Name and briefly describe two other situations in which computer simulation might reasonably be used. (4)

Chapter 33

1 (a) A hospital uses a fleet of ambulances. The hospital uses a computer-based model of the surrounding area to decide which ambulance should go to an emergency.

(i) This is part of the map of the surrounding area the model displays. The numbers are the average time in minutes for an ambulance to travel that section of the map. Which ambulance should be sent to the emergency? (1)

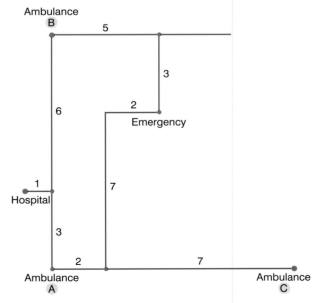

(ii) Tick two boxes to show the information the model should provide to help the hospital decide which ambulance to send.

	Tick **two** boxes
The time it will take for each ambulance to get to the emergency	☐
The distance each ambulance will have to travel to get to the emergency	☐
The name of the patient	☐
The amount of petrol the ambulance will use	☐
An indication of whether the medical supplies carried will allow an ambulance to deal with the emergency	☐

(2)

(iii) The model has to make some assumptions about the ambulances. For example, the model assumes that all the ambulance drivers are fully trained.
Describe two other assumptions the model would make. (2)

(b) A spreadsheet is used to manage the medical supplies carried by an ambulance. This is part of the spreadsheet:

	A	B	C	D	E
1	Description of item	Unit cost	Quantity		
2	stretchers	707.50	2	1415.00	
3	bandages	2.00	50	100.00	
4	medicines	5.50	40	220.00	
5					
6			Total value =	1735.00	
7					

(i) Write a formula that will work out the value in cell D3. (1)
(ii) Write a formula that will work out the value in cell D6. (1)
(iii) Complete these sentences, using the terms from the list.

a byte
a cable
a formula
a matrix
a number
text

Cell B2 contains _____
Cell C6 contains _____
The value of _____ may be recalculated when the value of a number in a cell is changed. (3)

(iv) It is decided to reduce the total value of the medical supplies carried by an ambulance to below $1,400.
Explain how the spreadsheet could be used to decide what medical supplies will be carried. (3)

(c) The computer-based model and the spreadsheet are separate information systems. The hospital wants to integrate all its information systems. A systems analyst is asked to carry out a **feasibility study**.
Complete the sentences, using terms from the list.

buildings
costs
problems
reports
stores

The systems analyst finds out what the _____ _____ are by talking to users.
The systems analyst looks at all the possible ways of integrating these information systems and works out the _____ of each option.
The systems analyst _____ the findings of the feasibility study to management. (3)

2 Betterview, a firm of opticians, used to keep **manual** records of the sales of each of the eight shops.

A computer model was needed to give an improved breakdown of financial details and to predict future profits, based on previous sales, with greater accuracy.

Betterview now uses a spreadsheet to record the sales information. Part of this spreadsheet is shown below.

	Branch 1 Predicted sales	Branch 1 Actual sales	Branch 2 Predicted sales	Branch 2 Actual sales
Number frames sold	1832	2546	7712	6775
Original buy-in price	36342	41454	53156	47651
Final profit (pre-tax)	27124	31239	36453	29987

(a) Explain what is meant by *computer model*. (1)
(b) Describe THREE features of spreadsheet software which make it suitable for computer modelling. (6)

(c) (i) Using the information shown above, describe **two** features of the relative performances of the two branches of Betterview.

    (ii) Betterview wants the spreadsheet to report automatically about the relative performances of the branches. Describe how the spreadsheet could be extended to do this. (4)

3 A company which designs and fits bedrooms is planning to buy a graphics package to produce designs that can be printed and given to its customers. Outline **five features** (other than saving and printing) that you would expect the package to have. (5)

4 A company which designs and fits bedrooms is planning to buy a graphics package to produce designs that can be printed and given to its customers. Outline **five** features (other than saving and printing) that you would expect the package to have. (5)

Chapter 34

1 A school has recently bought a new graphics package. The package has tools that carry out various tasks. Five of the different tools that are available in the graphics package are given below. Explain clearly the purpose of each.
(a) Freehand drawing (1)
(b) Pre-defined shapes (1)
(c) Text (1)
(d) Copy (1)
(e) Palette (1)

2 'CAD – computer-aided design – is one of the most widely used commercial applications of computer graphics.'
(a) Name two different applications of CAD programs. (2)
(b) Give three features/facilities you might expect a CAD program to contain. (3)

3 Drawing packages have many different tools with which to draw.
(a) Name **four** tools commonly found in a drawing package. (4)
(b) Describe a feature of a computer-aided design (CAD) package that you would not normally find in a drawing package. (3)

Full course Higher tier questions

1 A large health centre decides to replace its manual information system with a network of computers.
(a) Give **three** advantages a network of computers could give the health centre rather than using stand-alone computers. (3)
(b) (i) Suggest a suitable *general purpose* software package that could be used by the health centre accountant. (1)
    (ii) Give **two** different uses for this software in the running of the health centre. (2)
(c) One of the doctors requests that an *expert system* should be used to help with medical diagnosis.
    (i) What is an expert system? (2)
    (ii) State **three** benefits an expert system might give patients or doctors. (3)
    (iii) Give **two** drawbacks of using an expert system. (2)
(d) Give **two** different datafiles that could be used by the doctor in the treatment of patients. (2)

2 A software company sends information to its customers by personalised letter. These letters are created using mail merging.
(a) Describe the processes involved in mail merging. (3)
(b) The company is considering using electronic mail to send information to its customers. Describe the process of sending and receiving electronic mail. (3)
(c) Describe the relative benefits and drawbacks of using electronic mail to order and pay for goods. (4)

3 Satellites are widely used in communications. Most satellite dishes are permanently fixed to receive signals from just one particular satellite, but some are capable of rotating to receive signals from different satellites. This is achieved by using a microprocessor linked to a motor to rotate the dish, an analogue sensor to evaluate the signal received and the principle of feedback to maintain the strongest signal possible.

(a) What is a microprocessor? (3)
(b) What item of hardware is needed to allow the microprocessor to process the signal from the analogue sensor? (2)

This control system uses the principle of 'feedback'.
(c) Explain the principle of feedback. (3)
(d) Give two reasons why feedback is necessary for most control systems. (4)
(e) Apart from television communication, give one other purpose for which satellites are used. (2)

4 Complete Bedroom Design is a firm which makes, designs and installs bedroom furniture.

The firm uses information technology methods to:
- produce a catalogue of equipment and prices
- design the best arrangement of bedroom furniture
- help with financial matters and stock control.

(a) A two-way communication link is necessary between the main office and the design staff, who spend a lot of time away from the office with customers.
  (i) Name a piece of computer software that staff need to make this communication possible. (1)
  (ii) State a use for this piece of software. (4)
(b) Name **three** other types of software that Complete Bedroom Design needs, apart from your answer to (a)(ii).
  Describe a use for each type of software you have given. (6)
(c) The senior management of Complete Bedroom Design decides to change to the use of information technology methods to perform the payroll calculations for all their staff.
  Some staff are part-time and some are full-time.
  (i) They intend to buy new hardware to record and input automatically the working times of all the staff into the computer system. State the name of **one** piece of hardware that would be suitable for this task. (1)
  (ii) Describe **two** advantages to the firm of making this change. (4)
  (iii) Describe **two** disadvantages to the firm of making this change. (4)

5 Systems diagrams are used in documentation to convey the overall design of a system. These diagrams often show the processes that are performed on the data and the devices and storage methods used. Below is an incomplete systems diagram for processing electricity payments and bills.

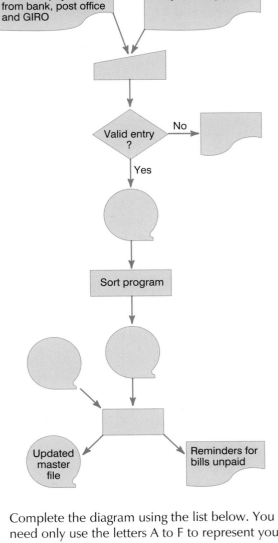

Complete the diagram using the list below. You need only use the letters A to F to represent your choice.
A Sorted payments transaction file
B Masterfile
C Payments transaction file
D Input using keyboard
E List of invalid entries
F Update program (6)

6 Computers will not function without an operating system.
(a) What is an operating system? (1)
(b) Give **three** functions of an operating system. (3)
(c) A multi-access, multitasking operating system is installed on a large computer which is also used for batch and real-time transaction processing. Give the meaning of the following:
  (i) multi-access (1)

(ii) multitasking (1)
(iii) real-time transaction processing (1)
(iv) batch processing. (1)

7 An estate agent is going to transfer all the details of her houses for sale from paper files to files stored on a computer.
(a) Suggest an input device she would need to buy to input the pictures of the houses into the new computerised system. (1)

The estate agent decides to store the pictures of the houses on the hard disk of a computer in a compressed form.
(b) (i) Give two advantages of using compression in this situation. (2)
(ii) Give one disadvantage of using compression in this situation. (1)
(c) Give three reasons why it may be easier to misuse data when they are stored on the computer system rather than when they were stored on paper. (3)

Full course Foundation tier questions

1 A school is going to buy a number of laptop computers for pupils to borrow and use at home. Give **three** problems that this may cause. (3)

2 Ben and Shaazia run a small firm supplying computer hardware and software. They have a small shop and a mail order business.

Customers can:
- call at the shop
- fill in forms from the catalogue
- ring up to make an order.

(a) Each item of hardware and software in the shop has a barcode on it. The barcode is a unique identifier to a piece of hardware or software. List **three** pieces of information that will be stored in the computer file for this item of hardware or software. (3)
(b) Give **two** reasons why Ben and Shaazia use barcodes on their goods. (2)
(c) When customers ring up with their orders, Ben uses a screen input form to collect details of:
- the customer
- their order
- the method of payment.

New customers are given a customer number. Existing customers are asked to give their customer number. Ben uses a different screen input form for the new customers. Give **two** reasons why Ben uses a **different** form for new customers. (2)
(d) Design a screen input form that Ben could use for **new** customers ordering computer goods from the mail order catalogue. (7)
(e) Ben and Shaazia own a business that sells computer hardware and software.
(i) They need to know from which parts of the country most of the mail orders come. Name the data item that must be stored so that they can identify these parts of the country.
(ii) Ben and Shaazia want Fernando to join the management of the business. Fernando says that he wants to see information about the sales made during the last year. Describe, in detail, how a computer system could be used to present this information to Fernando. (5)

3 When a new computerised system is developed it is important that it is properly tested and documented.
(a) A package processes examination marks. When the marks are input they have to be validated with a range check. Marks are allowed if they are in the range 0 to 100. Give **three** numbers you would use to test that the range check worked correctly. Explain why you would carry out each of your tests. (6)
(b) Documentation supplied with a system should provide instructions for normal use. Describe **three** other topics which should be included in the user guide. (3)

4 A computer company uses mail order to sell its goods. A new computerised system is to be introduced.
(a) Describe **two** steps involved in implementing the system. (2)
(b) Describe **two** items of documentation which would be supplied with the system. (2)
(c) Describe **two** verification methods the company could use when the data are entered into the computer. (2)
(d) Give **two** reasons why the company uses codes to store data about the goods being sold. (2)

(e) Describe **two** methods used to ensure that the data are not accidentally lost. (2)

5 A new system is to be introduced into a school for pupils to pay for their dinner using computer cards. Describe the steps taken in the analysis and design of this system. (6)

6 An *operating system* is a program.
   (a) Name **two** tasks the operating system does. (2)
   (b) Name **one** operating system used by computers. (1)
   (c) Microcomputers can carry out *multitasking*. Give the meaning of the term multitasking. (1)
   (d) Computer hardware can be linked up to form *networks*. Draw a diagram of a network you are familiar with. (4)
   (e) Give **two** advantages a network has over a number of stand-alone computers. (2)
   (f) Networks create security problems because of the increased number of users sharing the system. Give **three** security measures to make the system more secure. (3)

7 Under the terms of data protection laws, give **four** legal obligations of any company storing personal data on a computer file. (8)

8 The Silsden Tennis Club is having a dance to raise funds.
   (a) The Secretary uses desktop publishing (DTP) software to design a poster to advertise the dance. Complete the sentences using terms from the list.

         clip art
         columns
         fonts
         pixels
         sizes

   DTP software helps the Secretary lay out text and graphics in _____ on the poster.
   DTP software allows the Secretary to use different _____ and _____ for the text on the poster.
   The Secretary can import _____ into the DTP software. (4)
   (b) The Secretary prints the poster on a laser printer. Tick one box to show why a laser printer is used. (1)

	Tick **one** box
A laser printer costs less to buy than a dot-matrix printer	☐
A laser printer costs less to run than a dot-matrix printer	☐
A laser printer is environmentally friendly	☐
A laser printer prints good quality text and graphics	☐
A laser printer prints good quality text but cannot print graphics	☐

   (c) Name one hardware device that is useful for DTP, other than a keyboard, a disk drive, a monitor, a mouse, a printer and a processor. Describe what the hardware device is used for. (2)
   (d) When the Secretary bought the computer, it was supplied with an operating system and some utility programs.
      (i) Tick **two** boxes to show the tasks done by an operating system. (2)
      (ii) Tick **two** boxes to show the tasks done by utility programs. (2)

Enters information into a database	☐
Displays a screen saver when the computer is not being used	☐
Cleans the computer room	☐
Alerts the police when burglars break into the computer room	☐

   (e) The computer was also supplied with a user manual.
      (i) Complete the sentences, using terms from the list.

            dictionary
            hardware
            index
            puzzle
            tripod

      You can also use the _____ in the manual to help you find the information you want.
      You may have to read the section on setting up the _____ before you can use the computer. (2)
      (ii) Tick three boxes to show the features of a good user manual. (3)

Tick **three** boxes

The language used should be easy to understand ☐

The manual should be large ☐

The manual should have a picture on the front cover ☐

There should be a word search at the end of each chapter ☐

There should be no missing instructions ☐

It should be easy to find the information you want. ☐

(f) Some Tennis Club members believe that the Secretary should not use information technology. Tick three boxes to show why the Secretary should not use information technology. (3)

Tick **three** boxes

Silsden is a thriving market town with a flourishing textile industry ☐

The Tennis Club has 12 members ☐

Multimedia is an application of information technology ☐

The hardware and software needed cost more than £2,500 ☐

None of the Tennis Club's members can use information technology except the Secretary ☐

When the fibre-optic cable has been laid, the Secretary can send email to other tennis clubs ☐

9 Members of a library are given a membership card when they join the library.

The membership card has a barcode on it.

Anytown
Library
Membership Card
HU P00043085 4

(a) Tick three boxes to show which of these statements are true. (3)

Tick **three** boxes

The number printed under the barcode is also stored in the barcode ☐

Different members have the same number on their membership cards ☐

Every member has a different number on their membership card ☐

The member's address is stored in the barcode ☐

Barcodes can be read into the computer without the need for data preparation ☐

The library computer would understand the barcode on a can of baked beans ☐

(b) When a member borrows a book, either the barcode on their membership card is read into the computer using a barcode reader, or, the librarian types the number on the card into the computer.
Tick three boxes to show which of these statements are true. (3)

Tick **three** boxes

Librarians can tell if a member has not returned all the books they borrowed by looking at their membership card ☐

It is faster to use a barcode reader than to type the number into the computer ☐

The librarian could make a mistake typing in the number ☐

The barcode reader is almost always accurate ☐

Barcode readers are too expensive to be used in libraries ☐

The librarian types the number into the computer if the barcode reader is not working ☐

It is faster to type the number into the computer than use a barcode reader ☐

(c) The barcode has a check digit in it. Tick three boxes to show which of these statements is true. (3)

	Tick **three** boxes
When you work out the check digit on a barcode, you should always get the same answer	☐
When a barcode is read, the check digit is worked out. If it is correct then the computer assumes that the barcode has been read accurately	☐
The number under the barcode does not contain the check digit	☐
If you know the check digit, you can find out the information stored in the barcode	☐
Different barcodes will have the same check digit	☐
Every barcode has a different check digit	☐

(d) Every book in the library has a different barcode on it.

(i) When a member borrows a book from the library, the barcode on their membership card and the barcode on the book are read into the computer. Explain why both barcodes are read. (2)

(ii) When a member returns a book, only the barcode in the book is read into the computer. Explain why only the barcode in the book is read. (2)

(e) Several barcode readers are connected to the library's computer. The librarian can use the computer to send electronic mail while it is reading barcodes. Tick three boxes to show the types of operating method the library computer uses. (3)

	Tick **three** boxes
online	☐
virtual reality	☐
batch	☐
multitasking	☐
multi-access	☐
gateway	☐

Short course Higher tier questions

1 The internet is often called the information superhighway. Every day new uses are found for the internet.

(a) A mail order company usually sends its customers a printed catalogue. Now it is considering using the internet to advertise its goods in an electronic catalogue.
Many of the company's customers already have telephone lines and computer systems (computer, disk drive and printer, word-processing, database and spreadsheet software), but would need **extra** hardware and software to access the electronic catalogue using the internet.

(i) Give **one** extra hardware device the customer must have in order to access the internet. (1)

(ii) Give **one** extra item of software the customer must have in order to access the internet. (1)

(iii) Give **one** advantage to the company of advertising on the internet. (1)

(iv) Give **two** disadvantages to the customer of accessing an electronic catalogue using the internet. (2)

(b) Once they are able to access the internet, the customer can use it to access many different services. Give **one** other different service that they could access on the internet. (1)

(c) Every day more and more uses are being found for the internet. Give **four** ways the internet could be used to help the police combat crime. (4)

(d) In addition to the internet we have other types of communications systems. One of these is broadcasted information.

(i) Name **two** broadcasted communication or information systems. (2)

(ii) Give **one** problem that can occur with broadcasted systems. (1)

2 A computer system is to be set up in a school laboratory.

(a) Identify two safety issues which must be considered. (2)

(b) Describe two sensors which could be attached to the computer to collect data from experiments. (2)

3 Describe how computers might be misused, giving rise to legal and moral problems. (4)

4 Discuss the advantages and disadvantages of using information technology in shopping. (6)

5 Describe how information technology can be used to design the layout of a computer room. (3)

Short course Foundation tier questions

1 The widespread use of IT has had a great impact on today's society. One benefit that the increased use of IT has brought is the creation of some new jobs.

(a) Give three examples of jobs that have been created by the introduction of IT. (3)

(b) Describe briefly three other possible benefits that this increased use in IT has brought. (3)

(c) Personal information, stored electronically, is potentially easier to misuse than that kept in paper files. Give two reasons why this is true. (2)

2 Computers can be used in science laboratories to collect data from experiments.

(a) Give three reasons why computers are used in this way. (3)

(b) Give one example of an experiment in which data logging is used. (1)

(c) Describe how information technology is used to create a report on the experiment. (4)

(d) What type of printer should be used to give high quality output? (1)

Glossary

Access To obtain data from a computer.

Actuators Hardware devices, such as motors, which react according to signals given to them by the computer.

ADC See Analogue-to-digital converter.

Algorithm A set of rules that gives a sequence of operations for solving a problem.

ALU See Arithmetic and logic unit.

Analogue A continuously changing quantity that needs to be converted to digital values before it can be processed by a computer.

Analogue-to-digital converter ADC. A device that changes continuously changing quantities (such as temperature) into digital quantities.

Application What a computer can be used to do.

Applications package A program or a set of programs to carry out a particular application, such as accounts or payroll.

Archiving Storing copies of important files for back-up or reference purposes.

Arithmetic and logic unit Part of the central processing unit. It performs all the arithmetic and logic operations.

Artificial intelligence The science of developing computers that 'think' like humans.

ASCII American Standard Code for Information Interchange. A code for representing characters in binary.

Assembler A program that converts assembly language into machine code.

Assembly language Low-level language where one programming instruction corresponds to one machine code instruction.

Automation The automatic control of a process or system without requiring a human operator.

Backing store Memory storage outside the CPU. It is non-volatile which means the data do not disappear when the computer is switched off.

Backup file A copy of a file which is used in the event of the original file being corrupted (damaged).

Bandwidth A measure of the amount of data that can be transferred per second over the internet or other network.

Barcode A code formed by lines on the side of goods, luggage, etc.

Barcode reader An input device used to scan a series of lines (called a barcode).

BASIC A high-level programming language.

Batch processing A method of processing where programs are run in batches and data are processed in batches.

Baud rate A data transmission rate: the number of bits per second.

Biometric A property of the human body, such as fingerprints or the pattern on the back of the eye, that can be used to identify a person.

Bit Binary digit, 0 or 1.

Bitmap An image represented by patterns of tiny dots called pixels.

Bitmap graphics Graphics formed by a pattern of pixels. The whole picture is stored as a series of dots.

Blog A website that allows comments to be posted.

Bluetooth A method used to transfer data wirelessly over short distances from fixed and mobile devices.

Broadband A high-speed internet connection.

Browser A program that is able to display web pages and follow links to other sites.

Buffer A storage area where data are temporarily stored. Printers have buffers so that the data can wait to be printed while the user gets on with something else.

Bug A mistake or error in a program.

Byte The amount of memory needed to store one character, such as a letter or a number. See also Kilobyte, Megabyte and Gigabyte.

C++ A general-purpose programming language which is easier to understand than assembly language but runs almost as fast. It is a development of the programming language C.

CAD Computer-aided design. A method of using the computer to produce technical drawings.

CAL (computer-assisted learning) The process of using computers for the instruction, training or testing of learners.

CD-ROM Compact disk read only memory.

Cell An area on a spreadsheet in which data may be placed produced by the intersection of a column and a row.

Central processing unit (CPU) The computer's brain. It stores and processes data. It has three parts: the arithmetic and logic unit, the control unit and the memory.

Changeover The process of changing from an old computer system to a new one.

Character Any symbol that you can type from the keyboard.

Check digit A number placed after a string of numbers to check that they have all been correctly input to the computer.

Checksum A check performed to ensure that all the bits in a transmission unit of data have been received correctly.

Chip An integrated circuit etched onto a thin slice of silicon.

COBOL A high-level programming language used mainly in business because of its good file-handling facilities. COBOL is an abbreviation for COmmon Business-Oriented Language.

Compiler Software that converts a high-level language program into machine code.

Continuous stationery Stationery in continuous sheets, for use, for example, with a dot-matrix printer. It may be pre-printed with company logos, etc.

Cookie A small text file downloaded to your computer, used by websites to collect information about how you use the website.

CSV Comma-separated variables. A way of holding data so that they can be transferred into databases or spreadsheets.

Data Information in a form that a computer can understand.

Database A series of files stored in a computer which can be accessed in a variety of different ways.

Data capture The way the computer obtains its data for processing.

Data compression Taking files on a disk and using software to reduce their size so that they take up less space on the disk.

Data logging A system that automatically collects data over a certain period of time. Remote weather stations use data logging.

Data processing Doing something with raw data to produce some form of useful output.

Data protection laws Laws that restrict the way personal information is stored and processed on a computer.

Debugging Removing all the errors from a program.

De-skilling The result of ICT making a task capable of being performed by anyone. For example anyone can prepare a perfect document using word processing, whereas in the past a very experienced typist would perform the task.

Desktop publishing Software that can be used to combine text and pictures on a screen to produce neat-looking posters, newsletters, brochures, etc.

Digital computer A computer that works on data represented by numbers. Most ordinary computers are digital.

Digital signature A way of ensuring that an email or document sent electronically is authentic. It can be used to detect a forged email.

Disk A storage medium used to hold data.

Document A text file produced by a word processor.

Documentation The paperwork that accompanies an information system explaining how the system works. The manuals that accompany a program.

Dot-matrix printer An impact printer that produces characters by using a print head with either 24 or 9 pins that punch through a ribbon onto the paper.

Download The transfer of a file or program from the internet to the user's own computer or portable device (e.g. mobile phone, PDA).

DPI Dots per inch. The term is used to describe the resolution of printers. A 600 DPI laser printer will produce a sharper image than a 300 DPI printer.

Dry run Writing down the results of each step of a flowchart or algorithm manually in order to check it.

EDI Electronic data interchange. A network link that allows companies to pay suppliers electronically without the need for paper invoices and cheques.

Edit Change something stored on a computer.

EFT Electronic fund transfer. The process of transferring money electronically without the need for paperwork or the delay that using paperwork brings.

EFTPOS Electronic fund transfer at point of sale. Where electronic fund transfer takes place at a point-of-sale terminal.

Electronic mail See Email.

Email Electronic mail. Email messages and documents can be created, sent and read without the need for them to be printed out.

Encryption The process of coding files before they are sent over a network to protect them from hackers. Also the process of coding files stored on a computer/storage device so that if the computer/storage device is stolen, they cannot be read.

EPOS Electronic point of sale. A computerised till, which can be used for stock control.

Ergonomics The science of the correct design of working equipment and the working environment.

Evaluation The process of determining the quality of software or hardware.

Execution errors Errors detected during the running of a program.

Expert system A program that behaves in the same way as a human expert in a specialist field.

Fact finding The investigation of a system prior to performing a feasibility study.

Fax A machine capable of sending and receiving text and pictures along telephone lines.

Feasibility study A study carried out by experts to see what type of system is needed before a new system is developed.

Fibre optics Thin strands of glass along which light signals pass for communication purposes.

Field A space in a database used for inputting data. For instance, you could have fields for surname, date of birth, etc.

Field check A check performed by a computer to see if the data are the right type to be put into a field. It would be able to check that only numbers are entered into numeric fields.

File A collection of related data; for example a student file would contain details of all students in a school.

File attachment A file that is attached to an email.

File server A network computer used for storing all the users' programs and data.

Firewall A piece of software, hardware or both that is able to protect a network from hackers.

Flat-file database A database that is able to use only one file at a time, unlike a relational database, which is able to use two or more files at a time.

Flowchart or Flow diagram A chart or diagram used to break down a task into smaller parts.

Font A style of type.

FORTRAN A high-level programming language.

Generation of files Every time a file is updated, a new generation of the file is produced.

Gigabyte Roughly 1,000 megabytes.

GIGO Garbage in garbage out. It means that if you put rubbish into a computer then you get rubbish out.

GPS (Global Positioning System) Another name for a satellite navigation system.

Grammar checker A program (usually part of a word-processing package) that checks a document for grammatical errors and provides suggestions for the corrections.

Graph plotter A device that draws by moving a pen. It is useful for scale drawings and is used mainly with CAD packages.

Graphics Diagrams, charts or graphs either on the screen or printed out.

Graphics tablet An input device that makes use of a large tablet containing many shapes and commands, which may be selected by moving a cursor and clicking. Graphics tablets are used mainly with computer-aided design (CAD) software.

GUI Graphical user interface. A way of allowing users to communicate with a computer that makes use of icons and pull-down menus. Windows is a GUI and Macintosh® computers use a GUI.

Hacker A computer expert who tries to break into a secure computer system.

Hard copy Printed output from a computer which may be taken away and studied.

Hard disk A rigid magnetic disk, which provides more storage and faster access than a portable disk.

Hard drive A unit containing a hard disk.

Hardware The components of the computer system that you can actually touch. These would include the visual display unit, processor, printer, modem, etc.

Hash total A meaningless total of numbers used to check that all the numbers have been entered into the computer.

High-level language A programming language where each instruction corresponds to several machine code instructions.

Home page A key page that you usually come to first when you connect to a website that a person or organisation has created on the World Wide Web.

HTML (hypertext markup language) The language used to create documents for the web.

Hypertext A way of linking a word in one document (such as a web page) to another document.

Icons Symbols displayed on the screen in the form of a menu.

Immediate access store Storage in the memory of the central processing unit.

Implementation The process of converting to a new system.

Information What we get from a set of data.

Information retrieval The process of recovering information after it has been stored.

Information technology The application of a combination of computing, electronics and communications.

Inkjet printer A printer that works by spraying ink through nozzles onto the paper.

Input Data fed into a computer for processing.

Integrated circuit Semiconductor circuits inside a single crystal of semiconductor.

Interactive A program or system that allows the user to respond to questions from the computer (and vice versa) and immediately acts on the answers.

Interface The hardware and software used to enable devices to be connected together (e.g. an interface would be needed to connect a joystick to a computer).

Internet A worldwide computer network of networks. The internet forms the largest connected set of computers in the world.

Interpreter A program that converts a high-level language into machine code. An interpreter is different from a compiler because it translates each instruction and then carries it out. Compilers translate the whole of the program first and then carry out each instruction separately.

Interrogation The process of getting information from a file.

Intranet A private network used within an organisation that makes uses of internet technology which only employees or certain people can gain access to.

Invoice A bill.

ISP (internet service provider) A company that provides you with a connection to the internet when you log on.

Joystick An input device used instead of the cursor keys or mouse as a way of producing movement on the screen.

K Short for kilobyte or 1,024 bytes. Often abbreviated as KB. A measure of the storage capacity of disks and memory.

Keyboard A computer keyboard consists of the standard typewriter keys plus calculator keys and some special keys.

Key-to-disk A way of inputting data directly into a computer and onto disk using the keyboard.

LAN Local area network. A network of computers on one site.

Laptop A portable computer small enough to fit on your lap. Laptop computers use rechargeable batteries.

Laser printer A printer which uses a laser beam to form characters on the paper.

LOGO A simple computer language which enables a 'turtle' to move according to the instructions given to it.

Loop A sequence of steps in a program which repeats.

Low-level language A programming language very similar to the machine language of the computer. Each low-level instruction can easily be converted into a machine code instruction.

Machine code The language the computer can understand without it being translated. Each type of computer has its own machine code.

Magnetic ink character recognition (MICR) A method of input that involves reading magnetic ink characters on certain documents. MICR is used on cheques by banks.

Magnetic media Media such as tape and disk where the data are stored as a magnetic pattern.

Magnetic stripe reader A device that reads the data contained in magnetic stripes, such as those on the back of credit cards.

Mainframe A large computer system with many dumb terminals attached.

Mainstore Memory inside a CPU.

Master file The main source of information and the most important file.

Medium The material on which data can be stored, such as magnetic disk, tape, etc.

Megabyte (MB) Roughly one million bytes (1,048,576).

Megahertz (MHz) One million cycles per second. The speed of the internal clock which controls the speed of the pulses in the computer is measured in megahertz. Chip design and clock speed determine the overall performance of the CPU.

Memory An area of storage inside silicon chips. ROM and RAM are two types of memory.

Memory cards Thin cards you see in digital cameras used to store photographs. They can be used for other data too.

Merge To combine data from two different sources.

Microcomputer A cheap but relatively slow computer that is able to work only on one program at a time. The memory is usually limited.

MIDI (musical instrument digital interface) Allows the communication between a musical instrument and a computer.

Modem MODulator/DEModulator. A modem converts data from a computer into a form that can be passed along a telephone wire and vice versa.

Monitor Another name for a VDU.

Mouse An input device which, when it is moved over a table, moves a cursor on the screen. Buttons on a mouse are pressed to make a selection from a menu.

MS-DOS Microsoft Disk Operating System. An operating system used by personal computers.

Multi-access system A system which allows many different users to access a computer 'simultaneously'. Each user appears to have sole access because of the speed of the CPU, although in actual fact the time is being shared amongst the users.

Multimedia Software that combines more than one medium for presentation purposes, such as sound, graphics and video.

Network A group of computers which are able to communicate with each other. See also LAN and WAN.

OCR Optical character recognition. A combination of software and a scanner which is able to read characters into a computer.

Off-the-shelf software Software that you can buy ready made, without you having to have the software specially written.

OMR Optical mark reader/recognition. A reader that detects marks on a piece of paper. Shaded areas are detected and the computer can understand the information contained in them.

Online/offline When a device is under the control of the computer it is said to be online, otherwise it is offline.

Operating system The software that controls the hardware and also runs the programs.

Output The results from processing data.

Package Sometimes called an applications package. A set of programs, with documentation, used to perform a task or a set of tasks.

Password A series of characters chosen by the user that are used to check the identity of the user when they require access to an ICT system.

Peripheral A device connected to and under the control of a CPU.

Phishing Tricking people into revealing their banking or credit card details.

PIN Personal identification number. The secret number that needs to be keyed in to gain access to a cash dispenser.

Piracy The illegal copying and use of software.

Privacy The rights of individuals to decide what information about them should be known by others.

Programmer   A person who writes computer programs.

Protocol   A set of standards that allow the transfer of data between computers on a network.

Pseudocode   A combination of English and a programming language used to express the flow of a program.

RAM   Random-access memory. A fast temporary memory area where programs and data are stored while the computer is switched on.

Range check   A data validation technique which checks that the data input to a computer is within a certain range.

Real time   A realtime system accepts data and processes them immediately. The results have a direct effect on the next set of available data.

Record   A set of related information about a thing or individual. Records are subdivided into fields.

Relational database   A database that consists of several files. It is possible to use a single file and access data in several of the other files.

Remote sensing   The process where sensors are connected via communication lines to a main computer.

Robot   A machine or device that has been programmed to carry out some (usually mechanical) processes automatically.

ROM   Read-only memory. Computer memory that cannot be changed by a program.

Satnav   Satellite-navigation systems – commonly just called satnav – enable maps to be displayed showing a location and guiding the person to their destination.

Screen dump   A printout of what appears on the screen.

Search   To look for an item of data.

Search engine   Software that finds information on websites on the internet based on input criteria.

Sensors   Devices which measure physical quantities such as temperature, pressure, etc.

Serial access   Accessing the data in sequence. The time it takes to locate an item depends on its position.

Simulation   The imitation with a computer program of some system (e.g. aircraft flight) or some phenomenon that can be described

mathematically (e.g. how the economy of the country works).

Smartcard   A plastic card which is 'intelligent' because it contains its own chip.

Social networking site   A website that is used to communicate with friends and family and to make new friends and contacts.

Software   The programs used in a computer.

Source documents   The original documents from which the data are taken.

Spam   Unsolicited bulk email – that is, email from people you do not know, sent to everyone in the hope that a small percentage of the recipients may purchase the goods or services on offer.

Spell checker   A program usually found with a word processor, which checks the spelling in a document and suggests correctly spelt words.

Spreadsheet   A software package which consists of a grid used to contain text, numbers or formulae. Spreadsheets are often used to produce financial predictions.

Spyware   Software that collects information, without consent, about the user of a computer connected to the internet.

Structure diagram   Diagram used to break a problem down into a series of smaller tasks, making it easier to find a solution to the problem.

Surfing   The process of looking around the internet.

Syntax error   An error reported by a computer due to the incorrect use that contradicts the rules governing the structure of the language.

Systems analyst   A person who studies the overall organisation and implementation of an IT system.

Tape   Magnetic media used to store data.

Telecommunications   The field of technology concerned with communicating at a distance (e.g. telephones, radio, cable).

Terminal   A computer on a network, or a keyboard and VDU connected to a mini or mainframe computer.

Test data   Data used to test a program or flowchart for logical errors.

Test plan   A set of test data which will test the solution to a problem that is to be solved using ICT.

TFT (thin film transistor) A thin screen used in laptops/notebooks or in desktops where desk space is limited.

Thesaurus Software which suggests words with similar meanings to the word highlighted in a document. Thesauruses are found mainly with word processors.

Toner Tiny black plastic particles used by laser printers as the 'ink'.

Top-down design The process of breaking down an overall task into a series of several smaller tasks. Each of these smaller tasks is broken down again into smaller tasks. The process is repeated until the small tasks can be easily solved.

Touchscreen A special type of screen that is sensitive to touch. A selection is made from a menu on the screen by touching part of it.

Tracker ball An input device which is rather like an upside-down mouse.

Transaction file A file on which all the transactions (items of business) over a certain period of time are kept. A transaction file is used to update a master file.

Translator A program used to convert a program written in a high- or low-level language into machine code.

Turnaround document A document produced by a computer, filled in manually and then used as the input to the computer.

UNIX An operating system used in multi-user computing.

Update The process of changing information in a file that has become out of date.

Upload The transfer of a file or program from the user's computer to a remote computer where that file or program is then stored.

UPS (uninterruptible power supply) Alternative power supply in case the mains supply fails.

User A person who uses a computer.

Username or User ID A name or number that is used to identify a certain user of the network or system.

Validation A check performed by a computer program to make sure that the data are allowable.

VDU Visual display unit. The screen on which data is displayed. Also called a monitor.

Vector graphics Graphics which are defined using co-ordinate geometry. They are easy to scale (make bigger or smaller) without any loss of resolution.

Videoconferencing ICT system that allows face-to-face meetings to be conducted without the participants being in the same room or even in the same geographical area.

Virtual reality Computer technology which creates a simulated multidimensional environment for the user.

Virus A nasty program that has been created to do damage to your computer system.

Visual display unit See VDU.

Voice recognition The ability of a computer to 'understand' spoken words by comparing them with stored data.

WAN Wide area network. A network where the terminals are remote from each other and telecommunications are used to communicate between them.

Web A shortened name for the World Wide Web.

Web address The address that points to a certain site on the internet. For example the web address for the publisher of this book is www.nelsonthornes.com

Webcam A digital camera used to capture still images or video and transmit them to a computer, where they are converted into graphic forms and can be published on a website.

Web logs (blogs) Blogs are websites that are created by an individual with information about events in their life, videos, photographs, etc.

Web page A single document on the World Wide Web, usually containing links to other sites.

Website A site on the internet containing information. It consists of one or more web pages.

WIMP (Windows Icons Menus Pointing devices) The graphical user interface (GUI) way of using a computer rather than typing in commands at the command line.

Windows A commonly found graphical user interface (GUI).

Word processor A word processor allows text to be typed and displayed on a VDU and to be edited before being printed out.

World Wide Web A huge collection of web pages and other material, such as files for downloading, that you can access. This material is held on millions of servers (called hosts) all around the world.

Index

Notes